THE UNOFFICIAL COMPANION

LAW & ORDER
SPECIAL VICTIMS UNIT

Susan Green and Randee Dawn

BENBELLA BOOKS, INC.
Dallas, TX

BENBELLA

BenBella Books, Inc.
6440 N. Central Expressway, Suite 503
Dallas, TX 75206
Send feedback to feedback@benbellabooks.com
www.benbellabooks.com

Printed in the United States of America
10 9 8 7 6 5 4 3 2 1

Library of Congress Cataloging-in-Publication Data is available for this title.
ISBN 978-1933771-88-5

Proofreading by Jennifer Canzoneri and Stacia Seaman
Cover design by Moxie Studio
Text design and composition by PerfecType, Nashville, TN
Printed by Bang Printing

Distributed by Perseus Distribution
perseusdistribution.com

To place orders through Perseus Distribution:
Tel: 800-343-4499
Fax: 800-351-5073
Email: orderentry@perseusbooks.com

Significant discounts for bulk sales are available. Please contact Glenn Yeffeth at glenn@benbellabooks.com or (214) 750-3628.

For my mother,
an artist haunted by the Holocaust
who embraced life until the end
—SUSAN GREEN

For all of the special victims,
who learn to be survivors
—RANDEE DAWN

TABLE OF CONTENTS

ACKNOWLEDGMENTS

Our deepest gratitude goes to Dick Wolf, a man who really knows how to make things happen. We also want to profusely thank *SVU*'s Neal Baer, Ted Kotcheff, David DeClerque, Peter Leto, Mike Ciliento (óur hero!), Jim Nickas, Meredith Petty, Ryan Spencer, and Gail Barringer—as well as all of the fine cast and crew who made our visit so delightful and pleasant and, well, yummy; Mariska Hargitay for going above and beyond; Lippin Group's Pam Golum and Audrey Davis; Peter Rubie of Fine Print Literary Management; Glenn Yeffeth, Jennifer Canzoneri, Yara Abuata, and Leah Wilson of BenBella Books; Wolf Films' Arthur Forney, Lydia Mayberry, Adrian Bassuk, and Kristel Crews; NBC Universal's Charlie Engel, Curt King, Amanda Ruisi, and Christy Havranek. Kudos to photographer Dave Allocca and artist Brandon Bird. And, as people in love with the written word, we must express our admiration for the storytellers behind a decade of episodes: Dawn DeNoon, Lisa Marie Petersen, Amanda Green, Jonathan Greene, Judith McCreary, Patrick Harbinson, Jeff Eckerle, Robert Palm, Robert Nathan, Paul Grellong, Michele Fazekas, Tara Butters, Dan Truly, and Mick Betancourt.

Susan: I have boundless appreciation for the support that comes from my wise daughter Jennie, who never lets me get away with anything;

the amazing Bob Green and Bill Coil; poet supreme Ryki Zuckerman of Buffalo; wonderful cousins Shirley and Sandy Guth and Dave and Judy Solomon; the erudite Deborah Straw and Bruce Conklin; the perceptive Suze Rotolo, friend for half a century, and the savvy Enzo Bartoccioli; photography genius Ron Levine in Montreal; my *sympatico* colleague Kevin Courrier in Toronto; the always creative Debra Weiner in Chicago; wittily observant Chris Booth, across the big pond; fellow "wild thing" Susan Connell, to be remembered forever; good neighbors Rick and Karen Sener; Pogo and Isabella, the best kitties a writer could possibly want.

Randee: Many thanks to my former employers at *The Hollywood Reporter*, who gave me the room to get this book made—including Stephen Galloway and Christy Grosz for their advice, encouragement, and support. To my longtime co-editor at *apocrypha*, Anne Sapko (and her amazing husband Jeff) for coming along on this now-fourteen-year-old *Law & Order* ride, to Michelle Loo who helps out every week keeping the list going, and to all of our longtime subscribers and readers. To my dear friends who have encouraged my writing over the years in all of its forms, including Julia Harrington, Rebecca Hoffman, Alexis Gerard, Valerie Mehta, Nadine Rufrano, Monica Gorlewski, and Cecelia Donohue—I finally have something for you to read that comes with a bar code on it! And finally, to my brother Craig and his beloveds Kris, Sydney, and Natalie, and my mother Lois, who made everything possible for me from day three up to this very moment.

INTRODUCTION:
DICK WOLF SPEAKS

The story of *Law & Order: Special Victims Unit* starts over ten years ago. At the time, *Law & Order* had just won the Emmy Award for Outstanding Drama Series and it was one of the top drama series on television. I was inspired by the show's success, and when *Exiled: A Law & Order Movie* was a ratings hit in 1998, I realized that the Law & Order brand was ripe for another spin-off, this time a new series.

COURTESY WOLF FILMS

Dick Wolf

Fortunately, Barry Diller, who was running the production studio at the time, agreed.

The inspiration for *Law & Order: SVU* goes back to the Robert Chambers case, the preppy murder in Central Park, which we did a variation of in the first season of *Law & Order*. I wanted to get deeper into the psychology of crimes like that, the role of human sexuality.

At the same time, I saw a chance to expand the Law & Order brand, to create a universe of characters that would run between the two shows, who have real ties that continue and change. It may sound pretentious, but I thought of *Law & Order* and *SVU* as a huge novel, like Dickens' London. And not only did *SVU* survive, it thrived.

At the time, the government was staunchly defending the V-chip. I was very outspoken against the V-chip, but not as a defender of violence. I was defending the right to free speech. So when I originally thought about calling the show *Law & Order: Sex Crimes*, Barry (Diller) disagreed with the title, and we changed it to *Law & Order: Special Victims Unit.*

So I wrote the pilot for *SVU* in early 1999, creating two intense, multi-faceted and complicated characters, Elliot Stabler and Olivia Benson. Stabler was a typical cop, a family man with four kids. Benson was the child of rape, so to her, working with special victims was a way to right the wrongs of her own life.

We read multiple actors for both lead roles, and we found our perfect match with Christopher Meloni (Detective Elliot Stabler) and Mariska Hargitay (Detective Olivia Benson). Ten years later, they have become one of the most popular and enduring partners on television. I also recruited two familiar characters to join the fold— Richard Belzer, whose Detective John Munch migrated from *Homicide: Life on the Street*, along with Dann Florek, who created the role of Captain Cragen as an original cast member on *Law & Order.*

Tackling the difficult subject matter of sex crimes was not easy. The darkness of the stories had to have some light, which the writers provided by helping me flesh out such likeable characters. The crimes committed were particularly heinous—they often involved children and other defenseless victims—and the stories were rich in social issues. Rape, incest, child molestation were regular themes.

By halfway through the second season, we had a new showrunner—Neal Baer, a Harvard educated M.D. and pediatrician who had been a writer/producer on *ER*. Neal's background in pediatrics and his talents as a brilliant storyteller were a dynamic combination. So it's no accident that he infuses the series with sensitivity and a burning desire to cure this world of its ills.

Over the years, we have added new and exciting characters, including the role of the ADA assigned to the special victims unit (three wonderful actresses—Stephanie March, Diane Neal, and the newest addition, a bright, young, and talented Michaela McManus). Ice-T, who I worked with previously on two series and a telefilm, plays the streetwise detective Odafin "Fin" Tutuola. And supporting actors B.D. Wong (forensic psychologist George Huang) and Tamara Tunie (M.E. Melinda Warner) have expanded their roles over time, to give the show one of the most diverse ensemble casts on television. Given the sensitive nature of the show, all of these actors and characters bring their own voice to the stories, which tend to be more graphic and emotional than those on the other Law & Order branded series.

All of this has made the show very popular, with an incredibly loyal fan base. A string of remarkable guest actors have graced us with their presence, including Ellen Burstyn, James Brolin, Chris "Ludacris" Bridges, Elle Fanning, Brian Dennehy, Kim Delaney, Abigail Breslin, Ming-Na, Hayden Panetierre, Matthew Modine, Martin Short, Jerry Lewis, Marlee Matlin, Joe Morton, Will Arnett, Khandi Alexander, Karen Allen, Natalie Cole, and Betty Buckley. Amanda Plummer, Leslie Caron, and Cynthia Nixon won Emmy awards for their work on the show; Robin Williams, Angela Lansbury, Marcia Gay Harden, Marlee Matlin, Barbara Barrie, Mare Winningham, Jane Alexander, and Tracy Pollan received nominations. We hope to continue the tradition of Emmy-nominated performances in years to come.

Mariska and Chris have both been nominated for Emmys, with Mariska winning the coveted award in 2006, along with the Golden Globe Award the same year. In the highly competitive world of network and cable television, just being nominated is an honor. Mariska has been nominated four years in a row and has won this honor, which is a testimony to her incredible talent, and the writing that has allowed her to shine.

I would be remiss if I did not also acknowledge the extraordinary work of everyone behind the scenes. In addition to Neal, the phenomenal director/producer Ted Kotcheff, who is the New York–based showrunner, as well as Peter Jankowski, who as head of Wolf Films is also an executive producer on the series and is the crucial link between the Los Angeles–based writing team and New York–based production. Another longtime friend and colleague is the amazing Arthur Forney, who heads post production in Los Angeles and has also directed multiple episodes. It is the combined vision from all of these hardworking and talented individuals, and every single crew member, writer, and staff member past, present, and future who has been instrumental in our past success, and will hopefully drive us to greater heights in the future.

So I invite you to enter the world of *Law & Order: Special Victims Unit*—from an insider's perspective, and I thank Susan Green and Randee Dawn for their devotion to this project and their unwavering commitment to accuracy and professionalism.

—Dick Wolf, *SVU* creator/executive producer

FOREWORD

"Art establishes the basic human truths which must serve
as the touchstone of our judgment."

—PRESIDENT JOHN F. KENNEDY, October 1963 speech

People whose cars sport those bumper stickers that read "Kill Your Television Set" probably assume the electronic system for transmitting transient images has the power to mesmerize the masses. But TV can be more than just a diversion that renders couch potatoes apathetic.

If the medium is the message, as philosopher Marshall McLuhan pointed out a year after JFK's salient observation about art, then perhaps the public perception of crime has been altered by any Law & Order series in ways that only history will determine. The Bible's 1 Corinthians advises that "for now we see through a glass, darkly." By the mid-twentieth century, that box with a picture tube in the living room was blessed with the power to illuminate.

For the authors of this book, *Law & Order: Special Victims Unit* seemed like an appropriate mirror to help understand the spirit of

RANDEE DAWN

SVU *crew hat*

the current millennium. In this time fraught with unprecedented concern about the human condition, we wanted to delve into the show because of both an intellectual curiosity and emotional attachment: How are these taut stories put together and why do they often leave us feeling so unsettled?

But the goal of studying *SVU* in print proved to be elusive. Although the idea was immediately greeted with enthusiasm by creator/executive producer Dick Wolf in 2003, all plans had to be tabled when NBC began merging with Universal, a process that lasted into May of 2004. By the time our book proposal was reshaped to account for that interlude, interest from a few initially keen publishers had fizzled—and in at least one instance, the publishing house itself had fizzled.

When our agent Peter Rubie eventually contacted us about a query from BenBella Books, the project was on the back of the back burner. We regrouped and began to envision a fall 2007 visit to the *SVU* set, only to have our notion evaporate when the Writers Guild of America called a strike. Once that hurdle was overcome four months later, the series needed to recharge its batteries. So, in order to allow the production some breathing space, we penciled in late April 2008 for an eight-day stint on what would be the last episode scheduled to shoot in season nine.

Fate intervened again. With Diane Neal and Adam Beach reluctantly leaving the show, we were told that even well-meaning interlopers like us might exacerbate tensions on the set. OK, but *SVU* would next be taking a two-month hiatus, which meant a significant disruption of our timetable. Just as we were beginning to despair, Glenn Yeffeth—BenBella's guiding light—kindly granted us an extension.

After watching more than 200 episodes (Randee took the odd-numbered seasons, Susan the even) throughout May and June, we finally made our way to Mecca: *SVU*'s North Bergen, New Jersey headquarters. Greeted with more warmth and conviviality than either of us had anticipated, at last it felt as if the arduous, uncertain five-year journey had been worth the effort. Perhaps, as the lyrics from "Choose Me" by Ringo Starr attest: "You've got to pay your dues if you want sing the blues."

While Randee interviewed actors, Susan trailed after producers, directors, and a slew of crew. Other key *SVU* figures past and present were reached by telephone or email. By August 2008, we had begun writing, writing, writing.

SVU has never been just another TV program for us. Since the early 1990s our lives have intertwined with the Law & Order franchise. In Susan's case that resulted in the original *Law & Order: The Unofficial Companion* (with Kevin Courrier); for Randee, that meant a lot of freelance articles celebrating the shows and a little fan website called *apocrypha*—thanks to which she met Green and Courrier when their book was first published in 1998.

SVU *season ten hat*

RANDEE DAWN

But so much time and effort could not have been invested in a series in which we had just a casual interest. *Law & Order* and, in its time, *SVU* have kept us on our toes for well over fifteen years, a testament to the unique quality of the shows or our own persistent inquisitiveness.

What you hold in your hands today is the result of those labors, those interests, those passions—behind the screen, on the screen, and at the keyboard.

—Susan Green and Randee Dawn / October 2008

CHAPTER ONE

THE RUDIMENTS

"A wonderful fact to reflect upon, that every human
creature is constituted to be that profound secret
and mystery to every other."

—CHARLES DICKENS, *A Tale of Two Cities* (1859)

Nurturing the New

While no violence is palatable, rape and molestation seem to bedevil society in a more insidious way than do most other illegal acts.

In the past, these crimes often were not taken seriously by cops, courts, or church hierarchy. And, since experts have yet to come up with a foolproof cure for people compelled to commit sexual assaults, rehabilitation has largely eluded the prison system. But compulsive deviant behavior isn't the only culprit. Sometimes it's a question of choice, whether for revenge or other misbegotten motives.

Moreover, the justice system is frequently too overextended and ill-equipped to make the punishment fit the crime or enforce even the most reasonable punishments.

Law & Order: Special Victims Unit was conceived as a responsible mechanism for addressing complex issues through the context of popular culture. The show is an entertainment that asks viewers to think about these problems, some of which may already have affected their towns or even their immediate families.

The idea for such a show stemmed from the notorious 1986 "Preppie Murder," in which Robert Chambers strangled a young woman during what he later claimed was consensual "rough sex" in Manhattan's Central Park. The event inspired executive producer Dick Wolf to write the story for "Kiss the Girls and Make Them Die," an episode that aired early in the original *Law & Order's* first season. But, for some reason, the case continued to haunt him.

"I wanted to go deeper into the psychology of crimes like that, (to examine) the role of human sexuality," he explains, referring to the 1999 genesis of *SVU*.

In the beginning, nobody involved knew if the exploration of such dark places would find an audience. Many people watch TV to escape the crueler realities of everyday life. So, it was essential to cast actors talented and sensitive enough to convey the deeply humane approach of police, prosecutors, forensic specialists, and psychiatrists assigned to protect the public from predators.

Also, this was a task that required skilled writers who understand the legal and moral dilemmas that can surface in such cases. The same qualities are necessary in episode directors. They must elicit stellar performances—frequently from very young guest stars—that delve into some terribly grim subjects.

Luckily, *SVU* has been able to benefit from the longevity of the original *Law & Order*, affectionately referred to as "The Mother Ship." That excellent track record helped persuade the studio and the network to take a chance on a show with an even bleaker topical sensibility. This was sure to be drama in which ripped-from-the-headlines tended to rip out the viewer's heart.

Like all Law & Order shows, (most of) the producers, writers, and editors work in Los Angeles, while the actors and crew shoot in New York—Dick Wolf's hometown and a city with unique personalities, cultural attractions, architecture, and events that fascinate people the world over. The Big Apple has inspired many of the greatest poems, books, plays, and movies, while continuing to nurture artists who call it home.

Landscape architect Frederick Law Olmsted's magnificent Central Park alone gives citizens a breath of fresh air and *SVU* writers acres of ideal locations. Their imaginations also swim in the Hudson and East rivers. In all five boroughs, neighborhoods can either glitter enticingly or represent urban decay. Everything needed is within reach, often a few subway stops away.

New York is also a place always struggling with how to keep 8 million residents and an untold number of visitors safe. On a daily basis, the NYPD encounters staggering calamities that would undoubtedly make the ordinary person cringe with horror.

Periodically, there are cops who think they're above the law. *SVU* unflinchingly scrutinizes that type of miscalculation, as well as the infamous "blue wall of silence" in which loyalty trumps legality.

Although Wolf wants the series to shed light on sexual maladjustment, nobody can say for sure what makes "perps"—as perpetrators are routinely called on the show—tick. The human mind remains a mystery that no one can afford to stop trying to unravel.

But this blight on a citizen's right to live a peaceful life is a cause television should champion. *SVU* attempts to accomplish that in the most caring way possible, without unnecessary prurience.

The series also contributes to the civic discourse essential for communities working together to find a solution . . . or a remedy. Executive producer and showrunner Neal Baer is a physician who specializes in pediatrics. So it's no accident that he infuses *SVU* with a desire to cure this world of its ills.

On the other hand, Baer also is a brilliant storyteller. And that's what makes the show so remarkable: With his guidance, the great yarns that are spun provide a compelling platform for the difficult themes that plague us all.

Make-believe has rarely seemed so real.

Rounding up the Brain Trust

Television screens may have gotten a little bit brighter when veteran film director Ted Kotcheff was recruited to work on *SVU* a decade ago. Despite a love of motion pictures, the medium that kept him busy from the early 1960s through the late 1990s, he was amenable to a professional detour when Dick Wolf beckoned.

"I was supposed to do a big film about Hitler, one of the two major obsessions of my life: Hitler and Shakespeare," recounts Kotcheff, a gifted raconteur. "We were looking for locations when it fell though at the very last second." The Third Reich and the Bard would just have to wait.

His agent told him about a new Law & Order series in the offing. "So I met Dick and we liked each other. We have the same sense of humor. I asked to see a script. If I was going to work in TV, I didn't want to do the same old thing. But it seemed as if *SVU* went into areas no show had gone before. It was breaking new ground," says Kotcheff, who was tapped to be in charge of the operation's East Coast sector.

The switch in his career path stunned people he knew in the industry, one of whom even teased him: "Hey, Kotcheff! I understand you've gone over to the other side."

COURTESY TED KOTCHEFF

Ted Kotcheff

The man who lured Kotcheff to the other side, Dick Wolf, remains certain of his decision. "When I heard that Ted was interested in doing television, I was both amazed and delighted," he writes in an email. "As the director of one of the greatest sports films in the history of American cinema, *North Dallas Forty* (1979), he is an extraordinary talent. Ted is very versatile—he has expertise in drama, comedy, and character, and his films, including *The Apprenticeship of Duddy Kravitz* (1974) and *Fun with Dick and Jane* (1977) speak for themselves."

The *SVU* launch also was graced by an experienced writer well known to Wolf: Robert Palm, who had left *Law & Order* after the first two seasons because "I got bored with the format. I was proud of my work there, but felt kind of handcuffed." Drum roll, please, for that law-enforcement imagery.

Palm went on to co-author several TV pilots with Wolf throughout the 1990s, though none were ever picked up. Then the two men had a falling out and stopped speaking altogether.

One day, Palm's agent called him about a pilot that his estranged *L&O* friend had written for a new series on sex crimes. "I told (Wolf Films president) Peter Jankowski, 'I will never ever work with him again.' He said, 'Please, just read the fucking script.' I did and, son of a bitch, it was brilliant. Later, Dick said to me, 'So, forever is five years, huh?'"

Palm, an L.A. resident at the time, became *SVU*'s first showrunner. As such, it was his idea to refer to the original *Law & Order* as the Mother Ship. "We made up stationery that dubbed our (new) show 'The Bastard Step-child,'" he recalls.

His goal was to give the series "a strong woman's perspective. I helped bring in female writers—more women than might normally be found in Wolfland, shall we say."

His former boss sees it somewhat differently. "Depending on the season, there are many female writers on all these series," Wolf contends. "We tend to have several female writers on *SVU* because of the subject matter."

Among the gender pioneers were Dawn DeNoon, now a co-executive producer, and her writing partner at the time, Lisa Marie Petersen. Their route to *SVU* was a bit circuitous, however.

Longtime fans of the Mother Ship, they reacted with glee when their agent delivered some good news: "*Law & Order* wanted to meet with us? Oooh! And this was not *SVU*, this was *L&O*," DeNoon recalls.

In May of 1999, the duo talked with René Balcer (then the *L&O* showrunner, now a consulting producer for USA's *Law & Order: Criminal Intent*) in L.A. "He said they weren't hiring staff, but they were doing a spin-off of *L&O* that year, which I couldn't imagine because it was such an institution, called *Sex Crimes*, which was the original title," DeNoon says.

She and Petersen subsequently met with Palm, who promised: "'You'll hear from me this week,' and we heard nothing."

Time passed. The two women had an interview for the CBS show *JAG*, which made them an immediate offer. Before they could respond their agent got a call with a second offer—from the fledgling *SVU*. "So there was no question over which one to take, not to say anything against *JAG*," DeNoon confesses. "We screamed when we heard we got a job with (the new) *Law & Order*."

Symbolically, it could have been a scream heard clear across the country. In New York City, Jonathan Greene was writing and producing documentaries on a freelance basis. In his spare time, he tried his hand at fictional scripts that never quite made it to the finish line.

Greene eventually paired with a former TV journalism colleague, Robert F. Campbell. He, in turn, knew David Burke, an L.A. resident who joined them in trying to pitch projects—without success—to what was then called Court TV.

Once Burke began working as an *SVU* executive producer during the first season, it wasn't long before all three men were immersed in Wolf World. "David says to Bob, 'We need stories,'" Greene says of the trio's reunion.

He dusted off one of his old scripts and, along with Campbell, rewrote what would become a season two episode, "Honor," about certain cultures that condone family members executing a young woman for any romantic relationship other than an arranged marriage.

Dick Wolf apparently was impressed. Still in New York, Greene and Campbell were promised other assignments and, maybe someday, staff positions.

Already on board the *SVU* express, Jeff Eckerle had longtime ties to the tribe. He describes rooming with Peter Jankowski after college in the late 1980s: "Just three guys in a tiny apartment."

That sounds like the premise for a sitcom, but both men wound up toiling in the trenches for the crime-drama hothouse known as the Law & Order brand.

"I went out to dinner one night with Dick and he said, 'Come work for me. Come be senior vice-president for my company and we'll put it in your contract to write three scripts a season,'" says Eckerle, a former producer. "When he offered me that opportunity, I jumped on it."

At the time, *SVU* was just getting started. "The first season, I was an executive," Eckerle continues. "After reading my script, 'Legacy,' Dick said, 'I think you should start writing for the show now.' So, I became a full-time writer in the second season (and) I went from producer to supervising producer."

He contends that his friendship with Wolf grew out of a mutual appreciation for their profession: "One reason Dick and I became pals is I knew what it felt like to stick your neck out, and put your talent and reputation on the line. It takes a certain amount of chutzpah."

Chutzpah is not an unfathomable personality trait for the exuberant Peter Leto. "I'd been such a fan of the Mother Ship and always thought: 'God, I would love to be part of that in the city where I was raised.' But that's such a tight-knit group, it's hard to find a job," says the current *SVU* supervising producer and episode director, who started in season one. "So I came to a crossroads in my career: pursue TV or movies? And then I got an offer for a movie on the same day an offer came from (the show). To hell with Hollywood! I wanted to tell these New York stories."

Amanda Green, now a co-executive producer, had been living her own New York stories for ten years in the law enforcement field by the time *SVU* began gearing up. "I was running a forensic psychology project that went between the DA's office and the NYPD," she recounts. "I was working with the detectives and the DAs and the victims of sex crimes, child abuse, domestic violence, homicide, you name it."

But one fateful day, show business came calling when *SVU* researchers learned about her expertise. "They said, 'Would you mind answering some questions?' I'll never forget it was like 10 or 11:00 on a Friday night. I was out on a case, sitting in Special Victims in Brooklyn. I hid in the captain's office for two hours and talked to one of the writers. And I came out thinking, 'Hmm, that was really cool.'"

Tinkering with the Concept

"Out of ego, I wanted my show to be different," recalls executive producer Ted Kotcheff. "I didn't want to be a step-child. I felt that for *SVU* you can't be detached. These are difficult emotions, dealing with children and people who are such a puzzle."

Creator Dick Wolf wondered whether or not the subject matter would frighten audiences away, according to Kotcheff. "Dick asked, 'Is there any way you can lighten this dark material?' But, as a cinephile, I wanted to head towards film noir. So it was push-me/pull-you, and out of that comes something new."

For co-executive producer Dawn DeNoon, hired in season one to write scripts, the push-pull was daunting. "It took pretty much the first year to figure out what the show was going to be," she says, adding that the Mother Ship had been conceived as "100 percent procedural, and anything personal was in the victims' or perps' lives. They really fought getting into the personal lives of the (lead) characters; you never went home with them."

Robert Palm

But *SVU* had a mandate to carve out its own identity with a formula that continued to require alterations. "This was going to be three-quarters procedural, one-quarter personal," DeNoon explains. "Even that was too much. It just didn't flow. We had a lot of trouble making that work."

Wolf recalls how the equation changed at the beginning of season two, when legal issues began to infiltrate the scripts: "I realized that adding a new dimension, the ADA assigned to the Special Victims Unit, (would provide) a new and interesting dynamic to the stories."

Well aware of the angst all around him, then-producer Jeff Eckerle was having fun as one of the people asked to help dream up a distinct template. "We felt deference for the Mother Ship," he says. "We respected the idea of what a *Law & Order* was: Clean, taut storytelling. But this is a deeper, more psychological show because

Squad room wall

we're dealing with more emotionally wrenching crimes. We had to figure out how to differentiate ourselves while still being in the genre. We kept trying to fine-tune this little gem, keep it out of the wake of the Mother Ship while staying in the same fleet."

Like Kotcheff, Eckerle refers to the *SVU* birthing as "a push-pull situation. One philosophy was: 'Just keep it on the case, stupid.' The other was: 'Come on, this is a golden opportunity to explore the personalities.' Over the seasons, it seemed as if we were shoehorning in personal stuff. We also struggled with how much courtroom time felt right. We thought of it as more of a cop show."

Wolf agrees that his *SVU* characters' off-the-job problems were being given more screen time, but with a caveat. "There is a more perceptible emphasis on personal lives," he says, "although with all the Law & Order series, the story is king."

Squad room with equipment

Royalty did not halt a period of readjustment. "There was a good deal of experimentation, while not tossing out the baby with the bath water once the show got its traction," Eckerle says. "We thought, 'God, this is all sex crimes.' Initially, that felt limiting. How many ways can you, pardon the expression, screw in a light bulb? So we slowly expanded the definition."

Executive producer Peter Jankowski remembers that even the decision to embrace the new program—then still *Sex Crimes*—as an identifiable part of the brand was not a given: "Some didn't want *Law & Order* in the title. Now we can't imagine these shows any other way."

Charlie Engel, executive vice-president for programming at NBC Universal, agrees that the *L&O* name wasn't a sure bet at first. "My recollection is that the network felt the advertisers would not want to be associated with *Sex Crimes*," he says. "And we thought, 'If *SVU* doesn't work, will it hurt the Mother Ship?'"

Wolf initially wanted to call the show *Law & Order: Sex Crimes*. "It was important for the brand to have *Law & Order* included and the consensus was that it made sense," he says. "Barry Diller, who was then head of Studios USA (the production entity), was concerned about *Sex Crimes*, so we changed the title of the show to *Law & Order: Special Victims Unit*, which is what the actual unit in the NYPD is called."

Ted Kotcheff was among the dissenters back then. "I must tell you that I resisted it, because I wanted to make a brand new series," he recalls. "I had no idea of coming in on the skirts of *Law & Order*. But (NBC and Wolf) felt it was commercially desirable to do such a thing. Now I don't think that was a mistake."

Assembling the Players

In the spring of 1999, casting for the lead characters of *SVU* was in full swing—a setting in which recently hired executive producer Ted Kotcheff says he felt like the odd man out.

"The grandees (*SVU* creator Dick Wolf with officials from NBC and USA) were at the final auditions for the two leads on the 60th floor of Rockefeller Center," he recalls. "I kind of sat in the back with the butlers and the maids."

The last round came down to six finalists: Samantha Mathis, Reiko Aylesworth, and Mariska Hargitay; Tim Matheson, Nick Chinlund, and Christopher Meloni. "Dick turns to me and says, 'Why don't you pair them up?' It was arbitrary: Tim and Samantha; Nick and Reiko; by happenstance, Chris and Mariska," Kotcheff explains.

Then came the moment of truth. "After the actors left, there was dead silence," he points out. "I didn't obey television rules when I blurted out, 'Oh, well. There's no doubt who we should choose— Hargitay and Meloni.' They all turned to look at me. Finally, Garth Ancier (then entertainment president at NBC) said he agreed and everybody jumped in."

Wolf's recollection is that the perfect duo seemed obvious. "It was apparent there was incredible chemistry the first time I saw them together," he says of Meloni and Hargitay. "They were the pair to beat, and they ended up being our first choice, and we made the right decision."

Maybe there was just something in the air that day. "The audition was so visceral," Kotcheff acknowledges. "You just know when it's the right chemistry. They were all good, but the melding of those two was special. You've got to have strong opposites: His intensity; her empathy. Sparks flew."

Those sparks apparently had already started ricocheting around the room where Hargitay and Meloni waited with other hopefuls for the auditions to begin.

"I was told by my agent that John Slattery was going to be there, and he's their client," Hargitay says. "And Chris walks in, and I see this guy who's all street New York, cocky—everything that he is now he was then. I jumped up and I go, 'Slattery!' And he goes, without missing a beat, 'Meloni!' Well, he and I, from minute one were (doing) all this shtick, and laughing. . . . It was nonstop chit-chat; couldn't stop talking. All of a sudden someone comes out and pairs us up: 'Mariska and Chris.' And I thought, 'I want to be with that guy!' Because we already had a thing."

Just think: Had the guy actually been John Slattery, Hargitay might have wound up as a long-suffering mid-twentieth-century wife or secretary on his current show, AMC's *Mad Men*, instead of as an early twenty-first-century cop alongside Meloni on *SVU*.

Meloni's knack for being himself in any setting surely helped nudge fate. "I'm like, 'Who's the chick with all the energy?' And nothing against the other two women, but I just knew that Mariska was going to be The One," he recalls. "They say (the audition pairing) was random, whatever. But I was in the middle of telling her this story, this joke. So we got up on the stage and I'm like, 'Hold on just a second, I'm going to finish telling this story.' Not being disrespectful, but this is important too. This may change my life, but the story is that funny. And I think that put us at ease, and unconsciously there was a connection you could see: That she was now my partner."

Selection of the other primary cast members flowed easily. "Dick had worked with Richard Belzer," Kotcheff says, referring to the Mother Ship's periodic crossover episodes with NBC's *Homicide: Life on the Street*.

This link had great significance, as it turns out. "When *Homicide* was canceled, I was in France with my wife and she said, 'Let's open a bottle of Champagne and toast; you did this character for seven years,'" Belzer says. "And then I remembered that Benjamin Bratt was leaving *L&O*, and so I called my manager and said, 'Call Dick Wolf—maybe Munch can become (Det. Lennie) Briscoe's partner,' because we had teamed for the crossover. So he called and Dick said, 'What a great idea, but I've already cast Jesse Martin to be the new guy.'"

Hope reared its lovely head again thanks to some quick reconfiguration, recalls Belzer. "My manager called me back and I said, 'Isn't *L&O* doing a sex crimes show?' and I said, 'What about that?'"

A few contractual glitches related to Munch's previous incarnation were soon overcome. But he needed a partner.

"Richard Belzer and I were good friends," says Dean Winters (former Det. Brian Cassidy). "(He) had always looked at me like a little brother, and he basically told Dick, 'Well, I'll do this new show of yours, *SVU*, only if you make Dean Winters my partner.' And that's exactly what happened."

Dann Florek—whose Captain Cragen appeared in the Mother Ship's 1988 pilot and later spent three seasons in that squad room—got an enticement from Wolf one day: "'How would you like to bring the character back?' And I said, 'What's going on?'"

The seasoned actor's next question was logical. "I asked, 'What am I doing, the same character? Similar?' Dick said, 'It'll be Cragen, but we'll fill in the backstory and all that.'"

Even so, Florek felt it was crucial to get Wolf's assurance that he did not have to audition for the role: "No way I'm walking into a room to read and be told that I can't play—*me*."

No such precedent existed for Stabler's long-suffering wife on *SVU*. Isabel Gillies was shopping for a wedding dress when a call came asking her to head over to the casting session. It wasn't exactly a convenient time, but she told them: "'This is the right role for me and I should have it.' And then I got the part and that was that. I was in the first episode."

Many Rivers to Cross

"There were no traditional studio spaces available in New York," says *SVU* producer David DeClerque, referring to the challenge of securing an appropriate edifice for the new show. "In Manhattan, we looked at a number of places but it was getting really expensive. Real estate was as hot as a pistol and most wanted five- to ten-year leases. We literally scoured two dozen possibilities. They'd be dirty or in noisy areas or there wouldn't be enough bathrooms. By late winter, we knew that when spring came we needed to have a home."

And, then, voila! North Bergen, New Jersey, glimmered like an unpolished gem. "Here, all the logistical things fell into place: an air-conditioning system; enough parking; 53,000 square feet, about two-thirds of it stage area. I told Dick, 'It looks like we're crossing the river.' He asked, 'A Law & Order show that's not in Manhattan?' I said, 'Just the internal sets would be here. We'll still think of this as a New York show.'"

RANDEE DAWN

David DeClerque

The Garden State facility made sense. "It had been sitting empty for a while," DeClerque recalls. "We got a one-year lease and the owner thought it might be fun to have a TV show in one of his properties."

Dick Wolf agrees that New Jersey has proved to be a blessing in disguise. "It was tough to find a full production facility in Manhattan that gave us the room and the resources that we needed," he says, adding that the arrangement "has worked out beautifully."

SVU started filming while construction of the sets continued at the East Coast headquarters, situated on what were once wetlands; cast and crew concentrated on location shoots until the work was completed.

As time went on, however, the accommodations got at least one negative review. "I wish they weren't based in North Bergen," says Stephanie March, who signed on in season two as the show's ADA Alexandra Cabot. "That is a pain in the neck to get to. (And) how depressing is that place? You're floating in the middle of Secaucus."

She saw a stark contrast between the Jersey Swamp Thing and the Mother Ship anchored at Manhattan's Chelsea Piers. "Every time we would shoot at the *Law & Order* stages—and we shot there a lot because we didn't have (our own) courtroom—I would think to myself, 'Why can't we shoot at the pier? It's six blocks from where I live. It's in the middle of Manhattan. Why not? Why not?' Nope, I have to get my sorry self through the (Lincoln) tunnel."

After reaching the other bank of the Hudson, March felt stranded in a gloomy building surrounded by an industrial wasteland. "That place is an energy sucker," she contends. "I remember when my mom came to see it, she said, 'Do you think they'll change the lighting?' I said, 'I don't think so, no.' . . . You're totally trapped out there, because you can't pop out and do anything else."

March disliked the marsh but others involved with *SVU* were less bothered by the bleak North Bergen ambiance as long as the faux squad room was correct. Writer Amanda Green, then a law-enforcement employee in real life, encountered a little bit of déjà vu all over again when she first visited the soundstage.

"My biggest concern was that the set looked right," she says. "I walked around that day and saw real wanted posters for cases that I'd worked on and I'll never forget going, 'Gosh, that guy looks familiar. Why does he look familiar? Right! Because I worked that case. I was there in the lineup and I was there when he got convicted at trial.'"

For Green, verisimilitude soon kicked in. "Looking at details in the squad room that the scenic designers had just copied from what they'd seen, I knew what everything meant and it was right. They don't even know why they've done it but they've done it right. So I was really impressed."

While inspecting the set, Green had also spent three hours with Dick Wolf, telling him what she thought about the show. "The next day my phone rang and it was Dick's assistant saying, 'Come out to L.A. and meet the writers.' I asked, 'When?' and she said, 'Tomorrow.' I told her, 'Are you kidding me? I'm on trial.' So that was that."

Not exactly. "Couple hours later the phone rang and they asked, 'So, when would you be available to come to L.A.?'" Green recalls. "And that started what became the next three years of my life—which was not telling a soul what I was doing because I was afraid it would undermine my credibility professionally."

Way Out West

Compared with the mammoth New Jersey soundstage, there's a smaller, tidier operation on the Universal Studios lot in Los Angeles, where the writing and editing of *Law & Order: Special Victims Unit* unfolds. It's nestled next to the gift shop and down the street from the commissary. (Recommended to visitors: try the peanut-butter cookies.)

All three L&O shows are housed in adjacent structures. *SVU* has set up shop in a one-story gray bungalow that's named—appropriately—in honor of Jack Webb, the creator and star of *Dragnet*. The legendary NBC crime show ran from 1952 to 1970, before being all-too-briefly resurrected by Dick Wolf in 2003 on CBS.

But the *L&O* empire now rules the roost, where just outside select parking spaces are available for the *SVU* personnel inside: executive producer and showrunner Neal Baer; co-executive producers Jonathan Greene, Dawn DeNoon, and Amanda Green; and some novices, supervising producer Daniel Truly and story editor Mick Betancourt.

The *SVU* quarters are little more than a long hallway with offices branching out to each side; depending on staff seniority, the capacity increases mightily. Truly and Betancourt seem lucky to have a window, desk, and whiteboard, while DeNoon, Greene, and Green enjoy enough space to make many a New York studio apartment dweller drool with envy.

Bookshelves line the walls, packed with thick ring-binders, one for each episode. Others have been devoted to source material, such as all those headlines that are ripped and now ready for the plundering. Desks, side tables, walls, and computer screens display personal photos posed with cast and crew, or awards earned for particular scripts.

There is no specific common space or coffee area; with the commissary so close, food can be easily foraged. But Baer's assistant, Ryan Spencer, has an office with a wide selection of snacks, should the urge come over anyone. In aggregate, the *L&O* workers potentially mean a lot of hunger.

"We have 50 to 100 people in three buildings close to each other," explains Peter Jankowski, president of Wolf Films.

A handful of those folks are astonishingly industrious writers.

CHAPTER TWO

GRAPPLING WITH UNCERTAINTY

W hile shooting the *SVU* pilot on New York's Upper East Side in the autumn of 1999, the show's two lead actors coasted on the thrill of a wonderful new opportunity, epitomized by an evening meal with their boss.

"Dick invited Mariska and me to dinner at a very fancy steak restaurant," Christopher Meloni (Det. Elliot Stabler) told *The Hollywood Reporter* in 2007. "For some reason, we had a boom box. After a little wine, we were feeling really good. As we were leaving, we flipped on the boom box and started dancing to a late '70s head-banger, 'I-like-to-rock' type song. We were so happy to be employed by Dick Wolf— and he didn't fire us the next day for our outrageous public display."

But it didn't take long for the crucible of episodic television to emerge. "It was tough in the beginning. I felt as if we were being

Mariska Hargitay and Christopher Meloni

pulled in many directions at once," says producer David DeClerque. "We had growing pains."

Arguably, few felt more anguish in that situation than the stars.

"I was not prepared for the weather; shooting exteriors, working fifteen-, sixteen-, seventeen-, eighteen-hour days in the beginning and all of a sudden this was my life and I had no other life," Hargitay (Det. Olivia Benson) laments. "It was all *SVU* all the time and dark and depressing and sexual assaults and rape, and the show hadn't found its voice."

The trial-by-fire was extraordinarily difficult for Meloni, as well. "You're prepared because you want it so badly, but the first four months or so, because I was so mentally and emotionally drawn and crispy from the hours and the subject matter and pouring all my heart and soul into it, I woke up two mornings shaking and couldn't get out of bed," he admits.

To this day, Meloni wonders if the stress nearly did him in: "I was sitting on the edge of the bed and I was shaking, and I remember thinking, 'Oh, my God, this is an emotional breakdown. And I'm not that (kind of) guy, so whatever, it's an anxiety attack, but I've never had one.' But I still think it was a mini-collapse. But—nothing a shower couldn't fix!"

The giddy notion of being employed by Wolf no longer prompted Meloni and Hargitay to dance with joy: "I was so sad, alone, and all of that," she acknowledges. "Even my work was suffering, I just wasn't happy. . . . I wasn't flying at the material."

After three or four episodes Wolf asked for an assessment from Kotcheff, who remembers the conversation that ensued:

Ted: "I'm not used to wall-to-wall verbiage."

Dick: "Yeah, (TV) is a writer's medium."

Ted: "In the 1960s I helped Michelangelo Antonioni edit *Blow Up*. His approach was, 'We think of dialogue as sound effects; we tell a story in terms of pictures.'"

In this regard, Kotcheff was the polar opposite of venerable word-smith Robert Nathan, on the Mother Ship during the early 1990s and with *SVU* as co-executive producer in the fifth, sixth, and seventh seasons. "*Law & Order* is a writer's dream," he suggested during a 1997 interview for a book about the original show, "because it's all about words."

Words can be fickle, however. "I know you're a creative person," Wolf told Kotcheff early in *SVU*'s season one. "But in a season of twenty-two shows, we'll do four great episodes, four terrible ones, and the rest lie somewhere in between."

The East Coast executive producer's response: "I can't approach a season in that frame of mind."

Somehow, the two frames of mind merged enough to impress the studio and the network.

"I thought for a while we would never get to episode thirteen, that it would turn into rape-of-the-week, child-molester-of-the-week, and I'd be out looking for work again," Kotcheff notes. "But we were asked to do nine more episodes, a full season. Then, we were invited back for another year."

The network's pat on the back eased any worries Wolf might have been having. "I don't think we had many growing pains," he says. "But there (was) some re-evaluation of stories and characters, which is normal."

Although Dann Florek had three seasons on the Mother Ship under his belt, he found *SVU* to be an entirely different experience. "There was definitely a sense of feeling our way," he notes. "And I also think if you go back and look, probably a handful of our weakest episodes were in that first year, when we were still figuring things out and getting the right writers for the style of the show, and where could we go, you didn't want to just be grisly."

Yet, grisly was almost the mantra in those early days with episodes that never seemed to stray from the horrific crime into the relative calm and, well, order of a courtroom. The victims were varied—a teenage model, a prostitute, a male travel writer, a college student, a Wall Street financier, a TV news reporter—but the somber caseload was unrelenting.

"I guess I felt we were struggling with the philosophy and how we were going to present that philosophy," Florek says. "I thought what we had happening was pretty good."

Audiences, which were not tuning in *en masse*, may have disagreed with his assessment. People he talked with would often disparage *SVU.*

"They'd go, 'Oooooh, that one, don't like it.' And I'd say, 'Give it at least three, maybe four or five episodes. It's different but it's smart and it's good. And it kept changing and changing," Florek says.

Wolf points out that *SVU* "is not about sex; it's about special victims, and the courage of police to prosecute these heinous crimes."

For the production team, perceptions of a sex-crimes show were sometimes formidable beyond the soundstage. "We had to take a very sensitive approach in the beginning, getting people to understand what the show is about," says Trish Adlesic, *SVU* location manager since season one's sixth episode. "One of my responsibilities is to communicate with the public. . . . We coordinate with city government, state government, tenants, superintendents, building electricians, co-op associations. I've been very fortunate, but in general people are a bit apprehensive. I have to be a diplomat."

While Adlesic continued blazing a path for their location work, the actors tried to muster the inner strength to cope with the show's pace.

Stephanie March, introduced as the ADA in the first episode of season two ("Wrong is Right"), contrasted the *SVU* schedule to the relatively easy demands of theater: "You have to sustain a certain low-level constant energy, and when I say sustain, I mean more than fifteen or seventeen hours. And that is so different from being in a play. I remember thinking the amount of time it takes to shoot one scene, I could have been done with my play by now. So it was so much harder than I thought it would be."

Nonetheless, March found a positive side to the arduous effort. "It was completely different muscles, it was a different kind of concentration, and sustenance and focus, and it was really wonderful for me and lucky for me to be a principal on a show where I could hone that over and over and over day after day," she surmises. "It was like being forged in fire, but it worked."

By then, the rigor was becoming at least somewhat routine for the others. "I think it took me a little over a year to figure it out," Meloni says. "Because the first year is the impending actors strike, so in order to get a jump on that we worked a whole year, we put thirty episodes in the can, and then the next two or three (seasons) we were working anywhere from sixteen to twenty-two hours a day. It was a matter of course."

For Hargitay, the East Coast had turned into an albatross around the neck of a California native. "I wasn't dating anyone, I just didn't have a life here. It was unbalanced and depressing," she says.

And where did Monique Jefferies, one of the original *SVU* detectives, go? "At first, we had Michelle Hurd as Belzer's partner, but (ultimately) man-woman, man-woman was too redundant," Kotcheff notes. Her character got in trouble with the NYPD and quit the job in frustration early in season two—not an ideal situation for the actress.

As the cast coped with various problems, life wasn't always smooth sailing for the show's producers. Showrunner Robert Palm had two young daughters at the time and "the subject matter was really getting to me. You dream of that shit. You wake up in the middle of the night. I didn't want that in my head anymore," he says of his decision to leave *SVU* at the end of season one.

The scribes were restless. "I remember Dick Wolf reminding us how high the bar was, and if any scripts weren't as good as a *L&O*,

you were fired," recalls DeNoon, who has penned teleplays for *SVU* from the start. "He pulled no punches and we left the room shaking. And they pretty much fired every single person by the end of the first season."

Another issue: Who got to rip what stories from which headlines? "We worried, 'What happens if the original *L&O* does a sex crime?' We had turf wars over story ideas," recounts Jeff Eckerle, a former *SVU* producer. "Now there's a central clearing house. They try not to have two shows cover the same case in the same season or at least do things differently. Whenever we reached an impasse, a decree would come down from the Wolfman."

As a veteran resident of the Wolfman's lair, executive producer Arthur Forney explains, "We got off to a rough start because we were dealing with sex crimes in a harsh, almost cinema-verite style that was maybe a little too graphic," he suggests. "As time went on, we brought in the medical point-of-view. On the Mother Ship, it's a dead body. On *SVU*, the victim is often still alive with damage done to their body and emotions. We were figuring it out as we went along. By the second season, Neal Baer really spearheaded that process."

For writers Jonathan Greene and Robert Campbell, a year had passed since their initial involvement with *SVU*. Then, one evening they were rather suddenly summoned to a meeting in New York with David Burke, the first season two showrunner, and Judith McCreary.

"David said, 'How soon can you guys be ready to move to L.A.?' And I was like, 'Huh?' They wanted to hire us (full-time). And six weeks later, that's exactly what happened. We moved out here (to L.A.) and came on the show," Greene says.

But there was an additional surprise: "Three weeks after that, David left the show and Neal Baer came and that changed the whole world."

CHAPTER THREE

HEALING THE WHOLE

I t's no secret that *SVU* was caught in a whirlwind of flux during the first two seasons, according to executive producer Ted Kotcheff. "We lost Robert Palm, our chief writer. He quit. David Burke—that just wasn't working for us. We had no writers. Then I read that Neal had parted company with (*ER* showrunner) John Wells."

Baer, an executive producer with the NBC medical series for seven seasons, was poised to leap from the hospital to the halls of justice. "I felt *ER* was getting very soapy and thought it was time to move on," he says. "I left the show on Friday, October 13 in 2000—a lucky day!—and started at *SVU* on October 20."

That sense of luck pervaded *SVU*. "This show to a certain extent started out being more sensational and what Neal really did was bring it around to being . . . more issue-oriented than (merely) the sex crime of the week," theorizes Jonathan Greene, now a co-executive producer. "He literally took this not just to the next level, but up five or six levels above that."

He calls the showrunner "our spiritual guru."

Series creator Dick Wolf says that "when Neal Baer joined the team, his background as a pediatrician added new insights to the stories and characters."

But Baer initially felt wary about the offer to join that team, given the tenor of *SVU*'s first season. "My wife told me: 'Don't take this job—it's too tawdry.' I thought it was, too. Bananas up the butt and all that."

This fruit assault takes place in an episode titled "Russian Love Poem." Earlier in the season, "Wanderlust" included another questionable shot that Baer describes as "panties stuffed in a dead guy's mouth."

Robert Palm bristles at the suggestion that the episodes were dissolute under his one-season watch as showrunner. "That's bullshit," he says. "It was raw the first year, not prurient. We tried to bring complexity to the stories but were constantly getting slapped down."

His theory was that it would be an oversimplification to merely demonize abusers: "It seemed too easy to just create monsters. But we were told, 'No, no, no. We want monsters.'"

Whatever the cause, in the opinion of NBC Universal vice-president for programming Charles Engel, the series was sinking. "We were doing some types of stories that, taken out of context, sound like a horrible show you wouldn't want to watch," he surmises.

Baer had discovered the daunting challenge ahead during his first *tête-à-tête* with several *SVU* higher-ups. "Dick said: 'I'll toss you into deep water and you'll either sink or swim.'"

But this cautionary statement did not sour Baer on the invitation to work for *SVU*, a risky decision that was rooted in an earlier chance encounter. "Primarily, I was drawn to it by Mariska," he acknowledges. "I'd been introduced to her by (longtime *L&O* writer who later worked on *SVU*) Robert Nathan in 1996. He did *Prince Street* (NBC, 1997–2000) with her. She was hoping to play Anthony Edwards' screwed-up girlfriend on *ER*. Despite being smart, funny, and beautiful, she didn't get the part. Then I ran into her on the (Warner Bros.) lot."

Hargitay was en route to demand that John Wells, Baer's boyhood pal growing up in Colorado, reconsider his decision not to cast her as Edwards' girlfriend—a tactic she would use later when insisting that Wolf choose her for the role of Olivia Benson.

Impressed by her determination, Baer had no qualms about intervening. "I told John, 'She won't take no for an answer.' She got the part and was wonderful on the show. So, when *SVU* had an opening (in season two), I thought I was destined to take the job."

But destiny was much thornier when it came to other matters on the show, as Baer discovered in what was ostensibly his job interview during the search for a new executive producer. "Some of us were nervous after the first season of *SVU* that it was being done in the wrong way," Engel recalls. "Dick, Peter Jankowski, and I were having a sort of meet-and-greet with Neal Baer. And at a certain point we realized—I could see it in Dick's eyes—that Neal was the guy. We basically told him, 'You've got to start yesterday.'"

Baer will never forget the sense of urgency in that get-together. "Dick told me there was a (season one) script, 'Pixies,' I had to have ready by Monday. And I had to do something about 'Runaway,' which was a disaster," he says. "To re-shoot it, Ted Kotcheff directed around the clock for twenty-four hours. I threw out all the original dialogue and put in long interviews with each character. That's the only episode ever broadcast just once on the network—because it was stinky."

He also deepened the *SVU* diagnoses by bringing on two physician characters. Baer replaced the psychologists, Elizabeth Olivet (Carolyn McCormick) and Emil Skoda (J.K. Simmons) with a forensic psychiatrist, Dr. George Huang (B.D. Wong). And Tamara Tunie came on as a pathologist, Dr. Melinda Warner.

Next, he made use of his passion for social change by encouraging Amanda Green, then a consultant, to begin writing scripts and relocate from the East Coast. "I wanted to cover more psychological and social issues," Baer notes.

Green (no relation to the co-author of this book) had been living a semi-clandestine existence, theoretically not allowed to hold a job outside the NYPD yet mentioned in the credits for each *SVU* episode. She had "a top-secret memo" to prove she was merely a consultant. "But I didn't tell anyone. I would just come out here on weekends and vacations and . . . have my brain picked for days. Finally, after like two and a half years, Neil asked: 'Can you write?' I said, 'Uh, I've written reports and documents and case reviews and plenty of stuff but I don't know TV.' He goes, 'Hey, you (already) give us the stories and dialogues and twists and turns and plot points. You're writing; you just don't know it.'"

She accepted the doctor's prognosis. In season three, "Counterfeit" was Green's debut as an official *SVU* employee.

Another Baer prescription was to reduce the surfeit of personal details about lead characters. "I felt that the show was going home with Stabler and Benson too much," he explains. "That detracted from solving the crime. You can explore their personal lives through the crime and don't have to interrupt the investigation. *SVU* needs to be about the very dark nature of the human psyche."

Baer seems to believe the human psyche can also be reflected in fashion. "(I wanted) no more espadrilles and bad beige suits for Stephanie March," he says. "She needed to be an Ice Queen in Armani."

The Ice Queen was not terribly confident. "I think the first season of any new thing is rocky," March says. "When (David Burke) was gone and Neal came in, I thought: 'OK, well, I guess this is how it is. Maybe they'll fire me too.'"

Instead, she remembers that Baer met with her and said, "'I'm really excited about your character; I can't wait to write for your character.'. . . It's such an obviously better show after that."

That forward movement also seems to have worked wonders for Mariska Hargitay, who remembers that, "I hadn't found my stride, I wasn't inspired. And I have to be inspired . . . *SVU* was still finding its way. We'd had a writer that was really kind of a negative. We had a second writer that didn't work out, didn't know our voices, and I thought nobody was doing well with the material. There wasn't a communication between the writers and the actors. The directors were different every week. There was no consistency. Dick wasn't really here. We had no leader, we had no vision."

Baer's reign apparently began to make life on the set, well, *bearable*. "When Neal came, it was an energy shift for the show and everything changed. We owned it, we were inspired, we cared," Hargitay suggests. "We all had the same vision. Neal brought amazing writers and all of a sudden we got excited. He's a great leader and accessible. I can get that man on the phone twenty-four hours a day."

She is comforted by the fact that "Neal has the excitement (level) of a seven-year-old. There's this beautiful collaboration. Everything started to gel, and then everyone was more invested. It's so fun to come to work. It all just takes time. It takes time."

Like Baer, Kotcheff appreciates Hargitay and her fellow thespians. "In my fifty-seven years as a director, some of that on live television, this is the nicest cast I've ever been with," he says. "No vanity, no egos, no bad behavior. They all come to work with energy and enthusiasm and great expectations."

Such energy and enthusiasm can't be all that easy to rally. "After these actors spend fourteen hours here," Kotcheff points out, "they have to go home and memorize six pages of dialogue!"

CHAPTER FOUR

THE GRIND

In 2000, the *Law & Order* patriarch explained how he expected his business to function. "I hire obsessive people, people who literally work sixty to seventy hours a week for months on end and who have fine-tuned detectors for what's good and what's bad," Wolf said in an interview with a quarterly magazine published by the Producers Guild of America.

Jonathan Greene, a co-executive producer who has been slogging through *SVU* workdays since season two, observes that there really is no typical daily structure: "It depends on how much time I have for an episode. I've had as many as six months and I've had as little as two weeks from beginning to end. When I'm researching, it's talking to people on the phone, it's reading a book."

Each with an office, writers are largely left on their own in L.A., though always aware of the looming deadline. While writing the script, schedules become more rigorous. "I'll generally get up and

Jonathan Greene

be in the office as early as five in the morning, no later than six if I can get myself out of bed," Greene says. "I do my best work in the mornings when I'm fresh. I have this rule: I never hand in work at night until I have time to check it in the morning."

Despite ubiquitous computers in the Studio City headquarters, many writers find it useful to put their thoughts down on whiteboards before creating "beat sheets" (on which the distinct rhythms of a story are charted) or more advanced drafts.

"There are some people who can write a script without a beat sheet, but I find the more detailed and thought-out our beat sheet is—the outline, if you will—the easier it is to write the script," Greene suggests. "Because you've taken care of all of the thinking. You still have to (invent) great dialogue, but you've taken the hard part, which is the story, out of the picture."

The going isn't always smooth, of course. "You get to shape it as you go along and, even when you have the best of intentions, you can write yourself into a corner," he says. "Then, the fun part is, 'OK, how do I get out of the corner?' That gets the juices flowing."

Juice or no juice, writing tends to be a solitary profession. And *SVU* more or less eschews the collective effort—called a "writers' room," in which everyone hashes out script ideas—that's favored by many other TV shows.

Judith McCreary prefers it that way. "In the Dick Wolf camp, you sink or swim on your own versus being in a room with other writers, putting all the beats up on a board as a group. That makes for lazy writing."

Tara Butters, employed at *SVU* from seasons three through seven along with writing partner Michele Fazekas, says that lack of a writers' room proved to be liberating: "As a result, there was no sense of competitiveness. We were working on our own, so it was like writing your own mini-feature."

As seen by a newcomer, Mick Betancourt (who joined *SVU* in season nine after working on several other shows), a writers' room is not always such a terrific idea. "I would have a meeting maybe once a week, which sometimes we do here, just to see where everybody's at, and have writers write—that's what they do best," he says. "If writers had tremendous personalities they wouldn't like the isolated experience of writing. (Put) five hermits in a room to socialize for fourteen hours?"

This more independent process at *SVU* initially can seem strange. Daniel Truly, who started on the show in time for season ten, had to readjust to the notion of flying solo.

"In some ways it's slightly lonelier, because you don't spend the first two hours every day sitting around telling what you did over the weekend," Truly says. "You can still do all that, but you get a lot of time to do research, which you need for your episodes, and to work over the stories."

Apart from his nostalgia for shooting the breeze with other writers, he appreciates *SVU*'s literary ambiance. "My experience has been you pitch an idea to Neal (Baer). He says, 'I like it.' You then pitch story beats to him as you go along and he says, 'Go write an outline.' You write an outline. He does notes (on it). You write a script. He gives you notes. . . . Neal and Amanda (Green) are always available, so if you need another writer to run stuff by, they're all over the place."

When former co-producer Paul Grellong started at *SVU* in 2005, he discovered that "they have a team of incredibly bright writers who are patient with new people."

The more seasoned staff watches out for the new kids on the block. "Amanda Green did that for me," Grellong says. "Neal and Amanda told me some of the areas they were interested in exploring. I wanted to write a script that was of the moment. That's one thing the show is really good at: of the moment."

Green relishes that mentoring role. "I supervise all the junior writers, so we have a process where I work with them to develop their ideas," she says. "I'm sort of the intermediate step. A lot of what

I do all day is working with younger writers, helping them find a way to tell the story they want to tell within the format of the show, within our conventions."

Those conventions can be turned on their heads every now and then. What starts out as a sex-crime investigation may veer into very different territory, with an overarching issue—racism, homophobia, greed, government corruption, for instance—as the final denouement.

When working on her own projects, Green becomes something of a bookworm. "(If) I'm working on an episode about manic depression, I'm going to read memoirs and news articles about it. I have a full-time researcher whose job is to find me, say, the voices of manic depression. Whether it's watching documentaries or reading books or whatever. Reading, reading, reading."

Judith McCreary likes the Internet. "I'm always Googling," she notes. "For example, I ran across a story about women who were

Executive producer Amanda Green on the set of season eight's "Underbelly" with members of the NYPD.

raped more than once by the same guy and that made me wonder if his biological clock was ticking ("Confrontation" season eight) . . . I troll Lexis-Nexis (a subscription service that provides legal, governmental, and high-tech information sources). Or I look at *McKinney's Consolidated Laws of New York Annotated* to understand the statutes. We don't really do ripped-from-the headlines. That's more the Mother Ship."

Longtime *L&O* writer and Baer's former *ER* colleague Robert Nathan (now with *Criminal Intent*), was on hand for the fifth, sixth, and seventh seasons of *SVU*. He found the process there quite different from that of the Mother Ship: "One's a sonnet, the other's free verse. *Law & Order* is structurally more formal. After eighteen years, it holds to its roots: solve a crime, then see if the legal system can do its job. *SVU* is more fluid. It can be a quiet meditation one week and a suspense movie the next. You never quite know what you'll get, which is one of the reasons the show remains so vibrant."

Grellong, who came to *SVU* by way of theater, observes that *SVU* "leaves no stone unturned. Accuracy is really, really crucial. One of my favorite things about working there was that every week they turn out a forty-two-minute mystery set in a new world populated by unique characters."

To make sure those mysteries are good, nobody at *SVU* is busier than showrunner Neal Baer. "I'm working on fourteen episodes right now, in various stages," he explains, before enumerating several upcoming season ten titles. "In the last two days, I looked at 'Lunacy,' took notes with Arthur (Forney, an executive producer), worked on a re-edit of 'Trials' and a third rewrite of 'Confession.' Dan Truly will pitch me a script tomorrow. I'm reading Jonathan Greene's episode about HIV, 'Deniers.' I'm communicating with (Casting Director) Jonathan Strauss about the parts we'll offer for that episode."

In addition, Baer is "always asking the script supervisor what the timing is on a show. I'm looking at cuts. Maybe asking people to re-shoot things I don't like. My researcher constantly emails me interesting articles."

Plus, he's involved with the publicity end of things otherwise expertly handled by Pam Golum and, until her retirement at the end of 2008 Audrey Davis of The Lippin Group, a bicoastal public relations firm that's been with Wolf Films since 1994.

"I have my hand in everything," surmises Baer. "I essentially rewrite every show but don't always get credit because I feel that's my responsibility as executive producer."

In the communications business, the color red historically symbolizes editorial oversight, but not at *SVU*. "Every writer gets notes in purple ink," he says of the script suggestions given to his team. "I have a big box of purple Pilot V-Ball pens. I got the idea from a neurosurgeon who wrote that way."

TV showrunning may not be brain surgery, but Neal Baer's hands-on approach probably comes closer than most. He's got a management style that seems to suit McCreary, at least. "Neal allows us a considerable amount of freedom to write what we feel most passionate about. I like to go to a place where the characters get irritated with each other. I like to explore aggressive tension between Fin and Stabler. . . . It gives us something to play with. Dick says verisimilitude is important. These things don't resolve themselves. Let's just let it stay there."

The *SVU* endeavor was "a learning curve," notes Michele Fazekas. "Having just one storyline is a huge challenge. Everything has to make sense and lead to the next thing. Doing a script is like boot camp. You have to be logical all the way through. Every scene had to be integral to the plot. That made me a better writer."

Tara Butters, Fazekas' writing partner, points out that the show has no specific formula, compared with the Mother Ship's cops in the first half and courts in the second.

"Neal told us, 'We don't have to do it that way,'" Fazekas says.

"Sometimes we'd start with meeting the killer in the teaser, or never meet him until the last scene," Butters adds. "It's a blessing and a curse as a writer. So much freedom can be daunting."

On the other hand, "It forces you to be more creative," Fazekas concludes. "Neal likes to grapple with issues. He wants the cops to be on opposite sides in an argument. . . . The only rules at *SVU* are: Don't be ordinary and don't be lazy. I love courts and case law but have a tendency to get into the legalese too much. Neal always said, 'Find creative ways to get around ordinary questions the cops or prosecutors ask.'"

Amanda Green's specialty is sticking to the quintessential facts. "We take liberties with timing," she says. "Obviously, cases don't go to trial five minutes later and DNA results don't come back in thirty seconds, but we never make up a technology that doesn't exist. We stay on the cutting edge. We research what's new and happening in forensics or law. I've gotten calls from lawyers asking me to explain how we did something."

Before he was hired, Mick Betancourt remembers being impressed by *SVU*'s commitment to topicality. "It was a show that was so good I was just entertained by it, which for someone who is a writer is a pretty unique thing, because usually you want to get in there and find the nuances, and I just took it for what it was," he says. "Which is more a compliment than anything because it was so airtight. And when I got hired I went through all the scripts and saw the character nuances that Neal likes to put in, socially conscious events and issues. . . . Not being heavy handed but just shining a light on these things."

That revelation gave him pause. "It was so perfect, I was a little intimidated," Betancourt acknowledges. "You don't write 200 episodes of television by accident. It was a humbling experience to be brought on and see how other people write, see what the process is, have them share it."

Former co-executive producer Patrick Harbinson, who arrived at the end of season three, knew Baer from *ER*, where Harbinson worked as a producer. "He was the brains and heart. He asked me to join *SVU* and I said, 'Yes, please.'"

Originally from England, Harbinson had done a series there about the special investigations branch of the armed services called *Red Cap*. "That was close (to *Law & Order*) in terms of tightly plotted procedurals," he suggests. "I love the strictness of the Mother Ship. There are rules, like a little dramatic sonnet. For *SVU*, Dick Wolf said we can break some of the rules. What writer wouldn't like that?"

Esat Coast–based producer David DeClerque thinks *Law & Order* is "a great whodunit, with twists and turns. *SVU* was going to be much more about the emotions of victims. We were still going to have those ka-chings. This show is similar to *L&O* in many ways, but with a little more beating heart to it."

A medicine man who knows how to keep hearts beating and beat sheets pumping, Baer says his intention is "to inspire writers. I give them the ideas. Some are better with emotional material; others with the twists and turns."

A sublime testament to the show's ethos may be the two leather signs on the well-appointed desk in Dick Wolf's office—the only things on his desk, in fact. One reads, "It CAN be done." The other: "It's the writing, stupid."

CHAPTER FIVE

TOGETHERNESS

O ur best writers are women," proclaims executive producer Ted Kotcheff.

The presence of so many females on the staff is "unusual for any show," says former co-executive producer Michele Fazekas. "There are always many more men. But I don't think this has been a coincidence on *SVU*, because women are a huge percentage of the viewing audience. It's a nice change."

Judith McCreary takes heart from Dick Wolf's compliment on her ability to transcend gender. "He once told me, 'You write like a man.' I felt like Dorothy Parker. It was always her aspiration to write like a man. A lot of women (writers) lean toward romantic notions," she says. "I'm by no means a feminist, though some might say I'm a rabid feminist. I tell them, 'Trust me. I'm a double-D. I need my bra.'"

Dawn DeNoon seems to think the feminine mystique is an *SVU* charm: "Ted Kotcheff has always loved female writers on the show, and we've gone through a lot of men. Turnover's big on men, and even talking to them, I hate to say, it's really hard for a man to get (the) mindset of being a victim and at risk to be raped . . . I'm generalizing; obviously there are men who can write for (the series), and Neal is running it."

Moreover, at *SVU* it's extraordinary that people in their prime are writing for primetime, given an industry milieu that worships youth. In a 2003 interview, Dick Wolf pondered this Hollywood phenomenon: "I've never understood the obsession with younger writers and dramas. Comedies I understand, but how do you write drama at twenty-three, you haven't experienced anything? . . . There are not many twenty-three-year-olds who can write about life-changing situations unless it's medical. That sounds weird, but there's not the mileage on the odometer to get under the surface. There are exceptions—(Charles) Dickens wasn't bad at twenty-three."

Whatever the age or gender, writing partnerships of all kinds have been a fairly common occurrence at the L.A. headquarters. After being teamed with Lisa Marie Petersen from 1999 through 2005, DeNoon found the work ethic a wee bit harder to muster on her own.

"It's a big difference if there's no one to come in and say, 'OK, we have to start writing now!' The procrastination lasts a little longer," she muses. "With another person, we're going to meet up at this time and we have to get to work. . . . Conversely, I was always a nighttime person. So when the idea comes to you at midnight you could start and run right through, but with a partner you're like, 'I can't call her at midnight, but this just hit me.'"

Fazekas, who went on to work with longtime collaborator Tara Butters on CW's sci-fi show *Reaper*, explains their method while at *SVU* from 2001–06: "We'd break a story together, figuring out every beat, write an outline, and split up to each write half. Then we switch halves. Tara gets less frustrated than I do. I'm like, 'If it's not working throw it out.'"

Butters remains committed to her bailiwick: "My favorite thing is dialogue."

Once his writing partner Robert Campbell left the show, after a stint that lasted from 2000–03, co-executive producer Jonathan

Greene soldiered on alone. "When you're doing it by yourself, you get to work more in your own head. You don't have to verbalize as much stuff," he observes. "So it makes it easier for me to go through whatever my wacky thought process may be, and to get it out there."

While still together, they would always use a whiteboard to plot their episode. As a solo act, Greene assumed, "I don't need the board; I can do this all in my head," until encountering a small hurdle. "I just started using the board again because I realized it helps me to look at something and not have to go to a computer. It's like anything else, your process evolves," he explains.

Across the country, close collaboration is a daily *SVU* regimen, generally involving clusters of people with expertise in various fields.

"We normally prep for eight days and shoot for eight days, so there's always a team prepping," says producer David DeClerque, who has to keep track of it all. "We constantly leapfrog that way throughout the year. It's high-energy. We can't ever lag. Sometime that means twelve- or thirteen-hour days. In the beginning, we had crazy hours to establish the look of the show and the characters. Now we're pretty well-oiled."

That term is frequently mentioned by the many human cogs in the *SVU* machine. Indeed, if the roof were removed to allow a crane shot looking down at the labyrinthine North Bergen operation, it might resemble elaborate wheelworks—or perhaps an ant farm. The hustle-bustle is constant, all the more so when scenes are being shot on the soundstage and everyone seems supercharged with a sense of purpose.

"We start with Uncle Ted's Story Hour (a weekly brainstorming session for each new script that's led by executive producer Kotcheff), going over our thoughts on the episode," DeClerque explains. "For example, what kinds of houses will we put the characters in? The assistant director breaks down the script to come up with a schedule. We discuss what guest stars might be available."

CHAPTER SIX

FINDING OTHER TALENT

"Uncle Ted's Story Hour" sounds like a cozy children's library event. But, at *SVU*'s New Jersey headquarters, it's a visit to the dark side of human nature via a brainstorming session led by executive producer Kotcheff for each new script. About a dozen people gather in a conference room or squeeze into his office to evaluate everything from plot to potential sets.

"We go over our thoughts on the episode," producer David DeClerque explains. "For example, what kinds of houses will we put the characters in? The assistant director breaks down the script to come up with a schedule. We discuss what guest stars might be available."

The search is always on for an *SVU* smorgasbord of victims, suspects, perps, witnesses, legal eagles, uniformed flatfoots, and city gumshoes with badges.

"We hold one or two casting sessions and 'offer out,'" says DeCler-que, referring to the way well-known performers are recruited for *SVU*. "If someone is not going to audition, we send them a script. We have a casting treasure trove in this city. There was a playbill for a Broadway show that referred to a cast member as 'one of the few actors in New York that hasn't done a *Law & Order* yet.'"

Casting Director Jonathan Strauss (who works with Lynn Kres-sell Casting, the company that oversees all three *L&Os*) likely has that list of theater people memorized. He started out on "the finance-marketing-computer track, but I always had a hankering for arts and entertainment."

Strauss heard about a number of production jobs that were open in the late 1990s. "One happened to be in casting," he says. "So, I got an internship and loved being on the buyer versus the seller side of things. As an assistant with a casting company for six or seven years, I did indie films and learned the ropes, then more TV. . . . In 2000, I received an Emmy nomination for casting on *Ed* [NBC, 2000–04]."

At his Chelsea Piers office in Manhattan, Strauss can now boast "a wall of videotapes—actor reels. There are 15,000 actor names with contact information and notes in my computer. When I started *SVU* [in season five], I watched and re-watched about 100 episodes to get a sense of who they had used, looking at the show through a casting director's eyes for the first time."

Occasionally, his enterprise devolves into a misadventure, such as what happened while casting "Design" in season seven. "We thought it would be a hoot to have Donald Trump as the prototypi-cal businessman," Strauss says. "He was doing *The Apprentice* on NBC. I went to his agent. Mariska, who's an acquaintance of his, put in a call. He agreed."

But the casting coup was soon scuttled. "We were all set to shoot, then four or five days before I got a call from Neal Baer: 'We can't use Trump.' Turns out there was some creative conflict in the script. I had to call to let the guy know. He'd even postponed a trip to Dubai for us. His assistant asked, 'Let me get this straight: Are you actually telling me that Mr. Trump has been fired?' That gave me cocktail party conversations for a lifetime."

CHAPTER SEVEN

OH, THE PLACES THEY'LL GO

"It takes a village," says location manager Trish Adlesic, referring to the support available to *SVU* from a city of 8 million and beyond. "I try to get what's written on the page and don't give up too quickly. I'm tenacious."

Her task is partly public relations, when she negotiates for use of a desirable home or business or park. "I have to keep the real and episodic worlds happy," Adlesic explains. "It's a balancing act, given the gritty New York life, the kinetic energy. It's also caring so much about the palette for actors and production designers."

She worked on the *Law & Order* pilot ("Everybody's Favorite Bagman") as a location coordinator, before joining the series for its first three actual seasons (1990–93). Adlesic then left to try her hand at feature films for nine years.

But early in season one of *SVU*, DeClerque invited her to rejoin the Dick Wolf fold and the show's location manager was born.

"I brought with me twenty-five boxes of files because I've had a fair number of jobs in which we canvassed New York," Adlesic says, enumerating "some of *SVU*'s more magnificent locations over the years: the old TWA terminal at JFK ('Angels,' season four); Reuters' 30th floor ('Pure,' season six); the Museum of Natural History ('Alternate,' season nine)."

She also likes to find "new, cutting-edge locations. I read *Architectural Digest*. I network. It's always an evolving situation in the city."

Executive producer Ted Kotcheff quotes Dick Wolf on the show's *mise-en-scene*: "He says the audience loves seeing New York—our skyscrapers, our yellow taxicabs—and hearing the New York accents. I just love exteriors. I often ask, 'Why don't we move it outdoors?' There's such an endless parade of interiors. It gets claustrophobic. Exteriors engage the eye."

For California-based producer Judith McCreary, the eye of the beholder is what counts and Manhattan exteriors just aren't up her alley. "When I returned to New York for 'Venom' (season seven), it was my first time back there in, like, two years," she recalls. "But it was really cold that winter and we were downtown, at 60 Centre Street, which is some sort of wind tunnel. I refused to go out and tried to change the script so we could shoot indoors. I didn't get my way."

Her New York nightmare was only getting started. "As I recall, the snow came; a horrible blizzard that dumped inches of snow and brought the city to a standstill," McCreary says. "And imagine my concern when some pedestrians that weekend actually lost their lives by walking on grates in the sidewalk and getting electrocuted from exposed wires because the salt had eaten away their protective coating!"

Neither rain nor snow will keep Adlesic from her appointed rounds, which begin every six or seven days by "getting a new script and starting to break it down immediately," she says of the "prep" phase. "I sit in on Uncle Ted's Story Hour (a session with Kotcheff and other key staffers) and tell them my ideas."

Adlesic and her team need to find roughly ten to twenty locations per episode. "We also have 'bottle shows' (shot primarily on

ATTENTION - READ CAREFULLY
YOU ARE BEING PHOTOGRAPHED

Please be advised that Universal Network Television LLC is
filming scenes in this area for a television production entitled
"Law & Order: Special Victims Unit"

Your entrance into this area will serve as your voluntary
agreement to appear in these scenes to be exhibited as part of
this or any other production in any and all media now known and
hereafter devised throughout the universe in perpetuity, including
advertisements and promotions.
We are sorry for any inconvenience and thank you for your
cooperation.

RANDEE DAWN

On the set of season ten's "Lunacy," Battery Park City, New York

the soundstage) that conserve money, because we have to pay for locations," she points out. "But 30 to 40 percent of *SVU* is shot on 'practicals' (locations)."

In terms of scouting, "I'm part of the assistant director's team, with about five people," Adlesic says. "We're the cornerstone of the production."

To pave the way, Adlesic asks writers to give her a heads-up "if they plan any challenging locations—like the subway—so I can hit the ground running. The Fire Department's training academy does have a platform with modern trains."

DeClerque works with Adlesic in this process. "The producer, episode director, production designer, location manager, first and second directors, we become joined at the hip," he says. "We try to find hub locations—the Museum of Natural Science, for instance—and build a full day of shooting around that. Can't find a doughnut shop the script calls for? Is it possible the guy could be in a bodega instead?"

And then there are those endless details, such as the distances an episode can travel without running up the cost. "I'm always mindful that the Screen Actors Guild rules specify only eight miles from the city for actors and the crew's trade union (IATSE 52) says they can't go beyond twenty-two miles. Otherwise, we pay penalties," Adlesic says.

To secure a site, Adlesic has other hoops through which to jump. "I have a sense of what's fair and within budget," she contends. "Most people will negotiate. We draw up a legal document, get insurance, coordinate the crew. It's remarkable how smooth that can be. But it's always deliver, deliver, deliver. There's not a lot of room for error. I have to be conscientious in every detail."

She knows chaos is lurking around every corner. "It's sort of like asking me to control the weather," Adlesic says. "It's the real world, with noises, airplanes, never-ending surprises. The New York City Mayor's Office (of Film, Theatre & Broadcasting) has a list of certain hot-spots, neighborhoods in which we can't film. We need to be very strategic: no hot-spot, no nearby construction going on, good parking. We try to make our impact as minimal as possible. We refer to this as 'letting it live.' That keeps the public happy."

And when all else fails, "we can change at a moment's notice," she vows. "I have a sort of sixth sense about pulling out quickly if a negotiation seems headed to a dead end. But we can't walk around with a crystal ball and imagine every scenario."

CHAPTER EIGHT

WHAT WASN'T THERE BEFORE

Every now and then Dean Taucher, *SVU*'s production designer since early in season one, has an interesting dilemma when called upon to make the Big Apple look worm-ridden. Or, as he puts it, "a taste of the 1970s when the city was collapsing."

Locations in today's cleaner, more tourism-friendly metropolis may not yield the sort of mean streets a crime show requires. "We needed junk-filled empty lots," Taucher says. "Can't find them anymore. So we have to make it look like South Bronx of the 1980s. Sometimes we need grit and darkness and scariness to capture a mood. I come from New York. I'm familiar with urban decay, so I found that very appealing."

His résumé indicates a propensity for crafting sets suitable for wrongdoers and the public servants who pursue them. While working as a visual consultant on *Miami Vice* (NBC, 1984–89), Taucher got to know that show's then-head writer Dick Wolf. This relationship opened the door to various production designer jobs, on such programs as *H.E.L.P.* (ABC, 1990) and *New York Undercover* (Fox, 1994–98).

After a short stint with the non-Wolf series *Dellaventura* (CBS, 1997), several commercials, and a few TV movies, Taucher enabled mobsters on *The Sopranos*. Though he was only with the beloved HBO drama during its first season, his magic touch remained thereafter. "A lot of those permanent sets were my creations: the backroom of the strip club, the pork store, much of Tony's house."

Bada bing, bada boom. Taucher was tasked with giving *SVU*'s characters a range of equally true-to-life destinations. "It all has to feel real," he says. "If not, that takes people out of the story."

To achieve that goal, he collaborates with the art department, the set decorators, the props people, the carpenters, the grips, the scenic team—"probably twenty-five of them each day but that number can double or more," Taucher points out.

The hotel set from season ten's "Lunacy," pre-filming

The "Gots Money" set from season ten's "Wildlife."

The collective endeavor to lend authenticity to fiction doesn't come cheaply. An extensive cave was essential for "Alternate," a season nine episode with guest star and subsequent *SVU* Emmy-winner Cynthia Nixon. "But there are no caves in Manhattan," Taucher says. "So we built one in our adjacent warehouse out of Styrofoam."

Unit production manager Gail Barringer notes that this indoor cave cost $50,000, and "would have been maybe twice that if we'd used one somewhere outside."

CHAPTER NINE

LEADING THE WAY

E arly on, while *SVU's* identity still seemed rather malleable, executive producer Ted Kotcheff was impressed by the innovative approach of a guest director: "In season one, Leslie Linka Glatter came (for 'A Single Life'). She had been a dancer and that was the way she staged scenes. She made a big impact on how we do the show."

Her style involved graceful circling and swooping movements of the camera, as well as choreographing everyday "bits of business," as actors call it, that frame the primary activity on screen. These ideas were enshrined by the time Peter Leto began taking the helm in season six. He had gone through quite a learning curve over the years, in fact, from key assistant director to first assistant director to production manager/co-producer.

"I was asked if I had any interest in directing," Leto says. "But I was quite happy producing. I was helping novice directors who came in."

Peter Leto

He wanted one more year as a producer before his directorial debut and apparent epiphany on "Goliath" (season six). "As clichéd as this sounds, a light went on in my head, in a dormant creative part of my brain," Leto says. "I never knew I had such an ability to visualize what's on the page. I got on-the-job training. My mentor is Ted Kotcheff—he's the greatest film school I could ever have applied to."

Showrunner Neal Baer also points out that "we have a movie director who makes actors very comfortable and it's one reason the big stars like to come on. They feel, 'Omigod, Ted Kotcheff!'"

Recently, Leto has been one of the people whose job mushroomed as *SVU* began to winnow down its freelance stable to provide more creative continuity. Although there are a few newbies each year, Leto remains among the few go-to guys. "When we started, I had maybe fifteen different directors a season," Kotcheff explains. "Now, Peter does eight episodes, David Platt does eight, and we bring in only about six others."

Baer is happy about the new arrangement: "It's very smooth, with Peter Leto and David Platt directing most of the episodes. We found that bringing in itinerant directors made it difficult to always get the fluid style of camera movement I love."

Platt went from boom operator to sound mixer on the original *Law & Order*, before he began periodically directing episodes during the Mother Ship's sixth season. His contribution to *SVU* was kept at a minimum until season five.

Three years later, Platt began to seem indispensable. In season nine, he was promoted to the rank of producer and continued to fashion a variety of episodes. "I can do anything they throw at me," he says. "There are certain writers I like to work with or maybe it has to do with a particular actor. Sometimes it's just luck of the draw."

Co-executive producer Arthur W. Forney, another in-demand director, says "Neal Baer and Ted Kotcheff decide who directs and in what order. They tell us a month before, while the script is still being written. In a TV series, you get what comes your way."

The same can probably be said of Forney's long history with Dick Wolf, having survived *New York Undercover* (Fox, 1994–98), *The Wright Verdicts* (CBS, 1995), *Feds* (CBS, 1997), and *Players* (NBC, 1997), among many others.

Forney started out as an editor and now supervises all Wolf Films post-production, editing, dubbing, and music "with the right part of my brain," he says. "With the left part, I direct episodes. Of course, once I look at my own work in the editing stage I want to shoot myself. What was I thinking?"

Perhaps the answer is an urge to yell "Action!" and "Cut!" His first directing assignment on the Mother Ship came in 1994, after which he did ten to fifteen episodes for the next three seasons. On *SVU*, Forney has been at the helm periodically since 2001.

"There's a great benefit coming from a *Law & Order* background," he says. "You know what style Dick wants."

Despite that foreknowledge, there's a routine he must follow. "I spend seven or eight days being with the script, to get it into my system," Forney says. "We have 'tone meetings' with the writers in New York. We do the casting. We scout locations. I block out the scenes. When do they walk over there and get coffee? When do they look at a computer? By the time we start shooting, I have a shot list. But we can always make changes when actors have ideas."

RANDEE DAWN

David Platt

His experience doesn't necessarily mean it gets any easier, Forney admits. "Every day as a director, you're always nervous, your stomach is growling."

Thank goodness for the support system. Two teams each of first and second assistant directors invariably are at the ready. Ken Brown and Howard McMaster were in the former category during season nine.

"I'm always with the same team—I work with Peter Leto, my producer," explains McMaster, who hitched his wagon to *SVU* in season three after working on features and a succession of TV series for about ten years. "My biggest responsibility here is the schedule. I break down each scene into its elements: sets, locations or (sound) stage, actors, stunts, costumes."

He must constantly consider "the overview of an episode" in collaboration with the location manager, the producer, and the production designer. "Where are we going? What sets do we need? We have to come up with answers pretty quickly. We break down the number of extras needed and what kinds per day," McMaster says. "I'm responsible for logistically managing it all."

When an episode is shooting, he's required to be in the fray. McMaster conveys the director's commands—"Cut!" and "Roll!"— and issues what's known as a "will-notify call" that summons actors to the set.

"A lot of my work is instinctual," he theorizes. "I'm like a stage manager in the theater. We do six to eight pages a day, so the pace is fast. In TV, it's very important to keep a rhythm going."

All the more reason for artistic precision, presumably honed in his early years as a New York actor. McMaster feels flattered that a costume designer once told him, "You schedule like a poet."

CHAPTER TEN

ESTABLISHING THE VISUALS

E xecutive producer Ted Kotcheff was concerned with how *SVU* could distinguish itself. "I wanted more cinematic storytelling," he says. "The (Mother Ship's) jiggly camera is documentary."

Episode director Peter Leto, now *SVU* supervising producer, agrees. "We started to move away from the tried-and-true *Law & Order* style. We're not really hand-held. I like to think we're a bit more cinematic. Ted was always pushing us in that direction."

Creator Dick Wolf embraces all his broadcast babies as equal yet different. "I think each of the individual Law & Order–branded series has its own unique feel," he says. "But they are cousins, so you can see the family resemblance. Any documentary-like comparisons are not really germane."

SVU's emphasis on less "jiggly camera" ushered in a big difference in terms of storytelling. "This show has very graceful shots," Producer/episode director David Platt says of an approach that enhances the ability "to get into the character's heads."

The Kotcheff-inspired shift toward Steadicam and dolly work evokes wistfulness in some *L&O* loyalists. "I've always loved the 16mm, gritty stories about this city," producer David DeClerque explains. "But for *SVU*, Dick (Wolf) says, 'I want to show the city as it really is. The colors. People on their way to work. But our subject matter is dark enough, we don't need a bleak look. Bad things can happen to good people in a nice environment.'"

The responsibility for conveying that nice environment was inherited by George Pattison after the departure of *SVU*'s original director of photography, Geoffrey Erb, during season eight. "We use a Panavision camera, same as in features," he notes. "We shoot a 35mm negative. A lot of shows are moving toward digital, but I still feel 35mm is the most reliable, best-looking, and fastest way to go. Ours is one of the last programs doing that. . . . Despite pressure from above to save money, Dick Wolf and our creative producers insist on sticking with a proven formula. Whether it's 100 or 0 degrees outside, these cameras work. And they give beautiful latitude compared with digital."

For Kotcheff, beauty comes across most powerfully in "a whole gallery of distinctive, colorful places. Every second should be entertaining. I tell our directors, 'Make it new.' If a producer says, 'That's not a very important scene,' I ask them: 'Oh, you want to do it badly and have the audience lose interest?'"

Failure is not an option in showrunner Neal Baer's purview. "Last year (season nine), we were too dark; we want better lighting (in future episodes)," he points out. "I'm looking for ways scripts can push our visual style and I believe nothing is verboten if it serves the story."

CHAPTER ELEVEN

THE CORRIDORS OF KA-CHUNG

I n the summer of 1999 Karen Stern was about to apply for an editing job at another Dick Wolf show, *DC*, when a friend told her a *Law & Order* spin-off in the pipeline would be "crewing up, as well."

The choice was easy. "I'd never missed an episode," she says of her viewing habits. "So I went for that interview instead."

A decade later, Stern and her fellow editors, Nancy Forner and Steve Polivka, work in a rotation; she covers every third show. Amoung them, they may be working on nine episodes in various stages at once.

Like the others, Stern is holed up in an *SVU* "cutting room" at the Verna Fields Building, which encompasses editors for all programs in the NBC Universal realm.

MATTHEW IMAGING

Peter Jankowski and Charlie Engel

"There are three editors and two assistants for each Law & Order show," explains Wolf Films president Peter Jankowski. "You walk down the hallway and hear that 'ka-chung' all day long."

The indelible electronic sound, originally created by Mike Post for the Mother Ship, also now demarcates scenes on *SVU* and *Criminal Intent*. He calls it "the clang"; at least one TV critic (*Entertainment Weekly*'s Ken Tucker) has referred to "an ominous chung CHUNG."

Post's ubiquitous "time/location signature" between scenes has prompted Wolf to playfully taunt him ever since: "Isn't it great that you worked all these years to become a serious composer and after you're gone they'll remember you for two notes?"

Stern keeps a copy of those two notes in a bin with other sound effects and musical interludes to insert into her initial edit. It's part of a system that requires bouncing episodes-in-progress across the country and back again.

Every night, the "dailies"—representing what the director decides to print from his twenty-four hours' worth of footage—are shipped from New York to Los Angeles, where a lab processes them. (The ratio of raw footage to each show's actual length of forty-two or forty-three minutes is approximately ten to one.)

The negative of the processed material is then transferred to digital video. Stern, who has by then read every successive draft of the script, begins to assemble her cut, which takes about three weeks. "My job is to give the director the best blueprint possible," she notes.

Executive producer Arthur Forney, who oversees post-production, says the next step is when "the editor's cut is sent to the director, who has four days to make his own (cut). We leave him alone to do his thing."

A first screening is then attended by Forney, showrunner Neal Baer, supervising producer Randy Roberts, the writer, and the editor, who together do the fine-tuning. "Most directors work on different types of shows, whereas the producers are there for all twenty-four episodes a season," Forney says. "We know the arc of the series."

At this juncture, they collaboratively determine "if it needs tightening, the story is too confusing, if we're giving away too much information, if the episode needs a little more suspense," Stern says. "We have to build performances that are absolutely true. I think our shows are quite seamless and very naturalistic in tone. So much of what we do is from gut feelings."

A final look from Wolf, Jankowski, and NBC Universal seals the deal. Associate producer Sheyna Kathleen Smith is in charge of all the finishing touches, such as sound mixing and color correcting. Stern enjoys mastery of the "locale cards," which indicate places where the detectives are going in their investigations.

"We tell the audience where we are without an establishing shot," she explains. "They situate the characters and give the viewer a chance to breathe. The script doesn't tell us where to put them. We pretty much know when they're necessary. I love locale cards."

Each address has already been vetted by *SVU* researchers so as not to portray any existing spot. But do the West Coast personnel really know the city where every *Law & Order* is set?

Although mistakes apparently are rare, Stern often is amused by the make-believe. "I'm from New York. I laugh when a locale card identifies, say, 706 West 45th Street: 'Oh, that's in the river!' But the audience generally will go with us wherever we take them."

CHAPTER TWELVE

THE TWAIN SHALL MEET

N ot quite a Hydra, the two-headed body that is *SVU* somehow functions with about six thousand miles in between each noggin. Is this bicoastalism ever a problem?

"Not at all," insists showrunner Neal Baer. "Ted (Kotcheff) and I talk five times a day. Mariska, three times a day. Chris, once a day."

East Coast–based executive producer Kotcheff says the dual nature of the series—like that of all Law & Order shows—can present a challenge. "Sometimes there are geographic mistakes," executive producer Kotcheff acknowledges. "I try to bring the writers here. I've lived in L.A., so I've got both an outsider's and insider's perspective. I see what's idiosyncratic about New York."

Otherwise, the arrangement is copasetic. "During Uncle Ted's Story Hour (the brainstorming session for each episode), I weed out things from a script that I think are incorrect," he says. "Then I speak with Neal and he speaks with the writers. We're like partners."

Producer David DeClerque, who works at the New Jersey soundstage, says this about *SVU*'s cross-country relations: "We ship, hopefully, wonderful footage to the West Coast and keep our fingers crossed that they're happy with it."

He was a New York location manager for features, TV pilots, and movies-of-the week before the Mother Ship appeared on his radar. "I wanted to get into the production managing field," DeClerque says. "They gave me the opportunity a few times. . . . But there didn't seem to be a full-time position. In the middle of (*Law & Order's*) season six, I landed a pilot with *Dellaventura* (CBS, 1997)."

Three years later, friends from *L&O* recommended him to Dick Wolf for the spin-off. "I felt these guys know how to make television shows," DeClerque says. "They taught me how to do episodic TV."

His *SVU* counterpart is unit production manager and producer Gail Barringer, who began as a production accountant on the show in 1999. "Dave and I alternate (responsibility for) episodes," she explains. "We both oversee operation of the facility, the crew, and

the needs of actors. We report directly to studio executives. We're in charge of budgets and amortization. We make deals for crew, equipment, purchase orders. We oversee studio policies and procedures."

Better yet, "I'll ask them if we can afford to blow up a car."

Kaboom. Barringer hesitates when asked about the cost per episode. "Well, we're given a template that the studio allows us to tweak," she says. "On 'Lunacy' (season ten), the special effects budget is over the norm. That happens with stunts, using

Gail Barringer

the Hudson River, a lot of blood. We have no wiggle room this year."

According to Barringer, *SVU* has approximately twenty-five vehicles, ten to fifteen trucks or trailers. She adds, "Our fleet includes some hybrids. We've had to double our fuel budget lately (due to rising fuel costs). We always want to shoot in New York City, even though it's more expensive than working on our stage. We just happen to be in a facility that costs less than it would in Manhattan."

When the inevitable glitches occur, she may be forced to get tough. "On 'Doubt' (season six), which Ted Kotcheff directed, there was a truck in the shot that wouldn't start," Barringer recalls. "It was at night and we had a long delay, went really late. It's the worst feeling to keep looking at your watch. We want it all to be perfect, but your watch just screams at you. There are times when I look at Ted or (episode director) Peter Leto and say, 'This is your last take. I'm sorry.'"

CHAPTER THIRTEEN

TEARS AND LAUGHTER

There's no doubt *SVU*'s tales of human depravity can be disturbing for writers, producers, actors, and crew members. They've all searched for ways to coexist with scripts about exceedingly loathsome situations.

"It's tough," says former co-executive producer Patrick Harbinson. "That's why I tended to do more of the issue stories. My own shield against depression is to tell a story with social relevance. But sometimes at the start of a new year I'd think: 'God, not another sex crime.'"

And another and another and another.

"It absolutely does get to you," acknowledges George Pattison, the director of photography. "You build up a callus, but any human being would be affected."

Tamara Tunie's *SVU* medical examiner is awash in body parts and some of the show's most graphic dialogue. "I think certainly my awareness of the heinous things that one human being can do to another has become keener," she acknowledges. "But we know it's pretend while we're doing it, and when the camera's not rolling, it's very much a light feel on the set. It doesn't get too maudlin or heavy. So there's a certain part of me that remains able to detach myself when I'm not in it. But at the same time, I'm still affected emotionally, by the reality of humanity against humanity."

With real-world experience, co-executive producer Amanda Green may have a more profound vantage point than do others at *SVU.* "I spent four years working in a maximum-security federal prison, in outpatient settings with all sorts of victim populations, and in domestic violence shelters. . . . Working with HIV positive victims in 1989 when AIDS was a death sentence, I learned that these people were going to die, and were going to die awful, undignified, painful deaths. You have to learn to separate yourself."

Executive producer Ted Kotcheff knows that nothing presented on *SVU* could ever be as horrific as what cops witness every day in real life, evident in a field trip before the show began. "I went to an actual Manhattan *SVU* and sat there all day long," he recalls. "Richard Belzer came, as well. We saw some terrible stuff. Two Hispanic women were weeping and a girl of about five or six had a bandaged hand. Her father had been frying bacon as the child was dancing around. He told her to shut up, then burned off all her fingers on the hot stove. How can detectives stand hearing such things?"

Some cannot. "The police told us no one can bear the abuse of children," Kotcheff says. "The job span there is two years. They get out. They can't take it."

He cites a second incident that has remained with him (and is the subject of season one's "Nocturne" episode). "A piano teacher in Harlem had been giving free lessons but for ten years molested kids and videotaped them. . . . Detectives had to watch hours and hours of footage and testify in court. The next day, one guy quit and requested to be transferred back to drug crimes."

The fictitious *SVU* detectives have been able to keep going for a decade, but not without scarred souls. Green sees it as something of a cause.

RANDEE DAWN

Props from the SVU *set*

"People watch our show and they take the information we present and they act on it," she suggests.

Years ago, at an event honoring the series, Green met a man who recounted a true story. A young woman had walked into his office to report a rape two weeks after the fact. His reaction: "My face fell, because I knew all the evidence, forensics, the DNA, was all lost."

When he started to explain to the victim why it would be tough to find the perp without that evidence, she held up a bag that had all her clothes in it from the night of the attack. Nothing had been washed.

"He asked how she knew to do that and she said, 'I saw it on *SVU*,'" Green explains.

One of her fellow co-executive producers, Jonathan Greene, discovered much the same path for addressing the human toll of sex crimes. "Everything evolves," he suggests. "As you learn to do something, you learn how to do it better and better . . . And it was a question of learning how far we could take this. I remember there were a lot of times we'd say, 'Are we going to be able to come up with enough stories for each season?' And as it turned out, it wasn't a matter of finding the stories, because they're out there, but the question is how can you tell these stories in such a way that they will somehow make a difference?"

One answer has been the fact that Mariska Hargitay (Det. Olivia Benson) started a charitable organization for victims of sex crimes. "Often, she will send the writers emails she will get from victims that say *SVU* helped them realize this or change that," Greene explains. "It's one thing to have a great job like this, writing on a show that you not only care about but believe in, where it's not just a paycheck."

The same sense of higher purpose apparently is important to actor Richard Belzer. "We've all been affected in one way or the other, and have befriended people who do what we do. . . . I'm amazed at some of the victims I've met, who maintain their humanity," he says. "So it's very moving. It's not like I'm just doing some stupid cop show."

Dann Florek (*SVU*'s Capt. Don Cragen) suspects each person working on *SVU* has found a different way to deal with its most

COURTESY LAW & ORDER: SVU

Director Peter Leto mugs with a special guest star on the set of season ten's "Wildlife."

wrenching themes. "First of all, you know it's not real, but it's based on what is real. . . . Even though you know it's fake, you're looking at pictures of a lot of hurt people, and some of them are hurt children. And sometimes those just pop into my head at night. (Or) I'll see a kid on the street who looks like a kid who was in makeup to look hurt."

That burden is lessened for him when he meets people who watch the show with their children "because they feel these are lessons to be learned," Florek says. "(Episodes) can serve as cautionary terms. The best way I can describe the show is: We shine a light in a very dark place. And I think that's good. I know we're entertainment, but we can enlighten."

Dawn DeNoon found a recipe for staying sane when working on a bleak story with her former writing partner, Lisa Marie Petersen.

"(We) used to do the sitcom version along with it," says DeNoon, a co-executive producer. "We didn't write it down, but we'd do the sitcom. We'd say the wacky version, which is hard to do with sex crimes. . . . It's like what the cops do in real life, their gallows humor. Even in real life they do a lot more than we're allowed on (*SVU*), because it looks so bad. But there's no way to deal with it otherwise. If you didn't find some humor in it, you'd eat a gun."

Comic relief on the written page has been a coping mechanism for DeNoon, as well. She gives an example of patter the detectives would use to lighten the heavy load before a court appearance: "'Oh, I have to go testify in this weenie-wagger trial.' They weren't the hard core cases; they were the sillier cases. You couldn't do that for a whole episode."

On the set, wisecracking has been raised to an art form.

One example: On location at a Manhattan park for a scene in "Lunacy" (season ten), episode director Peter Leto describes NBC's attempt to become more eco-friendly as a "green effort." Actor Ice-T (Det. Odafin Tutuola) chimes in with: "No trees were harmed in the making of this episode."

Any personnel experiencing emotional harm from the wretched crimes depicted on *SVU* hopefully can continue to find solace in off-camera levity. "We're blessed here," suggests first assistant director Howard McMaster. "It's extremely rare to have a show without at

PHOTO COURTESY AMANDA GREEN

Christopher Meloni, Gail Barringer, and executive producer Amanda Green clown around on the set of season eight's "Scheherazade."

least four assholes. But this core group of actors likes to cut up and have a good time."

Script-wise, periodic wit certainly helps viewers digest unsettling sequences, as well as complex moral and legal issues.

In "Birthright," a season six episode written by Jonathan Greene, when Detective Munch refers to a van ferrying suspected serial sex offenders as "their very own perpmobile," it's a small moment that goes a long way. Ditto for the line that Star Morrison (played by Marcia Gay Harden) is given for Dawn DeNoon's "Informed" in season eight, as Stabler tosses a soda can in the trash: "You keep doing that and the eco-terrorists win."

CHAPTER FOURTEEN

WILL THEY OR WON'T THEY?

A persistent question on the minds of ardent *SVU* viewers brings a range of answers from those most closely associated with the characters: What's with the personal feelings between police partners Elliot Stabler and Olivia Benson?

Enticing clues have been introduced over the years, reaching a peak with several key developments during season eight. On "Infiltrated," after being knocked unconscious she wakes up muttering his first name ("Elliot . . . Elliot . . ."). Meanwhile, separated from his wife, he's messing around with Benson's temporary replacement (played by Connie Nielsen) in "Underbelly" and "Cage." By "Annihilated," a glimpse of detective rear-end is a clue that Stabler may be trying to rekindle his marriage.

Flash forward to season nine and "Paternity," in which Benson helps deliver the recently reunited Stablers' newborn amidst a car-crash scene. Many fans were looking for signs in the postpartum hug between Stabler and Benson at the hospital.

Perhaps father knows best. Listen to Christopher Meloni, whose family-man Stabler never quite comes to terms with his feelings for perpetually single Benson: "I'm the man in her life. I'm the solid guy, maybe the shoulder to cry on," he says. "It was very interesting, you know, when she delivers my wife's baby. We're rehearsing the scene, and I said, 'Guys, I have to hug her. This is the only time this is going to happen, this is the only opportunity where I will initiate physical contact with this woman.' . . . That to me was the crux. Why? What comes (out) is 'Thank you.' Not 'I love you.'"

And Mariska Hargitay is fine with that. "(Stabler is) her rock, her protector. Olivia has never had anyone to protect her . . . He's the one who makes her feel safe and loved. He puts his life on the line to keep her safe. . . . No other man measures up to him. But I absolutely do not think we should be together romantically. That would be a different show. It's not this show."

The guy whose job it is to keep a finger on the pulse of the fan base weighs in. "The writers keep it interesting with sexual tension," surmises Mike Ciliento, who assists the show's line producer and administers the *SVU* blog on NBC's website. "When he hugged her after the car accident, the next day the blogs were flying. All that personal stuff is a way to take the weight off the show's darkness. The (NBC) blog has opened my eyes to what the audience wants—they want Chris and Mariska to get together."

And probably none more so than "livi_wells," an excited *SVU* romantic who posted this (verbatim) plea on fanpop.com: "ELLIOT AND OLIVIA BELONG TOGETHER!!!!!!!!!!!!!dont you think?i meen.......they make a very,very,very cute cuple!and it would be great for the show!!!!!!!!!!!!!!!!!!!!!!!!!!!!!!!!!and the way they look at each other in the show!!!!!!!but if they dont i will dieeeeeeeeeeeeeeee!!!!! !!!!!!!!!"

Alas. Even with this spelling-challenged girl's life in the balance, it's highly unlikely Dick Wolf—who named the characters after two of his children, Elliot and Olivia—would budge. "*SVU* is a procedural crime series and not a soap opera," he insists. "There is tremendous chemistry between the characters, but they are working partners, not sexual partners."

But let some other experts speculate about where these two star-crossed detectives may be headed:

"Early on, we tried to figure out the nature of their relationship," says former *SVU* writer Jeff Eckerle. "Were they antagonistic? Did they have animosities? Jealousies? We wanted to get away from their home lives to reveal character through their work. It was an unspoken idea that they were professionals. Let's not turn this into a soap opera."

Co-executive producer Amanda Green has a slightly different take: "I think that a partnership between two cops is about as intimate a relationship as you can get. . . . So what does that mean for men and women that work together in those situations every day? There's something they share that they don't share with others. In some ways Stabler has two wives."

Peter Leto, an episode director, has much the same opinion. "She and Stabler are a married couple, of sorts," he says.

But supervising producer Judith McCreary demurs. "I've written a backstory for Benson and Stabler that hasn't really been shared much with the others," she points out. "They have been intimate and will always be intimate. That's how I play them. That's how I like them."

Cops, she adds, spend more time with their partners than with their families. "The adrenaline's pumping. It's a recipe. On *SVU*, I wanted this to be the subtext, the undercurrent, not just ordinary sexual tension. Mariska and Chris laugh at me when I tell them about this. Their characters love each other."

And there may a psychological *ménage à trois*, in McCreary's view. "Stabler's wife is resigned she will never really have him to herself. . . . To me, his family's immaterial. His wife's a bit player. He's miserable without Benson. I always see them as incredibly intimate in every single way."

Not so fast. According to Michele Fazekas, an *SVU* writer in seasons three through seven, "their work is more important than their feelings for each other. In some scenes, she's more vulnerable. In

COURTESY MARISKA HARGITAY

Mariska Hargitay and Christopher Meloni

another, it's him. They do get jealous about each other. That's fun to play with. Just a hint of a romantic dynamic. The actors like to play with that as well."

Her writing partner, Tara Butters, has the same belief: "I've always believed their love was genuine. They'd die for each other and that superseded the sexual stuff."

Co-executive producer Dawn DeNoon is among the contingent that thinks the duo will never engage in hanky-panky. "I remember being shocked when Neal Baer allowed (the Stablers) to separate," she says. "I do see that, as much as he loves Benson, she's the one who's still looking for the love of her life; he's found it. . . . Dick would never allow that. It goes back to the *Moonlighting* (ABC, 1985–89) curse. As soon as you get them together, the show's over."

Former *SVU* scribe Patrick Harbinson: "It's sublimated love, no question at all. They've never had sex and never will. The series would be over. But it's a good way to end it when the time comes. . . . Connie Nielsen gave the show an excuse to look at Stabler and Benson in love, but through a surrogate."

Executive producer Ted Kotcheff: "If Benson and Stabler had sex, they realize their police partnership would be over. When he and Connie Nielsen kissed, we were deluged with angry mail: 'How could you allow Stabler to betray Benson?' Will they ever get together? It's impossible. We've shown him to be a devout Catholic. But we've gone through so many boyfriends with her and not one of them worked out. So maybe that's what interferes with her being involved for long with other men."

As season ten was about to start, showrunner Neal Baer could predict the future. "They do not have sex but they will be in a compromising position," he says.

During an episode titled "Wildlife," Stabler goes undercover for a sting. He's in a motel room being watched by thugs who warn him not to have contact with anyone else, but Benson comes there to talk with him about something. When the criminals burst in to confront him, she comes out of the bathroom in panties and a bra, pretending to be a prostitute. "We like a little touch (of sexuality) every so often," Baer notes.

Season ten cast, from l.-r.: Tamara Tunie (Dr. Melinda Warner), Richard Belzer (Sgt. Det. John Munch), Ice-T (Det. Odafin Tutuola), Mariska Hargitay (Det. Olivia Benson), Christopher Meloni (Det. Elliot Stabler), Dann Florek (Capt. Don Cragen), Michaela McManus (ADA Kim Greylek), B.D. Wong (Dr. George Huang)

Arthur Forney, co-executive producer

Ice-T and wife/manager Coco, 2005

Christopher and Sherman Meloni, 2004

George Pattison, director of photography

RANDEE DAWN

Mariska Hargitay on Benson St. in New York City

COURTESY MARISKA HARGITAY

Christopher Meloni and Matthew Modine (as Gordon Rickett) in season six's "Rage"

Mariska Hargitay and father Mickey Hargitay (as Michael) on the set of season five's "Control"

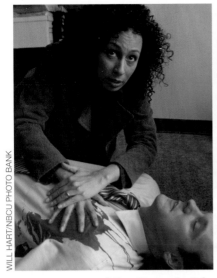

Tamara Tunie and Tom Verica (as Jake Hunter) in season seven's "Blast"

On the SVU set: cop lockers

Johnny Messner (as Guard Lowell Harris) and Mariska Hargitay in season nine's "Undercover"

The Stabler family home, as used in season ten's "Lunacy"

Christopher Meloni and Dean Winters (Det. Brian Cassidy)

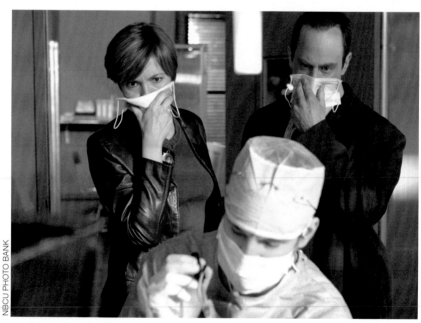

Mariska Hargitay, Gale Harold (as Dr. Lang), and Christopher Meloni in season four's "Perfect"

The Men in Black: Ice-T and Richard Belzer in character on the set of season four's "Lust"

RANDEE DAWN

Ice-T (center), filming season ten's "Lunacy"

PHOTO COURTESY AMANDA GREEN

*From l.-r.: Producer Gail Barringer, Christopher Meloni, second asst. direc-
tor Denis Doyle and writer/producer Amanda Green get in the habit on season
eight's "Scheherazade"*

Mariska Hargitay and monkey used in season ten episode "Wildlife"

Jonathan Strauss, casting director

Season four cast, from l.-r.: Ice-T, Richard Belzer, Mariska Hargitay, Dann Florek, Christopher Meloni, B.D. Wong, Stephanie March (ADA Alexandra Cabot)

From l.-r.: First asst. director Ken Brown, executive producer Amanda Green, Christopher Meloni, unknown crew member, and key production assistant Brian "Monkey" Campe in the Rockaways in Queens for season ten's "Swing"

Mariska Hargitay and Mickey Hargitay, with Mariska's friends, at the 2005 Emmys

Richard Thomas (as Daniel Varney) restrained by guards in season two's "Scourge"

Christopher Meloni and "August's Mommy" director chairs

Connie Nielsen (Det. Dani Beck) and Elle Fanning (as Eden) in season eight's "Cage"

Mariska Hargitay and husband Peter Hermann in 2005

Neal Baer, showrunner/executive producer

Diane Neal (ADA Casey Novak) and executive producer Amanda Green heading to the Emmys in 2006

Law & Order *franchise creator Dick Wolf and Mariska Hargitay at the 2005 Emmys*

From l.-r.: Richard Belzer, producer David DeClerque, and Ice-T

Christopher Meloni and Mariska Hargitay going "undercover"

From l.-r.: Jesse L. Martin (Det. Ed Green), Jerry Orbach (Det. Lennie Briscoe), Mariska Hargitay, Richard Belzer, and Christopher Meloni in season one's "Entitled"

SVU Viewing Party, season one. From l.-r.: Bill Butler, Mariska Hargitay, Christopher Meloni, Sherman Meloni, Richard Belzer, Dann Florek

CHAPTER FIFTEEN

THE NERVE CENTER

S trangely, I'm the most senior member of the production office (staff)," reports Mike Ciliento, a former NBC page who's been with *SVU* since 2004 and now coordinates scripts, clearances, and publicity, among other responsibilities.

People who came before him in the show's hectic nucleus have either moved up or moved out due to the killer pace. "The toughest thing here is the quick turnaround," he says. "Movies have months of pre-production; we usually get seven days."

He hung in, progressing from a production assistant to "a position with script coordination duties that took on more and more responsibility. I now coordinate scripts with the West Coast and New York. I'm a research assistant for the writers. I work on publicity and award submissions. And I maintain the *SVU* site on the network's blog."

There are moments when all of *SVU* appears to converge on him at once. "Everybody wants information as soon as possible and

RANDEE DAWN

Mike Ciliento and Meredith Petty

(we're waiting for) the scripts to come from the West Coast," Ciliento says. "It's crazy. If you don't date someone within the industry, you'll never see them. But we're like a family—and like your grade school!"

Somehow, the young man's equanimity never seems to waver. "I'm good at problem solving," he contends, adding that the executive producers often rely on his techno-savvy. "It's nice to be appreciated."

Whenever shooting on location goes haywire, Ciliento is part of the mix trying to make things right: "On an episode ('Night,' season six) about skateboarders who find a trail of money, we had to keep clearing the set of snow during a blizzard. It was around Christmastime. One of those mayhem things."

To make matters worse, he says, "Ted Kotcheff came in from L.A. and his plane landed in six feet of snow. We check the weather hour by hour. The wardrobe department keeps backup outfits if it's raining. When I watch the show, I'm remembering everything that went into it."

Production office coordinator Faith Brooks holds down the fort. "Mike works closely with the writers and goes over timing with the script supervisor," she says. "I'm responsible for equipment rentals, insurance certification, films stock, camera batteries. I do a lot of juggling and troubleshooting."

What kind of trouble? "Getting lifts to a location during a snow-storm," she explains. "It took four hours. And after all that, they never made it into the episode. Another time the Lincoln Tunnel was shut down and the cast stranded on the other side. Or that day when the water main broke on the set."

On a normal day, Brooks creates "production reports—what scenes were shot, page counts, crew times, what actors are coming in. That's for the studio. . . . I send them the script supervisor's notes, the sound roll, the film. They later stream it all back to us. We get the dailies cut, the broadcast version. We are the liaison. This is a clearinghouse."

CHAPTER SIXTEEN

GOOD GRUB

N apoleon Bonaparte supposedly once proclaimed that, "An army marches on its stomach." Two centuries later, that has become a sort of mantra for *SVU*, where the eats are abundant, tasty, and available at all hours of the day and night.

Lisa Brown has been making sure the troops are well-fed since four months into the first season. Shooting Stars Catering, which she owns with husband Brian, is the prime source of nourishment for both *SVU* and *CI*.

"I serve three entrees," Brown says of her daily meat, fish, and poultry lunch options. "Most caterers do only two. Also, we always have two starches and two vegetables."

And then there are her specialties. "If I don't make chicken cutlets and meatballs for a while, they ask for them," she points out. "(Episode director) Peter Leto will tell me, 'I have to have a chicken cutlet.' And everybody wants a Mexican day."

Ole! In addition, Brown provides "crafts service" (the multitudinous snacks and beverages available throughout the day on any movie or TV set) and hot meals when shooting continues late into the night.

"All the delicious food Lisa makes for us is not cheap," notes cost-conscious unit production manager Gail Barringer. "But I just leave that alone because keeping (cast and crew) fed keeps them happy."

The cooking takes place in trucks that are able to travel to locations. "We have two ovens, six burners, nine refrigerators, and three sinks," Brown explains.

Waistline consciousness is a factor at times. "Right after New Year's, I know to buy more egg whites," she says. "Come January, everyone makes resolutions. By February, they're back to the way it was."

And other holidays tend to guide the menu. "Around Thanksgiving, I serve sweet potatoes and turkey. For St. Patty's day, it's corned beef and cabbage."

Some people appreciate her gourmet skills. "Chris (Meloni) loves fresh tuna seared with wasabi sauce," Brown notes. "Mariska (Hargitay) eats real healthy. Ice-T? Whatever's there, he's happy. He'll eat anything as long as there's meat. I am really blessed with a very nice cast and crew."

She also probably qualifies as a workaholic. "I have to be there three or four hours before the crew, so I often have to leave my house at 2 or 2:30 in the morning. I stay until lunch is over—and lunch can be at 4:40 P.M. or later—then two to three hours more. I'm always a-movin' and a-groovin'."

CHAPTER SEVENTEEN

GOOD LOOKS

T o capture the realism that gives *SVU* its primetime punch, the performers have to accept people constantly fussing over them. A brigade of hair, makeup, and wardrobe specialists must be available at the start of each workday and for as long the cameras are rolling.

Whether at the New Jersey soundstage or in a trailer on location, these wizards of physiognomy ensure that the mere mortals in their care come across as enduring TV characters.

Rebecca Perkins, head of the makeup department, and Brian Badie, her counterpart for hair, share a cramped room also frequented by their respective staffs along one of the winding *SVU* New Jersey hallways. It's where they tend to the regular cast and guest stars.

"We've got five chairs in here and they're full all day," explains Badie, who joined *SVU* in season nine. "We switch (the actors) between hair and makeup."

Perkins, on board the show since the end of season five, points out that "Chris and Mariska often have to be ready first thing in the morning . . . And one of our team will always go to the set when they're shooting."

Indeed, stylists armed with powder, blush, spray, combs, and such gather behind the director until he stops the action, then swarm over to the players to check their faces, coifs, and clothing. The person from costumes can usually be identified by the collection of safety pins dangling from her belt—presumably for any sudden wardrobe malfunctions.

Perkins and her helpers generally lavish more attention on Hargitay, especially before the day's emoting begins. "Mariska has to look like she's a cop, but she's a beautiful woman. We decided never to get in the way of that. I usually spend a half-hour on her. Chris? Seven minutes."

For Badie, the time frame is almost reversed. "Mariska's hair has to fit with her bone structure. It looks best medium length. She likes it long. . . . When I cut, Chris' hair takes the longest time. I'm really particular. I ask him for a half-hour. Mariska's more like twenty minutes, max."

As for the other two detectives, Badie says Ice-T's previously long locks were independently shorn in season nine—"He did that on his own."—and Richard Belzer "is really into the textured look for hair."

The bigger challenges sometimes are reserved for visiting actors. Perkins recalls. "Brian once had to do Orthodox *payes* (the sideburns worn by Hassidic men)," Perkins recalls. "And in another episode, a guest star had to look like a street urchin."

CHAPTER EIGHTEEN

CLOSE SECONDS

I've gone gray while working on this show," laments Kent Cassella, who's been with *SVU* from the beginning.

His *Law & Order* odyssey started with "my first audition for the Mother Ship in 1997 or 1998. David Platt was directing an episode about a toxic terrorist threat. Then, in July 1999, I got a call from (*SVU*) Extras Casting to be a stand-in for Dann Florek. They saw from my head shot that I was also going bald. I'm a little shorter than he is but that didn't seem to matter. I wear clogs and maybe that made us closer in height."

Ever since, Cassella has been a temporary Captain Cragen while the crew adjusts lights for the next scene. "The main thing is they know I'll be there when they need me," he says. "The show prefers to have people they can count on who know the business. It's not rocket science."

Kent Cassella

Except in season ten's "Lunacy," that is, the story of an errant astronaut.

Cassella also gets to go before the camera from time to time. "I played a character named Eddie Love in 'Runaway' (season two)," he recalls. "That was the big joke on the set: 'It's Eddie Love! Eddie Love's here!' The next year, I did three episodes as Eddie Palmieri, a detective, but everybody still called me Eddie Love."

As Mariska Hargitay's quasi-doppelganger since season four, Ellie Scully appreciates the steady gig but regrets that "we're always on our feet for what can end up being a sixteen-hour day."

Rick Johnson, subbing for Richard Belzer since 1999, is glad the show helps him fill in the income gaps of his career as a singer-songwriter.

Storm Chambers, who has been doubling for Ice-T since the second season, periodically does *SVU* extra work as, say, a jury foreperson. Otherwise, the job leaves him time to audition for roles elsewhere, "because you don't want to be a stand-in for life."

CHAPTER NINETEEN

OUT THERE IN TELEVISIONLAND

An objective television news icon like CNN's Anderson Cooper travels the globe to report on the most important issues of the day, yet in a September 2008 interview with *USA Weekend* he revealed that there's somehow still time for him to catch one of his three favorite TV programs: *Law & Order: Special Victims Unit*.

A more subjective source, identified only as "hazel" on the specialvictimsunit.org fan site, observes that "watching (*SVU*) is like going on a roller coaster ride at times."

This roller coaster may be planetary in its reach. The show has been licensed to more than 200 territories worldwide (though not necessarily airing in all of them right now), including such far-flung lands as Sri Lanka, Fiji, Macau, and Botswana. The Kalahari Desert comprises 70 percent of that African nation, where the wildebeest and the antelope roam, so perhaps *SVU*'s themes can transcend almost any geographic or cultural divide.

Back home, another American enthusiast—"chloethereturner," posting on the svufans.net blog—announced she was writing a college paper about "which psychological aspects are used in the construction of the main characters of the series in the search for identification with the public."

That academic mouthful, perhaps a topic more appropriate for B.D. Wong's on-camera shrink to tackle, is offset by less cerebral devotees of the show who periodically chat about their desire for an *SVU* convention. Sans Spock ears or Klingon lingo, what would such a gathering entail? A murder-mystery scenario worthy of dinner theater? A fake mass arrest of attendees?

Nonetheless, the idea caught fire in the svufans.net chat room, with one apparent teenager ("Myhumps") moaning that "I doubt my parents would let me go all the way to New York."

It's difficult to reconcile the frivolity of some *SVU* followers, who frequently post giddily detailed messages about meeting the stars, with the wrenching facts of any sex crime depicted on the program. So viewer euphoria is something of a sticky wicket. While those who swoon for Meloni, Hargitay, or other performers are surely aware of the show's profound nature, it could be that the line is blurred between grit and fluff if the actors are attractive enough.

"It's a very tricky fine line that we walk—and no one has been able to walk it more successfully than (showrunner) Neal Baer," suggests *SVU* casting director Jonathan Strauss. "He's brilliant at blending the two realities, allowing the audience to get a little more attached by giving tidbits of the characters' personal lives without getting too far away from the procedural essence of the show."

And luckily, Mariska Hargitay never forgets *SVU*'s sagacity. Ordinary fan adoration is matched, maybe even outpaced, by communications from real-life rape victims, many of whom clearly perceive her as a kindred spirit.

"As the show got more popular, I received so many emails from so many survivors," she recalls, "They were identifying so much with my character, identifying with this lion, this strong powerful (Olivia

Benson). And then I had thir-
teen-year-olds going, 'I want to
be you; you are my role model.'
Hundreds of emails going, 'I
want to be a cop when I grow
up.' And I thought this character has touched something so
deep in women and provided a
safe place to go. . . . I felt I had a
responsibility."

Neal Baer sums up *SVU's*
double-edged appeal. "Mariska
and Chris are the yin and yang of
the audience," he suggests. "(She)
represents the empathy one feels
towards the victim . . . She pulls
the audience with her, particularly women. And men think
she's hot. So she's the empathy
we feel; Chris is the rage we
feel about what's happened. The
audience can identify with both

One of the SVU Valentines *by
acclaimed California pop artist
Brandon Bird, an avowed Law &
Order fan.*

of them in very deep ways, which makes them quite popular in real
life . . . They stand in for ourselves, I think, and how we feel about
these things."

And how does he, as the showrunner of a serious drama, feel
about the roar of the crowd in America's celebrity-obsessed culture?
"I do read all of the fan sites," Baer concedes. "I even go on(line) once
in a while—I won't say what my handle is . . . It's interesting to get
the gestalt."

For the man at the top, fan zeal eventually boils down to a hard-
wired business rationale. According a March 2006 article in the *San
Francisco Chronicle*, Dick Wolf told some assembled media critics:
"You've got an actress sitting up here (Mariska Hargitay) who has
received two consecutive Emmy nominations for a show (*SVU*) that
everybody would describe as mature. I didn't see that much fuss
made about it. You read about who's hot, who's not. These shows are

never mentioned. We're not looking to be the hot show. That's not what the Law & Order brand is about. It's about longevity and about repeatability and about staying on the air and being a profit center for NBC for years to come."

CHAPTER TWENTY

A WEEK IN THE LIFE ·OF AN EPISODE

"A long pull, and a strong pull, and a pull all together."

—CHARLES DICKENS, *David Copperfield* (1849)

MONDAY, JULY 14

9 A.M.

"The stage is in an industrial area on a swamp," explains Teamster Mario Berritto, driving a *Law & Order: Special Victims Unit* van from Manhattan's West Side to the set in New Jersey. "They're always pulling bodies out of the swamp."

Hopefully not those of the authors, about to begin our first day of observing the initial episode shooting for season ten.

Also riding to the Garden State are a few actors joining the cast of "Lunacy," about the murder of a female astronaut.

"I'm a lesbian," says Therese Plummer, referring to the character she'll play in her TV debut. "I'm the girlfriend of a victim named Marga. Friends ask me if I'm the dead body and I tell them, 'I'm the lover of the dead body.' I've got a two-page scene in the morgue with Benson and Stabler."

Briana Marin will appear as "an uber-feminist making anti-Muslim rape porn videos. I'm supposed to be a Dominican girl pretending to be Middle Eastern."

Both women agree that a L&O appearance is a stepping stone for New York thespians. "It's a rite-of-passage," notes Marin.

In a sense, so is this chronicle by two outside observers given an opportunity to peek behind the curtain of a popular NBC series in the ubiquitous Law & Order universe.

9:30 A.M.

"Get ready to experience the sights, sounds, and smells of New Jersey," announces Mario, as the van draws closer to the show's North Bergen headquarters. "We've got a sewage plant coming up on the right."

Inside the sprawling, one-story, nondescript L&O structure, some corridor walls are posted with real and fake memorabilia: A genuine snapshot of Mariska Hargitay (Det. Olivia Benson) with Robert Redford. Others with every member of the crew individually posing with her 2005 Golden Globe award. A note to her from co-star Christopher Meloni (Det. Elliot Stabler): "Congratulations from your fellow sex detective . . . Love, hugs, and handcuffs, Chris."

10:25 A.M.

A production meeting gets under way around a long conference table.

Howard McMaster, "Lunacy" first assistant director: "Scene one, Exterior. Battery Park. As a young man pops the question, his girlfriend sees a woman's body floating in the water."

Tina Nigro, costume designer: "Is she wearing clothes?"

The answer is yes.

Peter Leto, supervising producer/"Lunacy" director: "But we'll try to expose as much skin as we can."

SVU never flashes too much flesh or reveals the truly grisly visual aspects of a grisly crime. An NBC Universal Program Standards and Compliance Script Report for "Lunacy" cautions: "Please exercise your usual taste and discretion when showing corpse bobbing in water and on examining table."

McMaster: "Scene twelve. We're in the morgue . . . One of Marga's eyes is not so good. How do we do that?"

Leto: "Marine organisms and feeder fish and eels have gotten at her eyeballs."

McMaster: "How are we doing on the eels?"

Anthony Munafo, prop master: "Five made it through the weekend."

Later, in the production office . . .

Munafo says he spent "eight man hours" hunting for the slimy creatures: "I contacted the only eel farm in the United States, in North Carolina. But they don't grow them until May. I tried pet stores and Internet sites."

Dann Florek (Capt. Don Cragen): "You didn't go to Eels 'R' Us down the street?"

Munafo: "I had no luck at bait stores. They're no smaller than seven inches on the Jersey shore. We need three to four inches. Finally, a pet shop in San Diego had 'zigzag eels.' They sent them overnight for $8.95 an eel, plus the $40 shipping cost. I got a fish tank, hoping they would survive over the weekend. I used

Peter Leto and season one shirt

tweezers to feed them dried blood worms. They grow up to eighteen inches. I hate to see them go after all I went through."

TUESDAY, JULY 15

9:50 A.M.

Stabler is interrogating two male suspects who created a faux-rape porn video and simultaneously overlooked a genuine rape-murder happening on the same block. But their video camera may hold a clue.

Outside the interrogation room, director Peter Leto and script supervisor Stephanie Marquardt watch two side-by-side monitors that show similar images of the cast. Writer (and supervising producer) Daniel Truly, in from Los Angeles, keeps an eye on events. By take four, Leto paces up and down a bit, takes a deep breath, sits, and calls out "Action!"

10 A.M.

Dann Florek arrives and hugs Meloni. This is the cast's first day back on the set after a two-month hiatus. Hargitay shows up and

Stephanie Marquardt

kisses Florek on the cheek. As she starts to rehearse, her two-year-old son August—"Mr. Hermann" is printed on his T-shirt—tugs at her, pleading: "Mama out! Mama out!" (August's father, Peter Hermann, who recurs as defense attorney Trevor Langan on the show, is married to Hargitay.)

Another interrogation scene. This time Vince, a hopped-up addict (young novice actor Dane DeHaan), is the suspect. He's alone in the room, trying to peer through the one-way mirror.

Vince: "Hello? Someone gonna come talk to me? I can hear you watching me. Yoo-hoo! Come in, Calcutta."

Cragen (on the other side of the glass): "Where'd this guy beam down from?"

Stabler: "The planet Methamphetamine . . ."

RANDEE DAWN

Plaque indicating Capt. Cragen's promotion

10:25 A.M.

With his nanny nearby, August toddles through the production office while mom's in front of the camera elsewhere.

10:40 A.M.

Leto points to the bottom of the monitor to show Truly where the annoying network promotions inevitably will be and says, "Next week on NBC!" A final, successful take of Vince's scene is cheered by Leto: "Cut! Hee-hee-hee!"

11 A.M.

Meloni and Hargitay are guided through the blocking. Leto: "This will be the scene where Warner takes us places." That means Medical Examiner Dr. Melinda Warner, played by Tamara Tunie, will walk the detectives from one spot to another in the morgue and indicate evidence she has analyzed. All the angles and reaction shots are what take up the time; in the script, it's only three pages.

11:20 A.M.

Back in the U.S. from his home in France, Richard Belzer (Det. Sgt. John Munch) enters the room and gestures with his hands to encourage applause: "Ladies and gentlemen!" A leash and dog collar dangle around his neck. Bebe, the little poodle–fox terrier mix he adopted from a shelter, trots after him. More hugs among the humans.

RANDEE DAWN

Morgue phone—with surprising speed dial names

12:05 P.M.

The make-believe lifeless body of Marga (Kristina Klebe) lies on a slab in the morgue.

12:20 P.M.

After a snack, filming resumes. A juvenile eel—about the size of a garden worm—swims in a plastic Ziploc bag filled with water. Some of us choose to call it Neal, though the writer of this episode, Dan Truly, insists the tiny creature's name is actually Larry.

Leto (inspecting Neal/Larry): "No animals were hurt in the making of this episode, marine life or otherwise."

Hargitay: "That's the eel?"

Tunie: "Imagine how surprised I was."

Meloni looks at the eel and pretends to vomit. . . . The normally nocturnal Neal fails to move on cue after several takes under bright lights.

Hargitay: "This guy is so fucking tired."

Leto (suggesting another take): "It's just for the eel moment."

When they check out poor Neal, this time around Meloni and Hargitay mime regurgitation in unison . . . After introducing August to Bebe, Belzer asks if the child remembers his name.

August: "Belzer!"

Hargitay (amazed, proud): "He just said, 'Belzer!'"

1:45 P.M.

Following a lunch break, technical problems cause a delay.

2:10 P.M.

Meloni wanders into the holding room and makes a beeline for fruit on the snack table. "Cherries! All right! Who's my daddy?"

Stand-ins for Belzer and Ice-T (Rick Johnson and Storm Chambers, respectively) rehearse a sequence involving an evidence bag full of urine. Leto wants it held higher for the camera. "Show me the pee!" he says. "Show me the pee!"

2:25 P.M.

Belzer saunters onto the set again, singing a *West Side Story* tune: "Could it be? Yes, it could. Something's coming. Something good."

Suddenly, something's not so good. He swears. His eyeglasses are broken. The actor tells Leto he could sport sunglasses instead, but crew members provide a fix. Ice-T (Det. Odafin "Fin" Tutuola) arrives, concentrating on his BlackBerry.

2:35 P.M.

A tongue-twister requires several attempts by Ice-T, as he grasps that bag of urine. Eventually, the word "epithelials" is changed to "skin cells" and everything flows smoothly.

3:15 P.M.

It's time for Uncle Ted's Story Hour, as everyone calls the weekly session when executive producer Ted Kotcheff conducts a read-through of whatever episode is prepping. The title of this one is longtime *SVU* writer Dawn DeNoon's "Trials," in part about a hyperactive foster child subjected to experimental drugs, that's slated to be the season ten opener. A conference room in which the group normally gathers is too close to the set where "Lunacy" is now shooting, so ten people are instead crammed into Kotcheff's office to avoid noise problems.

David Platt, director (surveying the crowded conditions): "Ten years and this is the best we can do?"

The reading commences. They reach scene twelve, two pages in which Cragen, Munch, and Fin walk down an SVU corridor with their suspects.

Kotcheff: "That scene is way too long."

Platt: "We don't have enough hallway."

Producer David DeClerque suggests that the transition from a hospital back to the SVU is too abrupt, but Kotcheff says he's not bothered by the pace.

DeClerque: "If Ted Kotcheff thinks there's no problem, there's no problem. I agree with you completely, Ted." Everyone laughs.

Belzer pops in to say hello, then offers an idea for his conspiracy-obsessed character: "A can of soup falls on Munch's head in a bodega and he wakes up in Paris. No! It's black-and-white. November 22, 1963. And he's a Dallas cop."

The character's squad room desk is decorated with several mementoes of John F. Kennedy, including a vinyl record album of highlights from the assassinated president's speeches.

3:20 P.M.

Leto cradles Bebe in his arms while directing a rehearsal.

5:10 P.M.

The morgue, again, for various reaction shots. The scene concludes after much eel-wrangling. "It proved more slippery than expected," Truly quips.

(Days later, Tamara Tunie confides: "It was was so funny because we walked past a sushi place last night. I was like 'Eel. Hmm. Yummy.'")

6:25 P.M.

A scene from "Lunacy," with Benson interrogating the suspect named Rosie who was discovered making rape-porn videos.

Leto: "Is this the line when they ululate?"

Hargitay: "Is that when they ovulate? Maybe in a week."

The merriment ends when another take begins.

Rosie: "Wanna hear me ululate?" Without waiting for an answer, she does.

Benson: "I wanna hear how you can sleep at night making anti-Muslim rape porn."

7 P.M.

Fatigue is setting in, but the interrogation continues. In the script, Rosie's comment about her erotic entertainment empowering women provokes Benson to snap back with, "Being raped is empowering? On what planet?"

Hargitay: "This line is not ringing true for me. I can feel it right here (indicating her gut). That's my button, my empathy, my passion. It's not a fucking joke to me."

Truly: "Try saying, 'You are an idiot.'"

Hargitay: "That might work."

WEDNESDAY, JULY 16

7:30 A.M.

The day begins for cast and crew with a seminar on sexual harassment, as well as race and gender issues. *The authors have decided to skip this early morning session. Too bad, as it turns out.*

Mike Ciliento, the office production coordinator, later reports that the otherwise serious discussion was illustrated with clips from NBC shows *The Office* and *30 Rock*. A spoonful of television sugar apparently helps the medicine go down.

10:25 A.M.

Someone has brought homemade brownies. Dean Taucher, the production designer, enjoys a bite before providing a tour of his not fully assembled secondary sets. A crew member hammers down carpet in a hotel room painted in gray with white edging. The rug has padding underneath because there's going to be a brawl between Stabler and James Brolin's character, Dick Finley. Taucher points to where the fight will end, when the two fall on top of a table that looks real—but is really just made up of flimsy balsa wood and special breakaway (or "candy") glass.

Elsewhere, there's a screen painted to represent the interior of a spaceship, where soon-to-perish Marga will be seen floating in zero gravity. This can be accomplished by dangling her from wires, while moving the entire set back and forth on casters.

10:50 A.M.

Hargitay, holding the kind of black plastic bowl available on the set during meals, tells a crew member that it's not eco-friendly. "Can't they find something greener?"

Veteran actress Betty Buckley is dressed in a black suit and carrying a briefcase to portray Vince's defense attorney. Her character—attorney Collette Walsh, described in the script as "the legal lioness"—has been seen on *SVU* several times before.

James Brolin arrives. He's been cast as astronaut Dick Finley, Stabler's fellow former Marine and longtime mentor.

11:10 A.M.

Hargitay tells Dan Truly she's seen James Brolin and is thrilled that the script calls for him to ask her character out on a date. Olivia goes for his type, in her estimation. Ditto for the role of Benson's boyfriend that Bill Pullman inhabited in "Closet" (season nine).

Hargitay: "I won't lie. James Brolin is hot!"

Someone jokes that his wife, Barbra Streisand, might come looking for her.

Hargitay (with bravado): "I'm not frightened."

RANDEE DAWN

Daniel Truly

11:17 A.M.

Between takes of a scene with Vince, Buckley recounts how her lawyer character's SVU cases have turned out over the years. "I represent all losers," she surmises.

NOON

Meloni suggests to Leto that junkie Vince "clearly is still in that whack place" and should therefore blurt out his willingness to help the cops, rather than say so in the course of normal conversation. It's a good call, so they convey this to DeHaan.

Several women on the crew sport T-shirts emblazoned with Hargitay's name; they're souvenirs of *The Love Guru*, a 2008 film in which star Mike Myers repeatedly utters "Mariska Hargitay" as his mantra. She has a cameo role in the comedy and began selling the shirts, along with other merchandise, on her website.

12:15 P.M.

Chris Martini—the editor of *Dirty Movie*, a 2008 feature written and produced by its star, Christopher Meloni—watches the proceedings.

Leto, starting to show signs of being pressed for time: "With any hope, we can get this done. Come on, you silly freaks!" They make him happy in three takes.

1:50 P.M.

A prop person shows up with a four-inch model of a rocket that Dick Finley will give to Stabler's son Dickie, named in honor of the astronaut. The toy will bear a fingerprint that yields key evidence.

Leto wants to continue shooting but the mandatory lunch break is only ten minutes away. "Two days back (from hiatus) and it's like the wind is knocked out of me," he laments.

4:12 P.M.

Leto, finally finished with Vince's interrogation scene, announces: "Cut! Let's get out of this room quick." Perhaps that's because it feels like 100 degrees Fahrenheit under the lights on this oppressive July afternoon.

4:16 P.M.

Ted Kotcheff watches camera tests for Michaela McManus, who is replacing Diane Neal as the new ADA (Kim Greylek). A slinky brunette, she has remarkably high cheekbones and dazzling blue eyes. Key hair stylist Brian Badie sprays her tightly upswept 'do. Costume designer Tina Nigro has dressed the actress in a tailored black suit over a gray blouse. They all seem to be going for an Ice Queen look.

Kotcheff asks if there'll be "any accoutrements." McManus has small pearl earrings on but otherwise no jewelry or accessories.

(Hargitay later comments: "I got a great vibe from the new girl. And she's gorgeous.")

4:50 P.M.

Rehearsal of the morgue scene in which Andrea (Therese Plummer) must identify Marga's body. When Truly expresses concern that her reaction ought to be more emotional, Leto says it's just the rehearsal. With a mock Yiddish accent, he adds: "You vant she should spend it all now?"

5:20 P.M.

The atmosphere in the room has become tense. Today's shoot is running late with take after take. In between, Meloni and Hargitay rest in their high director-style chairs; hers has "August's Mommy" printed on the back.

RANDEE DAWN

SVU's morgue set

5:40 P.M.

Dan Truly mentions that his father (U.S. Navy Vice Admiral Richard H. Truly) is an actual former astronaut who flew on two NASA shuttle missions (in 1981 and 1983).

6 P.M.

Dann Florek appears in the holding room, where meals are served and extras await their moment in the sun. He chats about working in *American Buffalo*, a play by David Mamet.

6:15 P.M.

During a scene in which Benson talks about the discovery of Marga's earring, she indicates her own ear. This amuses Leo and Truly, who point to their necks, wrists, and other areas of the body where jewelry might go. They're a bit punchy.

7 P.M.

Leto (after a scene is filmed): "Ah! Oh! The horror, the horror."

7:20 P.M.

Puge Ruhe, a production assistant who handles the "background"—or non-speaking—extras, rounds up a gaggle of rather seedy-looking men who have been sitting in the holding room for hours: "All my lineup dudes, let's go!"

7:30 P.M.

The lineup dudes, in identical beige baseball caps, rehearse a scene with DeHaan, Hargitay, and Florek looking at them through the one-way glass window. These possible perps are joined by Chris Elliott, a guest star playing an unhinged stalker obsessed with astronauts.

7:35 P.M.

Electrician Ronnie Paul, an *SVU* staffer from the beginning, recalls that his daughter was six months old when she took her first steps in front of Meloni's dressing room. The girl later portrayed a Romanian orphan in "Poison," a season five episode. "You know, forty-eight kids have been born to this show since we started," he says wistfully.

7:50 P.M.

George Pattison, the director of photography, proclaims: "C'est bon!" This take of the lineup scene meets with his approval.

THURSDAY, JULY 17

NOON

The Emmy nominations have been announced. In addition to two guest stars from season nine (Cynthia Nixon for "Alternate" and Robin Williams for "Authority"), Mariska Hargitay is on the list again. Her "people" are reportedly on the set, urging her to do some canned video quotes for shows like *Access Hollywood*.

August is visiting and he charms everyone. Ice-T notes that his son, now sixteen, also grew up among adults, but in the recording studio.

12:10 P.M.

In the SVU squad room, astronaut groupie Anton (Chris Elliott) is being interrogated near Cragen's office. Leto's sipping a large iced coffee from Dunkin' Donuts, while Brolin quietly rehearses his lines.

Under intense questioning from Stabler, Anton sweeps the articles on a desk to the floor, as Cragen and Dr. Huang watch. This is B.D. Wong's (Dr. George Huang) first day on the set for the episode.

12:30 P.M.

Script supervisor Stephanie Marquardt says Chris Meloni, who plays Elliot Stabler, had mused, "Could there be a more confusing actor to have on this show than someone named Chris Elliott?"

12:35 P.M.

The same scene is reconfigured to shoot again, but from a different angle. Filming takes up perhaps 10 percent of the day; everything else is moving furniture and equipment or rehearsing.

1:05 P.M.

The SVU squad room, painted a drab green, boasts real and mock law enforcement posters. The place looks coolly authentic but the temperature is hot, hot, hot. The North Bergen building does have

A/C, but it's switched off in the soundstage areas when cameras are rolling because of the ambient noise that's created. Someone suggests the problem is exacerbated by the fact that the facility is just a retrofitted warehouse.

Between takes of their scene, Dann Florek says to B.D. Wong: "They've been lying to us about the air conditioning for ten years, bro'."

Truly suggests to Leto how lucky Brolin is to have become "a silver-haired lion" on camera.

Cot and hat props, inside Capt. Cragen's Office

1:15 P.M.

A prop man brings Leto two identical mugs for an upcoming scene in which Stabler, Benson, and Brolin's Finley drink whiskey while eating Chinese food. But the director wants them mismatched and "from the cupboard," not new.

A crew member shows his laptop with clips from real-life Apollo launches to Leto, who is humming MTV's theme song. He wants space shuttle footage, as well. Someone refreshes the ever-present 35-pack of Poland Spring water bottles that rests next to the cart holding the monitors.

1:30 P.M.

Leto emerges from the interrogation room: "It's a well-oiled, rusted machine," he says, in a slight variation on the cliché everyone uses to describe all Law & Order shows. Looking at Cragen, Huang, and Finley on the monitor, he notes: "There's a three-shot that's never been seen before in *SVU* history."

1:45 P.M.

The holding room is packed with actors, primarily middle-aged, dressed as uniformed cops or detectives. They'll be the seen-but-not-heard occupants of the squad room when the script dictates. Meanwhile, several of them are playing cards to pass the time.

2:45 P.M.

Leto is on the squad room floor with the monitors, while the actors sit around a table with containers of Chinese take-out up in the lounge. Hargitay: "This is real food, right?" Leto: "Yeah, but don't eat it." A prop man mentions later that they spent $80 on the meal, in case more than what's initially laid out is needed.

2:50 P.M.

Hargitay calls down: "Stephanie, what time is it?" Marquardt: "9:30." It's not yet 3 P.M., of course, but they're talking script hours. The room is darkened, so night seems realistic.

3 P.M.

While Hargitay waits for shooting to begin, she chats with fellow actors, explaining that it took her a year of marriage to stop calling her husband Peter Hermann "Chris," and Meloni counters by saying how difficult it was to stop calling his wife "Peter." Always a naughty clown, he adds: "Just said I was referring to my penis."

5:25 P.M.

Leto joins Mike Sime, the show's video assistant, in an area of the soundstage where the crew has begun creating Marga's zero-gravity sequence. In the episode, this is going to be watched by schoolchildren. The strong wires they've hooked to each side of her blue space suit will later be digitally erased from the frames. Suspended in mid-air against the backdrop of a shuttle interior, she is coached on how to move her arms and legs as if floating.

Although fascinated, Leto quips, "OK, I'm going back to where the action is."

5:50 P.M.

Back at the lounge, where the action is, everyone's besieged by the intensifying heat and humidity. Hargitay wipes perspiration from her brow. "I'd rather act when it's cold than when it's hot," she vows at the start of a scene with Meloni and Brolin.

On the day Hargitay's been nominated for an Emmy at 8:30 A.M., she's still sweating under the lights at 6 P.M.

6:15 P.M.

The space station video shoot gets under way. Truly takes photos of the suspension process.

6:30 P.M.

In the production office, prop man Anthony Munafo shares a taste of the novelty freeze-dried space "ice cream" that he purchased for Anton to eat in the episode. There are twenty-five bags of the stuff, just in case. It tastes a bit like sweet cardboard.

7:02 P.M.

In the holding room, the fake cops are still playing cards.

Trailed by August, Hargitay walks briskly along a hallway while telling her enthusiastic son: "Let's go see everybody! Let's go see everybody!"

7:10 P.M.

Hargitay shows August around "where Mommy works." He goes up to the lounge with her. The boy is perched on a seat in front of the gigantic camera and allowed to hold the guiding arms of the apparatus. A little later, she brings him down to Benson's desk.

August likes to be called "Augustino" but, when someone calls him "Auggie," Hargitay chides them: "Don't corrupt my child." Mother and son sit at her desk, singing the alphabet song. She also trills "You Are My Sunshine" to him and explains the meanings of "astronauts" and "cut" and "action!" He then goes around chanting, "Cut! Cut!"

7:50 P.M.

With the camera behind her, Hargitay's in the lounge leaning over the staircase to talk with Ice-T standing on the steps. This brief scene requires numerous takes. Leto has referred to it as "The famous derriere shot." He says to Pattison: "We're looking at her tush for ten seconds." Hargitay, "This is so hot." It's not clear if she means the saucy shot of her rear end or the temperature.

FRIDAY, JULY 18

9:30 A.M.

It's a cops-and-perps day on the New Jersey set. Background extras are slated to be the main focus of a complex, chaotic scene in the halls outside the squad room.

11:10 A.M.

The big scene is being blocked, but a Hannah Montana concert in Bryant Park has reportedly delayed actress Betty Buckley's arrival. When she does appear, Leto explains how he'd like her to walk from the interrogation room into the hallway. Her client will be getting shot, so she'll have to back away through an oncoming sea of armed SVU detectives.

Leto is wearing a red T-shirt with an image of two blazing pistols, from which long strands of smoke entwine to form a heart. He's also singing "Happiness Is a Warm Gun," a 1968 Beatles tune.

Three takes are sufficient, but Leto tells DeHaan: "Because I'm a paranoid freak, one more time exit left."

11:25 A.M.

The hallway is "broomed"—all of the furniture is removed to make way for the next scenes.

Buckley wonders who sent the beautiful flowers to her dressing room. The answer: Hargitay. The recipient later marvels that, "Mariska's just the perfect woman."

11:30 A.M.

The key actors, standing in a circle, are doing a read-through of their lines. First assistant director Howard McMaster handles the part that will eventually be recited by Jeffrey Scaperrotta, the young recurring cast member playing Dickie Stabler, who tells Benson that he prefers to be called Dick now. There's much guffawing over the notion of a grown man reading the "aw shucks" dialogue of a teenager.

11:35 A.M.

Leto gives an extensive walking tour through the series of shots that will take up most of the day. He winds up on the floor to illustrate where the shooting victim should fall. Brolin asks: "Want to go over that again?" McMaster cautions: "Don't encourage him."

11:50 A.M.

Truly says his father read the script and, though also an astronaut named Dick, he was fine with the fictitious astronaut Dick being a killer. Did the real guy ever have a stalker like the "Lunacy" character Anton? Not exactly, Truly recalls, but there was some woman who caused trouble for a while.

12:05 P.M.

Someone from the wardrobe department holds up three identical gray shirts like the one Vince wears in the scene. The team needs to figure out precisely where he gets shot.

12:20 P.M.

Meloni talks to Truly about Stabler's impending fight scene with Dick Finley and reveals an actual bruise on his arm from a recent tussle. "I'm getting too old for this," the actor suggests.

12:30 P.M.

Jeffrey Scaperrotta is on hand and ready to perform in his role as Dickie. Leto inspects photos of Marga, while she's still alive, and selects the "most professional" one.

12:50 P.M.

Meloni pulls Hargitay into the squad room, saying: "I have another saga to tell you about." "People will talk," she quips. They chat quietly.

1:40 P.M.

Leto, working on reaction shots of Chris Elliott as Anton, tends to become giddy when things go well.

2:15 P.M.

Things are not going so well now. Brolin is having some trouble remembering his lines. Perhaps he's not accustomed to much episodic TV.

2:35 P.M.

While "Lunacy" continues shooting in New Jersey, auditions are under way at Manhattan's Chelsea Piers for an episode to kick off season ten that David Platt will direct, "Trials." He's in a room with EP Ted Kotcheff, first assistant director David DeClerque, casting director Jonathan Strauss, and a few others.

They're seeing boys between the ages of seven and twelve for the challenging role of a foster child with hyperactive behavior. The first child to try out for the part is a diminutive kid with round wire-rim glasses that give him a Harry Potter look. With a clear voice and convincing delivery, he even has all the lines in one scene memorized.

"He's adorable," Strauss says when the wizard-like lad leaves the room. "But maybe not red-faced enough."

The character is required to throw tantrums. That would seem to be perfect for Boy Number Five, a prepubescent with a rather menacing demeanor.

"That kid's going to grow up and be a car thief," Platt later suggests.

"An eight-year-old method actor?" muses DeClerque.

Strauss has arranged for Kotcheff to see some other boys in Los Angeles on Monday, so no decision will be made until then.

3:30 P.M.

Pressed for time, Leto doesn't want to wait ten minutes while the crew removes a light fixture in the hallway so that the boom mike can be better accommodated. The fixture comes down anyway.

The inner wrist of Belzer's left arm bears a tattoo that reads, "Don't panic." It was inspired by the identical catchphrase in *The Hitchhiker's Guide to the Galaxy*, Douglas Adams's 1979 sci-fi novel.

3:40 P.M.

Belzer notices that the squad room floor has been replaced during the recent hiatus. Someone makes a comment about how *SVU* can afford new floors but not staff raises.

3:50 P.M.

For the sequence that requires gunshots, Leto yells "Bang!" on cue. Buckley's Collette Walsh is pushed aside by the SVU cops so they can apprehend the shooter. People are referring to it as "the Betty Buckley Abuse Scene."

6:30 P.M.

A thick padded mat has been put down to cushion the fall when Finley tackles Anton Thibodeaux.

RANDEE DAWN

Welcome back sign for cast and crew, season ten

8:30 P.M.

A yellow cake with chocolate icing is brought out to celebrate James Brolin's birthday.

9:30 P.M.

Make-believe corpses in body bags are wheeled out on gurneys. Leto experiences some frustration in trying again and again to get the shot right.

9:40 P.M.

Pizza is on the way and, presumably, a kiss of the hops: The production assistants regularly bet in a card game that funnels some of their winnings to the purchase of beer on Friday nights.

9:50 P.M.

"Three more shots and we're out of here," Leto promises. "Maybe four?"

10 P.M.

Maybe more than four. Irritated, Leto throws down his earphones and transmitter in disgust. "I'm good for one of those an episode," he says by way of explanation.

10:25 P.M.

Pizza arrives. One of the makeup people mentions that Ice-T is the "Zen master" of the show. Apparently, he's never in a bad mood and always has some bit of wisdom to share. "Every day I'm not in prison is a good day," Ice-T has reportedly told his colleagues.

MONDAY, JULY 21

11 A.M.

At the southern tip of Manhattan, just a stone's throw from where the World Trade Center once stood, the Battery Park waterfront is a familiar setting from all the Law & Order shows. On this morning, curious locals and tourists watch the *SVU* production in progress, often snapping photos.

It's excruciatingly hot, despite a breeze off the Hudson River. In addition to iced Poland Spring water, there's a large tub with various brands of sunscreen. Tamara Tunie is trying to stay cool under a white umbrella. Meloni's dressed in what would be a normal men's business shirt—except the sleeves have been cut off. This adjustment won't show up on camera once he dons a dark suit jacket when shooting begins. Hargitay acknowledges that she's "roasting" in black pants, a top and a vest, over which her jacket will go when necessary.

Background extras in police uniforms are everywhere. Kristin Krebe, playing Marga, is doing her swan song as the dead body is fished out of the Hudson. The scene in which she's discovered floating in the water was shot earlier. We're told that a motorized raft had circled nearby and stuntmen were submerged in the river to make sure the actress was safe.

Now that raft has been relabeled with "NYC NYPD" and has a single stunt man inside. They bob in the background as filming continues. "That's a two-fer," says producer Gail Barringer, referring to a prop that does double duty.

11:05 A.M.

Production assistants ward off a video camera–wielding member of the public. It's not allowed.

11:10 A.M.

Helicopters and motorboats frequently buzz the area, but are only periodically considered interference.

11:25 A.M.

Stabler and Benson cross the park to look at the body. Everyone's uncomfortable on this dog day of summer. Hargitay asks for help from the makeup people: "Just a little Blotty von Blotstein, thanks." Pattison is almost drowning in his own perspiration. And no wonder: He's got to carry the Steadicam on a harness strapped around his chest and it weighs about seventy-five pounds.

The crew trails him as he closes in on Marga's body and someone sets a wooden crate down so he can sit.

11:30 A.M.

It's so hot out today that the metal frame containing Marga's body—purportedly pulled directly from the water—and the blanket surrounding it are drying out, so a crew member is on hand to re-wet the contraption for verisimilitude. He uses what's called a "Hudson Sprayer," which resembles an insect exterminator's equipment. That's the actual name of the device, not a nod to the river from which it's drawing water.

NOON

The camera is reloaded, which takes time. Leto joins the actors. When someone mentions a cinematic "freeze frame," he starts humming the early 1980s J. Geils Band song with that title.

12:05 P.M.

Tunie finishes work for the day and the episode. There's applause from her colleagues. Kristin is also done being Marga. Hargitay tells her she did a good job.

The crew and the equipment are relocated further down the river promenade for scenes with Belzer and Ice-T, neither of whom is here yet. Hargitay seems to have disappeared, until the raft comes zooming back to shore: She's in it, along with one of the stuntmen and her assistant. They've just gone for a ride. "That was so much fun," she shouts. "I wanna join the Coast Guard."

1:30 P.M.

After lunch, setup begins for the day's last series of scenes at a building with a sign out front that reads, "Hugh L. Carey Battery Park City Authority." But the set designer apparently has added frosted glass engraved with the words "Hotel Argus" to the doors.

Tracks are laid for a dolly shot. When asked, Ice-T talks about the "Zen master of the set" designation given him Friday by the makeup people: "I have my priorities straight," he says, explaining that most of his friends are in jail. Some years ago it even felt as if his own luck was running out and the time had come to get his act together.

2 P.M.

Speaking of getting an act together, Belzer is here now and The Men in Black—as the crew refers to him and Ice—have a scene at the Hotel Argus. Munch walks outside to find Fin checking for clues in a sidewalk trash bin.

Between takes, nearby gawkers take pictures, prompting Ice to announce: "Paparazzi! Ice-T Fired From *Law & Order*! Exclusive!"

Leto says, no doubt humorously: "We've got ten hours to shoot this scene. Let's use it!"

2:15 P.M.

In front of the hotel again, Munch has to weave around a luggage cart piled high with suitcases. There's a car now parked there, as well, with background extras enacting Hotel Guest and Valet.

A prop man later explains the vehicle belongs to someone on the crew; as always, the owner is paid $120 per day for its use.

Belzer's step-daughter, Bree Benton, arrives with two friends. She's a willowy ash-blonde who has done some acting, including on a 1999 episode of his former series, *Homicide: Life on the Street.*

2:30 P.M.

There's some serious choreography needed this afternoon. Not much can be done to avoid noise from helicopters above and water taxis in the Hudson. But production assistants do try to keep the public out of the promenade sequence, again and again allowing joggers, bicyclists, moms or nannies pushing babies in strollers and summer-camp kids with backpacks to pass before each take of a scene. *SVU* has its own background extras in similar garb, however, once the camera rolls. This hilarious mingling of fact and fiction makes for a long day in the blazing sun.

A tourist is heard asking his wife, "Isn't this the highlight of your trip?"

A short while later, Ice echoes that idea when another swarm of visitors stops to watch the spectacle: "Hello! This is the most exciting thing you're going to see on your trip to New York except for the Naked Cowboy. He's next!"

Prop sign from on location set for "Lunacy"

2:45 P.M.

Somewhere in the midst of a scene that demands more than a

Computer Screens in Squad Room, used during season ten's "Lunacy." Director Peter Leto and writer Daniel Truly appear as astronauts in the lower center screen.

dozen takes, Ice jokes about the show's decade-long existence: "Ten years without reading a script." Belzer, pretending to cringe: "Shhh!"

After several unsuccessful takes, Leto says, "We're over-thinking it; that's our problem."

Before another try, camera operator Tom Weston informs him that a guy sitting on a bench within the shot is not a background extra.

Ice-T: "Hard to regulate New York." Nonetheless, he makes an attempt at crowd control by telling one group: "Back up a bit." They obey.

Belzer's a bit blunter with a family obliviously wandering into camera range: "Move, move, move! *Mach schnell!*"

He then politely asks a man in a yarmulke to back away, before muttering to himself: "Get your ass outta here!"

Despite all this angst, the two actors are soon glimpsed on a bench, posing with their arms around strangers who request snapshots of themselves next to The Men in Black.

3:05 P.M.

"Men in Green! Men in Green!" Ice proclaims, as New York City park employees in cucumber-colored uniforms come into view. One of them shakes his hand, saying: "I'm a big fan. A big fan."

Belzer is ensnared in a canine altercation, as little Bebe and a gigantic black Lab snarl at each other.

When someone points out that they're shooting an episode about astronauts one day after the 39th anniversary of the first moon landing (July 20, 1969), Ice-T says: "Fun facts." It happens to be one of his lines in this very scene.

3:30 P.M.

Leto says he hopes the Hudson River's water is clean because a stuntwoman has swallowed some.

4:05 P.M.

McMaster to Leto, who's eating pretzels and sipping a can of iced tea while Ice-T and Belzer wait for their marching orders: "Peter, your Men in Black need a little direction."

4:15 P.M.

Leto: "Good energy now and action! . . . Cut! . . . OK, here we go. Good pace, good pace . . . Cut! Check the gate . . . Oops, no. One more, one more."

TUESDAY, JULY 22

10 A.M.

SVU has fanned out into a second borough, at the New York Hall of Science in Queens. The setting for some of today's scenes involves two gigantic Atlas and Titan rockets on display outside amid a landscape that's overgrown with plant life, crying out for a gardener. This is intentional, it turns out (the museum, based near Flushing Meadows, is letting the grasses grow wild). But the look is untidy for filming purposes. "Benson has fuck-all for background," Leto complains.

In the script, the detectives seek information about Marga's murder at a space symposium discussing a return to the moon. So another part of the grounds they plan to use has been given a dais, where dignitaries are supposed to give speeches, and bleachers for the spectators.

10:35 A.M.

The show has recruited an unusually large group of background extras. About 125 of them are assembled in a cavernous second-floor area that's the location's equivalent of a holding room. Some are outfitted in either NASA or military uniforms. This might be confusing to the museum's regular patrons—mostly kids—who excitedly browse the interactive exhibits.

As they set up a scene outside, cast and crew don't have leisure time for such educational pursuits, but do understand one fundamental scientific truth: 90 percent humidity is profoundly uncomfortable, especially for those constantly on the move lugging heavy equipment or dressed in costumes befitting late autumn.

Moreover, mosquitoes have moved in, though the prepared-for-anything props department is stocked with repellent. Other crew members have had to venture into the dense meadow in order to do some preparations and they're now imitating monkeys in the jungle.

11:15 A.M.

Background extras are in the bleachers or at the podium. One of them, George Wilkinson, is dressed as a Navy commander. He's been on the show four or five times over the past two years, ever since retiring from the electric emergency services field and enrolling in an acting course at Nassau Community College.

"I was watching *Law & Order* and saw a jury filing into the courtroom," he recalls. "I told myself, 'I can do that.'"

The crew shoots B-roll footage of the rockets.

Yesterday, the noise was due to choppers and water taxis. Now, it's the frequent fliers above us from nearby LaGuardia Airport.

McMaster tells the crew to move all the equipment to the opposite side of the road. They're situated too close to the busy museum loading dock. "Welcome to the first cluster-fuck of the day," he says, waving his arms for emphasis.

11:35 A.M.

Meloni has a sleeveless business shirt on again. His upper left arm sports a large tattoo with a religious theme. Hargitay tries to beat the heat with a personal-sized, portable fan.

On July 27, the *New York Post* publishes a photo of him this way, with a cutline describing the tat as "a self-designed depiction of Jesus Christ's crucifixion." A few days later, the newspaper shows Hargitay alongside "Trials" guest star Luke Perry; he's got a portable fan in each hand, one aimed at her face and the other at his.

12:10 P.M.

Out of the blue, Leto starts singing a snippet from "Back in the U.S.S.R.," another 1968 Beatles hit: "Flew in from Miami Beach BOAC; Didn't get to bed last night . . ." Could this be in reaction to the intrusive LaGuardia flight path? In addition to the air traffic, trains rattle past not too far away from the shoot.

Dan Truly explains that while writing the script he'd envisioned the Hayden Planetarium in Manhattan, "but this site offered more opportunities." And more planes.

Even here, humanity is an issue. Pedestrians and cars periodically disrupt filming. At one point, a bare-chested Asian man so thin his ribs stick out pedals by on a bicycle rigged up as a sort of truck filled to the brim with detritus. A junk collector, perhaps? Leto asks a member of the crew to give him several bottles of cold water.

12:35 P.M.

Museumgoers, many of them school-age children, have gathered in the weeded area to take pictures and watch filming of a two-camera scene.

12:45 P.M.

The sun's directly above and everyone is dripping, especially the actors who wear heavy clothing. "I feel so sorry for those extras in sweaters," Leto says, "but we air in the fall, so the episode has to look that way."

1:05 P.M.

While in character for a scene, Meloni introduces Benson to Dick Finley as "Olivia Stabler." Leto: "Whoa, Freudian slip!" Gail Barringer: "Save that for the gag reel."

1:10 P.M.

More planes, trains, automobiles, and non-*SVU* people interrupt the shoot. Leto: "We'd do better on Lexington Avenue." Nearby, a police car has pulled up that's marked "Movie TV Unit." *Now, there's a tough beat.*

1:51 P.M.

Cast and crew are on hold, waiting for Meloni to return from elsewhere. "Something's not right with him," Hargitay says, then turning to the authors: "Put that in the book."
    Yes, ma'am.

2:25 P.M.

A child screams in the distance. A car honks insistently. Delays, delays, delays. Heat, heat, heat.
    Hargitay to Leto: "I'm hanging in there like a champion, but sweat is just dripping down my back."

4:20 P.M.

Child extras are placing a teddy bear in a space helmet on a makeshift memorial to Marga that includes flowers, condolence cards, and Belgian flags. Stabler and Finley spot Anton Thibodeaux, clutching a prized autograph book. He's bragging to anyone who'll listen about the famous astronaut names therein, but with each successive take Chris Elliott improvises slightly different dialogue that refers to renowned pioneers of space flight. The guy seems to know his NASA history.

4:40 P.M.

Leto asks Meloni to step into the frame, an angle not previously planned. The actor playfully asks the director: "You want a piece of me now?"

There's a long debate among Leto, camera operator Tom Weston, script supervisor Stephanie Marquardt, and James Brolin over where Anton should direct his gaze at the end of a one shot in order to match the placement of actors in the next one.

5 P.M.

Leto announces that Chris Elliott's work is done. Cast, crew, and extras applaud him.

6:15 P.M.

In the holding room, PA Drew Wood reads names from a list in an effort to round up several child extras for a "Lunacy" scene that will have them watching the Marga-in-zero-gravity video. A few don't respond right away and there's confusion about what they all should be wearing.

One little girl peppers him with questions: "Should we take notes?"

Wood: "No, you're just watching a video."

Inquisitive Girl: "Can we take notes about the video?"

Finally, everyone is ready. "Follow me. Here we go," Wood says like a Pied Piper leading the ambitious kids to their acting destiny.

6:47 P.M.

The shoot has finally gotten away from the direct sun by going indoors, but the temperature in this enormous chamber of a room—three stories high—keeps the sweat glands pumping. It is beautiful, though. Curved in and out like waves, the walls are studded with irregular shapes of dark blue glass that block daylight.

7:05 P.M.

"Monkey" (Key PA Brian Campe), on how he got his nickname: "When I started four years ago, I was young and eager and wacky and trying to make an impression and maybe a little goofy."

8:20 P.M.

Leto hugs Hargitay, possibly as encouragement to endure the swelter and long hours.

Seated, Meloni hoists himself up several inches using just one arm on a museum pulley exhibit that allows people to try lifting their own weight.

A crew from TV's *Access Hollywood* has arrived to interview James Brolin.

8:30 P.M.

When longtime *Law & Order* publicist Audrey Davis mentions that the show's scripts are redone with local casts in several foreign countries, Meloni and Hargitay spring into a hilarious sketch comedy routine.

Germany? Their accents are pitch-perfect.

Russia? Hargitay: "Nyet."

England? In character, they deliver an increasingly raunchy version of *SVU*, telling the Queen that Benson and Stabler are there to see Her Majesty.

France? Meloni, as he mimes puffing a cigarette with insouciant *joie de vivre*: "Zat ees not a sex crime. For ze French, ees never a sex crime."

Everyone is in stitches.

10:05 P.M.

The laughter is long gone, as fatigue sets in. Hargitay yawns. The attempt to nail a wordy sequence drags on and on because

Brolin, possibly approaching heat exhaustion, stumbles over his lines. Lunacy, indeed.

Leto tells the crew to "warm Odafin up" for a scene in which he identifies Marga's necklace in a pawn shop—actually a sort of stall with props that's been constructed in the holding room. Poor Ice-T has been waiting to do this since 3 P.M. *Not a very fun fact.*

WEDNESDAY, JULY 23

10:30 A.M.

"We're in!" comes the call, which means everyone heads to the squad room so that Peter Leto can conduct a walk-through of the sequence. But only stand-ins are on hand—the actors haven't arrived yet—and it's as cold as a meat locker in here. Quite a contrast with yesterday's torturous heat.

10:45 A.M.

Just inside the main doors to the soundstage, a bulletin board displays "approved" articles about the show from the Internet. Today it has expanded—there's going to be a *Law & Order: UK* version with an actor from *Battlestar Galactica* appearing in it.

Quick, somebody cue Meloni and Hargitay about that interrogation of the Queen!

10:55 A.M.

Stand-ins are reading lines to themselves in the holding cell just outside the squad room doors. A crew member has modified a director's chair with pink tape and written "Tom Weston" on it. He's the camera operator.

11:25 A.M.

Belzer and Bebe stroll onto the set and initial rehearsals with main actors commence. During one of them, he is standing next to Brolin, whose line is: "Anything I can do . . ." Belzer adlibs a verse from an *Annie Get Your Gun* song: " . . . I can do better."

11:35 A.M.

The first takes go relatively well. Dan Truly, for whom this is the last day on the set, talks with Leto about which of Brolin's arms should be carrying a duffel bag. Three bells ring, as they do every time the camera rolls.

Bebe on the set of "Lunacy," season ten

11:45 A.M.

Leto re-frames his shot a tad inside the squad room, comes back out and examines it on the monitor: "That's a-nice a-frame," he says in an exaggerated Italian accent.

Meloni arrives on set in a shirt and tie—and shorts—for rehearsal. A recent college graduate, aspiring actor, and neighbor of Howard McMaster's has been invited on the set today and is eager to understand the whole process.

Meloni shakes his hand. "Who're you?"

McMaster's neighbor: "Sam."

Meloni: "I'm Chris."

Sam: "I know who you are."

But he's amused and delighted by the actor's casual attitude.

12:05 P.M.

Tomorrow's on-location shoot will return to Battery Park, where exteriors of the faux Hotel Argus were done on Tuesday. This will be a night shoot (as opposed to the original location shoot, which took place during the day). McMaster explains that they tend to save night shoots for Friday, so that they don't have to deal with union-mandated turnaround time for the crew, since Saturdays are rarely on the schedule. The requirement: ten hours off between workdays; actors get twelve.

1:15 P.M.

With the squad room scenes done, everything and everyone relocates to the interior of the Hotel Argus, situated elsewhere on the set. There's a closed blocking rehearsal, and then it takes a very long time to light the room.

The authors must flee, but learn later that the indefatigable SVU people wind up going until about 12:30 A.M.

THURSDAY, JULY 24

11 A.M.

On this cloudy morning with intermittent rain, the show relocates to a lovely neighborhood in Fort Lee, New Jersey—specifically, Abbott Boulevard, which has houses on either side of a street bisected by a wide grassy, tree-lined median. Chairs, tents, and equipment are parked all along the strip, which also serves as a kind of park or promenade. Trucks line the streets, which are closed to traffic and monitored by local cops.

The whole setup occupies a good three to four blocks, not counting the holding area, which is even further away. The sun is fighting to come out but we're all hoping it'll stay in.

(Weeks later, location manager Trish Adlesic notes that "Lunacy" director Peter Leto hails from Fort Lee: "We call it 'Fort Leto.'")

11:15 A.M.

An ode to Crafts Services: They are awesome! Eat like a Teamster! Now it's clear why so many of those folks are, shall we say, on the large side. Cooks inside the trailer make food to specifications. Blueberry pancakes? No problem. Egg/bacon/cheese quesadilla? Coming right up. Turkey club? Certainly. And there's a table with other tempting items, from oatmeal to biscuits to fresh fruit to kielbasa sausage.

Jeffrey Scaperrotta, who plays Dickie "I Just Go By Dick" Stabler, is here again today.

11:30 A.M.

At a private residence that will serve as Stabler's home, the crew has lined the floor with thick paper. Someone says *SVU* is probably paying about $3,000 for the day to rent the place, and that the production will be gone before the owners return—likely from work. Leto explains that this house is one of many they've used as Stabler's domicile over the years.

Today he's got on a black shirt with a crudely drawn chalk outline of a body whose crooked leg makes the "V" and whose bent arm makes the "U" in the words *Special Victims Unit*. "This is old-school," Leto notes, "from, like, season one."

11:45 A.M.

More prep in progress, no shooting yet. Meloni is going over lines with Jeffrey on the edge of the lawn. Pattison again wears his Steadicam harness.

12:05 P.M.

The scene with Stabler and his son getting out of a car and going into the house works well and is done quickly.

12:10 P.M.

Neighbors have assembled to watch filming. Truly has gone back to Los Angeles. Leto and Barringer both express regret about that; it's always preferable to have the writer on hand—especially later, when Meloni has issues with something his character is saying.

When it starts to drizzle, the crew springs into action, laying sheets of plastic over everything and pushing equipment into tents or—in the case of the sound man and his cart—under a tree.

12:40 P.M.

While they wait for the shoot to begin, Meloni directs Jeffrey, suggesting motivation and explaining the scenes. They try two different ways of expressing something: In one, Dickie is amazed dad "got mom pregnant." In the other, he says his father "knocked mom up."

1 P.M.

After the authors interview Scaperrotta, Meloni asks: "He said I was the greatest actor he's ever worked with, right?" *Mais oui, French* SVU *detective.*

In yesterday's fight scene, which was restricted to just a few observers and workers, Meloni came out "un-dinged." But, he says there may have been damage when he bent down to pick up a "230-pound stunt guy" and felt something move in his gut, before pulling back to avoid a hernia. He's a bit tender today.

Meloni manages to keep in shape. "Some mornings it's roll out of bed, work out, half hour with the family, come out here, go home, roll into bed." This routine is a frequent regimen.

1:30 P.M.

The company has relocated to the side of the house, in the driveway. The area with the TV monitors is called the "Video Village," so that's what has moved. The action is now inside the home.

2:40 P.M.

Everyone shifts again, this time across the street to the other house, where a man washing his taxi will be questioned by Stabler and Benson. Hargitay is here; she and Meloni rehearse with the actors playing the cab driver and his wife. The male character is supposed to look as creepy as possible, so he's unshaven with a script-mandated beer gut hanging over tight shorts.

2:45 P.M.

A crew member brings Meloni his lunch—basic spinach, rice, and some kind of crumbly meat—wrapped up between two plates. He walks away with the food after rehearsal finishes.

Another setup, for a dolly shot this time, is in progress. "Let's lay this track and beat this storm," says Leto, squinting up at the sky. "We're gonna do this scene in an hour."

Hargitay trots after Meloni: "I took a boat ride without you!" she taunts him, referring to the other day at Battery Park.

MONDAY, JULY 28

When what's normally an eight-day shoot SVU shoot was extended to ten, the authors realized they would be unable to stick around till the bittersweet end. So, this section of the diary is provided by Rick Johnson, a singer-songwriter, Richard Belzer's regular stand-in, and our surrogate fly-on-the-wall for the final countdown of "Lunacy."

7 A.M.

Cast and crew gather with light conversation as to what everyone did over the weekend. The main topic is the movies that opened, specifically *The Dark Knight* versus *Step Brothers*.

9 A.M.

Benson and Stabler are in the interrogation room questioning suspect Orlando McTeer.

11:30 A.M.

A rehearsal of the scene in which M.E. Warner informs the detectives that the victim, an astronaut, was named Marga Janssen.

11:50 A.M.

Leto and the DP are shuffling back and forth from the squad room to the interrogation room. For use in the next three scenes, they're shooting with the B (secondary) camera to create five inserts: the picture of Vince that Benson will send from her cell phone to Fin's; Stabler's hands holding Anton's autograph book; and Marga's missing necklace under a magnifying glass at a pawn shop.

1 P.M.

The actors are again chatting about their weekend activities, such as the stand-up comedy show that Belzer did in New York and Ice's trip to Vegas for a musical performance.

1:10 P.M.

Leto reins in Florek, Belzer, Ice, Meloni, and Hargitay, reminding them they have a lot more work to do in "the hot zone" under the lights. This takes place in the squad room, where they must gather around the "multiplex"—a display panel with six screens that will show pictures of the victim, the crime scene, and the inserts that are still being shot.

2:15 P.M.

Lunch is called. Leto has blocked the scene as a "oner," meaning all the dialogue is caught in a single continuous movement of the Steadicam. He and Pattison continue overseeing the B-camera inserts in progress.

2:55 P.M.

An espresso/cappuccino machine has been set up for a few hours in the holding room for cast and crew, compliments of writer Dan Truly.

5 P.M.

The sequence of Marga Janssen in space. Due to technical difficulties with the multiplex and video equipment, Leto has to shoot the second half of the scene first, with Cragen joining the detectives.

7 P.M.

A tall stand-in for Brolin off-camera will provide someone for the other actors to look at and talk to in a rehearsal.

7:15 P.M.

Leto and Pattison are shooting B-camera inserts of the hands belonging to "photo-doubles' in place of Meloni, Hargitay, and Ice-T.

8:19 P.M.

Inserts finished. B-camera wraps.

8:22 P.M.

A-camera wraps and Leto thanks everyone for a wonderful episode.

And thanks to Rick for standing in as our eyes and ears. Come to think of it, thanks to an amazing SVU cast, crew, and production team for a wonderful—albeit a wee bit toasty—visit to your world.

CHAPTER TWENTY-ONE

ACTORS AND THEIR CHARACTERS

"He who knows others is wise; He who knows
himself is enlightened"

—THE WAY OF LAO-TZU, 604–531 B.C.

POLICE

Mariska Hargitay (Det. Olivia Benson, 1999–Present)

Originally From: California
Other Wolf Films Associations: *Law & Order: Trial By Jury* (Det. Olivia Benson, 2005); *Law & Order* (Det. Olivia Benson, "Flaw," "Fools for Love," and "Entitled: Part 2," 2000)

JUSTIN STEPHENS/NBCU PHOTO BANK

Mariska Hargitay (Det. Olivia Benson)

Selected Other Credits: (Film) *Perfume* (Darcy, 2001), *Lake Placid* (Myra Okubo, 1999); (TV) *Prince Street* (Det. Nina Echeverria, 1997–2000), *ER* (Cynthia Hooper, 1997–98), *Tequila and Bonetti* (Officer Angela Garcia, 1992), *Falcon Crest* (Carly Fixx, 1988)

Upcoming Project: (Film) *Thira* (associate producer, 2009)

Just the Facts

About Hargitay: She may have gotten an early start on a prime-time soap, but there was something about Mariska Hargitay that told casting directors she really ought to be in police work. The daughter of 1950s icon Jayne Mansfield and former Mr. Universe Mickey Hargitay, Mariska—a toddler asleep in the car when her mother was killed in an automobile accident—went on to pursue acting in high school and at the UCLA School of Theater, Film and Television. She then bounced around in film, finding a home on TV, even if her parts rarely lasted a season.

"I think acting is really hard," Hargitay says. "Some people are naturally gifted, and I've had to work on it. My father would tell me I was this champion, and I was going to be the best, but I struggled so long and I didn't think I was the best—and I still don't." A turning point came when she finished an extended stint on *ER* and got a pilot script from her agent, who noted that it was very dark. "It was a done deal from the moment I read it," she says of the *SVU* script. "I felt so connected to it; I knew this was my role somehow."

Since joining the force in 1999 Hargitay has married a fellow cast member (Peter Hermann, who occasionally plays defense lawyer Trevor Langan), had a child with him, and earned six Emmy nominations and one win (in 2006). The win was a bittersweet moment, as it came just weeks before her ailing father's death. Says Hargitay, "Because he'd been my coach in real life and because he was the person who told me not to quit and because I thought I was really bad—it was such a beautiful ending to the story, this forty-year story of somebody believing in you when you didn't believe in yourself."

About Benson: As the product of her late mother Serena's rape, Benson tends to live in the moment while simultaneously living to seek out her past—so details on her are sketchy. According to Hargitay, "She's on one side driven, focused, feel-the-fear-but-do-it-anyway, brave, courageous, obsessed with justice to a fault. On the other side she's this empathetic, compassionate female mama-woman that's so fragile and sensitive." Here's what's emerged over the seasons: Born in 1967, Olivia Benson has a half-brother named Simon Marsden, whom she met much later in life during a rape investigation. Her mother dies early in season two from a drunken fall, having never fully recovered from being raped.

Olivia attended Sienna College and in season one is said to have been with the SVU for a year and a half; her badge number is 44015. Her love life is spotty—mentions of dates or boyfriends are frequent but they have the shelf life of fruit flies. She sleeps with Det. Brian Cassidy in season one but it is clearly a drunken booty call. In truth, the real loves of her life are first, the job and, second, her partner, Det. Elliot Stabler—even if there's never been any physical evidence of it, and even if it will never be consummated. "He's her rock, he's her protector. Olivia has never had anyone to protect her," says Hargitay. "He's the one who makes her feel safe and loved and it's pure. It's such a deep love, they stay together no matter what. He is her partner and I don't think she's in a relationship because no other man measures up to him."

In season six, the partnership takes precedence over the job, which leads to the two splitting up briefly while Benson goes first into the computer crimes unit, then on an undercover assignment in Oregon. In season eight she meets her half-brother, a New Jersey pharmacist, when he comes under suspicion for multiple rapes, and learns that her father was depressed and an alcoholic (as well as being a rapist). She helps Marsden escape and is later investigated and suspended at the end of season eight, but returns for season nine—during which she reveals that she'd like to have a child, but has been turned down by adoption agencies. Hargitay says that showrunner Neal Baer has told her the next time she gets pregnant in real life they'll "definitely" write it in. Stay tuned.

The Rest of the Story

Not only did Mariska Hargitay know she wanted the role of Olivia Benson—she was ready to fight for it. When she came back after the initial auditions for what's known as a "work session" and spotted a beautiful actress in the hallway, Hargitay saw red. "I panicked," she admits, explaining she strode right into the meeting room and said, "Let me explain something to you: This is my role. So you can tell her—outside—that she is going home now. Because this is my part, and I'm so doing this part."

Fortunately, it turned out that the actress in the hallway was just meant to be a secondary player in the first episode, but clearly from day one Hargitay was committed to being Benson: "It was a dream that she was complex and compassionate and an empathetic character who wasn't shoved into a box. Not one dimensional: She's a cop! Or one dimensional: She's a doctor! You have to shut down and do your job! It was just such an opportunity to do it differently."

Early days in New York were a challenge for the California girl, even though she says it was long her dream to live in Manhattan as a stage actress. But that decision meant she had to leave everyone she knew behind, the weather was depressing her, and ultimately she felt her work was suffering. "This was all I ever wanted, and I was miserable," Hargitay says. "There was a darkness (in me)—I can see it in the photos when I look back at the time."

What snapped her out of it was twofold. The first season is a challenge on most sets; *SVU*'s season one, for example, saw a purge of many writers and producers, and executive producer Neal Baer stepped in to lead the show in season two. "With Neal I started getting excited about the material, and it was an energy shift and energy change for the show," recalls Hargitay. "Everything changed when Neal came. He's a great leader and a great writer."

The second bit of good fortune was meeting Peter Hermann, who began appearing as a defense attorney midway through season three. "There was this energy between us, charged. And so everyone was a little bit like, 'What's with them?'" she recalls.

Reinvested in the show, Hargitay earned SVU's first lead acting nomination in 2004; outside *SVU*, she was starting to become something of a champion, particularly for survivors of assault and rape. She received emails from survivors and was approached regularly by women who thanked her.

"Just walking down the street, I'd have women grab me, going, 'Your show changed my life. I wish you were the detective on my case. I wish someone would have believed me,'" says Hargitay. "Because from a police department point of view, your job is to get the information—and one tactic is to have the victim repeat the story several times. But that is a way of ultimately re-injuring (a sexual trauma victim) and hurting them more."

She started the Joyful Heart Foundation to help raise awareness of the kind of issues dealt with on the show, and to provide resources for survivors of sexual assaults, child abuse, and domestic violence. Hargitay's personal website (mariska.com) has the usual information on the actress, but is permeated by self-help and women's empowerment discussions and information. In some ways, scrolling through Hargitay's online presence is like taking a trip into an alternate universe powered by Olivia Benson.

"It made me sad that people were emailing a character on a TV show because they didn't know where to go," she says. "Dick Wolf is trying to entertain, that's what he's doing, but the show educates. That's why people watch the show, because it's so smart and it's a thinking person's show. I felt like God put me on this show for a reason."

Some of Hargitay's God-given qualities have long impressed Robert Nathan, a former *SVU* co-executive producer who also worked with the actress on two non–L&O series, and who says, "Generosity, emotional and artistic and every other kind, is in her DNA. It's just who she is."

In 2005, Hargitay became pregnant and *SVU* opted to keep Olivia without child, which led the production team to hide her growing belly while she made some very athletic moves—and even while just walking across the squad room. "I was very lucky in that my face maintained (its size), which we all couldn't believe because I got ginormous," Hargitay says with a laugh. "But we got into a rhythm of it—everyone knew to hold their files up high (to block her stomach) and it became a fun thing, sitting me at desks, there were all these tricks we did."

August was born in July 2006, and today he's like an off-camera cast member, roaming the set between takes with his mama and nanny in tow. "The fact that I was allowed to bring my child to work. . . was like I hit the jackpot," says his devoted mother

And in many ways, she has: In September 2008, Forbes.com named her the sixth top-earning primetime TV actress, pulling in $6.5 million between June 1, 2007 and June 1, 2008, including funds from her clothing line. But she didn't fall into that money pile; it's thanks to a lot of hard work and an Olivia-esque obsession. Luck may play a part, but Mariska Hargitay tends to make her own luck. "Everything has been such a gift," she says. "Neal came, I met Peter, I was in love the first year, then marital bliss the second year, then pregnant for the third year, then August—so it's been a really amazing five years. The first five were rough, I'm not going to lie, but the second five . . . they've been *beyond*."

Christopher Meloni (Det. Elliot Stabler, 1999–Present)

Originally From: Washington, D.C.

Other Wolf Films Associations: *Law & Order: Trial By Jury* (Det. Elliot Stabler, 2005); *Law & Order* (Det. Elliot Stabler, "Fools for Love" and "Entitled: Part 2," 2000)

Selected Other Credits: (Film) *Harold & Kumar Go to White Castle* (Freakshow, 2004), *Runaway Bride* (Coach Bob Kelly, 1999), *Fear and Loathing in Las Vegas* (Sven, 1998); (TV) *Oz* (Chris Keller, 1998–2003), *NYPD Blue* (Jimmy Liery, 1996–97), *The Fanelli Boys* (Frankie Fanelli, 1990–91)

Upcoming Projects: (Film) *The Stepfather* (2009), *Dirty Movie* (producer/director, 2008)

Just the Facts

About Meloni: He's held his share of off-camera sustenance jobs, but Christopher Meloni has always intended to eventually be center stage. "People say, 'How did you become an actor?' And I say, 'I didn't want to, I had to,'" he explains. After growing up in the suburbs of Washington, D.C., Meloni studied acting first at college, then in New York with the acclaimed coach Sanford Meisner.

Christopher Meloni (Det. Elliot Stabler)

But getting that big break required a prison term—as sociopath Chris Keller on HBO's *Oz*, where he bared his soul and certain parts of his anatomy during much of the series six-season run.

It was during that show's lifespan that he picked up a second major gig on *SVU*, and for a time he had to juggle the two jobs simultaneously. That meant on some days Meloni would work twenty-two hours straight, go home for four hours of sleep, then hit another set for fifteen to sixteen hours. But he kept his perspective: "When I got *Oz*, I'd ride my bike to the set at Chelsea Market (where the show filmed) on a spring morning and I had to repeat to myself, 'I am the luckiest actor, working on a quality edgy show in Manhattan.' Then I got *SVU* and now I've won the lottery." *Oz* may be long gone, but *SVU* remains, as does Meloni—who in person is, thankfully, far more affable and relaxed than his alter ego, Stabler.

About Stabler: The irony of being called "Stabler" is that—well, Elliot Stabler is possibly one of the least stable characters in the squadroom. Meloni has a different spin: "He was intentionally named 'Stabler' as a stabilizing influence on his more neophyte partner Benson, but he's got a fragility, a weakness—he's growing." Much of that growth has come over the past ten seasons; viewers likely know more about Stabler than any other character in the history of the Law & Order franchise.

Here's a summary of the Elliot Stabler résumé, as of season nine: He grew up Catholic with two sisters and three brothers—and a controlling policeman father who beat him. He knocked up his girlfriend Kathy while they were still teens, married her (seventeen years ago, as revealed during season three) and joined the Marines in time to serve in Operation Desert Storm while his firstborn was a toddler. When Stabler returned to civilian life, he earned a B.A. at night school and worked in a bar; he became a cop (sixteen years ago, as noted in season nine, but eighteen years ago in season eight, so the viewer can take his or her pick) and now he and Kathy have five children: Maureen, Kathleen, twins Elizabeth and Dickie (who were eight years old in season three), and new baby Eli (as of season nine). The family lives in Queens on Stabler's modest salary of $68,940 (as of season four).

His badge number is 6313. He's had at least three partners: One killed himself after becoming frustrated about his inability to solve a case (though whether they were partners at the time of death is unclear); another, named "Alphonse," retired to Florida; and Det. Olivia Benson appears to have succeeded Alphonse (in season seven, he and Benson have been partners for seven years). Stabler and his wife split in season six and in season seven she began divorce proceedings, though they ultimately reconciled. He's an often-absent father and a good cop with anger-management issues; his 97 percent case-closure rate is evidence that he's doing something right.

Explains Meloni: "He's a meat-and-potatoes guy who understands very clearly the ideas of loyalty and justice, and that's where his troubles in life stem from—because he knows what's right and wrong and the world doesn't match up to these very clear concepts he has. He's such a 'man' that he's also like a child. Maturity is about understanding that life is a big shade of gray with a lot of compromises along the way, and it's that uncompromising position that's difficult and weighs on him."

The Rest of the Story

There's something to be said about working for one boss while trying to score a second job from that boss's friend. Christopher Meloni auditioned for *SVU* while still doing *Oz*. He emerged from the casting session, thinking, "I did a great reading, and that's that." But three weeks passed and he had heard nothing. So while on the set of *Oz*, he approached executive producer/creator Tom Fontana, one of Wolf's longtime friends. "I said, 'You know this guy, tell this son of a bitch, "Is it yes or no?" Because this is killing me,'" recalls Meloni. "So God bless Tom Fontana; he makes a call and ten minutes later comes back and says, 'Yeah, he'll be calling you.'"

When the second audition came around, Meloni read for Wolf and then-showrunner Robert Palm, but again weeks passed without word. He and his wife had just landed in Hawaii for a trip when the call came to screen test in New York. He learned he had the part before returning to his hotel room. Hawaii, here we come! Except once Meloni was back on the islands, "I immediately got a gall bladder attack, had my gall bladder removed, and went back home."

Some things were just not meant to be, like that trip, but in the case of Elliot Stabler, some things truly were. It hardly seems that anyone else could have filled the brogans of that character better than Meloni, who can flip in a heartbeat from being comforting and sensitive to a perp's greatest nightmare, and who serves as the ideal yin to the yang of Mariska Hargitay's Det. Olivia Benson.

He's also become heavily invested in making Stabler real; early on, recalls Meloni, he tended to be "note-crazy" with the writers, commenting left and right on every word Stabler was meant to utter in a script. He's dialed back since then, and picks his battles. "Part of my job is to be a better interpreter," Meloni explains. "Now these aren't ego notes but notes of 'help me understand.'"

Playing Stabler requires other choices, and other battles that need to be selectively chosen. "Every victim can't bring tears to your eyes," Meloni says. "You're on a procedural type show, and you have to pick your shots. You're playing a cop, so you have to pick that place where you let your heart out and reveal it."

Without question, he has had plenty of opportunity to do that over the years, and has an Emmy nomination for the role to prove it. But Meloni claims that awards themselves don't hold a great deal of importance to him, even though his co-star Hargitay has multiple nominations and even a win for her role. "I do appreciate them," he says with care, "and I do understand it from a business side that it means a lot. But I did get a lot of shit for my attitude when I got nominated."

Namely, he was out water-skiing the morning nominations were announced in 2006. Called to the phone to talk with showrunner Neal Baer, Meloni pulled over and got a hearty congratulations. "I was like, 'Cool! I'm going back to ski.' And I tell that story because we all know the hype and hoops we're going to have to jump through, and the big party that's going to be great, and when I got it, I was like, 'All right.' I told my dad, and I told him I was having a hard time placing it, because I'd never expected it. It wasn't part of my universe. And he listened to me and he said, 'These are the sort of things you accept with grace.' It's such a simple thing. Someone's giving you a gift, accept it, thank you. Thank you for the party. I was having a hard time moving my own framework of what was important out of the way—and I finally got it."

Less easily resolved, however, is just how long he'll continue to stay with the show. The last time contract negotiations came up, Meloni says, "they were unhappy on my part. Hostile." But, he qualifies, "That's because of a changing dynamic in the business." In the end, it worked out well: In 2007, *TV Guide* reported that both Meloni and Hargitay now make $350,000 per episode, making them among the highest-paid actors on broadcast primetime television.

And after a decade, Meloni says he truly enjoys the job, despite the long, intense days. "I truly love the people I work with," he says. "I enjoy the collaborative effort both on the set and with the writers; I love being in New York as a well-paid, working actor, and I enjoy being on a show that on the street is well-respected. No one is phoning it in, and I just can't believe it after ten years. It's always nice to be in a place of passion."

Dann Florek (Capt. Donald "Don" Cragen, 1999–Present)

Originally From: Michigan

Other Wolf Films Associations: *Exiled: A Law & Order Movie* (Capt. Donald Cragen, 1998); *Law & Order* (Capt. Donald Cragen, 1990–93)

Selected Other Credits: (Film) *Sweet Liberty* (Jesse, 1986); (TV) *The Secret Diary of Desmond Pfeiffer* (Abraham Lincoln, 1998), *L.A. Law* (David Meyer, 1988–93)

Upcoming Project: (Film) *Thira* (Trent Parker, 2008)

GORDON TRICE

Dann Florek (Capt. Donald Cragen)

Just the Facts

About Florek: After an early start as a musician in the 1970s, Dann Florek alternated between theater, small feature film parts, and TV spots throughout the 1980s, first truly standing out as nebbishy Dave Meyer on *L.A. Law*. But once *Law & Order* got hold of him, it's been hard for the showrunners—or Florek himself—to disentangle for long. He originated the role of Capt. Don Cragen on the original *Law & Order* until he was ousted on orders from the network to beef up the female component on the show.

Nevertheless, he retained a friendly relationship with creator Dick Wolf, and Florek has directed three episodes of the Mother Ship over the years, as well as appearing occasionally back on his home turf. "The odd part was I was trying to get off the (original) show for a while, because I said, 'You're not using me.' And they said 'no,' and the next thing I knew it was like, 'You're off the show, because we're bringing in women' or whatever," he says. While away from the L&O family, Florek continued his TV/feature roles, but when Dick Wolf created *SVU*, Florek was first on board.

About Cragen: Cragen's backstory includes his *L&O* days, including his alcoholism recovery, but his marital status changed abruptly when he first appeared on *SVU*—his wife Marge, once even seen in a Mother Ship episode, was said to have died in a plane crash. There's some confusion over whether his alma mater is St. Raymond's or St. John's but a few other things are clear: He likes his snacks, attends AA, is childless, and has issues with the psychiatric profession. Cragen has alluded to fighting in Vietnam, and for a time would pop open a switchblade while thinking ("I liked it but the network said we can't have a captain with a knife," Florek says).

He's also loyal to his underlings, despite the fact that they routinely violate his orders. "Everyone refers to him as 'no-nonsense,'" says Florek. "I try to take that literally—the clothes are Brooks Brothers; it's something simple. He's a cop, he's a father figure, he's a politician, he's a rabbi, he's a mentor. I always like to think he was kind of a rogue guy himself. He's a guy you think is sitting in the corner and not paying attention, but he knows every fucking thing going on in the room. He knows what you said, he knows what you think you said, and if push comes to shove, he might be able to break your arm."

The Rest of the Story

The backbone of *SVU* may well be Detectives Benson and Stabler, but Cragen was the first one cast, bringing Florek back to a franchise he never thought he'd be fully involved with again.

Not long after appearing in *Exiled: A Law & Order Movie*, Florek got the call to appear in the new show, *Sex Crimes* (as *SVU* was being called then), and says he had to think about it: "My problem initially was I never felt I had enough to do. So if there was more to do, and I could really get my hands dirty, that would be great. And also, it was like going to the closet and pulling out an old suit—I didn't know if it was going to fit. And then when I did put it on it not only still fit, but it felt better."

Being on *SVU*, he says, is "the best set I've ever worked in, ever, in television and film." And that includes the last *L&O* set, which in its early days featured fractious actors trying to establish a hierarchy within a format that had only just been created. "Part of it was we were going up a mountain and we didn't know if you slipped and you fell if someone was going to catch you," he remembers. "That's almost completely antithetical here, now."

Not that it's been smooth sailing at *SVU* from day one, either. Florek acknowledges that some of the series' weakest episodes came out of that first season, but he had the sense that "we were on to something. . . . I never felt they were going to pull the plug on us." In that first season, he says people would hear which show he worked for and would say, "You're on the bad *Law & Order*." And by the fifth season, that had changed: "All I heard people talking about was *SVU* and 'the old one.'"

When asked how long he plans to stick around in the *SVU* squad room, Florek recalls the late Jerry Orbach (*Law & Order*'s Lennie Briscoe), who used to say "never leave a hit show." Florek signed a three-year contract in 2008, so there's nothing much to discuss at the moment. But in the end, he admits, "I'm a blue-collar work-horse. I'm a pro. I do the best I can and I'm always prepared. I look at it from episode to episode. I never thought nineteen years later I'd still be wearing this suit. But this show is as consistently good as anything that's ever been on, and if they keep on pumping out great stories and keep giving me enough to do, what's wrong with that?"

Richard Belzer (Det. Sgt. John Munch, 1999–Present)

Originally From: Connecticut

Other Wolf Films Associations: *Law & Order: Trial By Jury* (Det. John Munch, "Skeleton," 2005); *Law & Order* (Det. John Munch, crossover episodes with *Homicide: Life on the Street*: "Entitled, Part 2," 2000; "Sideshow," 1999; "Baby, It's You," 1997; "Charm City," 1996)

Selected Other Credits: (Film) *The Groove Tube* (various, 1974); (TV) *Homicide: Life on the Street* (Det. John Munch, 1993–99), *Saturday Night Live* (various episodes, 1975–1980; also served

PAUL DRINKWATER/NBCU PHOTO BANK

Richard Belzer (Det. John Munch)

as warm-up comedian in the show's first season); (Books) *I Am Not A Cop!: A Novel* (with Michael Black, 2008), *Momentum: The Struggle for Peace, Politics, and the People* (By Belzer and Marjorie Mowlam, 2002), *UFOs, JFK, and Elvis: Conspiracies You Don't Have To Be Crazy To Believe* (1999), *How to Be a Stand-Up Comic* (1988)

Upcoming Project: Belzer is working on a musical version of Jerry Lewis' 1963 classic *The Nutty Professor* with the octogenarian.

Just the Facts

About Belzer: "A lot of Munch is me, except that I've been happily married for twenty-four years. He's a little more depressed and cynical than I really am, but it's very close to how I was at one time. And all the conspiracy stuff is right up my alley." So says the comedian-turned-actor, who has been a presence on the stand-up comedy circuit, in films, and on TV since the 1970s. He's been on *National Lampoon* albums, had his own radio and cable TV shows (in 1985, on *Hot Properties* he was notoriously put in a sleeper hold by Hulk Hogan and passed out on camera; the ensuing lawsuit was settled). Belzer has authored four books (including one on conspiracy theories).

But in the 1990s he was cast on the gritty NBC Baltimore cop drama *Homicide: Life on the Street* as Det. John Munch, and attributes landing the role to putting a different spin on the character. Left in a room with other aspiring Munch actors' audition tapes, he watched some: "Every one played it dead serious, earnest, and I brought this comic madness that I saw in the character, and the person my character is loosely based on (Sgt. Jay Landsman) is like that, too."

Real life and fictional personalities merged and he has since become not only the longest-running character on U.S. primetime TV, but also the only fictional TV character to play the same role on eight series in total (*Law & Order, The X-Files, The Beat, Law & Order: Trial by Jury, Arrested Development, The Wire,* and of course, *Law & Order: SVU*). So when will the character be done for him? "When the fan mail stops, I guess," Belzer says.

About Munch: Munch was established during his *Homicide* days, namely that the character is a former hippie with a cynical streak—who became a Baltimore homicide detective. He's had a string of bad romances and four marriages and flirts incessantly with the ladies, but he's not a cad—just unlucky—and his softer side emerges when the women in his life seem to need him.

He's originally from New York City's Lower East Side, speaks semi-fluent Russian, and became a sergeant in season nine after taking the exam a year earlier. He lives at 80 West 183rd St. According to David P. Kalat's *Homicide: Life on the Streets, The Unofficial Companion*, Munch's father was a "cop, killed in the line of duty, and that led the one-time hippie to join the force himself." On *SVU*, however, Munch had an emotional scene in season five where he explains his father committed suicide (a detail that is true in Belzer's real life, as well); later on it is reiterated that Munch was thirteen when that happened. Regardless, Munch remains both the resident conspiracy theorist, sometime court jester, and always compelling presence in the squad room.

The Rest of the Story

Without Howard Stern, *Homicide* executive producer Barry Levinson might never have heard enough Richard Belzer (who regularly appears on Stern's radio show) to consider him for the part way back when. But thanks to that concordance, Belzer went in for the role and, despite network brass's desire to cast someone like Jason Priestley, he was in. But when *Homicide* was canceled, Belzer wasn't ready to see the character ride off into the sunset and asked his manager to call Dick Wolf to see if Munch could become Lennie

Briscoe's new partner on *L&O* when Benjamin Bratt exited. Jesse Martin had already been cast—though the mind reels at imagining Munch and Briscoe hitting the streets on a weekly basis—and Belzer came up with Plan B: The new sex crimes show Wolf was developing.

Wolf loved that idea, too, but there was still another obstacle to overcome: licensing. Munch was a character owned, in part, by several individuals and entities. The legal setup of how Munch came to *SVU* is something of a *Rashomon* situation, but in essence it required agreements from David Simon (who created Munch based on a real-life homicide sergeant named Jay Landsman in his book, *Homicide: A Year on the Killing Streets*, which ultimately became *Homicide*) and Tom Fontana and Barry Levinson (who brought *Homicide* to the small screen). Notes Fontana, he and Levinson waived their royalties. Now, he jokes, "If I'd known (*SVU*) was going to run this long, perhaps I wouldn't have been so generous with my money!" He laughs. "But no, I'm happy we did it." In Simon's case, his contracts had clauses dealing with spin-offs from his book, and with Munch a main character on a new show, that clause kicked in. Simon gets certain royalties every time Munch appears on *SVU*.

So, nearly ten years later, Munch remains on *SVU*, and over the years, he's been instrumental in finding roles for his fellow comic friends on the show, including Jerry Lewis (who played Munch's uncle in season eight) and his real-life cousin, Henry Winkler. But not all professional humorists are made for dramaturgy, he admits: "A lot of comics are wonderful comics but they're not good actors, and a lot of famous comedians can't act. There's not a day that goes by that I don't realize how lucky I am, and how thankful. Not that I don't have talent, but in this business it's full of sharp turns and chances. I was on the radio, I got *Homicide*, who would have known? My career was fine before that, but then it kicked into another hemisphere."

Season nine showed a marked drop in Munch's appearances on *SVU*—he shows up in just over half of the episodes. "I was a bit mystified," Belzer says, "but I do have a lot of other things (to do) so everything worked out. It's like yanking the tonsils out of the gift horse if I complain too much. I've been lucky over the years, the press has been very kind to me, and there was a lot of *TV Guide* (articles) and websites wondering, 'Where's Munch?' So that was flattering. But, *c'est la vie*: I'm not starving."

Ice-T (Det. Odafin "Fin" Tutuola, 2000–Present)

AKA: Tracy Lauren Morrow

Originally From: New Jersey

Other Wolf Films Associations: *Exiled: A Law & Order Movie* (Seymour "Kingston" Stockton, 1998); *Players* (Isaac "Ice" Gregory, 1997–98); *New York Undercover* (Danny Up, 1995)

Selected Other Credits: (Film) *New Jack City* (Scotty Appleton, 1991), *Breakin'* (Rap Talker, 1984); (TV) *Ice-T's Rap School* (2006); (Books) *The Ice Opinion: Who Gives a Fuck* (1994); (Music) *Gangsta Rap* (2006), *Body Count* (1992) (as Body Count), *OG: Original Gangster* (1991), *The Iceberg/Freedom of Speech . . . Just Watch What You Say* (1989)

Ice-T (Det. Odafin Tutuola)

COURTESY ICE-T

Upcoming Project: (Film) *Darc* (Brown, 2009); producing a documentary about Iceberg Slim

Just the Facts

About Ice-T: He's a polarizing figure, but most will agree that Ice-T is a man of many talents. After growing up in California, he headed into the Army post-high school, then dove into rapping, helping pioneer what would become the gangster rap version of hip-hop. Rapping (and a charismatic persona) pulled him toward acting, where he alternated playing a musician or a hard case, with exceptions like *New Jack City*, in which he appeared as a cop.

His heavy metal-meets-rap band Body Count released a song called "Cop Killer" in 1992 that made the group notorious in law enforcement and political circles. But any residual controversy didn't keep Dick Wolf from hiring him on as a guest star on *New York Undercover* (which Ice calls "a rip-off" of *New Jack City*) and the two formed a professional rapport that ultimately brought him to *SVU* in 2000. "I say in life there's people who cost you money, and people who make you money," says Ice. "I made Dick Wolf money, he made me money, so we cool."

About Tutuola: "(My character) is a street-smart narcotics cop," explains Ice, "who understands the streets, but he's still a little blown away by this rape stuff. He looks at these cats as real weirdos. He's pretty cut and dry." Fin comes to the SVU squad in the second season, having worked in narcotics (sometimes undercover as "Terry Brown") and a former partner took a bullet that was meant for him. (In season eight, Tutuola is revealed as having been a cop for twenty-two years.) His badge number is 43198.

He has an adult gay son named Ken Randall from whom he was estranged for many years; his ex-wife, Teresa ("Tessie"), had a baby at the age of sixteen and let her mother raise the boy—but Tutuola never knew about this until the child, Darius, was grown. As for his unusual, Nigerian-heritage name? Notes Ice, "I think my parents were supposed to have been black activists, and I was supposed to have been some type of guy who went to law school but didn't take the bar (exam). It just ended up with 'Ice-T, run these cases through your brain and play it out the way you would play it out.' So really, I'm playing myself."

The Rest of the Story

In the early days, TV was not for Ice-T. "I was on some arrogant, 'I ain't doing no TV-show shit,'" he recalls. "I'm like, 'I do movies.'" But then a call came while he was hanging out with hip-hop pioneer Fab Five Freddy and it was from Dick Wolf's people, asking him to come do a stint on *New York Undercover*.

But why Ice? "I think Dick Wolf likes reality," he says. "If Dick Wolf could cast real rapists, he would. It's more attractive to him than what he would call a corny actor. Also, he dug my work ethics, which are very simple: Once we make the deal and make an agreement, I'm gonna do it. One time, he told me, 'Ice-T, you are the least problem in my ass.'"

After *Undercover, Exiled: A Law & Order Movie,* and the short-lived *Players* (which Ice co-created), the least problem in Dick Wolf's ass was running an Internet record label when the opportunity for *SVU* came up. At first he only agreed to do four episodes, but the ensemble nature of *SVU* made it more attractive, and by the end of the four-show run Ice had relocated to New York.

"I reevaluated my life, and I thought, 'This is not such a bad gig,'" says Ice. "In music you don't have any security. You spend a year making a record and you pray to God people like the record. You can't forecast your life." Also, he says, "I didn't understand a word called 'residuals.' It doesn't pay if you're a guest star, but we're at (over) 200 episodes (on *SVU*) and Law & Order shows like three times a day. OK, now you're talking about a little money machine."

Certainly, there's an irony that the man behind "Cop Killer" makes a living playing a cop, but he hasn't found that Tutuola hurts his credibility in the rap community. "I don't think people think I've turned into some real right-wing Republican and I'm out picketing with (the late) Charlton Heston or something. In my community, hip-hoppers were excited to see somebody on TV. And people like the cop I play—even the worst criminals agree they need those kind of cops. So when they see me with a child molester, everybody is like, 'Smack the shit out of him, Ice!' It's the perfect place to be."

Word around the set is that while all of the regular cast members are utmost professionals, Ice appears to be the least pain in *everyone's* ass, not just Wolf's. He's got a cool, low-key demeanor, whether sitting in a director's chair waiting for the next take, or joking with passers-by while on location. He even has his wife and manager Coco on the set with him; while he reads lines, she's doing the business work in their corner dressing room.

"Would Ozzy (Osbourne) have a dollar if he didn't have Sharon?" asks Ice. "I was like, 'I need a woman who can handle some business around here.' And I met Coco and she said, 'That's what I really want to do. I can put modeling on hold.' And she's on the set now every day."

Over the years, Ice has grown comfortable with being considered—in part, at least—a TV actor. And he plans on sticking with *SVU* for as long as it remains fun, especially if he can let some of his pals in on the gig, too. "All my friends who do movies started calling me, trying to be on TV. Everybody knows Will (Smith) is working. But other than that, everyone else is going from gig to gig, all the black actors I know. A few of them are winning, hitting, but it's rough."

As for Ice, he knows he's got a good thing. "I went from, 'I don't know how long I can do it,' to right now, 'I'll be on this show until they throw my black ass off.'"

Michelle Hurd (Det. Monique Jefferies, 1999–2001)

Michelle Hurd (Det. Monique Jefferies)

GARRET DILLAHUNT, USED WITH PERMISSION

Originally From: New York City
Other Wolf Films Associations: *Law & Order* (Angela Roney, "Entrapment" 1997); *Players* (Laura Jenkins, "Con Amore," 1997); *New York Undercover* (ADA Reynolds, 1994–97)
Selected Other Credits: (TV) *Gossip Girl* (Laurel, 2007–Present), *ER* (Courtney Brown, 2006–07), *Leap Years* (Athena Barnes, 2001), *Malcolm & Eddie* (Simone Lewis, 1997–98)

Just the Facts

About Hurd: Michelle Hurd had leapfrogged her way through several of Dick Wolf's shows before landing on the *SVU* lily pad. The Greenwich Village–born actress (whose father is stage actor Hugh

L. Hurd) started out on the soaps, but quickly picked up roles on various TV shows while appearing in various theater productions, where she met husband and fellow actor Garret Dillahunt. When she was tapped to join *SVU*, Hurd recalls that Dick Wolf told her, "I've got this character, think of her as a flower, she'll bloom later, but for the pilot she's just got a scene." Hurd's stay was short-lived, however, and there was no blossoming. She left in season two to join the cast of *Leap Years*, and later *ER*, among other shows, and now enjoys a semi-regular gig on *Gossip Girl*.

About Jefferies: Jefferies partners with Det. Brian Cassidy and even Det. Ken Briscoe briefly, but ultimately settles with the one man she seems barely able to stand—Det. John Munch—once Cassidy leaves the unit. Traumatized by a car explosion during an investigation, Jefferies begins sabotaging her career by sleeping with a suspect, which ultimately forces her out of the rotation while she undergoes therapy. Desk duty does not agree with Jefferies, who threatens to leave, but is then transferred to Vice.

The Rest of the Story

Hurd has no sour feelings about her time on the show, possibly because she immediately landed in a better spotlight, even if her next job didn't last very long: As the second season of *SVU* rolled around she and husband Dillahunt were both cast on Showtime's *Leap Years*. "It was a rare opportunity," she says. Unfortunately, the show was canceled in the general industry malaise following 9/11.

"The thing about Dick Wolf," she explains, "is he's a quintessential producer. He has created a vehicle that is strong regardless of who is playing the part, and he's not going to hold someone if they want to go. I bump into him all the time and we have nothing but a good rapport—I'd do another show with him in a nanosecond."

Though *SVU* left her open to do theater work in the evenings, Jefferies was a sorely underutilized character, which Hurd realizes. "I just read instructions," she says. "And yeah, there's an art form to be able to say, 'Take the screwdriver, put it in the hole, turn left, turn right, unlock door.' I'm glad I can do that, but there are other things I can do."

It became clear that the show needed someone as a permanent partner for Det. Munch, and Hurd was having a hard time proving she was the right person in the slot. "I understand the industry, and what networks want, and they wanted someone to have an impact, a rating," she says. "I did think that in a sex crimes unit you'd want to have more women."

But she understands the role that Ice-T plays today (on *Players*, Hurd portrayed Ice's character's lover). "I adore him," she says. "You walk down the street with Belzer, he gets a lot of accolades. But there's nothing quite like walking down the street with Ice-T. He's one of the most interesting creatures you're going to meet. I think it's just sad they didn't have faith to stick around with me—but at the same time, when all of this was happening, Showtime came knocking. That's probably where I felt somebody was looking and saying, 'I want her.'"

Dean Winters (Det. Brian Cassidy, 1999–2000)

Originally From: New York City

Other Wolf Films Associations: *Law & Order: Criminal Intent* (Mike Stoat, "Purgatory," 2008); *Deadline* (Des, "Shock," 2001); *New York Undercover* (Paul, "Rat Trap," 1998)

Selected Other Credits: (TV) *Life on Mars* (Vic Tyler, 2008–09), *30 Rock* (Dennis Duffy, 2006–Present), *Terminator: The Sarah Connor Chronicles* (Charley Dixon, 2008–09), *Rescue Me* (Johnny Gavin, 2004–07), *Oz* (Ryan O'Reily, 1997–2003), *Sex and the City* (John McFadden, 1999), *Homicide: Life on the Street* (Tom Marans, 1995–96)

Upcoming Projects: (Film) *Splinterheads* (Reggie, 2009)

Just the Facts

About Winters: Dean Winters makes an impression wherever he goes: He's been Sarah Jessica Parker's "fuck buddy" on *Sex and the City* (HBO); the scary, manipulative Ryan O'Reily on *Oz* (also HBO); and—of course—the secretly terrified newbie of the sex crimes unit Det. Brian Cassidy on *SVU*, where he didn't quite make it through a full season. Born in New York but partially raised in Arizona,

Winters came to acting in his late twenties, and made friends with two key people: *Homicide: Life on the Street/Oz* executive producer Tom Fontana and future *SVU* partner Richard Belzer. And after an appearance on *New York Undercover*, he also knew Dick Wolf.

According to Winters, Belzer told Wolf: "I'll do this new show of yours (*SVU*) only if you make Dean Winters my partner." "That's exactly what happened," says Winters. Unfortunately, he also had a role on *Oz* at the time (as did *SVU* castmates Christopher Meloni and B.D. Wong) and while he was contractually obligated to HBO, the *SVU* part was initially meant to be only a few episodes. When HBO came calling, he had to leave. But he's bounced back nicely, with a recurring role on Fox's *Terminator: The Sarah Connor Chronicles* and a recent appearance (not as Cassidy) on *Law & Order: Criminal Intent*. He jokes: "I think I'm the only actor in New York City who hasn't been on the original show!"

Dean Winters (Det. Brian Cassidy)

DAVE ALLOCCA

About Cassidy: Young Det. Brian Cassidy is ill-equipped in the special victims unit from day one—lacking both the emotional maturity to deal with SVU crimes and the language with which to describe them. One night he and Det. Olivia Benson have a drunken booty call of which he'd like to make more, but she cuts him off. When it becomes clear that he might not be long for the unit, Capt. Cragen sends him solo to check up on a teen rape victim. The girl's story unhinges Cassidy and he transfers to Narcotics. "I wouldn't say that Cassidy was dim," says Winters, "but maybe a little naïve. I did voice to (executive producer) Ted Kotcheff that I wanted to make sure this guy wasn't the dumb blond of the department, because I guarantee you there are no dumb blonds in the real SVU."

The Rest of the Story

A quick conversation with Dean Winters reveals a perhaps surprising lack of bitterness that *SVU* didn't work out. Sure, *Oz* ended before *SVU* and, sure, Cassidy was never really given a third dimension, but he comes across as easygoing about the vagaries of the business. "In fairness to (the *SVU* writers), it was the first chunk of the first season and they were trying to flesh people out—and if I had stuck around I'm sure they would have found plenty for me to do."

Also worth noting: Unlike Meloni, Winters never had to shoot scenes for *Oz* and *SVU* in the same time period. "I remember Chris would work all night on an *SVU* and then go back to *Oz* at 8 A.M., they were giving him a workout—but it was Chris's show. Me, I never worked on them at the same time; the first season I did we shot *SVU* in the summertime and we had finished *Oz* in the springtime."

Still, he recalls that the two shows were not all that different in their demands. "I've never worked on a show that ran more like a Swiss clock than *Oz*. In six years we shot one day over twelve hours. *SVU* is pretty much on par—they know what they're doing, everyone has a shorthand, everyone has worked on the other (L&O) shows, so they know how to get the shows in on time. Dick can do it. Dick is Dick and Dick is the man. And anyone should give Dick whatever he wants for the rest of his life; he's got to be responsible for a quarter of NBC's profit at this point."

Connie Nielsen (Det. Dani Beck, 2006)

Originally From: Denmark
Selected Other Credits: (Film) *Battle in Seattle* (Jean, 2007), *The Ice Harvest* (Renata, 2005), *One Hour Photo* (Nina Yorkin, 2002), *Gladiator* (Lucilla, 2000)
Upcoming Project: (Film) *Between the Lines* (Cora, 2010)

Just the Facts

About Nielsen: The multi-lingual Danish actress grew up surrounded by the business thanks to her actress mother, and first appeared in a 1984 French film starring Jerry Lewis (with whom she was re-paired in season eight's "Uncle"). She moved to the United States and in the late 1990s immediately took roles in films like *Rushmore* and 2000's *Gladiator*. In 2007 she welcomed a son with longtime beau (and fellow Dane), Metallica drummer Lars Ulrich.

About Beck: Despite only being on *SVU* for six episodes, Nielsen couldn't help but have a major impact—she was replacing Det. Olivia Benson when Mariska Hargitay departed on maternity

Connie Nielsen (Det. Dani Beck)

leave. Det. Beck (like Nielsen, a Danish-born multi-linguist) is a warrants detective assigned to SVU while Benson is on temporary reassignment, and is very devoted to her previous job. "There was a certain obsessiveness to her that I thought was interesting," remembers Nielsen. "She doesn't want to dress up, she wants to feel free and be able to run and kick down doors, whatever she has to do."

Beck's marriage to Michael Dooley, who she met while he was serving in the military in Germany, ended after he was killed on the job (he became an NYPD cop). She and Stabler get a bit cozy as partners, but nothing ever comes of it. Overwhelmed by the SVU crimes, ultimately Beck returns to Warrants.

The Rest of the Story

Connie Nielsen is a rising star in her own right; still, it never hurts to have a connection or two when trying to break into television. According to the actress, her manager also has as a client *SVU* executive producer/showrunner Neal Baer, and the message got through once a replacement for Hargitay was needed: Was Nielsen up for the job?

Certainly—two of the three current L&O shows are her favorites. "I actually really like *Law & Order* and it's the only thing I really watch on TV," Nielsen says. "I never have the time to watch TV, so it really means something to me when I say I've seen something on TV that's unique and different."

Her time on the set was enjoyable, but, she adds, "It was the hardest thing I've done in my life. Sixteen hours a day, for two months, and sometimes they only have Sundays off. I just thought, 'How can they do ten months of that?' So I have an enormous amount of respect for people who can keep up with that kind of pressure and still do a great job with the characters."

Would she return? Not for those hours. "I don't think I would sign on to anything where you would have to work like that," Nielsen says.

Adam Beach (Det. Chester Lake, 2007–08)

CHRIS HASTON/NBCU PHOTO BANK

Adam Beach (Det. Chester Lake)

Originally From: Manitoba, Canada

Other Wolf Films Associations: *Bury My Heart at Wounded Knee* (TV) (Charles Eastman, 2007)

Selected Other Credits: (Film) *Flags of Our Fathers* (Ira Hayes, 2006), *Windtalkers* (Private Ben Yahzee, 2002), *Smoke Signals* (Victor Joseph, 1998); (TV) *Moose TV* (George Keeshig, 2007), *North of 60* (Nevada, 1993–95)

Just the Facts

About Beach: Adam Beach grew up in Manitoba, Canada; he is of Salteaux (a branch of the Ojibwa First Nation) descent. He got his first break at eighteen on a TV miniseries, and appeared in the 1998 indie feature *Smoke Signals* and the 2006 Clint Eastwood–directed

Flags of our Fathers, among other productions. He connected with Dick Wolf while making the Wolf-produced HBO film *Bury My Heart at Wounded Knee* (a role that earned him a Golden Globe nomination) and shortly thereafter signed with *SVU*.

"Adam is a superb actor," Wolf told *The Hollywood Reporter* in 2008. "I was knocked out by his commitment, dedication and total immersion in the film's most crucial role." At the end of season nine, Beach and the show parted ways. The actor declined to be interviewed for this book.

About Lake: Lake is a Native American of Mohawk descent, and his family has lived in New York for generations—all of the men being iron workers for the past three generations. Lake himself was at one point a foster child. He came to Manhattan SVU by way of Brooklyn SVU, and in his spare time competed non-professionally as a mixed martial artist (called "Naptime"); he abandoned fighting as a career after an injury.

He loves rare books, has insomnia, and as is learned in his final episode, likes to join fellow law enforcers in Philadelphia to share information on cold cases. He is arrested in the episode after shooting and killing a police officer in New York, and a jury fails to convict him. But Lake is again discovered with a dead body, and exits the show with police removing him from the scene.

The Rest of the Story

Adam Beach is a rising star who just never fully clicked with *SVU* viewers. For one thing, the presence of his character seemed designed to muscle out one of two longtime favorites—either Ice-T or Richard Belzer—and that did little to endear him to the audience.

Still, initially it seemed as if all would go well; Beach told Andpop.com in 2007 that he felt the part would be good for his career: "That role is definitely laying the groundwork to say, 'You know what, there's nothing bad we can say to Adam. He not only did it on a feature film level but now he's doing it on a hot TV show. And he's on one of the top TV shows as a regular!'"

And, he added, it should be good for all Native Americans: "This is sending a message every week that we are a part of society. It's going to open the doors of, 'Wow, Adam is really doing good for that show, now we need another Native American in one of our shows.'"

Unfortunately, his "dream role," as he called it, was not meant to last. Notes showrunner Neal Baer, "We felt there were too many cops, and we were getting deluded in how we were playing Ice-T, (Richard) Belzer, and Adam. We wanted to bring the focus back to the main characters. And Adam had lots of things he wanted to do, movies. It was a very amicable departure."

Beach's final comments on his exit were simple and to the point: "I very much enjoyed my year on *Law & Order: SVU*," Beach told *The Hollywood Reporter* in 2008. "Now I'm looking forward to new adventures."

Chris Orbach (Det. Ken Briscoe, 1999–2000)

Originally From: New York City
Other Wolf Films Associations: *Law & Order* (Finkle, "Securitate," 1993; Jason, "Matrimony," 1997; Augie, "Ambitious," 1999)
Selected Other Credits: (Film) *Clear Blue Tuesday* (Dave the Picard Fan, 2008), *Blue Moon* (Frank Junior, 2000); (Music) *Secession* (album, 2008) *Safely Through the Night* (album, 2004)

Just the Facts

About Orbach: The son of the late Jerry Orbach (Det. Lennie Briscoe, *Law & Order*) got his feet wet early in the franchise's history, with small roles in three separate episodes on the Mother Ship. But his heart really lies in music (he records his own songs and performs live in New York City), while his paycheck comes mainly from voice-overs for clients like L'Oreal.

About Briscoe: Ken is the nephew of Det. Lennie Briscoe, and largely serves a background function of fetching files, along with a little investigative work. After eleven episodes in the first season of *SVU*, Ken just vanishes.

The Rest of the Story

It's hard to tell the story of Chris Orbach and *SVU* without weaving his father into it. It got even harder in August 2008 when a *New York Post* reporter published a personal letter Chris had sent

Chris Orbach (Det. Ken Briscoe)

to his widowed stepmother, Elaine Cancilla-Orbach, that excoriated her for donating his father's eyes post-mortem and laid bare some financial details from Jerry Orbach's will that had previously not gotten much public airing.

But to go back in time: Chris Orbach had wanted to be an actor for many years, and had many discussions with his father about it. "Acting was something he'd been through the wringer with for decades," says Chris. "When it came to my songwriting his reaction was nothing but unabated joy."

He's frank about the genesis of his role on *SVU*: "I got the gig because of my old man, and the thing is it put me in a weird position—I thought I was up to the task," he says. "But the feeling I got was that everybody knew that and nobody liked it. Especially Dick Wolf; I felt like the guy couldn't stand the sight of me. What I thought was going to be a fun gig was needlessly loaded."

Since he had the voice-over work and his songwriting, Orbach turned to those skills once a second season failed to materialize. He recorded an album in 2008, and says, "I always keep thinking I could act again," but it doesn't seem a serious pursuit: "My relationship with acting has always been, 'If someone asks me. If someone has a play reading or a low-budget film.'"

PROSECUTORS

Stephanie March (ADA Alexandra Cabot, 2000–03; 2005, 2009–Present)

Stephanie March (ADA Alexandra Cabot)

Originally From: Texas
Other Wolf Films Associations: *Conviction* (Bureau Chief Alexandra Cabot, 2006)
Selected Other Credits: (TV) *Grey's Anatomy* (Jane, 2007), *Death of a Salesman* (Miss Forsythe, 2000); (Broadway) *Talk Radio* (Linda MacArthur, 2007), *Death of a Salesman* (Miss Forsythe, 1999), *The Treatment* (Julia, 2006)
Upcoming Project: (Film) *This Side of the Truth* (2009)

Just the Facts

About March: Texan Stephanie March connected early with the theater crowd, and after a few feature films, *SVU* turned out to be her first-ever television appearance. "It's an old-fashioned story," she says. "It was really just by the book. I'd never done anything but theater, and I was right off the street." March played the series' first regularly appearing ADA, but after five seasons she departed for the feature world. The L&O universe doesn't let go easily, however, and March returned to the new Wolf Films show, *Conviction*, reviving Cabot for thirteen episodes before NBC canceled the show in 2006. Additionally, March (as Cabot) returned to *SVU* in 2009 for several episodes.

About Cabot: March didn't even know her character's name until two days before she began working on the show. Her glasses were courtesy of the actress' own poor vision and inability to wear contacts. Cabot is unmarried and childless on the show, and in season five enters the witness protection program when a felon makes the case personal by trying to shoot her. After living in Wisconsin as "Emily," working in an insurance company and dating a claims adjuster, she emerges in season six to help with a case related to her previously feigned demise.

How she ended up back in the DA's office on *Conviction*, however, was never fully spelled out before the show got the axe. "She's very much a work-first kind of person, and she would be tough to be in a relationship with and tough to be best friends with," March says. "But you would always want her on your side. And I bet she's really good at tennis. I always thought she'd be a tennis player."

The Rest of the Story

Not only had Stephanie March not appeared on TV before she was hired at *SVU*, she really didn't watch much TV—and that included any of the Law & Order shows. When she got the job, though, it was time to do a little research. "It was so violent!" she recalls. "I was terrified. I thought, this is morbid. It is better than playing somebody's stupid girlfriend, but still . . . I thought, 'There's no way this show is going to last very long.'"

Beginners' luck later, she had the role of Alexandra Cabot. March trailed the head of the Manhattan DA's genuine sex crimes unit and author Linda Fairstein to get a sense of how Cabot's real-life counterparts would behave, and says what she learned most from those days was an understanding of "gallows humor. That's how you deal with (the horrible things that happen). You have to make it funny, or you cry."

Shortly after March began, Neal Baer joined *SVU* as showrunner, and she had reason to be excited about her character's future. "Neal said (to me), 'I can't wait to write for your character,'" she recalls. "And it was a much better show after that."

That said, March slowly realized that while Cabot may often do more than just present cases, there wasn't likely to be much exposition of her as a person, or her backstory. Such is a pitfall of not being familiar with the Law & Order universe ahead of time. "It's very plot driven, it's not overly emotional, and its longevity is based on the fact that you don't suddenly turn it into a soap opera," she says. "But as a performer—this is part of the reason I left—after three seasons you start to feel like a hamster in a wheel."

In the end, she realized she'd come to the end of where Cabot was likely to develop, and decided to get out. "When I got the job I wasn't even old enough to have graduated from law school; it's so funny," she says. "The guy I questioned in my first question-the-witness scene was supposed to be a kid—and he was a year older than I was. I really enjoyed my time there. I just felt from an acting standpoint that that's all there was, or ever was."

Fortunately, the series opted not to kill Cabot, just safely tuck her out of the way until she was needed again or until March agreed to return, which she did for a single episode. She recalls that her send-off was amazing, complete with a cake, a party, and people flown in from California just to wish her well. "It really was a wonderful experience," March says. "I don't have enough wonderful things to say about it. I had just come to a place in my life where it was over for me. And they understood that and couldn't have been more accommodating."

Few exited characters get an epilogue the way Cabot did; she made one more appearance on *SVU*, then showed up as a bureau chief on *Conviction*. She says she was promised more to do on *Conviction*, and that there would be an emotional backstory for her to play. "It was an interesting challenge," March recalls, "and one you don't often get. So when it didn't materialize and the show was canceled, I was like, 'Enough.'"

Today, March is making films and the occasional TV appearance, but her heart still lies in the theater. But when *SVU* comes to call, she seems to be ready to answer. In the middle of the tenth season, March returned as Cabot while the show's resident ADA Kim Greylek (played by Michaela McManus) went mysteriously AWOL. "Neal (Baer) called my agent and said the show was kicking around some ideas to excite the second part of the season, and would I consider a nice, juicy character arc," says March.

Whether this latest return will last was not determined when this book went to print. But as March says, "If the timing is right, if

the planets line up, if the money is good and you are desired somewhere, it's foolish not to consider it."

Diane Neal (ADA Casey Novak, 2001–08)

Originally From: Virginia
Other Wolf Films Associations:
Law & Order: Trial By Jury
(ADA Casey Novak, 2005);
Law & Order: SVU (Amelia
Chase, "Ridicule," 2001)
Selected Other Credits: (Film)
Dracula III: Legacy (Elizabeth
Blaine, 2005), *Dracula II:
Ascension* (Elizabeth Blaine,
2003); (TV) *Ed* (Vanessa,
2001)

Just the Facts

About Neal: Though she ended

Diane Neal (ADA Casey Novak)

up staying with *SVU* for more
than 100 episodes—making
her the franchise's longest-lasting ADA—Diane Neal was a relative
newcomer to the acting business when she first signed up with the
show. The Virginia-born, Colorado-raised actress studied medicine,
archaeology, ice skating, and modeling before turning to acting. A few
guest roles on shows like *Ed* and *The American Embassy*, plus a slew of
B-movies attracted the attention of the *Law & Order* universe with a
guest role in "Ridicule," a 2001 *SVU* episode.

"My experience was limited, so I had no idea whether or not I'd
performed well in the audition, but I was lucky enough to get the
part," she explains in an email interview. "I never thought it could
lead to anything else, especially within the franchise." Surprise—
not long after the guest role, Neal was hired as ADA Casey Novak,
the show's second full-time ADA, replacing Stephanie March.

Her departure at the end of season nine came suddenly for viewers; an article in *TV Guide* (April 28, 2008) reported that Neal told crew she had been fired, which Neal denied having said. According to showrunner Neal Baer, "The character had run its course. It was not a reflection on her ability as an actor in any way, shape, or form. But going into a tenth year it was time to bring on a new character who could create some conflict, and any time you bring on a new character it causes you to tell stories in a new way. Also, she's a great comedienne and she wanted to spread her wings, try new things before she got so identified with the part that it would be hard to try other things."

Neal declined to answer questions about her departure for this book.

About Novak: Formerly with a white collar crime unit, Casey Novak is not happy when she's transferred to Special Victims cases—though the unit grows on her. She de-stresses by hitting baseballs, and rides her bike to work. She has a mentor in Ret. Judge Mary Conway Clark, for whom she used to intern. "She was a tomboy with a very working-class background," recalls Neal. "I always thought of Novak as the kind of broad who never wore heels unless she had to—I always walked like I was uncomfortable in heels, therefore so did Novak—and she probably bought her only suit the day she had her first interview out of law school. She was single-minded in the pursuit of justice and was never influenced by self-protection, promotion, or what others thought. You can truly admire a lady like that." In her final episode, she was on the verge of being disbarred.

The Rest of the Story

Diane Neal knows exactly what she wore to her casting session for Casey Novak: Her favorite red Dolce & Gabbana suit "from Loehmann's, on sale" and "a really uncomfortable pair of shoes. When I left the room I had no sense of whether or not they liked me, I just knew I had to walk across town to another audition in those terrible heels!"

A few weeks later, she got the call, and reports she was "on cloud nine. A great show, in the city I lived in—what could be better?"

Naturally, the *SVU* schedule was a bear to wrestle with, but Neal says being young and not having responsibilities such as children meant it was less of an issue. "The only difficult part was not knowing much of my schedule in advance. I like to be a lady of my word, but when you belong to an organization with demands on your time, you end up canceling a lot of dates/events/dinners that you would have loved to attend."

So is she a fan of the show? Hard to say. Neal hadn't watched *SVU* before her guest role on the show, but admits she "started watching intermittently" after that. "I loved the cast and the stories, but typically I watched—and still do—more shows like (Fox's) *Family Guy*. You know, something a little funnier than crime and punishment."

Michaela McManus (ADA Kim Greylek, 2008-09)

Originally From: Rhode Island
Selected Other Credits: (Film) *The Beautiful Lie* (2006); (TV) *One Tree Hill* (Lindsey Strauss, 2008)

Just the Facts

About McManus: Some actors cope with minimum-wage jobs for years before their big break; Michaela McManus' golden opportunity came while she was still in a New York University graduate program for acting. McManus—who says she grew up with a stage-actress mom she says "instilled the love of theater in me"—was approached by an agent after a student film she was in won an award, and ultimately left school to pursue acting. She'd

Michaela McManus (ADA Kim Greylek)

NICOLE RIVELLI/NBCU PHOTO BANK

just made up her mind to move permanently from New York to L.A. when The CW's *One Tree Hill* hired her, and that—in essence—is her pre-*SVU* career history.

About Greylek: According to McManus, Greylek was nearly "Polly Sturges," but that seems to be a bullet her character dodged. Notes showrunner Neal Baer, "I named Casey Novak (Diane Neal) after Kim Novak. And our new ADA (Michaela McManus) is Kim Greylek. Kim for Kim Novak and Greylek for the character she plays in (the 1955 film) *5 Against the House*." Speaking in character, McManus says: "I'm a young hotshot Washington, D.C. up-and-comer, married to a lobbyist, and in D.C. I've been dealing with the policy making side of sex crimes—like legislation to protect victims. But there's been a rift with my husband, and we've separated. I really want to make a difference, so I move to New York and work for SVU." Fortunately, Greylek appears to have had no issue passing the notoriously difficult New York State bar, simplifying her early-career crisis.

The Rest of the Story

To provide a little perspective, McManus was just getting her driver's license when *SVU* originally debuted. The age issue came up in her audition, as well—she was twenty-four in her audition and twenty-five when she got the job—after her first tryout she was informed she was too young for the role. But she still got a screen test invite. "You can imagine my surprise," she says, recalling how she was now up against eight other applicants. "So I went in, and honestly I think that helped me—thinking I was too young, they wouldn't pick me anyway—so I had fun, and I played. Normally in an audition you're in a big boardroom with a bunch of executives, but in this case they put us on the set with cameras and everything. We did a bunch of different takes, so I was able to play and have fun."

And she knew what she was getting into, having been a longtime *SVU* fan. "It's my favorite (of the Law & Orders)," she says. "You can hop into it at any point, you don't have to follow characters' stories. So I was well aware of the content."

She's in a role that will require her to sound like an expert, while letting legalese roll off her tongue. "Playing a lawyer, there's a whole education I don't have. It's really tricky. This character has a lot of brain power and her vocabulary is different than mine," says McManus. "There's a lot of research to do, and it never really seems like it's going to end."

Still, she has the cast and crew, who have been welcoming and helpful, she says. "I adore the hair and makeup crew!" she laughs. "They're the sweetest. I know I'm still learning and getting comfortable. But every new script is another puzzle piece in trying to figure out who my character is."

Who that character is seems very agreeable to McManus: "It's so great to play a woman who's strong and independent and fighting for these victims," she says. "She's fighting to put the bad guys away. What a role to sink your teeth into—I'm just thrilled. It's hard, but bring it on."

Unfortunately, after spending just about half of the season at *SVU*, McManus—and Greylek—vanished from the show (details, no doubt, will be forthcoming later), replaced on a temporary basis by Stephanie March, reprising her ADA Alexandra Cabot role. Of the departure, showrunner Neal Baer would say only, "She's moved on. Sometimes the part and the actor just don't mesh. It was a mutual decision."

PROSECUTION EXPERTS

Tamara Tunie (Dr. Melinda Warner, 2000–Present)

Originally From: Pennsylvania
Other Wolf Films Associations: *Law & Order: Trial By Jury* (Dr. Melinda Warner, "Day," 2005); *Feds* (Martha Kershan, "Missing Pieces," 1997); *Law & Order* (Caroline Bennett, "Deadbeat," 1996)
Selected Other Credits: (Film) *Eve's Bayou* (Narrator, 1997), *Wall Street* (Carolyn, 1987); (TV) *24* (Alberta Green, 2002); *As the World Turns* (Jessica Griffin, 1987–2007); *NYPD Blue* (Lillian Fancy, 1994–97); (Broadway) *Spring Awakening* (producer, 2006)
Upcoming Project: (Film) *See You in September* (director)

NBCU PHOTO BANK

Tamara Tunie (Dr. Melinda Warner)

Just the Facts

About Tunie: Early on, Tamara Tunie found a great part for herself and stuck with it, as attorney Jessica Griffin on *As the World Turns*. She created the role in 1986, left in 1995 and then returned to in 2000—finally departing for good in 2007. Along came *SVU* in 2000 with a one-shot, possibly recurring role as the medical examiner.

Little did she realize that it would finally outlast her daytime job and ultimately make her a regular cast member. Nor did she abandon her multi-tasking along the way: Tunie has produced such Broadway shows as *Julius Caesar*, *Radio Golf*, and *Spring Awakening*, the latter of which earned her Tony and Drama Desk Awards in 2007. Now, with *See You in September*, she's able to add "director" to her résumé; as this book goes to print the feature—about a group of therapy patients who band together when their therapist go on vacation during the month of August—has no distributor, but she's ever hopeful.

About Warner: The first and only thing Tunie knew about the character she was to play was that her name was Melinda. Over the years, more has come out—her last name, of course, plus the fact that she was married with a child, once worked in a methadone clinic, served two tours of duty in the Air Force during Operation Desert Storm (she was stationed at Germany's Ramstein Air Base), and once lived in Paris. Says Tunie, "She's incredibly smart. Professional and caring. Level-headed and keeps her cool. Which probably sounds like every character on the show!"

The Rest of the Story

There's just something about Tamara Tunie that works on Dick Wolf-created shows. Tunie appeared on *New York Undercover*, the Mother Ship and *Feds*, and after signing on at *SVU* she even ended up on an episode of the short-lived *Law & Order: Trial By Jury*. So when her agent alerted her that *SVU* would be hiring a medical examiner, Tunie was initially irked by being asked to audition—she had a previous engagement. "I said to my agent, I've done (nearly) every Dick Wolf show that's aired on television. Either they want me to do it or not, but I can't get there. She called me back the next day and said, 'You should be your own agent, because you got the job.'"

Not that this immediately made life easier, as she ended up doing double-duty with her soap, *As the World Turns*. Fortunately, both shows parsed out her schedule so there would be little to no overlap—there were only two conflicts over the years. And it must have worked for all parties, because at one point Tunie was not only doing the soap *and SVU* and also recurring on the first season of *24*, which films in Los Angeles—and when that was over with she was doing her Broadway producing, and the soap, and the show. "It was a little crazy," she admits.

As Warner, some of the biggest challenges come from having to stay in character all day and remember lines that can be loaded down with what she calls "technojargon." Many of her scenes also involve spouting complex dialogue and words as she moves around props or points out evidence, and the combination can be exhausting. "I have days that are light and breezy where I can pop off some stuff, and then I have days where I can't even turn on the television (between takes) in order to maintain what I have to say," she says.

But Tunie adds, it's not about memorization; it's rarely having a real conversation with any other character that can be hard. "It's all expository," she says. "I'm just always there to deliver the facts. When I was playing the attorney (on *ATWT*) it was a similar thing in the courtroom—it's all question and answer and then you have to figure out your own through line so you remember what the next question is. That's a skill you develop."

Ultimately, it all came together well enough that Tunie got moved into the show's opening credits and group shot (a promotion the franchise's other, even longer-running medical examiner, played by Leslie Hendrix of *L&O*, has never received). "It's been a real blessing," Tunie admits.

And, in at least one case, it's had some side benefits: When the family dwelling was broken into a few years ago, the police showed up to take down the details before Tunie got home. One officer noticed a photo of the actress, and asked, "Is that Dr. Warner?" Her husband—jazz singer Gregory Generet—acknowledged it was. "The next thing you know there's four patrol cars swooping into the neighborhood and an unmarked car pulled up and a couple of detectives got out," says Tunie, laughing. "Then the detectives called me the next day to make sure everything was all right, gave me his card. All because they recognized Dr. Warner!"

B.D. Wong (Dr. George Huang, 2001–Present)

JIM COX. USED WITH PERMISSION

B.D. Wong (Dr. George Huang)

AKA: Bradley Darryl Wong
Originally From: San Francisco, Calif.
Selected Other Credits: (Film) *Mulan II* (Shang, 2004), *Mulan* (Shang, 1998); (TV) *All-American Girl* (Dr. Stuart Kim, 1994–95); (Book) *Following Foo: The Electronic Adventures of the Chestnut Man* (2000)
Upcoming Project: (Film) *Showing Up* (Himself, 2010)

Just the Facts

About Wong: An actor since childhood, B.D. Wong majored in theater at San Francisco State University, but left after two years. On the East Coast, he landed a plum role as Song Liling in the 1988–90 Broadway show *M. Butterfly*, a slot which earned him Drama Desk, Theatre World, and Tony awards. Most non-theater audiences first got a glimpse of him as Father Ray Mukada in HBO's *Oz*, in which he appeared from 1997–2003.

By then he already was doing double duty on *SVU*, like fellow *Oz* cast members Christopher Meloni and Dean Winters. In 2000,

Wong's book *Following Foo: The Electronic Adventures of the Chestnut Man* served as a public coming-out for the actor, as he retold the story behind the birth of his twin sons (one of whom died shortly afterward), conceived in surrogacy with his then-partner Richie Jackson.

About Huang: An FBI forensic psychiatrist, Huang is an outsider brought into the Special Victims Unit to provide a different perspective for the detectives. Little is known about the character except that he can serve as an interpreter for Chinese speakers (Wong himself is not fluent) and he has a low-key, intense-but-gentle approach.

Says Wong, "One, he's really knowledgeable and two, he's really into it. He likes to try and figure out why somebody would do something or what they would do next, and he knows a lot about conditions people have, including their proclivities, fetishes, infinite different states of mental health and mental disease. I think he likes to be a part of the puzzle-solving process himself. His compassion is not really active—Dr. Huang is simply there for (victims). He's always able to say, 'I'm really sorry about what happened,' and mean it, but he's not crying. And they believe him when he says it. And I don't know anybody like this."

The Rest of the Story

In certain respects, Huang is a proxy for showrunner and executive producer Neal Baer, a Harvard Medical School graduate and former full-time practicing doctor. With Baer in control up top, says Wong, a medical point of view for the show was required.

"They asked me to come and do four episodes as a kind of audition, to see if it worked, and after those four episodes they asked me to stay on," Wong recalls. "They weren't 100 percent sure the character would stick, so they didn't make a big deal out of who they were going to put in the slot for four episodes. Because it was an experiment on a lot of levels, it was a lot easier than going to a lot of auditions and having other people be in competition."

Wong's appearances on the set are infrequent, but can provide the linchpin for any given episode. His character may be taciturn, but Wong insists that's really not like him: "I'm really a very gooey person. I like hugging people."

In his time between *SVU* appearances, Wong appears on stage ("I've done a play almost every year that I've been on the show," he explains) and has another career as a public speaker. "I'll talk about any number of different things—choosing a career in the arts, being an ethnic minority, being a gay person, or any of all three of those things. It depends on who invites me," he says.

He's generally pleased with the show's racial mix and approach to racial matters in the storylines. "It's pretty rare to have a television show with ethnic diversity that doesn't really flinch, doesn't really call attention to itself, or that doesn't labor itself in being 'diverse,'" he says. "It just is. Which is unfortunately not really common. It's nice that a show that takes place in New York is as diverse as it is, because I think it's important for people to understand even if they don't live in a diverse community what that means and how valuable and interesting that can be."

And certainly, he'd like to have more to do as Huang, but Wong understands where his character fits in the mix—and besides, if he had more to do there might be fewer plays, or speaking engagements, or even books. "I think I've found a rhythm now that's rather pleasant and that I really like and that I really enjoy, and it allows me to do all these other things, so I try not to complain too much about it," he says. "As a creative person, as an actor, you're always looking for more, but I'm at the point now where I feel it's not really in the cards (on this show), so I try and enjoy it for what it is. And I do think he's valuable to the show, so I enjoy that aspect of it."

Wong hasn't given any real thought to potentially leaving. "I don't really have a plan. If you told me I was going to be here for twenty more years, which you never could do, I'd have to say I'd have to think about that!"

FORENSICS TECHNICIANS

Mike Doyle (Forensics Tech Ryan O'Halloran, 2002–09)

Originally From: New York City
Other Wolf Films Associations:
Law & Order: SVU (Asst. M.E. Karlan, "Prodigy," 2002)
Selected Other Credits: (Film) *Laws of Attraction* (Michael Rawson, 2004); (TV) *Oz* (Adam Guenzel, 2002), *Sex and the City* (Mark, 2000), *ER* (Michael McKenna, 1999)
Upcoming Project: (Film) *Rabbit Hole* (2010)

GABRIEL GOLDBERG. USED WITH PERMISSION

Mike Doyle (CSU Tech Ryan O'Halloran)

Just the Facts

About Doyle: Manhattan-born but Connecticut-raised, Mike Doyle has appeared in feature films and television for the past fifteen years, including *ER* when future *SVU* showrunner Neal Baer was still working there, and a stint on *Oz* with Christopher Meloni. But *SVU* fans have come to enjoy his dozens of appearances as the show's resident forensics tech. He's also a filmmaker who produced and starred in 2003's limited-release *Cutter* and who wrote, produced, and directed the 2006 short *Shiner*. "Some girls in Sweden started an unofficial fan site (for me), and I get a lot of people who say, 'How do I know you?'" he says. "Though recently, people have been like, *Law & Order* man, *Law & Order*!'" he says about his recognizability factor.

About O'Halloran: For most of his six-year run on the show, there wasn't much to know about him except that he was nearly called "Tim." "The first season (he was on), nobody used his name," explains Doyle. "Then the first time they used his name 'Ryan,' Christopher

Meloni said, 'Wasn't your name Tim?' And they used to write for O'Halloran as if he were from the Midwest; there was a scene where we were talking and I said something like, 'Back on the farm . . .' and Meloni's like, 'Back on the farm in Flatbush?'"

O'Halloran was murdered by a homicidal colleague at the end of season ten.

The Rest of the Story

Doyle's first *SVU* shot came in season three, as Assistant Medical Examiner Karlan in "Prodigy," brought on when Tamara Tunie (M.E. Warner) was out. "There were some reshoots that needed to be done—so they asked if I could play the part. Then I was bragging to all my friends that I had this recurring role on *SVU*—that never recurred," he says.

Doyle praises Baer and executive producer Ted Kotcheff for "creating an atmosphere of respect and safety so everyone can do their work." But he also reveals that "it's one of the funniest sets I've ever worked on—Chris and Mariska (Hargitay) are two of the funniest people, and you'd never know it from the show. There's a sense of playfulness and fun, but then things get serious for shooting and everyone steps it up. There's a lot of shtick going on."

When he learned his character was to be killed off, Doyle remained sanguine. He knows showrunner Neal Baer from their days together at *ER*, and says, "He's always been a big supporter of mine. He said, 'Your character is getting killed. It's not because I don't like you or your character, but we're making changes to the show and we wanted to make sure your character went out with a bang.'"

Grins Doyle, who's used to having his characters die: "I'm not unfamiliar with the territory of death. On TV, that is."

Joel de la Fuente (TARU Tech Ruben Morales, 2002–Present)

Originally From: Chicago

Selected Other Credits: (TV) *Canterbury's Law* (AAG Upton, 2008), *All My Children* (Seamus Wong, 2007), *100 Centre Street* (Peter Davies, 2001–02)

Upcoming Project: (Film) *Showing Up* (Himself, 2010)

Joel de la Fuente (TARU Tech Ruben Morales)

SABRINA USHER. USED WITH PERMISSION

Just the Facts

About de la Fuente: Joel de la Fuente plays Hispanic roles as often as Asian ones—and he clears up his heritage right away: He's Filipino. Since 1992 the actor has appeared in such projects as an *Afterschool Special* to *ER* during future *SVU* showrunner Neal Baer's tenure, a fact he shares with his fellow recurring co-star Mike Doyle. De la Fuente co-wrote the short film *Life Document 2: Identity* in 2002.

About Morales: "Morales is the 'computer cell-phone guy,'" explains de la Fuente. "(He) spends most of his time in the lab, but is very devoted to his family. Over the last few seasons he has shown a grumpy side when his technology isn't being acknowledged as a valid part of solving the crime." Morales appears prominently in season seven's "Web"—he reveals that his nephew Freddy was raped after meeting someone from the Internet, and Morales feels guilty for having bought him the computer.

The Rest of the Story

Had Joel de la Fuente not stepped into the role as the TARU Tech (TARU stands for Technical Assistance Response Unit), the character would most likely be called "Burt Trevor." That was the name de la Fuente was given when he auditioned. And though he says it would have been amusing to play a character with such an Anglo name, he appreciates that the show "wanted to match a name to me."

Several TARU Techs had floated through the *SVU* continuum before they settled on Morales, and part of the reason he's pretty sure they kept calling him back was his facility with the challenging language and the need to manipulate props while delivering lingo. "You have to convey information in a very condensed way, in a way that no one—even tech guys—speaks," he says. "And you have to do it while carrying nine pieces of machinery or doing something you've never done before until two minutes before you start shooting."

But he must have been more than just competent, because ultimately he played a large part in "Web" that few recurring actors get. De la Fuente only learned of the extent of his contribution when he arrived on set that day; he was teased mercilessly by some of the crew when it turned out his usually mild-mannered character would be beating up a suspect. "Everyone was so amused that Morales suddenly had a deep-seated anger and a temper."

RECURRING REGULARS

Judith Light (Bureau Chief/EADA/Judge Elizabeth Donnelly, 2002–Present)

JEFF KATZ, USED WITH PERMISSION

Judith Light (Judge Elizabeth Donnelly)

Originally From: New Jersey
Selected Other Credits: (TV) *Ugly Betty* (Claire Meade, 2006–Present), *Phenom* (Dianne Doolan, 1993–94), *Who's the Boss* (Angela Bower, 1984–92), *One Life to Live* (Karen Wolek, 1977–83)

Just the Facts

About Light: From her earliest days as a bored housewife-turned-prostitute on the ABC soap *One Life to Live* to her stint as a very different kind of mom on *Who's The Boss*, Judith Light has played comedy and drama with equal aplomb, and even won two Daytime Emmy Awards. In 1996 she portrayed a slightly less iconic role in the TV film *A Husband, A Wife and a Lover*, which became the contact point for her future *SVU* career since future *SVU* executive producer Ted Kotcheff directed the film. They reconnected once he was in the L&O fold, and she was made a bureau chief in the Manhattan District Attorney's office. Since then, she has a taken on a regular role on ABC's *Ugly Betty*.

About Donnelly: Other than her career trajectory (she became a judge in season seven), little is known about Donnelly. Nevertheless, she's a steely presence with a sure moral compass. "She's powerful, discerning, and working to not come from any of her personal emotions," says Light. "She's in love with the law, and connected to doing what's right and using the law to make the world a better place. She is incorruptible. Also, there's her mentorship: When she sees someone who has potential, she jumps in there to be supportive of them so they can go into the world and exercise that potential as much as they can."

The Rest of the Story

"Working on the *SVU* set is the highest caliber you can get, down to a person," says Light. "From directors to camera operators to lighting—all of that. It's a great cast that's very connected, and loves doing this job. It runs like a perfectly timed watch."

And she was a fan of the program even before joining the cast: "New York is home for me, and I love seeing New York—but I also thought the stories and actors were extremely powerful. You can see when you watch a show like this the level of professionalism going into it."

But don't expect Donnelly to make more appearances just because *Ugly Betty* has relocated in order to film solely in New York City—it is on a rival network, after all. "If I could, I'd love to do both," she says. "They had become my New York family in terms of work—you do get that when you work on a show for a long period of time, you do get connected to everybody, and you do take pride in that being your family."

Isabel Gillies (Kathy Stabler, 1999–Present)

Isabel Gillies (Kathy Stabler)

Originally From: New York City

Other Wolf Films Association: *Law & Order* (Monica Johnson, "Bad Girl," 1998)

Selected Other Credits: (Film) *I Shot Andy Warhol* (Alison, 1996), *Metropolitan* (Cynthia McLean, 1990); (TV) *The $treet* (Alison, 2000), *Sex and the City* (Elaine, 1998)

Upcoming Project: (Book) *Happens Every Day* (2009)

Just the Facts

About Gillies: "During this show I've been engaged, married, had two babies of my own, got divorced, got remarried, got pregnant again," says Isabel Gillies. And viewers thought Kathy Stabler had some challenges! In fact things have been almost as busy off-camera as on for Gillies, who has been working since 1990 in largely independent films.

Her children are six, five, and four, which means the part-time job she's held at *SVU* for the past ten seasons is "perfect." "I can't do a TV show or a movie in Los Angeles or Vancouver because I have these kids, and for a long time I was a single mother so I really couldn't go anywhere," she says. "So I just do this and I got married to a wonderful man, and I don't know—nice life!" Still, far from static: Her memoir, *Happens Every Day*, is due out in June 2009.

About Stabler (Kathy, that is): "Long-suffering" doesn't really do Kathy Stabler justice. That said, she's probably one of the most tolerant and believable cop wives ever shown on television. She and Elliot married young (after he knocked her up), and as an SVU cop he's rarely home, leaving Kathy to raise four children for most of the series (baby made five in season nine).

Stress pulled them apart for a time in season six, leading to the brink of divorce. She initially had her suspicions about her husband's partner, but now believes Det. Benson to be no threat to their union. "Kathy really has her family, and she wishes it was more intact sometimes, and can be disappointed," explains Gillies. "But I think Elliot and Kathy have a nice marriage; they get it about marriage."

The Rest of the Story

Apparently, a little bullying works wonders with *SVU* creator Dick Wolf: Like Mariska Hargitay, Isabel Gillies knew she wanted the part, and wasn't shy about telling him he'd better not hand it off to someone else. "When I went in (for the audition), Dick and Ted (Kotcheff, executive producer) were there, and I remember saying, 'Listen, this is the right part for me, and I'm missing my kid to be at this audition so you'd better give me this role.'"

Something about that seemed to tweak the powers that be— and because of the nature of the crimes, a single male lead detective could come off as perverted or strange, which meant Kathy and the kids were key roles.

"I love seeing what happens to (Elliot) in terms of the family," says Gillies. "So many people watch it who have children, and worry about what would happen if something dreadful happened to them, so the family is comforting in a way. It would almost be too cold for the lead detective to have no reflective sensibility."

But many fans are invested in an eventual Stabler/Benson hookup. "Over my dead body!" Gillies jokes about the possibility of them having a relationship, then acknowledges that that scenario would be fine with some loyal fans. "There are people (on the Internet) who are like, 'I wish she'd died in that (season nine) car crash!' Which is a little bit weird; I mean, don't wish death on anybody."

Even though she's usually on only a handful of episodes a year, Gillies is always happy to be asked back. "I love it," she says. "The thing about *SVU* is the humanity of it. I like that the family has a part in that, because it brings more humanity to the show. I feel incredibly proud to be a part of it, the whole franchise. It's a good example of how entertainment can work for people in their lives."

•

CHAPTER TWENTY-TWO

THE EPISODE GUIDE

"The more laws and order are made prominent, the more
thieves and robbers there will be."

—THE WAY OF LAO-TZU, 604–531 B.C.

"The world abounds with laws and teems with crimes"

—ANONYMOUS, 1775

SEASON ONE

September 1999–May 2000

Regular Cast: Christopher Meloni (Det. Elliot Stabler), Mariska
Hargitay (Det. Olivia Benson), Richard Belzer (Det. John Munch),
Michelle Hurd (Det. Monique Jefferies), Dean Winters (Det. Brian

CHRIS HASTON/NBCU PHOTO BANK

Season one cast, from l.-r.: Dean Winters (Det. Brian Cassidy), Dann Florek (Capt. Donald Cragen), Mariska Hargitay (Det. Olivia Benson), Christopher Meloni (Det. Elliot Stabler), Michelle Hurd (Det. Monique Jefferies), Richard Belzer (Det. John Munch)

Cassidy), Dann Florek (Capt. Donald Cragen), Leslie Hendrix (M.E. Elizabeth Rodgers)

Recurring Cast: Isabel Gillies (Kathy Stabler), Chris Orbach (Ken Briscoe), Erin Broderick (Maureen Stabler), Jeffrey Scaperrotta (Dickie Stabler), Patricia Cook (Elizabeth Stabler), Holiday Segal (Kathleen Stabler), Welly Yang (Tech/Medical Examiner's Assistant), Reiko Aylesworth (Assistant District Attorney Erica Alden), Angie Harmon (ADA Abbie Carmichael), Jerry Orbach (Det. Lennie Briscoe), Peter Francis James (Judge Kevin Beck)

SEASON ONE OVERVIEW: As with any new show, a first season can be a whirlwind of adjustment, as cast members find their characters' voices and writers settle on a tone. *SVU* premiered with a further handicap: It wasn't a spin-off, but it was a continuation of Dick Wolf's Law & Order brand, which meant the carry-over audience from that show (about to begin its eleventh season when *SVU* debuted) would come with expectations. Translation: No personal lives, and a crime for which solving didn't end with an arrest, or even a confession. So while the show included the familiar *L&O* door walk-through group shot in its opening credits—featuring from left to right Capt. Don Cragen, Det. Olivia Benson, Det. Elliot Stabler and Det. John Munch—*SVU* was left to reconvince its audience that it was possible, and satisfying, to forgo those two key elements. But the transition didn't wholly take, and as the season went on, scripts spent more and more time in and around the courthouse, with ADAs popping up as recurring characters. Fortunately, the cast clicked almost immediately: Mariska Hargitay's Benson and Christopher Meloni's Stabler had an instant chemistry, while the other detectives—most especially Richard Belzer's Munch, imported from another NBC show, *Homicide: Life on the Street*—went underused, but provided a solid underpinning of support. There were some early great episodes, and at least one throwaway, but overall there was no question: This was the start of something big.

Ratings Recap for Season: 8.1 rating / 14 share / 11,169,000 viewers

EPISODE DESCRIPTIONS

Episode 1: Payback

Original air date: September 20, 1999
Teleplay by Dick Wolf, directed by Jean de Segonzac

Additional Cast: Mili Avital (Marta Stevens), Elizabeth Ashley (Serena Benson), Judy Del Giudice (Judge Elizabeth Masullo), Ned Eisenberg (Kloster's Lawyer), Gordana Rashovich (Anya Rugova), Tina Benko (Mrs. Panacek), Ronald Guttman (Gallery Owner), P.J. Brown (Bremmer), Ramsey Faragallah (Taxi Driver), Mark Nelson (Robert Stevens), Jeremy Bergman (Nicholas Stevens), Matt Skollar (Victor Spicer), Mark Zimmerman (Mr. Dupree), Irma St. Paule (Aunt Jashari), Sevanne Martin (Ileana Jashari), Bill Driscoll (Mr. Kloster), Vivian Nesbitt (Farley)

Reviewing the Case: Detectives investigate the stabbing of taxi driver Victor Spicer, which kicks off the series using the template, tone, and dark sense of humor of the original *Law & Order*. Spicer is the pseudonym for a man who headed up a Yugoslavian ethnic cleansing unit, so detectives locate some of his local victims. But when Benson sides with one of them, she lands in hot water with Cragen.

Noteworthy Discoveries: The story goes first to Stabler's home, where he is married with four children; then to lunch with Benson and her mom Serena. Benson is the product of her mother's rape.

Relevant Testimony: "I was sad about losing Munch (when NBC's *Homicide* was canceled in 1999), that was an amazing experience. It was a minor miracle that everything worked out, in terms of so many entities (who had a stake in Munch) agreeing on something, and that's a testament not to me personally but the character and the affection for the character everyone had and still has."—Richard Belzer

Episode 2: A Single Life

Original air date: September 27, 1999
Teleplay by Miriam Kazdin, directed by Lesli Linka Glatter

Additional Cast: Michael Nouri (Dallas Warner), Dennis Boutsikaris (Dr. Mark Daniels), Laila Robins (Ellen Sidarsky Travis), Paul Hecht (Robert Sidarsky), Walt MacPherson (Det. Mourad), Leslie Lyles (Dr. Chatman), Liam Craig (Hawkins), Douglas D. McInnis (Trent Peterson), Virginia Louise Smith (Page), Clyde Baldo (Little Suit), Matthew Arkin (Mr. Daniels), Michael Gaston (Woody)

Reviewing the Case: Benson and Stabler investigate the death of Susan Sidarsky, a writer who plunged from her apartment. The cinematography is notable here for its quiet poetry, as the detectives stare wordless at the body in the moment before opening credits begin. Sidarsky was molested as a child, and Benson talks her sister Ellen into confronting their father in the hopes of learning who's behind Susan's death. But the late writer leaves behind an epilogue that surprises everyone.

Noteworthy Discoveries: Benson resides in Manhattan; Stabler in Queens with wife Kathy, children Maureen, Kathleen, Elizabeth, and Dickie. Stabler's previous partner, "Alphonse," retired to Florida, so Benson is new to him. On the stand, Cassidy proves uncomfortable with—and ignorant of—graphic sexual terms. Cragen's flight attendant wife, Marge, died in a crash that parallels the 1996 ValuJet downing in the Everglades.

Episode 3: . . . Or Just Look Like One

Original air date: October 4, 1999
Teleplay by Michael R. Perry, directed by Rick Rosenthal

Additional Cast: Jesse L. Martin (Det. Eddie Green), Bebe Neuwirth (Nina Laszlo), Carolyn McCormick (Dr. Elizabeth Olivet), Catherine Dent (Deborah Latrell), Ritchie Coster (Carlo Parisi), Rica Martens (Mrs. Johnson), Gary Klar (Lt. Joey Poole), Saidah Arrika Ekulona (Dr. Lakhmajara), Elizabeth Van Dyke (Attorney Harris), Ray Virta (Schecter), Lawrence Woshner (Dr. Sullivan), Peter Marx (Tom Burgess), Laura Poe (Sue Burgess), Todd Stashwick (Ricky Blaine), Damian Young (Hampton Trill)

Reviewing the Case: A model named Jasmine is raped and dumped in a parking lot. While investigating photographer Carlo Parisi, who had kicked the girl off the set for being too heavy, Benson recognizes his disfigured partner, who once testified in a stalk-and-attack case. *SVU* detectives run into *L&O* cops Lennie Briscoe and Eddie Green investigating a related crime, and share information. What emerges is how a blackmail threat from Jasmine turned into a beating . . . from an unexpected source. But just as the confession arrives, the story takes a tragic turn.

Noteworthy Discoveries: Stabler takes a belated concern in his eldest daughter's weight obsession, and talks to Dr. Elizabeth Olivet (from *L&O*).

Relevant Testimony: "I was happy to be working in New York City, I knew what my part was and I was happy to be part of the show. So I didn't moan about it, but after a certain time I started to get frustrated when other people would be brought on and they had things to do."—Michelle Hurd

Episode 4: Hysteria

Original air date: October 11, 1999
Teleplay by Dawn DeNoon and Lisa Marie Petersen, directed by Richard Dobbs

Additional Cast: Garrett M. Brown (Peter Ridley), Joe Lisi (Sal D'Angelo), Frederick B. Owens (John Henderson), Brad Beyer (Dennis Caulfield), Lisa Summerour (Carol Henderson), Delphi Harrington (Evelyn Caulfield), Gloria Sauvé (Jacelyn Myers), Page Johnson (Harry Rosen), Redman Maxfield (Charles Caulfield), Susan Willis (Mrs. Overton), Dan Snook (Bill Griswold), Selenis Leyva (Lorinda Guterrez), Sondra James (Agnes Rosen), David Newer (Defense Attorney), Judy Del Giudice (Judge), Tom Gerard (Fredo Valenti), Jillian Bowen (Rose)

Reviewing the Case: The detectives take over a smothering death of apparent prostitute Tracy Henderson when the vice cop who caught the case, Sal D'Angelo, calls it a "NHI" (no humans involved) case. But other deaths fit the M.O., and attention points first to Henderson's boyfriend and then back to D'Angelo. But Briscoe (who used to work in his precinct) tells Cragen that it's D'Angelo's partner, Ridley, who's the psycho. Ridley comes clean to some crimes while denying Henderson's killing—and to solve that crime, detectives must search their souls—and some soles.

Noteworthy Discoveries: The early episodes show a significant lack of cast integration and screen time: Jefferies and Cassidy have virtually nothing to do. Stabler's middle daughter tells him she's still a virgin, which tweaks him out.

Episode 5: Wanderlust

Original air date: October 18, 1999
Teleplay by Wendy West, directed by David Jones

Additional Cast: Lynn Collins (Virginia Hayes), Patricia Richardson (Annabel Hayes), John Dossett (Tom/Scott Dayton), Henry Strozier (John Freeman), Lisa Tharps (Prosecuting Attorney), William Westenberg (Ed Sostek), Marisa Redanty (Dr. Ramsdale), Anne Hubbard (Allison LoGreco), Kamal Marayati (Patel), Michael David Mantell (Jimmy Delmonico), Bruce Barney (Richard Schiller)

Reviewing the Case: Dead travel writer Richard Schiller is discovered by his landlord, Annabel Hayes; Stabler removes a woman's panties from his mouth. "Looks like he choked on his own words," says the detective, taking a page from Briscoe's joke book. Hayes' boyfriend turns out to be a convicted child molester, so detectives turn to her teen daughter Virginia, who had gone ballistic about "Schilly's" death. After a false molestation accusation and suicide attempt, however, Virginia has a new tale to tell.

Noteworthy Discoveries: Lovelorn Munch flirts with Schiller's ex-wife while interrogating her at the same time. Stabler again sees parallels between the teen Virginia and his teen Maureen going to the prom.

Episode 6: Sophomore Jinx

Original air date: October 25, 1999
Teleplay by John Chambers, directed by Clark Johnson

Additional Cast: Frank Deal (ADA), Novella Nelson (Mrs. Mosley), Kohl Sudduth (Riley Cougar), Al Sharpton (Himself), Lothaire Bluteau (James Henry Rousseau), Sean Squire (Chuck Mosley), Tom O'Rourke (Anthony Schlasser), Claire Lautier (Shelley Brown), George Martin (Father McCourt), John Elsen (Weatherbee), Bill Mitchell (Judge), Rose Stockton (Mrs. Gallagher), Barbara Caruso (Dr. Sara Goodnall), Carla Bianchi (Mrs. Dunbar), Michael Hobbs (Mr. Gallagher), Teri Lamm (Becky Underwood)

Reviewing the Case: This fast-moving collection of clues and class warfare is classic *L&O* but here gets an original *SVU* twist. A college student turns up dead after leaving a party with the basketball team, and two jocks are tested for DNA. When they don't match samples found inside the victim, detectives talk to the late student's professors, one of whom seems overly attentive. By episode's end, there may not even have been a murder . . . but there's still a comeuppance to be had.

Noteworthy Discoveries: Cragen's alma mater was St. Raymond's, where the victim is found. In 1964 Cragen broke his leg when a fellow named Anthony Schlasser drunkenly crashed into his car. Schlasser is now in the mayor's office, and Cragen still has a beef with him. Stabler went to Queens College.

Episode 7: Uncivilized

Original air date: November 15, 1999
Teleplay by Wendy West and Robert Palm, story by Robert Palm, directed by Michael Fields

Additional Cast: Stephen Bogardus (Bill Turbit), Ian Reed Kesler (Jimmy G.), Austin Lysy (Mike D.), Terry L. Beaver (State Attorney General Morris Klein), Torquil Campbell (Christopher James), Steve Ryan (Hank), Randy Danson (Dr. Greenblatt), Lisa Tharps (ADA), Adam Grupper (Dr. Malloy), Mike Hodge (Capt. Lloral), Bill Mitchell (Judge Connolly), Myk Watford (Mr. Davies), Caren Browning (Mrs. Davies), Joanna Wolff (Girl Scout), Elaine Formicola (Mrs. James)

Reviewing the Case: The "ew" factor that ratcheted up in episode 6, "Sophomore Jinx," surfaces again—but the script is really about shades of gray in a seemingly black-and-white situation. Here, young Ryan Davies is found in a park strangled and assaulted. The local child molester, Bill Turbit, is fingered as a suspect by neighborhood teens, and politicians want to use him as a test case for indefinite mental incarceration of sex offenders. But Turbit isn't their man, so Benson and Stabler instead turn to the teens that were so eager to lay the blame.

Noteworthy Discoveries: Stabler must find his life a bit creepy, because his children all seem to reflect his cases: Dickie disappears at a park for a few minutes, and his father goes ballistic. Cassidy seems to be having second thoughts about his precinct choice.

Episode 8: Stalked

Original air date: November 22, 1999
Teleplay by Roger Garrett, directed by Peter Medak

Additional Cast: Bruce Kirkpatrick (Richard White), Allison Mackie (Kimberly Phillips), Jack Hallett (Barlow), Charles Brown (Mr. Krim), Sandra Shipley (Lila White), Ben Lin (Tong), Linda Powell (Armstrong), Bruno Gioiello (Kenneth Maggio), Nat deWolf (Mr. Cummings), Dominic Fumusa (Det. Lopez), Don Creech (Atkins), Lorca Simons (Joan Simon), Mark Alan Gordon (Det. Carlyle), Joel Rooks (Grandfather), Barbara McCulloh (Mills), Adrienne Dreiss (Louise Billings), Steve Routman (Harold Levin)
Reviewing the Case: ADA Karen Fitzgerald is found raped and murdered in Central Park. Two convicts from her former cases pop up but only one seems viable: Richard White, who friends and coworkers say is a misogynist and a possible stalker prone to intimidating women to get what he wants. White flees, but calls Benson for a secret meeting, and she becomes concerned for her life.
Noteworthy Discoveries: Benson, who attended Sienna College, has been with the SVU for a year and a half.

Episode 9: Stocks & Bondage

Original air date: November 29, 1999
Teleplay by Michael R. Perry, directed by Constantine Makris

Additional Cast: David Jung (Tsumuru), Maria Tucci (Anne Briggs), Geoffrey Nauffts (Frank Martin), V. Craig Heidenreich (Fred Tucker), Lourdes Benedicto (Angela Torres), Christopher McCann (David Kelp), Francesca Faridany (Amy Tanner), Sean Arbuckle (ME), Monica Steuer (Anna Faust), Sarah Zhang (Debbie Minh)
Reviewing the Case: Financial whiz Leila Perry is hanged on her own bed, and no one's sure at first if it's suicide or homicide or accidental auto-erotic asphyxiation. Perry's boss, Frank Martin, seems likable but then turns out to be the master in multiple sex-slave relationships. Tucked into this episode is money laundering

through a charity, diamonds hidden in a bondage whip, and a child-hood buddy of Martin's who wants to play some of their old games. Confusing, yet ultimately exciting.

Noteworthy Discoveries: Stabler has a tattoo from his days in the Marines and he also may have a brother in the financial world. This is the first episode in the series that doesn't include his home life. Director Makris has been with the L&O franchise since its inception as cinematographer, director, and even co-executive producer.

Episode 10: Closure

Original air date: January 7, 2000
Teleplay by Wendy West, directed by Stephen Wertimer

Additional Cast: Tracy Pollan (Harper Anderson), Neil Maffin (Kenneth Cleary), Roger Bart (Benjy Dowe), Olivia Birkelund (Jane Tyler), Michael Kell (Sam Lardner), Michael H. Ingram (Super), Terry Serpico (Ron Johnson), Mary Sharmat (Older Woman), Liam Craig (Jeff McClintock), Keskhemnu (Det. Halligan), Rob Bartlett (Milton Schoenfeld)

Reviewing the Case: After Harper Anderson is attacked in her apartment, Benson walks her through the hospital process as the show turns more into a near-procedural show. But the case goes cold, and then the episode jumps ahead six months when another attack with a similar M.O. occurs. Anderson doesn't want to come in for a lineup, though she's clearly still scarred. "Closure is a myth," Benson tells her in a powerful speech, which convinces the victim to help. But there's still one last heartbreak she hadn't been expecting.

Noteworthy Discoveries: Benson and Cassidy have a one-night stand; she is dismissive of the idea that it could be more than that. Stabler catches on and says, "It happens." Pollan, best known as the wife of Michael J. Fox, will receive an Emmy nomination for this episode and go on to reprise her role in season two, "Closure: Part 2."

Episode 11: Bad Blood

Original air date: January 14, 2000
Teleplay by Dawn DeNoon and Lisa Marie Petersen, directed by
Michael Fields

Additional Cast: James McCaffrey (Jesse Hansen), Amy Ryan
(Lorraine Hansen), Stephen Barker Turner (Steven Hale), Peter Rini
(Joe Bandolini), Jerry Lanning (William H. Langdon), Leonid Citer
(Andre Lasnik), Anthony Mangano (Mancini), Irene Mazeski (Cindy),
Scott Robertson (Attorney Shore), Joseph Jamrog (Det. Pete), Alex
Sullivan (Mikey), Michael Early (Gerald), Ken Land (Bob), Stephen
Beach (Ray Gunther)

Reviewing the Case: Seth Langdon is found beaten and
splattered with seminal fluid on the roof of a residential building
after a party. One guest, Ray Gunther, is a former serial rapist staying with the super—who turns out to be his brother Jesse. DNA
initially points to Gunther, but final analysis indicates that it's just
someone in his bloodline. But the super is a straight-up family man,
and it takes some unraveling of twisted family dysfunction to reveal
what role he—and Ray—had in the killing.

Noteworthy Discoveries: Munch learns about Benson's
paternal heritage and researches the case. He comes up with a file
on a Carl Kudlack, but at the end of the episode she spies the now-
old man and insists he isn't her father.

Episode 12: Russian Love Poem

Original air date: January 21, 2000
Teleplay by Eva Nagorski, directed by Rick Rosenthal

Additional Cast: Olek Krupa (Alexander Strizhov), Nadine
Stenovitch (Katya Ivanova), Christian Lincoln (Adam Harlin), Russ
Anderson (Charlie Poe), Deborah Rush (Christina Harlin), Guy Ale
(Russian Cousin), Vitali Baganov (Bartender), Marin Rybchevsky
(Natasha), Russell B. Hunston (Andrew Harlin), Jonathan Sharp
(Bull Dozer), Michael Aronov (Spa Owner), Spiro Malas (Russian

Businessman), Snezhana Kushnir (Sonya Pietrovics), Allison Munn (Emily Harlin), Melissa Sagemiller (Becky Sorenson)

Reviewing the Case: A wealthy man named Andrew Harlin is strangled in his home, dressed in bondage gear with a banana inserted . . . well, you know where. The investigation draws *SVU* detectives into the complex world of Russian immigrants that Harlan was tangled up with, particularly the flirty, mysterious, obnoxious Katya (Stabler calls her a "Russian Tammy Faye"). Once Katya is cleared, she's wired up to catch the real murderer—until a game of Russian roulette goes awry. A confusing episode, compounded by impossible-to-distinguish Slavic names.

Noteworthy Discoveries: Munch can speak Russian, though not fluently.

Relevant Testimony: "In the first year and a half, one episode had a guy found tied up with a banana up his ass. That was 180 degrees from where we wanted to be. It was much too sensationalist and not dealing with any issues. There was no value to it. We all remember that as the straw that broke the camel's back. . . . But the network stuck with us and now *SVU* is a mega-hit."—Charles Engel, executive vice-president for programming, NBC Universal

Episode 13: Disrobed

Original air date: February 4, 2000
Teleplay by Janet Tamaro, directed by David Platt

Additional Cast: Frank Deal (ADA), Angie Everhart (Emily Waterbury), Kathryn Meisle (Gina Silver), Jack Gwaltney (Roger Silver), Bill Marcus (State Attorney General), Brenda Pressley (Carole Pinto), Lanette Ware (Sheena Reid), Judy Frank (Winnie Varella), Echo Allen (LaVonne), Otto Sanchez (Delfino Melendez), Pammy Martin (Jillian Silver), Charles Tuthill (Peter Tyler), Linda Halaska (Varella's Secretary), Kelly De Martino (Junkie)

Reviewing the Case: Judge Warren Virella—one of the "good guys," according to Cragen—is found shot in the head and groin on the docks. The ensuing investigation indicates that he was on the take from abusive perps hoping to reduce their sentences—and that he was on the take in a different way from their wives, who were trying to keep those perps in jail. Detectives zero in on the wife of one abuser, who didn't get what she wanted out of the transaction, and when her paroled husband comes back to his nest, he's ready for vengeance. The episode is a solid effort with winding turns and unexpected near-endings.

Noteworthy Discoveries: Shattered by a recent case, Cassidy takes Cragen up on his suggestion that he move to Narcotics.

Relevant Testimony: "Part of me wishes that I'd stayed (with *SVU*); I'd probably be a millionaire by now. I want to say, though, that when I left the show, they wrote this beautiful story for me. I had to find this girl that had been raped, and I come back to the office and (Cragen) sees how upset I am, and pours me a shot of vodka. I had to do that scene like nine or ten times, and cried my eyes out every single time. But it was all thanks to Dann (Florek)— he's such a gifted actor and I'm eternally grateful to him for that day. Dann seems to be overlooked in the praise department."—Dean Winters

Episode 14: Limitations

Original air date: February 11, 2000
Teleplay by Michael R. Perry, directed by Constantine Makris

Additional Cast: Isiah Whitlock, Jr. (Robbery Division Captain), Jenny Bacon (Jennifer Neal), Judith Hawking (Victoria Kraft), Leslie Ayvazian (Trial Judge #2), Jenna Stern (ADA Kathleen Eastman), Seana Kofoed (Lois Creen), John Driver (Police Commissioner Lyle Morris), John Doman (Dan Latimer), Harvey Atkin (Judge Ridenour), Tom Bloom (Andrew Garrick), Francesca Rizzo (Ruby Mazzanti), Michael Ornstein (Harvey Denis)

Reviewing the Case: Cragen is called on the carpet by his bosses to solve three connected-by-DNA rape cases, each with a statute of limitations about to expire. The episode is a thinly disguised (though well-made) polemic on why this legal measure can be a bad idea, and weaves in the judicial system more thoroughly than ever before. The investigation opens up old wounds for the three victims, but one has made a Quaker-like peace with her rapist and refuses to turn him over. Detectives track him down with mere hours to spare—then learn why he stopped at three rapes.

Noteworthy Discoveries: The episode opens up during a COMSAT (computer/statistical crime mapping) meeting between the commissioner and his underlings. It's a bit of jargon that spices up the show with realism.

Episode 15: Entitled (Part 1)

Original air date: February 18, 2000
Teleplay by Robert Palm and Wendy West, story by Dick Wolf, René Balcer, and Palm, directed by Ed Sherin

Additional Cast: Jesse L. Martin (Det. Eddie Green), Sam Waterston (Executive ADA Jack McCoy), Steven Hill (DA Adam Schiff), Katy Selverstone (Emily Shore), Jane Alexander (Regina Mulroney), Nahanni Johnstone (Helen Katish), Josef Sommer (Patrick Rumsey), Noelle Beck (Stephanie Mulroney), Sean Cullen (Arthur Pruitt), Betsy Aidem (Mrs. Brecker), Bill Hoag (Barry Rhinehart), Sophie Hayden (Dr. Winters), Allison Krizner (Julie Templeton), Dennis Higgins (Bailiff), Patrick Tovatt (Judge Barry Abrams)

Reviewing the Case: This is the first official two-part crossover with the Mother Ship, though the *SVU* episode holds up as a standalone. Salesman Dean Woodruff is shot in his car, and attention focuses on his former college girlfriend Stephanie Mulroney—the black sheep of the Kennedyesque Mulroney clan. But when another shooting that fits the M.O. occurs, detectives go after a man first referenced for these kinds of crimes in *L&O*'s season four "Mayhem" episode. Cragen eats crow over the premature arrest of Mulroney—but Munch has reason to believe there's more to the case.

Noteworthy Discoveries: Alexander is the wife of the episode's director, a familiar *L&O* talent, and served as chair of the National Endowment for the Arts under President Bill Clinton in the

1990s. She received an Emmy nomination for her joint role here and on the Mother Ship. The 27th Precinct case seems to continue from *L&O* season four's "Mayhem," in which the detectives searched for a "Mr. Peepers," arrested the wrong man—and never caught the right one.

Relevant Testimony: "Jane Alexander objected to (her matriarch character's) proximity to the Kennedys. I really had to go to the mat (with her) on this episode."—Robert Palm

Episode 16: The Third Guy

First aired: February 25, 2000
Teleplay by Dawn DeNoon and Lisa Marie Petersen, directed by Jud Taylor

Additional Cast: J.K. Simmons (Dr. Emil Skoda), Denis O'Hare (Jimmy Walp), Lance Reddick (Dr. Taylor), Katherine Borowitz (ADA Fahey), Eugene Byrd (Carlos Medina), Vincent Guastaferro (Stan Bosick), William C. Mitchell (Judge), David Adkins (P.D. Trax), Diego Lopez (Emmanuel), Francine Beers (Francis Reiner), P.J. Brown (Corelli), Teddy Coluca (Landlord), Michelle Hurst (Gloria Milton), Charlie Fersko (P.D. David Venko), Natalia Ortiz (Sonia Medina), Stu "Large" Riley (Johnny Schmidt), John Rafael Peralta (Hiphop), Rick Gonzalez (Alfonso Cardenas)

Reviewing the Case: Two teen toughs are targeted for tying up an elderly woman, sexually assaulting and then robbing her, but DNA found on the senior citizen—who dies of a heart attack—doesn't match the kids (who do 'fess up to the robbery). One of them points to a deliveryman in the apartment, and he in turn points to his partner Jimmy, who actually entered the place first. But Jimmy is borderline developmentally disabled. With the help of Dr. Skoda, the SVU detectives have to discern the gray areas between what a man does and what he is responsible for.

Noteworthy Discoveries: Cragen doesn't seem to care for the entire psychiatric profession.

Episode 17: Misleader

First aired: March 31, 2000
Teleplay by Nick Kendrick, story by Nick Harding and Kendrick, directed by Richard Dobbs

Additional Cast: Robert Foxworth (Dr. Ben Hadley), Anne Twomey (Sharon Hadley), Norbert Leo Butz (John Fenwick), John Benjamin Hickey (ADA), Bo Foxworth (Ben Hadley Jr.), Richard Thompson (Brad Weber), Jim Weston (Dr. Weeman's Lawyer), Michael James Gannon (Bartender), Kelly Deadmon (Lana Hoffman), Christopher D. Wells (Ben Weeman's Lawyer), Matthew Lawler (Povill's Lawyer), Kirby Ward (Brad Weber's Lawyer), Rich Hebert (Burglary Detective)

Reviewing the Case: A post-coital Sylvia Hadley is found strangled in her hotel room, and a serial hotel thief is hauled in. But the thief has just been trying to hack hotel security to make a point. Detectives look at the financial analyst who works for the Hadleys, but when DNA clears him they go even closer: Hadley's father-in-law. It takes Ken Briscoe to break this case, thanks to a lot of videotape viewing.

Noteworthy Discoveries: According to a detective with the burglary task force, among the rest of the NYPD, special victims cops are seen as almost as perverse as the people ones they arrest.

Episode 18: Chat Room

Original air date: April 14, 2000
Teleplay by Roger Garrett, directed by Richard Dobbs

Additional Cast: Paz de la Huerta (Karen Raye), Reed Birney (Harry Waters), Jenna Stern (ADA Kathleen Eastman), Siobhan Fallon (Melissa Raye), Rita Gardner (Doris Harrington), Ellen Muth (Elaine Harrington), Mark Zeisler (McClintock), Angela Bullock (Hammond), Wally Dunn (Michael Marolo), Ray Fitzgerald (FBI Agent Schreck), Mark Matkevich (Keith), John C. Havens (Johnstone), Ben Shenkman (Kenneth Brill)

Reviewing the Case: A teen's false claim that she was raped leads detectives to her computer, where they find emails that point to a pedophile named "The Yachtsman." Benson and Stabler haul him in, but the charges may not stick, so they hold their own *To Catch a Predator* trap. An end card announcing that "at any given time, there are 3.4 million anonymous chat room users on the Internet" make this dated episode more *Afterschool Special* than "trenchant look at a trend all parents should be warned about."

Noteworthy Discoveries: Stabler and the wife seem to finally realize that those junk emails they're getting might be going to . . . the children! So he reacts by reading Maureen's messages and putting a block on the computer, which she easily subverts.

Episode 19: Contact

Original air date: April 28, 2000
Teleplay by Wendy West and Robert Palm, directed by Michael Zinberg

Additional Cast: Audra McDonald (Audrey Jackson), Nicole Sullivan (Jen Caulder), Sal Viscuso (Sal Avelino), Bruce Bohne (Bruce Abbott), Tom McCarthy (Nick Ganzner), Bruce Birns (Bruce's Lawyer), Kamal Marayati (Ahmal), Rosalyn Coleman (Flower Vendor), Michael Broughton (Mr. Dewell), Leonora Gershman (Sidra Lonstein), Tracey Toomey (Sporty Spice), Dina Pearlman (Lisa Scopes), Michelle Parylak (Meek Pink), Tricia Paoluccio (Sal's Lawyer), John Littlefield (CPA Schreiber), Peter Appel (Det. Greenberg), Christine Todd Whitman (Detective)

Reviewing the Case: Women are being attacked in broad daylight on the subway, and when the cases attract some publicity, citizens arrest one sad sack, who is sent through the wringer by the detectives. But he's not their guy, so when another attack occurs a clue points Jefferies and Munch to the actual rapist's work. A problematic lineup ID is tossed by the judge, and the police need a new, untainted victim. They discover a young, pregnant woman who seems just a little too sanguine. What is she hiding?

Noteworthy Discoveries: Benson makes kissy-face with a *New York Post* reporter named Nick looking for a scoop on the rape case, and gets in trouble once he reads her files on the sly. Then–New Jersey Governor Christine Todd Whitman makes a brief appearance in the squad room as a background detective.

Relevant Testimony: "The cast includes a few old buddies of mine. Sal Viscuso (playing Sal Avelino) hadn't worked since *The Taking of Pelham One Two Three* in 1974. But the episode was not ripped from any headlines; it was definitely fiction."—Robert Palm

Episode 20: Remorse

Original air date: May 5, 2000
Teleplay by Michael R. Perry, directed by Alexander Cassini

Additional Cast: Jennifer Esposito (Sarah Logan), Josh Pais (Robert Sorensen), Christopher Evan Welch (William Lexner), Patrick Fitzgerald (Tommy McConaugh), Richard Petrocelli (Buck), Christa Scott-Reed (Producer), Sandra Daley (Rosa Farris), Jason Field (Mark Krieger), Juan Carlos Hernandez (Prison Source), Kristen Lee Kelly (Krieger's Date)

Reviewing the Case: When TV reporter Sarah Logan's own rape case goes cold, she takes to the airwaves to talk about it, and a viewer turns in her boyfriend. Munch becomes friendly with Logan and preps her for trial (like episode 10, "Closure," this story features detailed courtroom procedural). But she is blown up by a homemade bomb; the suspect tries to elude arrest and is killed in the same manner. Police examine Logan's fan mail and find one letter that leads them to a bitter stalker. It's up to Munch to persuade him to spill his guts when forensics aren't enough.

Episode 21: Nocturne

Original air date: May 12, 2000
Teleplay by Wendy West, directed by Jean de Segonzac

Additional Cast: Jerry O'Donnell (Off. Tulia), Wilson Jermaine Heredia (Evan), Kent Broadhurst (Larry Holt), John Benjamin Hickey (ADA), Marc John Jefferies (Jonathan), Tibor Feldman (Oslow), Joseph Edward (Jonathan's Father), Gregory Esposito (Ricky), Brian Guzman (Taylor Campbell), Bruce Birns (P.D. Lawyer), Barbara Tirrell (Judge Rothman), Nancy Ticotin (Evan's Mother), Alex Draper (Larry Holt, Jr.), Carole Shelley (Judge Pamela Mizener).

Reviewing the Case: The discovery of a piano teacher who offered services to low-income students that had nothing to do with tickling the ivories and videotaped his exploits with them for years is pretty bad. But it gets worse: Only one victim agrees to testify, and he's a twenty-one-year-old auditioning for Juilliard. Stabler takes the young man under his wing to help him cope, but then the tapes reveal that their new star witness is aping his teacher in more ways than one. This leaves prosecutors in a tragic quandary: Once you know where the abuser's abuse comes from, is he a victim or a perpetrator?

Noteworthy Discoveries: Guest star Wilson Jermaine Heredia won a Tony Award for originating the role of Angel in *Rent* (Off-Broadway/Broadway, 1996–2008) and also appeared in the 2005 film version.

Episode 22: Slaves

Original air date: May 21, 2000
Teleplay by Dawn DeNoon and Lisa Marie Petersen, directed by Ted Kotcheff

Additional Cast: Andrew McCarthy (Randolph Morrow), Mary Lou Rosato (Constanta Condrescu), Harvey Atkin (Judge Ronald Mannheim), Audra McDonald (Audrey Jackson), Susan Floyd (Mrs. Morrow), Layla Alexander (Ilena), Lance Reddick (Dr. Taylor), Natacha Roi (Lindsay Haver), Albert Makhtsier (Mircha Gabrea), Sharon Washington (Dr. Benedict), Peter Giles (Peter Haver), Mark H. Dold (Reservations Agent), Robert Carroll (Balloon Vendor), Evelyn Furtak (NYU Admissions Director)

Reviewing the Case: Tipped off by a Romanian vendor, detectives realize there's a young immigrant woman named Ilena in trouble. They interview her closed-mouthed aunt, who turns up dead hours later, then track Ilena's arrival in the country to businessman Randolph Morrow. The aunt's death leads them to Morrow's veterinarian wife, who crumbles. But he is a tougher nut to crack, telling them Ilena has disappeared. Can Stabler and Benson find her in time—or at all?

Noteworthy Discoveries: Audra McDonald returns as shrink Audrey, who evaluates all of the SVU detectives. The episode—and season—ends when she tells him one detective should be removed from duty to prevent a meltdown, but we don't find out who.

Relevant Testimony: "We were still in a state of flux and trying to find our way at the end of the first season. We felt some changes needed to be made, but we hadn't really decided on anything or anybody. I liked Michelle Hurd a lot, but we had Chris and Mariska, then we had Richard and Michelle, and I thought it diluted Mariska's and Chris' (characters') relationship if we have a mirror image of it, and that we should really make Mariska the only woman detective in the squad room. We had discussed that, but we hadn't decided it—Michelle was a lovely woman, and she worked hard."—Ted Kotcheff

SEASON TWO

October 2000–May 2001

Regular Cast: Christopher Meloni (Det. Elliot Stabler), Mariska Hargitay (Det. Olivia Benson), Richard Belzer (Det. John Munch), Michelle Hurd (Det. Monique Jefferies), Ice-T (Det. Odafin "Fin" Tutuola), Dann Florek (Capt. Donald Cragen), Stephanie March (ADA Alexandra Cabot), Tamara Tunie (M.E. Melinda Warner), J.K. Simmons (Dr. Emile Skoda), and B.D. Wong (Dr. George Huang)

Recurring Cast: Erin Broderick (Maureen Stabler), Isabel Gillies (Kathy Stabler), Welly Yang (CSU Tech Georgie), Harvey Atkin (Judge Alan Ridenour), Tom O'Rourke (Judge Mark Seligman), Joanna Merlin (Judge Lena Petrovsky), Tamara Tunie (Medical

Examiner Melinda Warner) Lou Carbonneau (CSU Tech), Ed Bogdanowicz (CSU), David Jung (Tech), Kent Cassella (Det. Palmieri)

SEASON TWO OVERVIEW: For its sophomore incarnation,
the show focuses less on the personal lives of Benson and Stabler, while
amping up that of Munch. Richard Belzer, in fact, serves as the heroic
and/or comic touchstone of several episodes. There are also quite a
few new characters to introduce: Tutuola eases out Jefferies; toward
the end of the season, Dr. Huang replaces Dr. Skoda as the preeminent
shrink; Warner ascends to the M.E. position; and Cabot becomes the
ADA, as the series puts more emphasis on prosecutors. As of the second episode, no more four-through-the-door: After the teaser, viewers
see a tableau of six in the squad room: Stabler, Benson, Cragen, Cabot,
Tutoloa, and Munch. Tensions abound as personnel are reconfigured,
but compatible relationships soon evolve. The writers begin to smooth
many of the kinks that made the debut season somewhat uneven,
finding a better balance of grit, pathos, and humor.

Ratings Recap for Season: 8.5 rating / 16 share / 11,944,000
viewers

EPISODE DESCRIPTIONS

Episode 23: Wrong is Right

Original air date: October 20, 2000
Teleplay by Jeff Eckerle and David J. Burke, directed by Ted Kotcheff

Additional Cast: Lance Reddick (Dr. Taylor), Adam Kaufman
(Michael Goran), Gerry Bamman (Craig Prince), John Driver (Police
Commissioner Lyle Morris), Paul Wesley (Danny Burrell), Nathan
Wetherington (Jason Sloan), Laura Regan (Denise Sandler), Michael
X. Martin (Principal Dietz), Denise Burse (Counselor Schneider),
T.J. Kenneally (Public Defender Eisenbrath), John Doman (Munch's
Informant)

Reviewing the Case: Stabler's adolescent daughter experiences nightmares after inadvertently witnessing a crime scene with
her father. The case winds up in his purview because the dead man,
Andrew Croft, was sexually mutilated. The investigation leads to a

NBCU PHOTOBANK

Christopher Meloni and Erin Broderick (Maureen Stabler) in "Wrong is Right"

teenager who confesses. But Croft, who was his guardian, worked for a shadowy defense contractor. Meanwhile, Cragen is under the gun at a police commission hearing about the problematic psychological evaluations of Jefferies and Stabler (the latter is briefly suspended). Although the tense episode seems packed with subplots—Pedophilia! Military-industrial shenanigans! Cops on the edge!—the whole is almost seamless.

Noteworthy Discoveries: Alexandra Cabot, the new ADA, initially clashes with Cragen ("Just what kind of unit are you running, Captain?"). In the closing scene, Ice-T reports for duty as Det. Odafin "Fin" Tutuola, newly transferred from Narcotics. This may not bode well for Jefferies, who remains under a cloud after supposedly sleeping with a suspect.

Relevant Testimony: "At the time, we were still exploring how to make *SVU* its own beast. The issue in this episode was partly how a cop leaves crime at the office when he comes home."—Jeff Eckerle

Episode 24: Honor

Original air date: October 27, 2000
Teleplay by Jonathan Greene and Robert F. Campbell, directed by
Alan Metzger

Additional Cast: Tom Tammi (Deputy Commissioner),
James Murtaugh (Gibson), Jennifer Hall (Annette Fleming), Frank
Girardeau (Tomas), Aasif Mandvi (Professor Husseini), Tim Kirkpat-
rick (Walson), Tony Hoty (Hollander), Jeff Branson (Chris Lyons),
Jeanne Lehman (Mrs. Weinberger), Tanya Berezin (Prof. Halber-
sham), Marshall Manesh (Saleh Amir), Susham Bedi (Aziza Amir),
Anil Kumar (Jaleel Amir), Firdous Bamji (Daoud Tarzi)
Reviewing the Case: "Honor" seems remarkably prescient,
now that America has been through 9/11 and its immediate after-
math. The Taliban looms unseen over the situation when a young
Afghan woman is stabbed and stoned to death. Her murder soon
embroils the detectives in a tangle of fundamentalist ideologies, with
suspects ranging from the girl's secular boyfriend to her rabidly
Islamic family. Cabot has a chance to shine as she challenges a
defense lawyer who is preempting all women and Jews from the
potential jury. The saga treads carefully through a sensitive topic
that can be a minefield and includes one of those wrenching twists
that are a trademark of the Law & Order franchise.
Relevant Testimony: "I was reading a *Time* magazine story
one day about honor killings and I said, 'That's it.' And it came into
my head right away, 'What if something like that that happened in
New York?'"—Jonathan Greene

Episode 25: Closure (Part 2)

Original air date: November 3, 2000
Teleplay by Wendy West, Judith McCreary, and David J. Burke, story
by Wendy West, directed by Jean de Segonzac

Additional Cast: Tracy Pollan (Harper Anderson), Ned
Eisenberg (Klein), William H. Burns (Lynch), Neil Maffin (Kenneth Cleary), Evy O'Rourke (Meredith Cleary), Doris Belack (Judge

Margaret Barry), Stina Nielsen (Lori Thatcher), Rob Barlett (Milton Schoenfeld), Polly Adams (Mrs. Walton), Amy Hart Redford (Susan Welch), Ron McClary (Det. Hammond)

Reviewing the Case: During season one's "Closure," Harper Anderson was the victim of a serial rapist but could not identify him. In this second go-round six months later, she engages in target practice at a firing range and relentlessly trails Kenneth Cleary, the perp who seems to be back in action. While trying to keep Harper from exacting vigilante justice, the detectives also turn up the heat on Cleary. His wife goes from denial to near-demonic fury. The guy is so smug that a viewer can't help rooting for his swift demise, rule of law be damned.

Noteworthy Discoveries: Tracy Pollan, wife of actor Michael J. Fox, received an Emmy nomination for her first time out as Harper in season one. When an exhausted Cabot accepts a drink and asks Cragen to join her, he declines with a simple explanation: "AA."

Episode 26: Legacy

Original air date: November 10, 2000
Teleplay by Jeff Eckerle, directed by Jud Taylor

Additional Cast: Craig Wroe (James Woodrow), Jennifer Dundas (Jamie McKenna), Yancey Arias (Denny Corea), Paul Michael Valley (Randall McKenna), Skye McCole Bartusiak (Jennifer), Kevin Gray (Henry Abadin), Adam Zolotin (Justin McKenna), Brian Keane (Dr. Peters), Divina Cook (Mrs. Fergus), Ann McDonough (Mrs. Dunlap), Jean De Baer (Lois Huntington)

Reviewing the Case: Jamie McKenna finds her seven-year-old daughter Emily unconscious with a grave head wound. Potential perps: Her teenage stepbrother, who resents his father's remarriage and the new sibling; Emily's hothead biological dad; a possible pedophile diplomat from Brunei. As the suspect count grows, so do the number of characters in comas. Caught up in this whirlwind of deceit, Munch—in a bravura performance by Belzer—is only certain of his compassion for Emily.

Noteworthy Discoveries: Munch grew up on the Lower East Side of New York. When a youngster laughs at his name, he tells her: "I guess if I ever have kids, I'd have to call them Munchkins."

Relevant Testimony: "The real-world inspiration was a newspaper or magazine story about a working-class child who had suffered abuse and the system utterly failed her. . . . Richard Belzer brings an interesting depth to his character. He uses acerbic wit as a defense mechanism to deflect emotion. I came up with a backstory about Munch as a kid having found out a girl in his neighborhood was murdered and thinking, 'I should have watched out for her.'"— Jeff Eckerle

Episode 27: Baby Killer

Original air date: November 17, 2000
Teleplay by Dawn DeNoon and Lisa Marie Petersen, directed by Juan J. Campanella

Additional Cast: Carlos Leon (Nicky Crow), Jeffrey DeMunn (Charlie Phillips), Carolyn McCormick (Dr. Elizabeth Olivet), Nicolas Martí Salgado (Elias Barrera), Josh Pais (Robert Sorenson), Sara Ramirez (Mrs. Barrera), Robert Montano (Barrera), Gloria Irizarry (Dorothea Strada), LaChanze (Ms. Pivik), Jalyl Ali Lynn (Jamal Morales), Donovon Ian Hunter McKnight (Tommy James), Gene Canfield (Det. Geary), Ming Lee (Kyung Kwan)

Reviewing the Case: In terms of poignancy, "Baby Killer" is reminiscent of "Mushrooms," a 1991 episode by Robert Palm on the original *Law & Order*. Both stories center on a child's murder caused by a terrible mistake with sociological implications. The *SVU* story involves the fatal shooting of a second-grade East Harlem classmate by little Elias. When the DA demands an aggressive prosecution, Cabot suggests: "Why don't you just apply for a change of venue to Texas so we can have him executed?" The boy's parents are decent, hard-working people, but the home of his elderly daycare provider harbors many secrets. There's yet another punch-to-the-gut ending in a series famous for them.

Noteworthy Discoveries: Cabot says that "the system failed Elias all the way down the line," and indeed almost every contemporary issue—poverty, healthcare, gun control, drug laws, ethnic tensions—is tapped.

Relevant Testimony: "This is the only episode I can think of that was censored. We originally included some statistics on handgun violence, but the powers-that-be were concerned it would offend 'certain people.' In the year we wrote this, firearms killed no children in Japan, 19 in Great Britain, 57 in Germany, 109 in France, 153 in Canada and 5,285 in the United States. I found that shocking and needed to write a story about it."—Dawn DeNoon

Episode 28: Noncompliance

Original air date: November 24, 2000
Teleplay by Judith McCreary, directed by Elodie Keene

Additional Cast: Kathleen Chalfant (Mrs. Nash), Kevin Breznahan (Mark Nash), Danny Mastrogiorgio (Earl Miller), William Youmans (Ben Moreland), Maryann Urbano (Dr. Klein), Byron Jennings (Matt Wooding), Helen Hanft (Mrs. Billings), Tony Campisi (Gary Wheeler), Chris Ceraso (Sanitation Manager), Lou Bonacki (Alvin Maddox), Laura Esterman (Mrs. Sandomir)

Reviewing the Case: A dead convenience store clerk has been raped. She was counseling mentally ill homeless people, some of whom come under scrutiny. A delusional schizophrenic brandishes a knife and appears to confess. But, he also confuses himself with the protagonist in Dostoevsky's *Crime and Punishment* and has stopped taking medications because of the dreadful side effects. His mother supports this decision. The murder eventually takes a backseat to the hot topic of optional versus mandatory pharmaceuticals for anyone who may pose a danger to society.

Noteworthy Discoveries: This is the first episode with Dr. Melinda Warner (Tamara Tunie), the medical examiner.

Relevant Testimony: "People have a right not to take medications. The other side of the argument is: Are they violent? I was showing a certain prejudice. We automatically assume people with mental

illness are violent. But they don't live in our world, so perhaps death is more palatable to them than the effects of these drugs. . . . I did a lot of research and tried to make everybody right. It's a paradox."
—Judith McCreary

Episode 29: Asunder

Original air date: December 1, 2000
Teleplay by Judith McCreary, directed by David Platt

Additional Cast: Nestor Serrano (Sgt. Lloyd Andrews), Peter Francis James (Judge Kevin Beck), Amy Carlson (Patricia Andrews), John Ramsey (Judge Walter Schreiber), Jerome Preston Bates (Clarkson), Tom Tammi (Deputy Commissioner), Mario Mendoza (IAB Det. Santiago), Mark Lotito (IAB Det. Howard), Brennan Brown (Brendan Walsh), Paul Stolarsky (Cyrus Parker), Dylan Price (Det. Danny Tatum)

Christopher Meloni and Mariska Hargitay in "Asunder"

Reviewing the Case: Spousal rape makes for a frenetic episode and a harrowing take on the institution of marriage. Patricia is the volatile wife of a manipulative cop. When one of their frequent arguments spills out onto the street, he drags her back to their apartment. Later, her claim of sexual assault and his contention that they simply indulged in passion keep the SVU detectives hopping—and disagreeing about which story is true. The trial is packed with police, some of them blatant misogynists.

Relevant Testimony:

"I know a lot of cops and sometimes they do bad things."—Judith McCreary

"Police are just a microcosm of our society."—David Platt

Episode 30: Taken

Original air date: December 15, 2000

Teleplay by Dawn DeNoon and Lisa Marie Petersen, directed by Michael Fields

Additional Cast: Jenna Lamia (Siobhan Miller), Derek Cecil (Russell Ramsay), Tim Hopper (Terrance Wilde a.k.a. Michael Berkman a.k.a. Kyle Kivlihan), Bill Winkler (Beau Miller a.k.a. Clayton Farnsworth), Nealy Glenn (Patty Ann Miller), Craig Braun (Allen Thorpe), Michelle Daimen (Ramsay's Public Defender), Susan Rollman (Terri Wilde), Steven Mark Friedman (Thorpe's Attorney), Ismail Bashey (Dr. Dhar)

Reviewing the Case: Benson and Stabler set out to find the stranger who raped Siobhan Miller, a seventeen-year-old from North Carolina registered along with family members at a posh new Manhattan hotel. In a lineup, she identifies an affable slacker in his twenties with a previous conviction for sleeping with an underage girlfriend. But apparent evidence on surveillance videotape may not be what it seems, and Cabot may lose out on what she thinks sould be a "slam dunk" conviction. This is yet another legal tangle with dreadful, unintended consequences.

Noteworthy Discoveries: Benson learns that her long-suffering mother, portrayed by Elizabeth Ashley in the series premiere during season one, has died in a drunken fall. Munch reveals that his brother is a mortician.

Relevant Testimony: "Ah, the Irish grifters. Yes, of course it's fun to write about grifters! I hate being conned . . . (The characters appear to be) this religious family but they're not; they're grifters. They are the opposite of what they look like."—Dawn DeNoon

Episode 31: Pixies

Original air date: January 12, 2001
Teleplay by Tracey Stern, directed by Jean de Segonzac

Additional Cast and Guest Stars: Philip Casnoff (Elya Korska), Kate Mara (Lori), Armand Schultz (Kyle Hubert), Steven Marcus (Willie Maxwell), Elaine Bromka (Nancy Meyerson), Richard M. Davidson (Sterner), Julia Mueller (Ann Brice), Terry Layman (Martin Meyerson), Ariel Arce (Danielle), Fidel Vicioso (Det. Reynaldo), Alba Oms (Mrs. Pappov), Courtney Jines (Hannah Miller)

Reviewing the Case: A dead Jane Doe, who appears to be thirteen, might have been a hooker. Instead, she was an Olympics hopeful training with a ruthless coach. His ambitious students starve themselves to stay thin and keep practicing despite injuries. The trail also leads the program's wealthy middle-aged benefactor, who buys expensive presents for these adolescent girls. The cops are successful in pinpointing the killer in this engrossing episode, but abuse in the guise of a popular sport continues.

Episode 32: Consent

Original air date: January 19, 2001
Teleplay by Jeff Eckerle, directed by James Quinn

Additional Cast: Michelle Monaghan (Dana Kimble), Craig Wroe (James Woodrow), Zak Orth (Wally Parker), Tammy Blanchard (Kelly D'Leah), David Jung (Lockhart), Chris Beetem (Joe Templeton), Marika Dominczyk (Tess Michner), Matt Kautz (Hank Ludlow), Alton Fitzgerald White (Nick Monroe), Mary McCann (Ms. Wilkerson), Brian Keane (Dr. Peters)

Reviewing the Case: The date-rape drug GHB is the focus of a case involving college students. When Kelly unwittingly drinks a chemical concoction, someone takes advantage of her during or after a campus frat party. Is it Harry, the vagrant spotted leaning over her unconscious body? Smug Lothario Joe Templeton? His hapless friend Hank? Awkward Wally Parker? Did the rapist also transmit the gonorrhea that now infects Kelly, previously a virgin? And what's with her conniving sorority sisters? Everybody's got an alibi but there are plenty of clues left behind at the crime scene.

Noteworthy Discoveries: Cragen has no children. The case prompts Stabler to worry about how dangerous college might be one day soon for his daughter.

Relevant Testimony: "There was a lot of news back then about the date-rape drug. One dealt with frat boys who drugged and gang-banged. I thought that this is such an interesting time in the life of a young person—their first chance to cut loose. But they face peer pressure. A lot of kids go to college unprepared. My thought was, 'Jesus, where were the parents?'"—Jeff Eckerle

Episode 33: Abuse

Original air date: January 26, 2001
Teleplay by Dawn DeNoon and Lisa Marie Petersen, story by Gwendolyn M. Parker, Dawn DeNoon, and Lisa Marie Petersen, directed by Richard Dobbs

Additional Cast: Hayden Panettiere (Ashley Austin Black), Carolyn McCormick (Dr. Elizabeth Olivet), Craig Wroe (James Woodrow), Leslie Ayvazian (Family Court Judge), Christine Andreas (Ricki Austin), Francesca Faridany (Sarah), Amy Bouril (Holly), Teresa Yenque (Housekeeper), Ryan Woodring (Dr. Mandolar), James Weston (Edwards), Fiddle Viracola (Mrs. Roqueford)

Reviewing the Case: This bizarre episode sifts from sexual abuse to celebrity privilege to what Olivet diagnoses as "corrective detachment disorder." After a boy's accidental death, there's a swift resolution of the red herring that points to a supposed pedophile.

But his parents, both self-involved pop stars, are guilty of neglect and their precocious daughter is very needy. So needy, in fact, that viewers might go from empathy to revulsion. Not Benson, though. She bonds with the girl against all reason, continuing to investigate even when Cragen decides to close the case.

Noteworthy Discoveries: Ashley is played by Hayden Panettiere, who grew up to inhabit the role of an embattled teen cheerleader on NBC's *Heroes*.

Episode 34: Secrets

Original air date: February 2, 2001
Teleplay by Robert F. Campbell and Jonathan Greene, story by Wendy West, Robert F. Campbell, and Jonathan Greene, directed by Arthur W. Forney

Additional Cast: Frank Deal (ADA Don Newvine), Dean Nolen (Philip Montrose), M. Neko Parham (Ethan Chance), Tom Bloom (Dr. Bennett Alston), Daniel McDonald (Dr. Byron Marks), Harry S. Murphy (Brian Denker), Omar Sharif Scroggins (Marcus Cole), Robert Patrick Brink (Host), Chevi Colton (Mrs. Cutler), Sophina Brown (Mrs. Williams), Saidah Arrika Ekulona (Principal)

Reviewing the Case: Teacher Marnie Owens has been honored for working wonders with inner-city teens on the Lower East Side, so her murder stuns the community. Even more shocking is that this apparently saintly educator had a dark, dangerous hobby: An addiction to frequent rough sex, often with multiple partners, many of them strangers. When did this woman get a chance to grade papers? The investigation encompasses her students, bedmates, internet porn, incest and proprietors of private clubs for "consenting adults" that encourage copious copulation.

Noteworthy Discoveries: Munch recalls an embarrassing experience in Baltimore, while still a *Homicide: Life on the Street* detective, that involved his ex-wife exhibiting a large photo of him in the buff. Asked if he has any secrets, Finn divulges his political preference: Republican.

Relevant Testimony: "I was a very loyal *Homicide* viewer and a very loyal *Law & Order* viewer. Once I got here I was, like, 'Wow, I get to write this stuff.'"—Jonathan Greene

Episode 35: Victims

Original air date: February 9, 2001
Teleplay by Nick Kendrick, directed by Constantine Makris

Additional Cast: Eric Roberts (Sam Winfield), Ann Dowd (Louise Durning), Rosemarie DeWitt (Gloria Palmera), Sylva Kelegian (Lindsay Branson), Phyllis Somerville (Mrs. Moss), Jay Christianson (Trent Wills), Rob Sedgwick (James Campbell), José Ramón Rosario (Mario Tomassi), Susan Pellegrino (Dr. Weddington), Tony Cucci (Erik Pulham), Joe Bacin (Det. Dalton)

Reviewing the Case: Predators released from prison have the misfortune of living in a community with a vigilant neighborhood watch organization. The group's leader is a former cop with a checkered history. Is he behind the shootings of some registered sex offenders or was it the vengeful mother of a traumatized young rape victim? When a third ex-con is targeted, all previous theories begin to unravel. Initially reluctant to work on the case, Stabler realizes he's the right man for the unnerving job.

Noteworthy Discoveries: When a cut on Stabler's hand comes in contact with the HIV-infected blood of a suicidal woman, he must start a regimen of anti-viral medication. His interrogation of Winfield includes a personal recollection of an old case, in which he almost shot a particularly evil but unarmed pedophile.

Episode 36: Paranoia

Original air date: February 18, 2001
Teleplay by Jonathan Greene and Robert F. Campbell, directed by Richard Dobbs

Additional Cast: Khandi Alexander (Sgt. Karen Smythe), Chris McKinney (Michael Towne), Isiah Whitlock Jr. (Todd Smythe), Kirsten

Sans (Lab Tech Felicia Young), Brennan Brown (Bates' Attorney), Liam Craig (ADA David Goreman), Jason Kolotouros (Mitch Murray), Brian M. O'Neill (Chief Sullivan), James Hanlon (Austin Bates), Dominic Fumusa (IAB Lt. Coates), Sam Coppola (Uncle Sammy)

Reviewing the Case: Although a bit convoluted, "Paranoia" brings back a favorite nemesis: Internal Affairs, which is interfering with the SVU investigation of a cop's rape. Sgt. Karen Smythe is assaulted while she and her partner are checking out an abandoned warehouse. The M.O. resembles that of an earlier crime in Queens. Nothing is quite what it seems, as Cabot must weigh sexual abuse versus dirty cops.

Noteworthy Discoveries: Stabler sweats out most of the episode waiting for results from his HIV test. Munch offers another of his anti-establishment observations about the NYPD keeping "secret files like J. Edgar Hoover." Give that man a raise! Although a fourteen-year veteran on the force and the woman who trained Benson, Smythe is still a beat cop?

Relevant Testimony: "Karen Smythe is a sergeant. We had a family friend who did not become a sergeant until he'd been on for twenty-five years so it's not uncommon for that to happen. . . . People like different things; some people like the streets, some people like being a detective."—Jonathan Greene

Episode 37: Countdown

Original air date: February 23, 2001
Teleplay by Dawn DeNoon and Lisa Marie Petersen, directed by Steve Shill

Additional Cast: Jeffrey Scaperrotta (Dickie Stabler), Frank Deal (ADA Don Newvine), Jeffrey DeMunn (ADA Charlie Phillips), Kent Cassella (Det. Palmieri), Patricia Cook (Elizabeth Stabler), Debbon Ayer (Mrs. Douglas), Andrea Bowen (Sophie Douglas), Jonathan Fried (Clayton Mills), Ray Iannicelli (Saul Garner), Ann Talman (Mrs. Lehr), Kristin Rohde (Det. Becker), Christine Toy Johnson (Dr. Anderson), Rafael Ferrer (Det. Trainor), Lisa Summerour (Defense Attorney Dylan), Jim Gaffigan (Oliver Tunney)

Reviewing the Case: As tense as episodic television gets, "Countdown" zeroes in on the frantic race to save a little girl from the serial rapist-murderer whose crimes always go like clockwork. After she's accidentally rescued from his clutches, her mother does not allow Benson to conduct a thorough interview. When another child is snatched, the entire squad spends three days with virtually no sleep trying to find the victim and identify her kidnapper. Tempers flare.

Noteworthy Discoveries: Benson must postpone a dinner date with someone named Michael. Stabler's twins are having a birthday.

Relevant Testimony: "It's fantastic to have a time clock. It just heightens the bar, you just immediately tense. The audience is counting down along with you. (Snaps her fingers) It speeds up the pace."—Dawn DeNoon

Episode 38: Runaway

Original air date: March 2, 2001
Teleplay by Nick Kendrick and David J. Burke, directed by Richard Dobbs

Additional Cast: Sean Nelson (Tito Frank), Darrell Hammond (Ted Bolger), Michelle Hurd (Jefferies), Reg Flowers (Lance Kanick), Kent Cassella (Edmond Love), Lance Reddick (Dr. Taylor), Dan Ziskie (Sgt. Frank Foster), Jared Blank (Will), Joseph Franquinha (Teen One), Kelly Karbacz (Jill Foster), Anna Kathryn Holbrook (Lorna Frankel), Kristen Griffith (Mrs. Foster), Baird Wallace (Jill's Brother)

Reviewing the Case: An amateur documentarian interviews street kids and posts his videos on the Web. An old friend of Cragen's spots his junkie-hooker daughter in the footage, but the girl's whereabouts are unknown. Her pimp is a convicted sex offender who organizes raves, where young people indulge in drugs and pornography. His sleazy attorney has a cocaine habit. An orgy-prone older woman is also immersed in this dirty business and Cabot offers her a deal in return for information: "You'll be out of jail before menopause." The outcome, however, is not particularly good for victims, witnesses, perps, or cops.

Noteworthy Discoveries: Benson and Jefferies dress as punks to blend in at a rave. Jefferies is back, despite having quit the force earlier in the season—evidence that the episodes are being broadcast out of their originally intended order. While going undercover to get information, Finn infuriates Munch by referring to him as "my Jew"—another sign that this story was meant to be seen not long after the detectives were first paired (episode 23: "Wrong is Right").

Relevant Testimony: "I told Belzer, 'If the Klan comes one day, all I have to do is worry about outrunning you.' But basically, in America, whether Jewish people, Asian people, there's some kind of bond."—Ice-T

Episode 39: Folly

Original air date: March 23, 2001
Teleplay by Todd Robinson, directed by Jud Taylor

Additional Cast: Patricia Kalember (Leslie DeSantis), Eddie Cahill (Tommy Dowd), Simon Jones (Darien Marshall), J. Tucker Smith (Gary Sutton), Linda Stephens (Mrs. Dowd), Marguerite MacIntyre (Darlene Sutton), Lee Bryant (Claudia Baines Marshall), Stuart Zagnit (Harrison Barnett), Mark Zimmerman (Attorney Katz), Debra Eisenstadt (Lab Tech Ellen Matthews), Amanda Naughton (Lisa), Jeff Robins (Bartender Bill)

Reviewing the Case: Pretty boys are dropping like flies as they unzip their pants to pleasure older women because someone has declared open season on male escorts from the Man About Town "companionship" service. Various well-connected New Yorkers come under scrutiny, but a strange obsession turns out to be the inciting factor in this case full of complex people in a tangle of carnal desires. Adroit viewers may easily guess what the final twist will be, but half the fun is in the process of getting there.

Noteworthy Discoveries: Skoda describes people afflicted with "folie à deux," a shared madness. Benson and Stabler debate the wisdom of keeping prostitution a criminal matter.

Episode 40: Manhunt

Original air date: April 20, 2001
Teleplay by Jeff Eckerle, directed by Stephen Wertimer

Additional Cast: Adam LeFevre (Walden Falls Police Chief), Dan Frazer (Ontario Province Judge), Mike Dooly (ATF Agent Gus Stone), Charlotte Maier (Ms. Michaelson), Anna Belknap (Sarah Kimmel), Robin Morse (Off. Cheryl Baxter), Paddy Croft (Aunt Mary), Tom Alan Robbins (Ed Kushner), Meg Hartig (Annie Tassler), Dennis Predovic ("Olive" Olivetti), Robert Westenberg (Colonel Marsden), Thomas Bolster (Sgt. Pierre), Paul Sparks (Marty Potter a.k.a. Marvin Posey), Luther Creek (Eldon)

Reviewing the Case: A woman's abduction in Manhattan takes the detectives to a bucolic upstate hamlet. Is she still alive somewhere in this snowy rural enclave? Is her kidnapping the work of "The Bowery Stalker," who Munch failed to catch during a previous flurry of rape-torture crimes? The only surviving victim from that earlier time is reluctant to ID suspects in a lineup. And it's Canadians to the rescue, as New York cops and prosecutors cross the border in hot pursuit.

Noteworthy Discoveries: While forced to share a shabby motel room with Munch, Finn recalls the glory days of Narcotics undercover work in the lap of luxury and reveals that is former partner "took a bullet that was meant for me." Munch compares his previous job dealing with murders (in NBC's *Homicide: Life on the Street*) to the current task at SVU: "Little did I know it's the living victims that rip your guts out."

Relevant Testimony: "I had read about a 1993 Canadian serial killer case. (A wife helped her husband rape and murder young women, including her own sister—crimes that also inspired the 2000 Mother Ship episode 'Fools for Love.') And this seemed like an opportunity to slip in character development with Munch and Fin. I wanted to watch these guys who didn't like each other at first be cooped up together . . . I liked the idea of small town because I grew up in one, but we actually shot the episode in New Jersey."—Jeff Eckerle

Episode 41: Parasites

Original air date: April 27, 2001
Teleplay by Martin Weiss, directed by David Platt

Additional Cast: Mili Avital (Irina Burton/Ava Paroulis), Victor Steinbach (Razvan Toscu), Michele Pawk (Valentina Valescu), Matt Servitto (Dr. Brad Stanton), Melissa Bowen (Pamela Stanton), Gary Basaraba (George Burton), Michael Berresse (Matt Sloane), Lance Reddick (Dr. Taylor), Neal Ben-Ari (Dr. Lowenstein), Peter Van Wagner (Al Shipley), Yuka Takara (Mahlin Amos)

Reviewing the Case: After the discovery of a buried skull and other bones, a few false leads soon give way to a bleak scenario involving Eastern European immigrants. The remains appear to be those of a mail-order bride of ill repute who has been missing for several years. Her sister is married to an American and the mother of their young daughter. Toss in a shifty Romanian diplomat with a passion for growing orchids and this becomes a case complicated by international relations.

Relevant Testimony: "(Guest star) Mili Avital flew in from California on the Red Eye and had to shoot her last, most emotional scene first. She arrived at 6 A.M. and by 7 was in makeup."—David Platt

Episode 42: Pique

Original air date: May 4, 2001
Teleplay by Judith McCreary, directed by Steve Shill

Additional Cast: Margot Kidder (Grace Mayberry), Bruce MacVittie (Colin Tandy), Rob Bartlett (Milton Schoenfeld), Doris Belack (Arraignment Judge Margaret Barry), Terry Alexander (Security), Chad Lowe (Jason Mayberry), Martin Kildare (ADA Malcolm Sanderson), Robert Turano (Sgt. Fuller)

Reviewing the Case: "Pique," a title with a double meaning, dips into unsettling territory. A married woman's rape and murder sends the detectives on a quest to comprehend the mind of her former co-worker. He's a guy with several conflicting alibis. What they eventually understand—thanks to profiler Dr. George Huang, in his first appearance on the show—is a disturbing psychopathology that would have made Freud cringe.

Noteworthy Discoveries: Margot Kidder, already acting for a decade before her 1978 big-screen turn as Lois Lane in *Superman*, plays the mother of all dysfunctions in this episode.

Relevant Testimony: "I thought it was interesting that a sharp instrument represents a man's penis—Vlad, the Impaler—and that an act of intercourse can be violent if you look at it clinically. I found the reference in DSM 4 (*Diagnostic Social and Statistical Manual of Mental Disorders*), a book that most psychiatrists use. I've read it cover to cover. I wanted to explore outside conditions that contribute to mental illness."—Judith McCreary

Episode 43: Scourge

Original air date: May 11, 2001
Teleplay by Robert F. Campbell and Jonathan Greene, story by Neal Baer, directed by Alex Zakrzewski

Additional Cast: Karen Allen (Paula Varney), Richard Thomas (Daniel Varney), Frank Deal (ADA Don Newvine), David Chandler (Malcolm Hunt), Kevin O'Rourke (Sam Tiffany), Donna Mitchell (Mrs. Lindberg), Brian M. O'Neill (Sullivan), Jim Weston (Quentin Lindberg), Liza Lapira (Rebecca Chang), Tasha Lawrence (Honey the Hooker), Kes Kwansa (Kabral N'Cuma), Kofi Boakye (Sekou Obeng), Jack McCormack (Arson Capt. Malloy)

Reviewing the Case: Mental illness once again takes center stage, albeit from a distinctly different angle. Mutilated and murdered women, some of them hookers, spark a citywide panic about a modern-day Jack the Ripper on the loose. A frenzied mob even beats up an innocent man. Dr. Huang's profile points to a schizophrenic with possible religious delusions. That's just what Daniel Varney initially seems to be, though his estranged wife claims he's basically a gentle person. The truth about his condition prompts one of those stunning revelations that give so many *SVU* dramas their third-act pungency.

Noteworthy Discoveries: Karen Allen, the tough female lead in 1981's *Raiders of the Lost Ark*, and Richard Thomas, John Boy on *The Waltons* during the 1970s, are memorable guest stars in this harrowing season finale.

SEASON THREE

September 2001–May 2002

Regular Cast: Christopher Meloni (Det. Elliot Stabler), Mariska Hargitay (Det. Olivia Benson), Richard Belzer (Det. John Munch), Ice-T (Det. Odafin "Fin" Tutuola), Dann Florek (Capt. Donald Cragen), Stephanie March (ADA Alexandra Cabot); Tamara Tunie (M.E. Melinda Warner); B.D. Wong (Dr. George Huang)

Regular Recurring Cast: Ron Leibman (EADA Stan Villani), Daniel Sunjata (CSU Tech Burt Trevor), Judith Light (SVU Bureau Chief Elizabeth Donnelly), Joanna Merlin (Judge Lena Petrovsky), Tom O'Rourke (Arraignment Judge Mark Seligman)

SEASON THREE OVERVIEW: For its third season, *SVU* did some fine-tuning, with shifting character roles, a dialing back of personal life stories, and a fleshing-out of the district attorney's office. They've abandoned the "walk through doors" group shot from the first two seasons and now have the lead cast (Tutuola, Munch, Benson, Cragen, Stabler, Cabot) continue to pose in the squad room—and in this post-9/11 season, the World Trade Center's Twin Towers no longer appear in the opening cityscape, which is now shown in reverse angle. But the content changes are what give *SVU* its own personality, with some extremely compelling stories this season that challenge conventional wisdom—despite a few that overreach and just become too complicated. There's a flurry of B-list actors filling out the guest roles, which can inject some fun into the show, but they can also merely serve as a flag proclaiming "Here There Be Villains." All in all, a very good season despite some growing pains.

Ratings Recap for Season: 9.3 rating / 17 share / 13,499,000 viewers

EPISODE DESCRIPTIONS

Episode 44: Repression

Original air date: September 28, 2001
Teleplay by Marilyn Osborn, directed by Henry J. Bronchtein

Additional Cast: Shirley Knight (Dr. Warton), Amy Irving (Rebecca Ramsey), Brian Kerwin (Evan Ramsey), Kelly Hutchinson (Megan Ramsey), Blythe Auffarth (Jody Ramsey), José Zúñiga (Forensics Tech), George Hearn (Charles Southerland), Jim Frangione (Richard Weiss), Steven Mark Friedman (Attorney Willington), Sarah Hyland (Lily Ramsey)

Reviewing the Case: Intensive—and possibly questionable—therapy leads an unstable young Megan Ramsey to blame her father for raping her as a child. The case seems shaky, but a search of the home turns up kiddie porn in her youngest sister's room, and daddy is arrested. The porn turns into a setup—and then dad turns up dead, with all signs pointing to Megan. Suddenly, there's another side to the story, and in a classic "gotcha" ending, all eyes revert to Megan's therapist.

Noteworthy Discoveries: This episode is the first since the September 11, 2001 World Trade Center attacks, and the final sequence of the title credits (which once showed the Twin Towers) has been altered so that they do not appear.

Episode 45: Wrath

Original air date: October 5, 2001
Teleplay by Judith McCreary, directed by Jean de Segonzac

Additional Cast: Ben Gazzara (EADA), Justin Kirk (Eric Plummer), John Doman (Rod Franklin), Lee Shepherd (Mr. Platt), Richard Joseph Paul (Adam Cordell, Jr.), Ebony Jo-Ann (Mrs. Harding),

Divina Cook (Mrs. Barrantes), Orlagh Cassidy (Valerie Plummer), Trey Wilson (Bruce Derricks), Jernard Burks (Russell Williams), Denise Bessette (Janice), John Bianco (Victor Klaussen), Stephen Paul Johnson (Mr. Lawrence), Brent Meyer (Michael), Rob Leo Roy (Mr. Talbot), Irene Mazeski (Shirley)

Reviewing the Case: This time, the woman in peril is . . . Olivia! OK, so the episode isn't quite that sensationalistic, but when a former convict who Benson helped put away (wrongly, as it turns out) decides to exact a little revenge, things take a melodramatic spin. It all starts when three unexpected corpses turn up on a body farm (where corpses are studied scientifically), all connected to Benson's old cases. The detectives journey through her old files, and find a lot of bitterness, which puts Benson on edge. But once the right man is pinned down, he's got a secondary agenda—and he needs Benson to help him see it through.

Noteworthy Discoveries: The SVU station house is in Precinct 16, and Benson's badge number is 44015. Although in season one it seemed fairly clear that the Benson/Stabler partnership was relatively new, one of Benson's convicted perps had already been in jail for seven years. It's an unusual canonical change, in that prior and subsequent episodes seem to indicate Benson was new to SVU in season one, but writer Judith McCreary travels to the beat of her own backstory drummer.

Relevant Testimony: "I played it that (Benson) was in SVU (when the initial crime in this episode occurred), so that in season three she had been a sex crimes detective for seven years. If other writers aren't paying attention (to the canonical history I established), then it says more about them than it does me. I'm sure some of the audience pays attention to those details in a very anal way, but we're more interested in the undercurrents and personalities clashing in the workplace."—Judith McCreary

Episode 46: Stolen

Original air date: October 12, 2001
Teleplay by Jonathan Greene and Robert F. Campbell, directed by James Quinn

Additional Cast: Celia Weston (Margaret Talmadge), Bruce Altman (Mark Sanford), Ted King (Tony Derichek), Rob Bartlett (Milton Schoenfeld), John Seitz (Herbert Talmadge), Josh Pais (Attorney Robert Sorenson), Linda Cook (Susan Young), Charlotte Colavin (Judge Serani), Jen Albano (Alicia Brown), Elizabeth Hanly Rice (Linda Cook), Ian Cronin (Tyler Blake/Stephen Talmadge), Ellen Parker (Erin Blake), John Sloman (Adam Blake), David Aaron Baker (Robert Cook), Devid DeBeck (Attorney Stern), Adrienne Dreiss (Rebecca Reiter), Kerri Green (Michelle)

Reviewing the Case: The grocery store kidnapping of a baby leads detectives first to the tot, then to the unscrupulous attorney who bought her from a crack addict. But the self-serving lawyer seems legit—until his files reveal an old child kidnapping case Cragen had worked on once. With Munch's help, Cragen tracks down Stephen Talmadge, who is now twelve years old and living with unsuspecting adoptive parents, then Stephen's biological father, who never knew his son existed. Cabot tries to help make sure the custody issues fall the right way. But who killed baby Stephen's mother . . . and why?

Noteworthy Discoveries: It's always a pleasure to re-visit the 27th Precinct (home of the Mother Ship's squad room), even if just through Cragen's eyes: The cold case he pursues had originally been Sgt. Max Greevey's, from a 1989 *L&O*.

Episode 47: Rooftop

Original air date: October 19, 2001
Teleplay by Robert F. Campbell and Jonathan Greene, story by Neal Baer, Robert F. Campbell, and Jonathan Green, directed by Steve Shill

Notable Additional Cast and Guest Stars: Audrie Neenan (Judge Marilyn Haynes), Jill Marie Lawrence (Cleo Conrad), Asio Highsmith (Malik Harris), Todd Williams (Rodney Thompson), Mylika Davis (Shareen White), Brenda Thomas Denmark (Judge Elmore), Adriane Lenox (Alva Tate), Dorian Missick (Leon Tate), Malachi Weir (Tommy Epps), John Ottavino (Burt Ferris), Jack Landron

(Darnell French), Trish McCall (Angela Dupree), Jamilla M. Perry (Mashika Morris), Kahshanna Evans (Vanessa Hill)

Reviewing the Case: Underage black girls are being assaulted and killed in a series of rapes occurring on rooftops near where Det. Tutuola grew up. Ice-T is particularly effective as Fin straddles being from the 'hood and being The Man at the same time. Initially, Stabler's sure their perp is a recently paroled sex offender, but then he turns up dead and the rapes intensify. An attempt to defuse a mob gets Tutuola in trouble with Cragen, but getting the DNA on their suspect admitted in court is a whole other story.

Noteworthy Discoveries: Tutuola says he didn't grow up Brooklyn, but in the neighborhood where the rapes are taking place—the Bronx, presumably—and that he was six during the 1968 riots following the assassination of Dr. Martin Luther King.

Episode 48: Tangled

Original air date: October 26, 2001
Teleplay by Lisa Marie Petersen and Dawn DeNoon, directed by Jean de Segonzac

Additional Cast: Jordan Gelber (Fritz Kestler), Lisa Eichhorn (Peyton Kleberg), Tuck Milligan (Phillip Karr), Geoffrey Wigdor (Jesse Kleberg), Justin Hagen (Vincent "Vinnie" Boyd), Liza Weil (Lara Todd), Tracy Sallows (Judy Trahill), Jennifer Dorr White (Sharon Filmore), Paul Geier (Warner Mason), Steve Pickering (P.J. Voltz), Elisabeth Noone (Marilyn Dunlap), John-Luke Montias (Martin Welker), Matt Stinton (Steve Callahan)

Reviewing the Case: The Klebergs, a married couple, are beaten to death (the husband) and raped (the wife), which prompts SVU detectives to look at the array of love interests Max had at the hospital where he worked. One, a secretary named Lara, points to her downstairs criminal neighbor Vincent—but before the cops can tie the guy to anything, Lara shoots him—in self-defense, she says. There's something Lara is hiding, and it takes a convenient videotape to unravel the full extent of the crime. Unfortunately, this late-in-the-game red herring used to tie up the loose ends undercuts the drama.

Noteworthy Discoveries: Stabler has been married seventeen years.

Episode 49: Redemption

Original air date: November 2, 2001
Teleplay by Jeff Eckerle, directed by Ted Kotcheff

Additional Cast: David Keith (Det. John "Hawk" Hawkins), Michael Knight (David Stedman), Anne Pitoniak (Ethel Berry), Kevin Chamberlin (Roger Berry), Ken Marks (Arthur "Artie" Blessard), Elizabeth Hobgood (Beverly Parsons), Joe Costa (Warren Johnston), DeAnn Mears (Phyllis Johnston), Maggie Lacey (Jane Merrill), Sarah Knapp (Darcy Chaney)

Reviewing the Case: The convenient cure for Stabler's sudden existential job crisis is his old academy teacher John "Hawk" Hawkins, who has an M.O. match for two rape/murder/mutilation cases that have the SVU detectives chasing their tails. Eighteen years ago, Hawk put a man named Roger Berry away using coercive interrogation techniques for crimes just like this, but as they investigate Berry, it becomes clear that he is innocent this time—and was innocent before. It takes the unearthing of an eighteen-year-old corpse to help Benson and Stabler nab the real killer.

Christopher Meloni and David Keith (Det. John Hawk) arrest a perp in season three's "Redemption."

Noteworthy Discoveries: The characters of Hawk and Stabler, plus a hot pursuit across New York rooftops, give this episode a retro cop-show feel.

Relevant Testimony: "There was some talk about spinning the Hawk character off into another series, but nothing ever came of it. The genesis of this episode was news that authorities may have caught the wrong Boston Strangler. I thought, 'Jeez, imagine a cop who thinks he nailed a case but maybe ruined a man's life and even contributed to the deaths of others.'"—Jeff Eckerle

Episode 50: Sacrifice

Original air date: November 9, 2001
Teleplay by Javier Grillo-Marxuach and Samantha Howard Corbin, story by Javier Grillo-Marxuach, directed by Lesli Linka Glatter

Additional Cast: Mark-Paul Gosselaar (Wesley Jansen), Elizabeth Banks (Jaina Jansen), Tom Gilroy (Cal Oman), Mia Dillon (Georgia Jansen), Rob Bartlett (Milton Schoenfeld), Joseph Murphy (Ray Borland), Kevin Geer (Phil Casner), Dylan Chalfy (William Mueller), Joseph Latimore (Det. Steve Nathan), Jon Korkes (Terrence Moore), Luke Reilly (Chester Jansen), Lucy Martin (Arraignment Judge Wende Kremer), Juliette Dudnik (Delia Sarton), Audrey Twitchell (Mara Jansen)

Reviewing the Case: Although the husband is estranged from his family, the Jansens have been struggling to pay for their daughter's cystic fibrosis care. Unfortunately, they've been paying for it by doing porn, and when husband Wesley is shot their lives come crashing down. Detectives put pressure on this crock-pot of a situation, which means something else is bound to blow. It's a tightly wound, intriguing premise (with a nice change of pace in the gender of one of the true baddies)—despite a blank performance from Gosselaar.

Noteworthy Discoveries: Tutuola's narcotics background rears up appropriately again as he takes a personal interest in a junkie witness.

Episode 51: Inheritance

Original air date: November 16, 2001
Teleplay by Kathy Ebel, Michele Fazekas, and Tara Butters, story by Kathy Ebel, directed by Juan J. Campanella

Additional Cast: Marcus Chong (Darrell Guan), Diane Baker (Margot Nelson), Nelson Lee (Johnny Chen), Billy Chang (Det. Matt Tsu), Wai Ching Ho (Susan Guan), Sharrieff Pugh (Michael Tatum), Lance Reddick (Dr. Taylor), Harvey Atkin (Judge Alan Ridenour), Kevin Louie (Dao Tran), Danny Maseng (Dr. Randall Coffey), Ron Nakahra (Sammy Sing), Miou (Jiang Li), LaDonna Mabry (Martha Shelby), Arthur French (Harold Starnes), Mona Chiang (Sonja Yung), Lynn Chen (Helen Chen), Eliot Chang (Larry Tang), Denise Burse (Pamela Tatum)

Reviewing the Case: Though inevitable that old cases from the first series seem to get a retread here (in this instance, the issues nature vs. nurture and "evil genes" got an initial airing in 1993 on *Law & Order*'s "Born Bad"), it's not a good sign when *SVU* appears to be rerunning a story it just told. Once again, there are ethnic-specific rapes going on—in episode 47, "Rooftop," it was black girls; here it's Asian women—and a racially mixed man is fingered for the crimes, as his defense attorney pleads he has a defective, violent gene.

Noteworthy Discoveries: This is a strong episode for B.D. Wong's Dr. Huang, who explores a dark side of Asian subculture. But it's even more so for Benson, whose buttons are pushed during the investigation; and Mariska Hargitay underplays her reactions beautifully.

Episode 52: Care

Original air date: November 23, 2001
Teleplay by Dawn DeNoon and Lisa Marie Petersen, directed by Gloria Muzio

Additional Cast: Piper Laurie (Dorothy Rudd), Colin Fickes (Glenn Rudd), Jamie Goodwin (Danny Marston), Keith Davis (Duke Henry), Erika LaVonn (Tashandra Adams), Robin Moseley (Adoption

Agency Caseworker), Parris Nicole (Tanya Adams), Kathleen Wil-hoite (Jane Rudd)

Reviewing the Case: A young girl is murdered and left at a construction site while in the care of a seemingly model foster-parenting situation, and at first her computer-game-loving, mildly retarded foster brother appears to be hiding something. But when the foster girl's birth mother reclaims her other daughter from the home and points to the foster family of Jane and Dorothy Rudd as abusive, detectives have to consider that the system has failed again. This is a clever episode with any number of twists, but features a real misstep in the unreality of the courtroom scene, which focuses on just three people: Cabot, the defendant, and her accuser.

Noteworthy Discoveries: The appearance of three-time Oscar nominee Laurie is a clever bit of casting; some of her best-known roles feature the actress as an apparent innocent hiding a beast inside.

Episode 53: Ridicule

Original air date: December 14, 2001
Teleplay by Judith McCreary, directed by Constantine Makris

Additional Cast: Diane Neal (Amelia Chase), Paige Turco (Pam Adler), CCH Pounder (Carolyn Maddox), Dianne Wiest (DA Nora Lewin), Leslie Ayvazian (Arraignment Judge Valdera), Pete Star-rett (Peter Smith), Andrew Heckler (Andrew Green), David Adkins (Attorney Barry Fordes), Patrick Quinn (Milo Walther), Crista Moore (Mandy Guevere)

Reviewing the Case: One of the strengths of the L&O fran-chise has always been to take a controversial theory, then walk it through the narrative paces; here, that makes for compelling view-ing. An apparent accidental auto-erotic asphyxiation propels the investigation toward the assault on a male stripper, who cries rape following a bachelorette party. But while male detectives—including Stabler—scoff at the very idea, Cabot and Benson want to see the law applied equally and take the case to trial. Just as it seems everything is lost, new forensic evidence has detectives thinking they may have a murder case on their hands after all.

Noteworthy Discoveries: Diane Neal, who will go on to play ADA Casey Novak two years later following the departure of Stephanie March as Cabot, has a meaty role as an accused rapist with a sangfroid temperament. As this episode was written, New York's law on rape had recently changed its wording from "woman" to "person."

Relevant Testimony: "Previously, rape was considered different than sodomy. In my opinion, that was absurd. To this day, they laugh at men who say they've been raped. The thinking is that men have more upper body strength. But rape is more psychological than anything else."—Judith McCreary

Episode 54: Monogamy

Original air date: January 4, 2002
Teleplay by Michele Fazekas and Tara Butters, directed by Constantine Makris

Additional Cast: John Ritter (Dr. Richard Manning), Bobby Cannavale (Kyle Novacek), Erin Broderick (Maureen Stabler), Audrie J. Neenan (Judge Marilyn Haynes), Peter Hermann (Trevor Langan), Fernando Lopez (Ramone Vargas), Marianne Hagan (Erin Sena), Tricia Paoluccio (Nicole Manning), Starla Benford (Carol Daley)

Reviewing the Case: The show was on a roll with this second-in-a-row of two excellent episodes, both chasing down controversy to propel plot. At first John Ritter's wholesome Dr. Manning seems genuine in his grief after his pregnant wife is attacked and her baby cut out of her, then disposed of. Still, when the case goes to trial, it all hinges on whether the baby ever took a breath to determine if the attacker can be tried for murder or not.

Noteworthy Discoveries: This episode introduces Peter Hermann's Trevor Langan to the rotating cast of defense lawyers; he takes on a second major role as Mr. Mariska Hargitay a little over two years later.

Relevant Testimony: "I've always been the welcome committee to *SVU*. Peter (Hermann) came on and I was like, 'Wow.' Then it went on for like three months or so, this flirty checking-it-out. He didn't work (on the show) that often, and then we started dating and the rest is history."—Mariska Hargitay

Episode 55: Protection

Original air date: January 11, 2002
Teleplay by Jonathan Greene and Robert F. Campbell, directed by Alex Zakrzewski

Additional Cast: Fernando Lopez (Ramone Vargas), Elpidia Carrillo (Maria Ramos), Jean-Luke Figueroa (Luis Ramos), David Zayas (Det. Milton), Louie Leonardo (Fredo Garcia), Dylan Price (Det. Danny Tatum), Sevanne Martin (Nurse Lisa), Zabryna Guevara (Annie Colon), Teresa Yenque (Graciella Hernandez), Otto Sanchez (Eddie Fuentes), Susan Pellegrino (Dr. Barrett), Michael Mosley (Ronnie), Bill Golodner (Sgt. DaCosta), Al Espinosa (Andy Penza), Paul Baron (Kevin McDonald)

Reviewing the Case: It's never a good sign when cops in a L&O episode promise they'll protect innocents from the criminals they're trying to convict. Here, mother Maria Ramos leaves her injured son Miguel alone in the hospital, and detectives have to untangle a complex web to first track her down, then identify the too-close-for-comfort shooter, and finally convince her to testify against the suspect. But Maria decides to take matters into her own hands, with tragic results.

Noteworthy Discoveries: Belzer turns in a thoughtful, surprising performance when Munch "talks ten-year-old" to Maria's other son.

Relevant Testimony: "The idea is that it's over for now, but it may not really be over. This was about the difficulty of sometimes keeping witnesses safe, and what a witness goes through. They want to do the right thing, and sometimes they get driven from doing the right thing into doing the wrong thing, and it can cost you to do the right thing."—Jonathan Greene

Episode 56: Prodigy

Original air date: January 18, 2002
Teleplay by Lisa Marie Petersen and Dawn DeNoon, directed by Steve Shill

Additional Cast: Jill Marie Lawrence (Cleo Conrad), Michael Pitt (Harry Baker), Brian Sullivan (Joe Poletti), Robert Clohessy (Vinnie), Michele Pawk (Daisy Baker), Antonio D. Charity (Albert), Ellen Lancaster (Dr. Di Remegio), Michael X. Martin (Ned Rubens), Mariann Mayberry (Candy Forrester), Guthrie Nutter (Scotty Wells), Lenore Pemberton (Edie Jenks), Jacob Smith (Phillip Mahoe), Shaheen Vaaz (Shaheen Puniwar), Katie Walder (Corey Thorne)

Reviewing the Case: A young sociopath named Harry who likes tormenting animals and collecting their skulls seems an obvious lock on the death of an animal cruelty officer, but the evidence—and a tip-off from the suspect—leads them to a less juicy, but not less guilty, suspect. It's a case that twists and turns satisfyingly—at least until the final act, which is bound to leave viewers wondering about Stabler's detection abilities.

Relevant Testimony: "Harry is a serial killer in the making. So we used him like (Clarice Starling uses Hannibal Lecter in) *The Silence of the Lambs.* This guy has the thinking of a serial killer because he's going to be one. The kid knows our killer more than we do, because this kid is him (eventually)."—Dawn DeNoon

Episode 57: Counterfeit

Original air date: January 25, 2002
Teleplay by Amanda Green, directed by Arthur W. Forney

Additional Cast: Robert John Burke (IAB Sgt. Ed Tucker), Michael O'Keefe (Marcosi), Khrystyne Haje (Francesca Jesner), Paul Regina (Jeffery Trapani), Armand Schultz (Ragolia), Jenn Thompson (Mandy Mangun), Rochelle Bostrom (Samantha Ragolia), Gordon Joseph Weiss (Brandon O'Keefe), LeAnna Croom (Stacia Green), Billy Strong (Phil Urzi)

Reviewing the Case: An intriguing script brings the refreshing temporary partnership of Benson and Tutuola, who spar while overseeing two rapes and one rape/murder tied together by an alleged cop demanding sexual services in return for not arresting his victims. In a nice piece of misdirection, however, the most recognizable guest star is not the perp, and detectives have to look outside the blue wall to chase down their man. But can they get to him before he kills his latest victim—who he "arrested" straight from her own home?

Noteworthy Discoveries: Munch, a hypochondriac, shows up with a bum foot injured while skydiving. Tutuola has an eighteen-year-old child. Green, who heretofore had been the series technical advisor, contributes her first script. She will quickly move up the ladder to co-executive producer.

Episode 58: Execution

Original air date: February 1, 2002
Teleplay by Judith McCreary, directed by Alex Zakrzewski

Additional Cast: William Hill (Allen Cooper), Laura Hughes (Hannah Cooper), Heather MacRae (Andrea Mason), Ty Burrell (Alan Messinger), Nick Chinlund (Matt Brodus), Timothy Wheeler (Robert Rule), Anthony Chisholm (Leroy Russell), Glynis Bell (Judge Whitemore), Martin Kildare (Wade Harris)

Reviewing the Case: In this format-altering story, Stabler and Huang race against the clock to tie an about-to-be-executed serial killer in New Jersey to a decade-old crime against another likely victim, but no one in their path is very helpful. It's an intriguing premise, to start off more or less at what would normally be the end, but does reduce the tension throughout the rest of the episode: Since viewers know they interview the killer, who attacks Huang and Stabler, just how they get there becomes a few shades less compelling.

Noteworthy Discoveries: As with episode 57, "Counterfeit," one of the lead detectives (in this case, Benson) has virtually no face time. Stabler reveals that his former partner killed himself after not being able to solve the case they are now pursuing. It isn't clear if they were partners at the time. This episode's format change enhances the storytelling.

Relevant Testimony: "The teaser is actually the climax, then we start at the beginning. But we don't actually find out (the cops') worst fears have been realized until the end of the show. They realize the guy won't outright confess—he wants the guard to beat him, because no state will execute an unhealthy man. Which is the dumbest thing I ever heard in my life."—Judith McCreary

Episode 59: Popular

Original air date: March 1, 2002
Teleplay by Stephen Belber, story by Kathy Ebel and Belber, directed by Jean de Segonzac

Additional Cast: Isabel Gillies (Kathy Stabler), Brittany Slattery (Cynthia Wilmont), Christopher Orr (Ross McKenzie), Billy Kay (Tommy Kessler), Jason Fuchs (Nick Radsen), Elena Franklin (Amy Bergen), William Charlton (Principal Charest), Allison Siko (Kathleen Stabler), Laura Interval (Darlene Wilmont), Ned Luke (Mr. Wilmont), Myra Lucretia Taylor (Principal), Craig Woe (James Woodrow), Scott Geyer (Mr. Bergen), Christy Baron (Mrs. Bergen), Sprague Grayden (Mia Kessler), Laura Marie Duncan (Carol Porter)

Reviewing the Case: A comment from Stabler's wife Kathy sends the detective searching for a fourteen-year-old rape victim who doesn't want to come forward, and what he and the other detectives learn is that some boys pimp their girlfriends even in middle school, and that oral sex isn't "really sex." The episode reveals a seamier underbelly to being popular than anyone wants to believe, which at the same time makes this an uncomfortably realistic tale of a very bad love triangle.

Noteworthy Discoveries: This is the first episode with Siko as Kathleen, previously played by Holiday Segal.

Episode 60: Surveillance

Original air date: March 8, 2002
Teleplay by Jeff Eckerle, directed by Steve Shill

Additional Cast: Emily Deschanel (Cassie Germaine), Peter Hermann (Trevor Langan), Rob Bogue (Kevin Wilson), Nate Mooney (Terry Willard), Lena Georgas (Valerie Baxter), Michael Nader (Robert Prescott), Michael Lewis Wells (Paul), Max Leavitt (Jeff Doolittle), Susan Pellegrino (Dr. Barrett), Wayne Pretlow (Ralph Grady), Joseph Adams (Ray Campbell), Jennifer Laura Thompson (Aimee Slocum)

Reviewing the Case: When a cellist is attacked in her apartment, investigators turn up hidden cameras—and the hidden love life of a tech-savvy stalker, who has set up his own shrine and Internet Web cam devoted to her. But after the musician is later shot, Benson and Stabler are left chasing the stalker and his actual girlfriend, while discovering that sometimes one sickness attracts another, even darker version. A harrowing and smart episode with a shocker of an ending.

Noteworthy Discoveries: This is an early performance by Emily Deschanel, sister of Zooey, who went on to the lead role in Fox's *Bones* in 2005. And soap fans should enjoy the appearance of a blond Michael Nader, who played the dark-haired Dimitri Marick on *All My Children*.

Relevant Testimony: "We were concerned all the bells and whistles (the gizmos used in the script) might take over the story. There are two sides to the coin, of course: Catch the cretins, but at what cost? From a writer's perspective, sometimes you bend yourself like a pretzel to service the technology in an episode."—Jeff Eckerle

Episode 61: Guilt

Original air date: March 29, 2002
Teleplay by Michele Fazekas and Tara Butters, directed by David Platt

Additional Cast: Ned Eisenberg (Roger Kressler), Beau Gravitte (Roy Barnett), Kay Lenz (Linda Cavanaugh), Bret Harrison (Sam

Cavanaugh), Lee Pace (Benjamin Tucker), Thomas Piper (Tommy Priore), Don Sparks (Dr. Phil Mitrano)

Reviewing the Case: It's a rule of law, or maybe just of *Law & Order* episodes: At some point, every major character will find a case that pushes his or her buttons and will do Whatever It Takes to secure justice. This time, it's Cabot's turn as she does her damnedest, including shading the truth on a warrant, to put a serial molester who lures adolescent boys behind bars for good. March (Cabot) is excellent, but gets upstaged by the introduction of Judith Light as SVU Bureau Chief Elizabeth Donnelly, who may just be the ballsiest character the franchise has ever invented—male or female.

Noteworthy Discoveries: Light's introduction lends depth to the DA's office and helps avoid the revolving door of otherwise unimportant EADAs to whom Cabot must report.

Relevant Testimony: "It was a group decision to have a bureau chief. We'd used Fred Thompson (who played District Attorney Arthur Branch on *L&O* at the time) and Dianne Wiest (DA Nora Lewin prior to Thompson), but it was hard to schedule them in. The *SVU* prosecution needed its own boss."—Michele Fazekas

Episode 62: Justice

Original air date: April 5, 2002
Teleplay by Lisa Marie Petersen and Dawn DeNoon, directed by Juan J. Campanella

Additional Cast: Keir Dullea (Judge Thornburg), Kathleen Goldpaugh (Sister Kay), Cloie Wyatt Taylor (Mary Elizabeth), Valerie Mahaffey (Brooke Thornburg), Michael Luggio (Tony Degalio), Bonnie Dennison (Heather Porter), Myk Watford (Tommy), Gina Nagy (Sharlene Degalio), Libby George (Beth Fischer), Jana Robbins (Emily Porter)

Reviewing the Case: A teenage girl who cries rape—and then dies from a head wound—turns out to be the troubled stepdaughter of a prominent judge in this initially interesting, but ultimately flat episode. Her death leads detectives to wonder first how the teen was connected to her rapist and killer, and then to figure out just what was making her act out so severely. Unfortunately, Cragen (a long-time friend of the judge) comes to learn that unhappiness starts at home.

Noteworthy Discoveries: In "Sophomore Jinx" (season one, episode 6), Cragen indicates his alma mater was St. Raymond's. In this episode, he says he and the judge attended St. John's. This contradictory information was a canonical mistake. Keir Dullea burst onto the scene playing an unlucky astronaut in the legendary *2001: A Space Odyssey* (1968).

Episode 63: Greed

Original air date: April 26, 2002
Teleplay by Jonathan Greene and Robert F. Campbell, directed by Constantine Makris

Additional Cast: Roy Thinnes (Curtis Johansen), Mary Beth Hurt (Jessica Blaine Todd), Henry Winkler (Edwin Todd), Rob Bartlett (Milton Schoenfeld), David Lipman (Judge Arthur Cohen), Sherri Parker Lee (Denise Johansen), Alex Feldman (Danny Ryan), Sarah Knowlton (Valerie Emerson), Michael Aronov (Andrei Gorsky), John Leone (Randy Taylor), Etya Dudko (Katarina Dinov), Nicolas Glaeser (Harold Karaka)

Reviewing the Case: Two similar burglary-rapes in a high-income neighborhood turn out to have a surprising connection: A pair of con artists interested in bilking their respective spouses. But when the scammers admit their crimes, spousal privilege kicks in, which makes prosecuting them impossible. At least, until a foreign credit card receipt gives detectives a second chance at making their case in a final act of legal hoop-jumping handled deftly by the script.

Noteworthy Discoveries: The episode pops with familiar faces, including Roy Thinnes, who played *L&O*'s original district attorney, Alfred Wentworth, in the 1990 pilot, "Everybody's Favorite Bagman," (which aired as the Mother Ship's sixth episode).

Episode 64: Denial

Original air date: May 3, 2002
Teleplay by Judith McCreary, directed by Steve Shill

Additional Cast: Martha Plimpton (Claire Rinato), Estelle Parsons (Rose Rinato), Mary Steenburgen (Grace Rinato), Michael Knowles (Arthur Felton), Sam Guncler (Gary Barbour), Danny Johnson (Sean Kramer), Andrew Polk (Dr. Phillip Devere)

Reviewing the Case: The discovery of a raped drug addict, Claire Rinato, is only the catalyst to open the closet on her troubled family history. Detectives investigate and learn that she is carrying the mummified finger of her sister, who died as a toddler—and who Claire says was killed by their narcissistic mother, Grace. But Grace is quick to, well, point the finger at Claire, saying she killed the baby in a jealous rage. Still there's even a third generation in Grandma Rose, who knows the rest of the story—and she's the most unreliable of all.

Noteworthy Discoveries: Martha Plimpton received an Emmy nomination for her role as Claire, which is amplified by Ice-T's heartfelt stoic performance. Tutuola's badge number is 43198.

Episode 65: Competence

Original air date: May 20, 2002
Teleplay by Jonathan Greene and Robert F. Campbell, story by Campbell, Greene, and Jeff Eckerle, directed by Jud Taylor

Additional Cast: Ned Eisenberg (Roger Kressler), Peter Hermann (Trevor Langan), Harvey Atkin (Judge Alan Ridenour), Jason Pensky (Andy McCollum), Ezra Knight (Kevin Caldwell), Darren Pettie (Joe Parker), Ray Fitzgerald (Ray Dunstan), C.J. Wilson (Scott Lucas), Matt DeCaro (Abe Cheney), Lois Smith (Rebecca Tolliver), Andrea Fay Friedman (Katie Tolliver), Badge Dale (Danny Jordan)

Reviewing the Case: A high-functioning young woman with Down syndrome is pregnant, and her overprotective mother cries rape. But trying to break through the layers of maternal "helicopter" and the young woman's naiveté about what sex actually is hampers the case—as does a competency hearing once mom decides she wants her daughter to have an abortion. Cabot comes up with a clever way to make sure the perpetrator pays for his crime—even if he never goes to jail.

Noteworthy Discoveries: Stabler's twins are eight. Cabot is childless. In real life and in this episode, guest star Andrea Fay Friedman has Down syndrome and she's an intriguing, unusual heroine.

Episode 66: Silence

Original air date: May 17, 2002
Teleplay by Patrick Harbinson, directed by Steve Shill

Additional Cast: Eric Stoltz (Father Michael Sweeney), Jayne Houdyshell (Judge Linden), Ned Eisenberg (Roger Kressler), Kris Eivers (Gus Yoder), Nance Williamson (Lara Retafian), Hardy Rawls (Det. Jimmy Moresco), Edward O'Blenis (Darius Retafian), Davis Sweatt (Todd Ramsay), Jordan Charney (Rory O'Halloran), Patrick Collins (Bishop Mallinson), Sean Dugan (Bobby Douglas), Robert Harte (Ben Campion),

Reviewing the Case: There's no keeping a juicy secret hidden forever in *SVU*-land, so when a transvestite is found murdered next to a smoldering confessional by resident priest Father Michael, the killing is fairly easily solved: It was an accidental slaying by Bobby, a vindictive former victim (or so it seems) of Michael's. But while he's a pedophile whose crimes were covered up by the Church, Michael never actually touched Bobby—he just failed to protect him from a much higher authority. Despite the subject matter, this season-ender lacks a compelling center.

Noteworthy Discoveries: Stabler is Catholic, and his son has recently become an altar boy.

SEASON FOUR

September 2002–May 2003

Regular Cast: Christopher Meloni (Det. Elliot Stabler), Mariska Hargitay (Det. Olivia Benson), Richard Belzer (Det. John Munch),

Ice-T (Det. Odafin "Fin" Tutuola), Dann Florek (Capt. Donald Cragen), Stephanie March (ADA Alexandra Cabot), Tamara Tunie (M.E. Warner), and B.D. Wong (Dr. George Huang)

Recurring Cast: Judith Light (SVU Bureau Chief Elizabeth Donnelly), Isabel Gillies (Kathy Stabler), Peter Hermann (Trevor Langan), Sheila Tousey (Judge Danielle Larson), Harvey Atkin (Judge Alan Ridenour), Tom O'Rourke (Judge Mark Seligman), Joanna Merlin (Judge Lena Petrovsky), Joel de la Fuente (TARU Tech Ruben Morales), Caren Browning (CSU Capt. Judith Siper), Daniel Sunjata (CSU Tech Burt Trevor), Lou Carbonneau (CSU Tech), Welly Yang (CSU Tech Georgie), Jordan Gelber (CSU Tech Layton)

SEASON FOUR OVERVIEW: This season's maturing *SVU* was a veritable guest stars-a-go-go. Apparently feeling comfortable in its own skin, the show invited more than twenty legendary, famous, or at least well-respected actors to appear in key roles over the course of two dozen episodes. From Jane Powell to Frank Langella to Illeana Douglas, the luminaries—playing victims or suspects or defense attorneys—added a distinct glow to some of the darkest topics imaginable. Meanwhile, the core cast did not change and this stability gave the series a safe harbor. In examining difficult subject matter, there's some degree of comfort seeing the same faces from week to week. The cases make the stomach churn, with pornographers, pedophiles, psychopaths and prostitutes among the leading contenders, followed closely by corrupt cops and calculating corporations.

Ratings Recap for Season: 9.4 rating / 17 share / 13,772,000 viewers

EPISODE DESCRIPTIONS

Episode 67: Chameleon

Original Air Date: September 22, 2002
Teleplay by Michele Fazekas and Tara Butters, directed by Jean de Segonzac

Additional Cast: Dianne Wiest (DA Nora Lewin), Sharon Lawrence (Maggie Peterson), Charlayne Woodard (Sister Peg), Lonette McKee (Meredith Greer), Dwandra Nickole (Mrs. Kerber), Magaly Colimon (Dr. Erica Olsen), Jurian Hughes (Krista Bertram), James Biberi (de Ricco), Lair Torrent (Cabrera), Sara Ramirez (Lisa Perez), David Lipman (Judge Arthur Cohen), Kent Cassella (Det. Palmieri)

Reviewing the Case: When prostitutes are sexually assaulted and murdered, the detectives pinpoint a known predator recently released from Attica. But a call girl who identifies herself as Deborah subsequently shoots him, supposedly in self-defense. Then she flees the hospital and her gun matches one used in a homicide committed six months earlier. Deborah is actually Maggie, either a traumatized victim or a conniving serial killer with a young son. Sharon Lawrence (from ABC's *NYPD Blue*) plays a reptilian character, fun to watch on TV but dreadful to know in real life.

Noteworthy Discoveries: This episode also features Sister Peg, a plainclothes nun who works to keep working girls safe. She seems to reappear on the series at least once a season.

Episode 68: Deception

Original Air Date: October 4, 2002
Teleplay by Michele Fazekas and Tara Butters, directed by Constantine Makris

Additional Cast: Sherilyn Fenn (Gloria Stanfield), Jill Marie Lawrence (Cleo Conrad), Harvey Atkin (Judge Alan Ridenour), Frank Grillo (Frank Barbarosa), Jonathan Bennett (Kyle Fuller), Gerry Bamman (Schaeffer), Darcy Pulliam (Fullers' Housekeeper), Jennifer Michelle Brown (Chloe Fuller), Tom Mason (Lawrence Fuller), Amy Bouril (Emily Savage), Melissa Murray (Vivianne Hendrix)

Reviewing the Case: Gloria, a self-involved actress, is sleeping with her seventeen-year-old step-son Kyle. His little sister caught them in the act and a housekeeper witnessed an inappropriate kiss. But who beat Gloria's husband to death? The startling revelations keep on coming: She's pregnant, has been raped by her personal trainer/lover, and the baby is not Kyle's! Yet another lethal chapter in the lifestyles of the rich and famous.

Noteworthy Discoveries: Sherilyn Fenn first gained national attention on ABC's eerie *Twin Peaks* (1990).

Relevant Testimony: "(Showrunner) Neal Baer is a big fan of (1940s and '50s big-screen siren) actress Gloria Grahame. She was married to the director Nick Ray and he caught her in bed with his teenage son. Years later, she married the kid. Neal's point was that if you marry a stepchild, that's not illegal, so there's nothing the law can do about it."—Michele Fazekas

Episode 69: Vulnerable

Original Air Date: October 11, 2002
Teleplay by Lisa Marie Petersen and Dawn DeNoon, directed by Juan J. Campanella

Additional Cast: Mary Kay Place (Hope Garrett), Jay Thomas (Joe Sherman), Jane Powell (Bess Sherman), Tom O'Rourke (Judge Mark Seligman), Andy Powers (Hal Shipley), Elaine Kussack (Lois), Leo Leyden (Leonard), Marilyn Raphael (Darlene), Arthur French (Jackson), Ryan Patrick Bachand (Andy Sherman), Patricia R. Floyd (Lori Helen Loy), Jason Weinberg (Attorney for Garrett)

Reviewing the Case: A senor citizen with Alzheimer's has been an unwitting cash cow for her son and grandson, but they may not be the perps who burned her with cigarettes. The detectives take a closer look at the assisted-living facility where she's relegated. There, the self-aggrandizing manager and an arrogant aide join the ensemble of obnoxious suspects. "Vulnerable" presents a strong argument for never growing old.

Noteworthy Discoveries: Septuagenarian Jane Powell, a charming star from Hollywood's Golden Age, makes a rare television appearance. Ever the dispenser of obscure pathologies, Dr. Huang describes something known as "malignant hero syndrome."

Episode 70: Lust

Original Air Date: October 18, 2002
Teleplay by Amanda Green, directed by Michael Fields

Additional Cast: Michael Gross (Arthur Esterman), James Doerr (Vartan Dadian), Kate Levering (Kate), Brian Rogalski (Roger Pomerantz), Jamie Sorrentini (Vincenza Agosto), Barbara Dana (Veterinary Tech Carol), Eric Michael Gillett (Dr. Portugal), Mike Babel (Brad), Christine Toy Johnson (Health Commissioner Chung)
Reviewing the Case: The Central Park rape-murder of a public-health physician might be related to her controversial research on the exposure patterns of people with HIV, work for which she was previously threatened. Her distraught husband seems eager to help the investigation, but tries to attack a big bruiser detained for questioning. A narcissistic AIDS patient who has willfully infected various partners is another suspect. Viewers are likely to guess the outcome, but enjoy all the shenanigans along the way.

Episode 71: Disappearing Acts

Original Air Date: October 25, 2002
Teleplay by Judith McCreary, directed by Alex Zakrzewski

Additional Cast: Pam Grier (Claudia Williams), Michael Kelly (Mark), Joe Maruzzo (Joe Tucci), John Heard (Peter Sipes), Thomas Guiry (Gavin Sipes), Caprice Benedetti (Amanda Curry), Grigory Gurevich (Sergei Perlman), John Henry Redwood (Judge Ernest Volpe), Barbara McCulloh (Lynn Moody), Michael Bolus (Michael Kerring)
Reviewing the Case: This is about as close to a classic police procedural as any *SVU* episode gets. The rape of an unscrupulous corporate executive leads to a man with ties to the Russian mob and his troubled son. The detectives lock horns with Claudia Williams, a U.S. Attorney. Benson and Stabler find their careers on the line from simply trying to do their jobs.
Noteworthy Discoveries: Stabler earns $68,940 a year. While being held by the Feds for seventy-two hours without access

to a lawyer, he's told this previously illegal time frame is "fallout from 9/11."

Relevant Testimony: "Every federal agency is under the umbrella of Homeland Security and none of them like to share information with local cops. And it's a numbers game for funding. They don't give a damn about getting drugs off the streets; they just want the money. . . . There are no more cartels. They operate now like terror cells—independent, nobody knows anybody else. But the Russian mob is still around."—Judith McCreary

Episode 72: Angels

Original Air Date: November 1, 2002
Teleplay by Jonathan Greene and Robert Campbell, directed by Arthur W. Forney

Additional Cast: Will Arnett (Tony Damon), Michael Hayden (Dr. Walt Massey), Pablo Santos (Ernesto Diaz), Kate Skinner (Laura Massey), Glenn Fleshler (Dr. Noah Kamon), Mike Hodge (Port Authority Supervisor), Gideon Jacobs (Shawn Massey), Patrick Cassidy (Dr. Stewart Lynch)

Reviewing the Case: When the body of an abused Hispanic boy is discovered in the luggage compartment of a bus, his good dental work provides an important clue. The apprehension of his Guatemalan friend leads detectives to the dead Wall Street lawyer who kept both kids locked up as sex slaves. His death, in turn, points to an extensive pedophile ring aided by a sleazy travel agent specializing in Central American sex tours.

Noteworthy Discoveries: "They operate in cells, like Al-Qaeda," Munch says of the well-organized pedophiles. He poses as a tourist with prurient interests.

Relevant Testimony: "God bless that child actor (Pablo Santos). He died in a plane crash in Mexico a few years later."—Arthur Forney

Episode 73: Dolls

Original Air Date: November 8, 2002
Teleplay by Amanda Green, directed by Darnell Martin

Additional Cast: Gloria Reuben (Violet Tremain), David Harbour (Terry Jessup), Barbara Andres (Eleanor Marshall), Ileen Getz (Mrs. Preston), Geoffrey Owens (Forensic Anthropologist), Cynthia Mace (Community Center Director), Susan Misner (Ronnie Marshall), Conan McCarty (Mike Flecker), Frank Medrano (Jake), Capathia Jenkins (Thelma Price), Michael Alexis Palmer (Peter Jackson), Ron Lee Jones (Rev. Allastair)

Reviewing the Case: A decomposing victim, dead for about eight weeks, is dubbed "Cherish Doe." A publicized forensic anthropologist's reconstruction of her face brings no tips, however. But a suspect named Violet, in rehab when her little daughter Nina disappeared, works with detectives to find what may be a serial pedophile. In the care of an elderly neighbor who died, Nina slipped through the cracks thanks to a negligent caseworker in an overwhelmed system. The perp, a man damaged by the demons of his own awful childhood, continues the circle of misery.

Relevant Testimony: "Part of that episode was based on a real tragic case out of Kansas City. 'Precious Doe' was (unidentified) skeletal remains that had been found . . . At the time in Florida, overworked caseworkers never bothered to follow up on a little girl who was living with this very crazy foster mother. Sadly, years after we did that show, they identified Precious Doe and it was her mother and her mother's boyfriend who killed her. And Florida overhauled its entire child welfare system after the case there."—Amanda Green

Episode 74: Waste

Original Air Date: November 15, 2002
Teleplay by Dawn DeNoon and Lisa Marie Petersen, directed by Donna Deitch

Additional Cast: Philip Bosco (Davis Langley), Bruce Davison (Dr. Mandell), JoBeth Williams (Mrs. Rawley), Rainn Wilson (Baltzer), Jill Marie Lawrence (Cleo Conrad), David Lipman (Judge Arthur Cohen), Rob Bartlett (Milton Schoenfeld), Judy Gold (Forensic Gynecologist), Henry Woronicz (Rawley), Steve Key (Wesley Dilbert), Lisa Pelikan (Dr. Garrison), Ian Kahn (David Anderson)

Reviewing the Case: Stephanie is pregnant, but has been left in a persistent vegetative state for the past year following a car accident. There are several suspects: Her fiancé, who often sneaks in the rehab center to visit her; her physician; a physical therapist; a janitor; and a mortician. But the surprising identity of the "father" taps into to a stirring debate about medical ethics, stem cell research, abortion, and the justice system's many gray areas.

Noteworthy Discoveries: Philip Bosco, a frequent guest star on the Mother Ship, shines as a man battling an incurable disease. Dr. Huang's question to Cabot: "You mean I could go to jail for stealing a toaster but not a woman's egg?"

Relevant Testimony: "We won an Edgar for 'Waste,' and I left the award at the cocktail reception. I have it now. It's not a pretty award, it's a bust of Edgar Allan Poe, not a gorgeous man, but still I was happy to get it."—Dawn DeNoon

Episode 75: Juvenile

Original Air Date: November 22, 2002
Teleplay by Michele Fazekas and Tara Butters, directed by Constantine Makris

Additional Cast: Illeana Douglas (Gina Bernardo), William H. Burns (Narcotics Officer), Becky Ann Baker (Mrs. Brice), Shane E. Lyons (Jeremy Brice), Connor Paolo (Zachary Connor), Jonathan Walker (Connor), Richard Topol (Dr. Hayman), Lisa Emery (Mary Ellen Lesinski), Toby Poser (Mrs. Connor), Robert Turano (Alfonso Corrales), Alysia Reiner (Cindy Kerber), Kyle Gallner (Marc Lesinski), Tony DeVito (Vincent Paglione)

Reviewing the Case: When 'tweens are involved in the rape-murder of a woman who runs a marijuana club for sick people, cops and prosecutors are stymied. At thirteen, one kid can legally be tried as an adult despite his extreme immaturity, while a twelve-year-old is probably a psychopath but only has to appear in family court. Complex legal maneuvers are unable to skirt a wrenching decision for everyone concerned.

Relevant Testimony: "I have a real problem with trying juveniles as adults. Even if you sound like an adult, you're a kid. . . . The idea for that episode came from Neal (Baer), who gave us a study and said, 'Do something on this topic.'"—Michele Fazekas

Episode 76: Resilience

Original Air Date: December 6, 2002
Teleplay by Patrick Harbinson, directed by Joyce Chopra

Additional Cast: Illeana Douglas (Gina Bernardo), Leslie Ayvazian (Judge Valdera), Jill Marie Lawrence (Cleo Conrad), Anna Berger (Karen's Grandmother), Drew McVety (James Randall), Justine Caputo (Sally Landricks), Cynthia Ettinger (Angie Landricks), Rachael Bella (Jackie Landricks), Titus Welliver (Tom Landricks), Billy Lush (Karl Serrit)

Reviewing the Case: After a distraught teenager tries to jump in front of a subway train, the detectives learn that the girl lives in a household from hell. She claims to have been kidnapped and raped by strangers, but the sexual abuse is far more twisted than that. Her seemingly normal parents may carry the notion of family love way beyond appropriate boundaries.

Noteworthy Discoveries: Munch and Fin have the unenviable assignment of spying on a young man's private parts while he stands at a urinal. In another of his always interesting psychiatric assessments, Dr. Huang describes a victim's mental state: "Regression in service to the ego." The episode takes its cues from the real-life case in England of Fred and Rosemary West.

Relevant Testimony: "There had been thirteen years of serial killings of adolescent women, many of whom entered into sadomasochistic relationships with Fred and Rosemary West. Some of their children wrote books about it. I wondered: 'How do you survive that?' . . . Some inner strength sustained the kids through their horrible journey."—Patrick Harbinson

Episode 77: Damaged

Original Air Date: January 10, 2003
Teleplay by Barbie Kligman, directed by Juan J. Campanella

Additional Cast: Erik Palladino (Dave Deuthorn), Max Vogel (Dr. Daniel Foster), David Bryant (Curtis), Mark Kachersky (Arthur Campbell), Keira Naughton (Sarah), George L. Smith (John Marcum), Ned Eisenberg (Roger Kressler), Dan Lauria (Peter Kurtz), Michael Gaston (Malcolm Field), Ari Graynor (Missy Kurtz), Glynnis O'Connor (Raquel Kurtz), Christopher Denham (Joey Field)

Reviewing the Case: An apparent video-store robbery goes bad when the masked thief kills innocent bystanders; the clerk then shoots him. Among the victims is six-year-old Rebecca, whose teenage stepsister seems genuinely distraught. But the little girl, on life-support, is a rape victim with gonorrhea. Who's to blame—her father, the family doctor, someone at school? This episode could easily have been titled "The Bad Seed," as it hurtles toward an unanticipated conclusion.

Episode 78: Risk

Original Air Date: January 17, 2003
Teleplay by Robert F. Campbell and Jonathan Greene, directed by Juan J. Campanella

Additional Cast: Robert John Burke (Ed Tucker), Matt Mulhern (Brad Kendall), Joe Murphy (Keith Gerard), Bryan Callen (Derek Pfeiffer), Paul Diomede (Frank Barry), Erica Tazel (Lynn Hauser), Robert Funaro (Philly Panzaretti), Laurie J. Williams (Laura Pfeiffer), Katherine Cunningham Eves (Mother), Maria Elena Ramirez (Abby)

Reviewing the Case: A few years before tainted products from China began showing up on the American market with regularity, *SVU* zeroed in on cocaine masquerading as baby food. But "Risk" is not actually about the dangers of globalization. Instead, the infant who dies from eating drug-laced formula alerts the squad to an international narcotics operation. Stabler goes undercover as a Wall Street–type to smoke out a bad cop involved with a smuggling ring that reaches into Mexico.

Noteworthy Discoveries: Benson wears a low-cut black dress and Stabler, in wire-rim glasses, an expensive suit to pose as customers at a bar where the high-end drug trade flourishes.

Relevant Testimony: "Baby formula comes with its own set of rules and regulations. . . . I think when we did this episode my daughter had just been born."—Jonathan Greene

Episode 79: Rotten

Orignal Air Date: January 24, 2003
Teleplay by Judith McCreary, directed by Constantine Makris

Additional Cast: William Mapother (Off. Luke Edmunds), Terry Serpico (Les Cooper), Peter Hermann (Trevor Langan), Joie Lee (Prison Nurse), Robert Stanton (P.B.A. Representative), Agustin Rodriguez (Hector Ramirez), Jason Catalano (Randall Grant), Gene Canfield (John Royce), Johnny Pruitt (Andrew Pennington), A.B. Lugo (Jose Ortega), Amy Landecker (Stephanie Grayson), Nathan A. Perez (Nathan Duarte), Jose Pablo Cantillo ("Willie" Angel)

Reviewing the Case: Grisly jailhouse culture is briefly explored before "Rotten" takes to the streets to look at drug dealers, disgruntled prison guards, corrupt city cops, and prosecutorial schemes. When a lowlife dies in the Tombs after being sodomized, SVU detectives follow a trail of evidence that snakes around several potential scenarios for the murder. The high command hopes to close the case quickly, sweeping inconvenient facts under the rug, but Benson perseveres in finding the truth.

Noteworthy Discoveries: This episode clearly takes inspiration from the 1997 attack on Abner Louima, a Haitian immigrant tortured by several Brooklyn police officers. Actor William Mapother, one of the creepy Others on ABC's *Lost*, is Tom Cruise's cousin. Joie Lee is director Spike Lee's sister.

Relevant Testimony: "All the rights are with the defendant in this system. If you put on a uniform, you're a target . . . The 'blue wall of silence' is designed to protect them. It's not malevolent in its intent, though it can be abused."—Judith McCreary

Episode 80: Mercy

Original Air Date: January 31, 2003
Teleplay by Christos N. Gage and Ruth C. Fletcher, directed by David Platt

Additonal Cast: Judd Hirsch (Dr. Judah Platner), Larry Bryggman (Attorney Rowan), Sheila Tousey (Judge Danielle Larson), Elizabeth Mitchell (Andrea Brown), Viola Davis (Donna Emmett), Gregg Edelman (Daniel Brown), Stephen Schnetzer (Rabbi), Ned Luke (Roger Swanson), Heather Goldenhersh (Ellen Swanson), Nathalie Paulding (Patty Swanson), Keno Rider (Dr. Klein), Gerry Rosenthal (Paul Howley), Allison Briner (Colleen Swanson), Michael Deeg (Frank Savvas)

Reviewing the Case: When a baby washes up in the Hudson River, a lethal dose of anti-depressants is determined as the cause of death. After a disagreement between Cabot and Bureau Chief Donnelly about privacy rights, detectives query students at a nearby college who have been pregnant and a fifteen-year-old who got an abortion. The fact that the infant showed signs of Tay-Sachs Disease narrows down the search to a particular woman and her pediatrician.

Noteworthy Discoveries: Elizabeth Mitchell is yet another *SVU* guest star who went on to become a regular on ABC's *Lost*. Judd Hirsch later signed on to the CBS series *Numbers*.

Episode 81: Pandora

Original Air Date: February 7, 2003
Teleplay by Michele Fazekas and Tara Butters, directed by Alex Zakrzewski

Additional Cast: Lothaire Bluteau (Erich Tassig), Dagmara Dominczyk (Kate Logan), Pam Grier (Claudia Williams), Billy McNamara (Sam Bishop), Stephen Gevedon (Nick Taylor), Zena Grey (Samantha Gilligan), Ellen Lancaster (Mrs. Van Wagner), David Deblinger (Ron Crowley), Alexis Dziena (Mia Van Wagner), Ben Bode (Mike Pearson), Gina Rose (Amy Taylor), Rob Grader (Gerald Lockhart), Jeff Blumenkrantz (Mike Schwartz)

Reviewing the Case: A dead woman who has been beaten, raped, and stabbed was investigating a cyber-porn ring involving adolescent girls, one of whom left the country to be with her much older online boyfriend in Prague. Stabler travels to the Czech Republic to find her, pairing with a local law enforcement official to visit a border region where it's everything-goes for sexual predators. Back home, he has teamed up with the boyish-looking Detective Bishop, whose enthusiasm often gets the better of him. U.S. Attorney Claudia Williams returns, but in this episode the Feds are cooperating with city cops.

Relevant Testimony:

"As soon as the wall fell, Eastern Europe became a magnet for child porn and the sex trade."—Michele Fazekas

"Ted (Kotcheff, an executive producer) said we'd have to go to Canada. I told him I could make it happen here. While walking my dog, I remembered the Spanish Institute in Manhattan has a phenomenal courtyard. I took a look and thought, 'Omigod, this is Prague!'"—Trish Adlesic, location manager

Episode 82: Tortured

Original Air Date: February 14, 2003
Teleplay by Lisa Marie Petersen and Dawn DeNoon, directed by Steve Shill

Additional Cast: Margaret Colin (Mrs. Krug), Illeana Douglas (Gina Bernardo), Frederick Weller (Preston Bennett), Charlie Hofheimer (Jerry Dupree), Steve Schirripa (Paulie Obregano), Paul Fitzgerald (Ryan Chambers), Latarsha Rose (Laurie Schneider), Ryan Postal (Brendan King), Jolly Abraham (Detchen Gyatso), Travis Guba (Marshall Brown), Sara Barnett (Greta Thorson), Erin McLaughlin (Clara Johnson), Judy Del Giudice (Judge Corwin)

Reviewing the Case: The issue of torture is once again examined, but is that really an essential element in the murder of a Tibetan woman who survived a nightmarish ordeal in her homeland? This tangled, unpredictable tale keeps viewers guessing. The victim's American husband becomes a chief suspect. Ditto for Paulie, a palooka implicated by virtue of a couch he may have tried to sell to the deceased. At a neighborhood bakery, other secrets rise to the surface.

Noteworthy Discoveries: Dr. Huang explains that a shoe fetish is "cross-wiring in the control map of the brain."

Episode 83: Privilege

Original Air Date: February 21, 2003
Teleplay by Patrick Harbinson, directed by Jean de Segonzac

Additional Cast: Erik Von Detten (Drew Lamerly), John Bolger (Douglas Lamerly), Sarah Wayne Callies (Jenny Rochester), John Ottavino (Tom Paysen), Tina Sloan (Camilla Hartnow), Scotty Bloch (Ms. Blundell), William Wise (Roger Burnbaum), Dan Snook (Angus Rochester), Malaya Riviera Drew (Susie Fleckner)

Reviewing the Case: Arrogant rich people are among *SVU*'s favorite targets. Carmen, a young woman dressed in a maid's uniform, has fallen to her death from a luxury high-rise in an apparent suicide. The detectives learn she was having a torrid affair with the scion of the wealthy family living there. He claims her pre-mortem injuries were the result of the rough sex she demanded. His grandmother fiercely defends him, but that testimony might not be such a good thing.

Noteworthy Discoveries: An ex-cop says, "SVU—I thought you were just the panty police."

Episode 84: Desperate

Original Air Date: March 14, 2003
Teleplay by Amanda Green, directed by David Platt

Additional Cast: Rob Estes (Dan Hoffman), Signy Coleman (Kim Hoffman), Max Weinstein (Tommy Hoffman), Haviland Morris (Dawn Trent), Adam LeFevre (Police Chief), Stephen Mailer (Mr. McGuire), Welker White (Jill Hoffman's Attorney), Sandra Bernhard (Priscilla Chaney), P. J. Benjamin (Lloyd Jackson), Richard Thomsen (Allen Wheaten), Mark Lotito (Mike Rizzo), Kate Goehring (Dr. Sally Ivers), Christy Baron (Ariana Kane), Michelle Hurst (Vita Weldon), Amy Love (Dana McGuire)

Reviewing the Case: Tommy, a small boy gone mute after witnessing the rape and murder of his step-mom, is the only real clue SVU detectives have. Turns out she was on the run from her slick husband Dan, whose first wife—Tommy's biological mother— went missing a few years back. The locals in upscale Rye think she was a slut. The detectives believe Dan's a serial abuser but the guy is a pillar of his community.

Relevant Testimony: "That's a favorite episode of mine. I loved working with that little boy, Max Weinstein. He's so sweet and we had a terrific rapport."—David Platt

Episode 85: Appearances

Original Air Date: March 28, 2003
Teleplay by Stephen Belber, story by Liz Friedman, Vanessa Place, and Stephen Belber, directed by Alex Zakrzewski

Additional Cast: John Cullum (Barry Moredock), Brian Kerwin (Stanley Billings), Eric Thal (Tommy Hedges), Julie Boyd (Sally Lathan), Susan Kellermann (Mrs. Hedges), Paul Doherty (Jeff Lathan), Michael Hobbs (Mr. Routhel), Gabriel Millman (Kevin

Routhel), Bailey Slattery (Amy Prescott), Ellen Whyte (Mrs. Prescott), Carolee Carmello (Sylvia Price), Chan Casey (Rob Canotti), Sherry Anderson (Mrs. McNamara)

Reviewing the Case: This episode's inspiration, the JonBenet Ramsey case, is mentioned early on by detectives investigating the rape and murder of an eight-year-old Long Island beauty queen. She had bleached blond hair and a nose job—the lengths to which her ambitious father was willing to go for success on the pageant circuit. But the evidence points to a registered pedophile taking testosterone to reverse his chemical castration. Cabot has much bigger fish to fry, namely a cyber-porn merchant who tempts predators with "youth-enhancement software" that transforms older girls posing legally into jailbait material.

Episode 86: Dominance

Original Air Date: April 4, 2003
Teleplay by Robert F. Campbell and Jonathan Greene, directed by Steve Shill

Additional Cast: Frank Langella (Al Baker), Ian Somerhalder (Charlie Baker), Jason Ritter (Billy Baker), Richard Bekins (Earl Briggs), Erik Palladino (Dave Deuthorn), Don Sparks (Renny Nix), Karen Trott (Brenda Nix), Andrew McGinn (Det. Stubel), Jen Ordham (Tara Burnett), Freddy Bastone (Ralph Sloan), George McDaniel (Harold Darling), Ciara Hughes (Marie Douglas)

Reviewing the Case: The crime scenes are incredibly perverse in an Upper West Side murder-robbery spree. Multiple victims have been forced to rape each other before they die. A building superintendent and his two sons come under suspicion. After tossing a little incest, ménage-a-trois, elder abuse, and sodomy into the mix, the episode creaks but still moves at a crackling pace.

Noteworthy Discoveries: Ian Somerhalder joins what is becoming the show's long line of eventual *Lost* castaways. Could the crash of Oceanic Flight 815 be merely a Dick Wolf dream?

Relevant Testimony: "Frank Langella told us, 'I don't do TV unless I need the money or I've never played that part.'"—Neal Baer, executive producer

Episode 87: Fallacy

Original Air Date: April 18, 2003
Teleplay by Barbie Kligman, story by Barbie Kligman and Josh Kotcheff, directed by Juan J. Campanella

Additional Cast: Robert John Burke (Ed Tucker), Fred Dalton Thompson (Arthur Branch), Katherine Moennig (Cheryl Avery), Bridget Barkan (Veronica), Tanisha Lynn (Ricky), Lonas Wadler (Jordan), Ariel Arce (Sarah Avery), Mary Elaine Monti (Annabella Avery), Nicholas J. Giangiulio (John Avery), Michael Garfield (Matt Roberts), Leland Gantt (Stew Matos), Chad Lindberg (Eddie Cappilla), Michael Lerner (Morty Berger), Karen Shallo (Judge Schechtel)
Reviewing the Case: At a party gone wild, Cheryl Avery appears to have killed Joe Cappilla in self-defense after he tried to rape her, despite the fact that she's been dating his brother Eddie. The girl's story starts to fall apart, which is what happens to her boyfriend when he learns she's actually a pre-operative transsexual. The episode isn't all that far-fetched, even though some of the events may seem preposterous. And Katherine Moennig's performance is mesmerizing.

Episode 88: Futility

Original Air Date: April 25, 2003
Teleplay by Michele Fazekas and Tara Butters, directed by Alex Zakrzewski

Additional Cast: Fred Savage (Michael Gardner), Audrie J. Neenan (Judge Lois Preston), David Lipman (Judge Arthur Cohen), Myndy Crist (Carrie Huitt), Tyra Ferrell (Bethany Taylor), Dana Eskelson (Karen Leighton), Lauren Ward (Erin Russ), Jenny Maguire

(Kimberly Gardner), Annie Burton Alvarez (Janet Todesco), Jennifer Riker (Renee Bassett), Ray Demattis (Artie Kabzinski), Adam J. Stern (Brendan Leighton)

Reviewing the Case: Unlike most episodes, "Futility" begins with the apprehension of a suspect rather than a crime scene. Michael Gardener, a smooth-talking yuppie, is a known sex offender whose M.O. has become apparent in the rape of four women. One of them is being advised by Bethany, a rape-crisis counselor. She winds up in jail after refusing to testify at Gardner's trial for fear of betraying her client's right to privacy.

Noteworthy Discoveries: Benson's morale hits bottom with this case: "There's always another child molester, always another rapist. So what the hell's the point?"

Relevant Testimony: "(Benson began) feeling like she was useless, but saving (even) one life matters. If you can help one person, it's all worth it."—Mariska Hargitay

Episode 89: Grief

Original Air Date: May 2, 2003
Teleplay by Adisa Iwa, directed by Constantine Makris

Additional Cast: Joe Morton (Ray Bevins), Jerry D. O'Donnell (Off. O'Brien), Ed Bogdanowicz (Sgt. Traymor), Paul Leyden (Perry Williams), D.J. Cotrona (Donovan Alvarez), Viola Davis (Donna Emmett), Michele Hicks (Kimmie Robinson), Sophie Hayden (Mrs. Kligman), Matt Servitto (Fred Hopkins), Linda Powell (Julie White), Larry Cahn (Prof. Schreiber), David New (Dr. Timothy Allston), Josiah Early (Peter Kligman), Martha Millan (Lindsey Hay)

Reviewing the Case: The rape-sodomy and shooting death of a cocktail waitress is is much murkier than it initially appears. Vanessa, a nineteen-year-old college student who had exhibited erratic behavior, leaves a trail of potential clues—like a cat covered in blood—and perps. Was she a druggie? Is her ex-boyfriend to blame? How about her sadistic boss? Vanessa's grieving single father wants revenge.

Episode 90: Perfect

Original Air Date: May 9, 2003
Teleplay by Jonathan Greene and Robert F. Campbell, directed by
Rick Wallace

Additional Cast: Robert John Burke (IAB Sgt. Ed Tucker), Barbara Barrie (Paula Haggerty), Laura Harring (Joan Quentin), Gale Harold (Dr. Garrett Lang), Kimberly J. Brown (Jessica Morse), Adriane Lenox (Mrs. Tassler), Chuck Cooper (Tassler), Brian Reddy (Ross St. Clair), Karen Ludwig (Marcie Kinderski), Anna Kathryn Holbrook (Karen Morse), Russ Anderson (Roger Morse), Benim Foster (Det. Jim Jordan)

Reviewing the Case: Cults are a lot of fun—not for the people suckered into them, of course, but such secretive organizations always provide great *SVU* fodder. Dr. Garrett Lang heads a group with messianic mumbo-jumbo about eternal life and perpetual youth. The detectives wonder if the death-by-dehydration of a runaway teenage girl can somehow be attributed to these true believers. A passel of other adolescents acting like Stepford Wives confirm that suspicion.

Episode 91: Soulless

Original Air Date: May 16, 2003
Teleplay by Dawn DeNoon and Lisa Marie Petersen, directed by
Chad Lowe

Additional Cast: Logan Marshall-Green (Mitch Wilkens), Ann Dowd (Sally Wilkens), Kieran Campion (Seth Wollford III), Danny Hoch (Morris Brandenberg), Matthew Bennett (Stark), Brette Taylor (Mrs. Dutton), Mark Jacoby (Phillip Dutton), Siobhan Fallon (Linda Leggatt), Daniel Letterle (Andrew Kenworthy), Ashley Burritt (Vienna Sterling), Ashton Holmes (Davis Harrington), Amber McDonald (Jenna Sterling), Eisa Davis (Vera Galeano), Peyton List (Chloe Dutton), Mary Beth O'Connor (Andrea Forbes), Denise Wilbanks (Dora Stark), Nicholas Hagelin (Bernie Thorkle)

Reviewing the Case: The guiltiest person in an array of guilty parties is sure to send chills up any viewer's spine. Nobody even peripherally involved with a teen who has been gang-raped, then drowned in a toilet bowl comes away innocent. The girl's friends and family are all despicable. But nabbing the worst of the worst proves to be elusive. Four young men under scrutiny keep blaming each other.

Noteworthy Discoveries: The notion of an irredeemable sociopath rears its ugly head, a situation that thwarts the detectives.

Relevant Testimony: "Stabler believes everybody has a conscience. Benson—who thinks there's something dirty, ugly, and bad inside her, as a child of rape—doesn't. Mariska was nervous about saying those lines because she does have that belief. I told her, 'I'm sure you do but Olivia Benson does not.'"—Neal Baer, executive producer

SEASON FIVE

September 2003–May 2004

Regular Cast: Christopher Meloni (Det. Elliot Stabler), Mariska Hargitay (Det. Olivia Benson), Richard Belzer (Det. John Munch), Ice-T (Det. Odafin "Fin" Tutuola), Dann Florek (Capt. Donald Cragen), Tamara Tunie (M.E. Melinda Warner); B.D. Wong (Dr. George Huang), Diane Neal (ADA Casey Novak)

Regular Recurring Cast: Fred Dalton Thompson (DA Arthur Branch); Stephanie March (ADA Alexandra Cabot); Marlo Thomas (Ret. Judge Mary Conway Clark); Peter Hermann (Trevor Langan); Audrie Neenan (Judge Lois Preston); Daniel Sunjata (CSU Tech Burt Trevor); Mike Doyle (Forensics Tech Ryan O'Halloran); Tom O'Rourke (Judge Mark Seligman); Joanna Merlin (Judge Lena Petrovsky), Caren Browning (CSU Capt. Judith Siper)

SEASON FIVE OVERVIEW: Opening with a fresh group shot in the squad room (Tutuola, Munch, Benson, Cragen, Stabler, Huang, and Cabot all gathered soberly around desks), the fifth season of *SVU* settles quickly into a comfortable, dependable framework in which episodes become more complex and ambitious, sometimes to their detriment. Certain episodes crackle, ensuring that the show more than warrants its emerging label as the best of the ever-expanding Law & Order franchise. Personal-life noise remains on low hum— Benson gets her own HIV scare this year—but when it comes to writing out Stephanie March's Alexandra Cabot, *SVU* takes a unique, if melodramatic turn that leaves room for her to come back (which she does in upcoming seasons, and on the brief flight of 2006's *Conviction* on NBC). But perhaps most importantly, this year marks the first in a series of lead-actress Emmy nominations for Mariska Hargitay, whose Benson is plagued with self-doubt and not a little loathing during a twenty-five-episode season. Thanks to Hargitay and two guest stars (Marlee Matlin and Mare Winningham, who also receive Emmy nominations), the show is being taken seriously at precisely the time it most warrants attention.

Ratings Recap for Season: 8.3 rating / 14 share / 12,059,000 viewers

EPISODE DESCRIPTIONS

Episode 92: Tragedy

Original air date: September 23, 2003
Teleplay by Amanda Green, directed by David Platt

Additional Cast: Kellie Martin (Melinda Granville), Gabriel Olds (Daniel Lester), Marisa Ryan (Laura Bergeron), Clarke Thorell (Sam Marlett), Karen Goberman (Annika Bergeron), Shirley Knight (Rose Granville), Tonye Patano (Sally), Adrianne Frost (Marva Taylor), Lou Martini Jr. (Moe), David Conley (Mike O'Brien), Tony Freeman (Dr. Crespo)

Reviewing the Case: Benson and Stabler race to find a pregnant woman who, for medical reasons, cannot give birth naturally before she goes into labor. At first they suspect a serial carjack-rapist, but quickly turn their suspicions homeward in a nail-biter of a season opener that more than justifies its title.

Noteworthy Discoveries: Stabler notes he once spent summers at Rockaway Beach, presumably as a child.

Episode 93: Manic

Original air date: September 30, 2003
Teleplay by Patrick Harbinson, directed by Guy Norman Bee

Additional Cast: Mare Winningham (Sandra Blaine), Rory Culkin (Joe Blaine), John Cullum (Barry Moredock), Bill Cwikowski (George Waddell), Daniel Jenkins (Dr. Carl Medwin), Stephen Schnetzer (Dr. Engles), José Ramón Rosario (Hector Recincto), Eric LaRay Harvey (Randy Fowler), Patrick Dizney (Dean Reynolds), Sharon Wilkins (Janice Tashjian), Amy Hargreaves (Jane Wellesley), Daniel Bentley (Derek Fowler), Pilar Witherspoon (Julia Hynton)

Reviewing the Case: A young boy takes the wrong medicine—with disastrous consequences—in this truly manic episode, which starts off with a school shooting and turns into an indictment of the drug industry's marketing techniques. It's almost too much information to absorb, but overall the casting is impeccable and the storyline compelling and fresh.

Noteworthy Discoveries: Mare Winningham receives an Emmy nomination for her role. Rory Culkin, brother of Macauley, earned plaudits in the 2002 movie *Igby Goes Down*.

Episode 94: Mother

Original air date: October 7, 2003
Teleplay by Lisa Marie Petersen and Dawn DeNoon, directed by Ted Kotcheff

Additional Cast: Jill Marie Lawrence (Cleo Conrad), Jon Abrahams (Robert Logan), Sherri Parker Lee (Christina Logan), Marisol Nichols (Natina Amador), Jimmy Palumbo (Mr. Ralsey), Susanna Thompson (Dr. Greta Heints), P.J. Marshall (Bennie Edgar Ralsey), James Lurie (Kenneth Heints), Emily Loesser (Amy Carr), Patrick Husted (Dr. Sheldon), Michael Pemberton (Jay Pamowski), Barbara

Sims (Dr. Natalie Baca), John Scherer (Reed Lynch), Naomi Peters (Keri Price), Neville Archambault (Bruce Horton)

Reviewing the Case: "Psychiatrist with unorthodox methods" is a character description designed for disaster in an *SVU* episode. In "Mother," a shrink regresses her rapist clients so they can have a clean parental slate—but then she's beaten and raped and loses her memory. Between her amnesia regarding the event and a suspect's history of fugue states, there's a lot of forgetting going on in this twisted, twisty episode.

Noteworthy Discoveries: Speaking of amnesia, someone forgot that in *SVU*'s "Uncivilized" (season one) Cragen railed against the "situational ethics" of committing a sexual offender to a mental facility indefinitely; here, he suggests a suspect should undergo civil commitment after his sentence.

Episode 95: Loss

Original air date: October 14, 2003
Teleplay by Michele Fazekas and Tara Butters, directed by Constantine Makris

Additional Cast: Mitch Pileggi (Jack Hammond), David Thornton (Lionel Granger), Charlayne Woodard (Sister Peg), Josh Hopkins (Tim Donovan), Jacinto Taras Riddick (Rafael Zapata Gaviria), Andre Royo (Felix Santos), Tibor Feldman (George Reilly), Mateo Gomez (Father Castrillon)

Reviewing the Case: *L&O* fans know there's nothing nastier than a Colombian drug lord, but when an undercover NYPD officer is raped and killed, a crusading Cabot has to learn that lesson firsthand. Anyone who sets a toe in the case ends up targeted by the cartel and there's a subtle but inevitable progression of disaster. But even when Cabot seems relieved of the case, there may still be a bullet with her name on it.

Noteworthy Discoveries: Stephanie March begins her slow phase out of the series, with an exit and re-entrance that drips with melodrama.

Relevant Testimony: "Dick Wolf told us, 'She can't die.' He always regretted killing off Jill Hennessy's character (Claire Kincaid) on the Mother Ship. We knew the Colombian mafia blows up cars, so we called Neal (Baer) and asked, 'Can we blow up a car?' He said, 'Sure.'"—Michele Fazekas

Episode 96: Serendipity

Original air date: October 21, 2003
Teleplay by Dawn DeNoon and Lisa Marie Petersen, directed by Constantine Makris

Additional Cast: Jack Gilpin (Ron Wolcott), MaryLouise Burke (Marcy Cochran), Martin Donovan (Dr. Archibald Newlands), Alexander Tufel (Peter Nestler), Jolie Peters (Molly Stratton), Nick James Sullivan (Dr. Dean Kern), Paulina Gerzon (Alicia Hahn), Bonnie Rose (Carol Lucero), Olivia Crocicchia (Courtney Jones), Barbara Garrick (Kelly Wolcott)

Reviewing the Case: A mother and her newborn turn up dead, and at first the one-night-stand baby daddy looks good for the crime . . . until he fails the paternity test. A silver lining from the test: He's a pedophile! But has he pulled a fast one on the cops—and on eager new ADA Casey Novak, who has a lot to prove?

Noteworthy Discoveries: Diane Neal steps in as former white collar crime ADA Novak, who earns the cops' derision when she interferes. Additionally, a new group shot debuts that includes Novak in the opening title sequence.

Relevant Testimony: "We must have talked (about creating the character of Casey Novak) but I don't recall that discussion at all. She was going to be a kind of tomboy; she was on the ADA's softball team. But all that sticks out now was that horrible hairdo they gave (Diane Neal). I thought, 'Who hated her?' That hair was a hazing for her."—Dawn DeNoon

Episode 97: Coerced

Original air date: October 28, 2003
Teleplay by Jonathan Greene, directed by Jean de Segonzac

Additional Cast: Beverly D'Angelo (Rebecca Balthus), Sheila Tousey (Judge Danielle Larson), James McCaffrey (Peter Forbes), Kate Hodge (Carolyn Forbes), Christina Kirk (Julia Walker), Joseph Siravo (Randall Haber), Nick Wyman (Michael Kelly), Marcus Neville (Ira Rosenman), Leland Orser (Kevin Walker), Adrian Martinez (Emilio Vasquez), Michael C. Fuchs (Eric Manning), Michael Danek (Steve Manning), Dylan Blustone (Adam Forbes), Spencer List (Tate Walker)

Reviewing the Case: A mentally ill man named Kevin Walker kidnaps a boy, believing he's his son. But after the child is recovered, Walker babbles about the murder of "Martha," a clue that Novak insists Stabler chase down. One crime becomes another, revealing a new villain and a whole new nest of victims.

Noteworthy Discoveries: Novak visits the batting cage in her spare time.

Relevant Testimony: "The question I wanted to talk about in this episode was how far do you go to save a life, because that's what Stabler basically does—he tries to drive the guy off the deep end so Huang has to medicate him to get the answer about where this kid is. (Executive producer/showrunner) Neal Baer has a medical background, and he's instilled in all of us this fascination with how the mind works, and the nexus of where the mind and the law cross."— Jonathan Greene

Episode 98: Choice

Original air date: November 4, 2003
Teleplay by Patrick Harbinson, directed by David Platt

Additional Cast: Shirley Jones (Felicity Bradshaw), Mariette Hartley (Lorna Scarry), Josie Bissett (Jennifer Fulton), Callie Thorne (Nikki Staines), Beverly D'Angelo (Rebecca Balthus), Ricky Aiello

(Craig Fulton), Victor Rasuk (Leon Ardilles), Lenka Peterson (Mela-nie Dunne), Elain R. Graham (Judge Sara Henning), Fred Burrell (Judge Howie Rebard), Ali Farahnakjan (Dr. Rohit Mehta), Victoria Clark (Margaret Melia), Chris Bachand (Joshua Fulton), Tod Engle (Tom Longleat), Kathrine Roberts (Lily Longleat)

Reviewing the Case: This focus on a woman who insists on boozing while pregnant has a whiff of *Afterschool Special* to it. But the fight over whether the expectant mother—a chronic drinker, if not full-blown alcoholic—should be locked up in a treatment facil-ity to ensure her baby's health is gripping and timely. The show hits both sides of the fetal life debate perfectly.

Noteworthy Discoveries: Beverly D'Angelo returns as the sassiest Legal Aid lawyer since Lorraine Toussaint's Shambala Greene (on many a *Law & Order* episode).

Episode 99: Abomination

Original air date: November 11, 2003
Teleplay by Michele Fazekas and Tara Butters, directed by Alex Zakrzewski

Additional Cast: George Segal (Dr. Roger Tate), Jonathan Tucker (Ian Tate), Daphne Zuniga (Emma Dishell), Michael Boatman (Dave Seaver), David Lipman (Judge Arthur Cohen), Peter McRob-bie (Judge Walter Bradley), James Otis (Rev. Mitchell Shaw), Tim Bohn (Dr. Phil Sona), Jeffrey Ware (Prof. Waldron), Don Stephen-son (Derek Singer), Andrea Cirie (Kelly Singer), Alison Fraser (Dr. Elizabeth Cahill), Kathleen Lancaster (Sandy Klein), Alice Schaerer (Laura Klein)

Reviewing the Case: Irony doesn't ride in subtly on *SVU*, so the minute a professor whose life's work involves proving homo-sexuality is all in the minds of damaged individuals shows up, you know there's a reckoning at hand. Sure his son is gay—but which of them is to blame when another gay man turns up naked after having sex, wrapped in a blanket and dumped on a street corner?

Noteworthy Discoveries: Novak rides a bike to work. Kudos to director of photography Geoffrey Erb and director Zakrzewski for a slick shot through a damaged wall to capture the cops' reactions while evidence is located.

Episode 100: Control

Original air date: November 18, 2003
Teleplay by Neal Baer, story by Dick Wolf, directed by Ted Kotcheff

Additional Cast: Jacqueline Bisset (Juliette Barclay), Samantha Mathis (Hilary Barclay), David Thornton (Lionel Granger), Eddie Korbich (Nick Petracho), Austin Pendleton (Horace Gorman), Mickey Hargitay (Michael), Joseph McKenna (Samuel), Ken Forman (Larry Delay), Linda Powell (Lauren White)

Reviewing the Case: Four years ago, Benson dismissed as too incredible the report by a junkie named Hilary Barclay that she'd been held in a dungeon and raped, but when detectives investigate the castration of an older man on a subway platform, they learn she wasn't lying. The older man turned out to be the jailer of the girls, and when he turns up dead, fingers point at Barclay, her estranged mother—and even at Benson.

Noteworthy Discoveries: For this major-milestone 100th episode, the big guns of Baer, Kotcheff, and Wolf come out in force for a real thriller. Hargitay's scenes, in which she doubts her judgment, are certainly Emmy-worthy, and her father Mickey makes his sole appearance on the show in the teaser.

Relevant Testimony: "Neal (Baer) just said, 'We're going to use your dad,' which for me was such a huge gift—and even more so in hindsight (Mickey Hargitay died in September, 2006)."—Mariska Hargitay

Episode 101: Shaken

Original air date: November 25, 2003
Teleplay by Amanda Green, directed by Constantine Makris

Additional Cast: Beverly D'Angelo (Rebecca Balthus), Olga Merediz (Veronica Nash), Nicole Leach (Sarah Rendell), Julie White

(Dr. Anne Morella), Cynthia Ettinger (Evelyn Prichard), Shaun Powell (Ian Felson), Richard Shoberg (Drew Farmer), Cynthia Darlow (Frances Clegg), Marty Grabstein (Ronny Ickles), George R. Sheffey (Dennis Papillion)

Reviewing the Case: The episode is post–Louise Woodward/pre–Terri Schiavo, but the subject covers both real-life stories as a nanny and then a mother undergo scrutiny for injuries sustained to a toddler. At first, it seems the guilty will get off thanks to a hung jury, but Stabler undertakes a mission to ensure that justice is done—even if that means removing the brain-dead baby from life support.

Noteworthy Discoveries: Meloni has a heartfelt scene in which Stabler regrets smacking his child once; he also reveals that he served in the Marines when his daughter Maureen was a toddler.

Relevant Testimony: "This episode really affected me and it really affected Chris (Meloni). There's a scene in a bar where (Cragen) has to pick up (Stabler) . . . and he tells the story where he smacked his kid once. It was some of the most emotional stuff Chris has done, and on a personal level. In those moments you have Elliot Stabler and Chris Meloni and you don't know where the line is—and when it mixes like that, that's very ethereal."—Dann Florek

Episode 102: Escape

Original air date: December 2, 2003
Teleplay by Barbie Kligman, directed by Jean de Segonzac

Additional Cast: Fionnula Flanagan (Sheila Baxter), Nancy Allen (Carin Healy), Craig Bierko (Andy Eckerson), Milo Ventimiglia (Lee Healy), Michael Kenneth Williams (Double D Gamble), Stephen Lang (Mike Baxter), Jack Noseworthy (Jeremy), Michael McCormick (Isaac Sage), Tana Sarntinoranont (Bret Kim), Andrew Steinmetz (Danny Healy), Lou Cantres (Albert Martinez)

Reviewing the Case: The destination may not always be clear on some episodes, but the journey is thrilling. Such is the case here, where an escaped convict blamed for raping his step-son drags the alleged victim, Benson, and his mother into his alibis. A sniper bullet knocks him down (though not out), forcing everyone to realize that this crime may have had more than one victim.

Noteworthy Discoveries: Fionnula Flanagan picked up an Emmy in 1976 for *Rich Man, Poor Man*; Nancy Allen has appeared in multiple films directed by her ex-husband, Brian DePalma; Milo Ventimiglia has recently been seen as a regular on NBC's *Heroes*.

Episode 103: Brotherhood

Original air date: January 6, 2004
Teleplay by Jose Molina, directed by Jean de Segonzac

Additional Cast: Gary Cole (Xander Henry), Serena Williams (Chloe Spiers), David Lipman (Judge Arthur Cohen), Craig Wroe (James Woodrow), Ned Eisenberg (Roger Kressler), Toby Moore (Rob Sweeney), Noah Fleiss (Nathan Angeli), Pell James (Alicia Morley), Elden Henson (Will Caray), Clayton LeBouef (Vernon Spiers), (Tyler Henry)

Reviewing the Case: When a fraternity brother who taped his conquests for streaming on the Web turns up anally raped, detectives question his former pledges—and then examine serious rot in the fraternity itself. A ledger and a sociopath frat brother provide easy mapping points for the script, but when the dead student's father gets his day in court, everything changes.

Noteworthy Discoveries: Veteran character actor Gary Cole is perfectly cast as the grieving father who seems as slippery as they come, then becomes to be the prosecution's best chance at winning the case.

Episode 104: Hate

Original air date: January 13, 2004
Teleplay by Robert Nathan, directed by David Platt

Additional Cast: Barry Bostwick (Oliver Gates), Linda Emond (Dr. Emily Sopher), Matt Salinger (Seth Webster), Reynaldo Rosales (Sean Webster), James Rana (Al-Shani Elbisi), Donnie Keshawarz

(Joshua Feldman), Lorraine Serabain (Jazlyn Elbisi), Annie Chadwick (Eleanor Webster), Peter Marx (David Schwartz), Joshua Annex (James Assad), Jeff Skowron (Jason Mullavy), Sean Moran (Ahmet Elbisi)

Reviewing the Case: A racist young man violates his victims and torches them, motivated by their ethnicity. His defense team says he's genetically programmed to hate Arabs, an idea that gets a hearing at trial—but the script tosses in a gotcha that nullifies the argument in the final minutes. That's a shame, because few series do controversial subjects better than *SVU*, and the idea of genetic hatred is one that deserves a fuller bashing than it gets here.

Noteworthy Discoveries: A scene in which Stabler, Benson, and Tutuola face off with the perp is a classic how-to in provoking a confession; all three actors are pitch-perfect. Revealed: Stabler was a student at the Sisters of Mercy parochial school before going into the Marines, then returned to attend night school to earn his B.A. His father was a cop, and he has two sisters and three brothers.

Relevant Testimony: "The link between genetics and specific behaviors is an ongoing debate in American medicine. The legal system has no simple solution for dealing with these issues. At one far end of the spectrum, some would argue that the insanity plea is for the most part meaningless. Far at the other end, the argument is that whether we define you as insane or not, this should have no effect on how the criminal justice system treats you. So the next question is: what's the appropriate punishment? In 'Hate' any answer a jury gave would have seemed definitive. Instead, we ended with extenuating circumstances, leaving each person in the audience to answer for themselves open questions for which there are no definitive answers."—Robert Nathan

Episode 105: Ritual

Original air date: February 3, 2004
Teleplay by Ruth Fletcher Gage and Christos N. Gage, directed by Ed Bianchi

Additional Cast: Michael Emerson (Allan Shaye), Barry Shabaka Henley (Asante Odufemi), Trini Alvarado (Maggie Shaye),

Sullivan Walker (Martin Bosa), Malika Samuel (Na'imah Haruna), Susan Blommaert (Judge Rebecca Steinman), Erika Alexander (Kema Mabuda), Diane Kagan (Marian Laymon), Abe Alvarez (Roberto Martinez), Bill Cohen (Agent Bruce Bigelow), Susan Willis (Rose Kern)

Reviewing the Case: An obscure religious ritual seems to blame when a boy is found dismembered and bloodless in a clearing, but as detectives dig deeper they come across importers who bring children over from Africa, and the well-off white people who buy them. It's a stomach-turning episode that's apparently based on all-too-real events.

Noteworthy Discoveries: Tutuola has a working knowledge of the Santeria cult thanks to some of his informants in Narcotics. Is there anything someone can't learn while working the drug beat?

Episode 106: Families

Original air date: February 10, 2004
Teleplay by Jonathan Greene, directed by Constantine Makris

Additional Cast: Jane Seymour (Debra Connor), Helen Slater (Susan Coyle), Michael Boatman (Dave Seaver), Patrick Flueger (Aidan Connor), Geoffrey Nauffts (Steve Abruzzo), Tom Mason (Jason Connor), Spencer Treat Clark (Brian Coyle), Michael Mulheren (Judge Harrison Taylor), Stefanie Nava (Lisa Faber), Jenna Gavigan (Shannon Coyle)

Reviewing the Case: A pregnant teen is killed, a situation made even more horrific when it turns out the child would have been the product of an ill-defined incestuous relationship. But then things get really weird when a father who has been living a double life is found shot in his car, and a mother makes plans to flee to Cuba. Viewers will need a scorecard to keep track of it all (and a good family tree chart might help) but sticking with this one is worth the hassle.

Noteworthy Discoveries: Nothing says fun casting like pitting Supergirl (Helen Slater played the Woman of Steel in a 1984 film) against Dr. Quinn (Jane Seymour, who received two Emmy nominations for the titular role she played in *Dr. Quinn, Medicine Woman, on* CBS from 1993–1998).

Episode 107: Home

Original air date: February 17, 2004
Teleplay by Amanda Green, directed by Rick Wallace

Additional Cast: Dixie Carter (Denise Brockmorton), Diane Venora (Marilyn Nesbit), Lauren Velez (Stephanie Jameau), Isabel Gillies (Kathy Stabler), Jeffrey Scaperrotta (Dickie Stabler), Larry Fleischman (Steve Krauss), Ebbe Bassey (Iris Jordan), Jennifer Piech (Poppy Conton), Laura Lehman (Polly Kester), Kevin Thoms (Daniel Nesbit), Marceline Hugot (Leslie Price), Joseph Cross (Adam Nesbit), Rose Arrick (Hazel Crane), Harvey Atkin (Judge Alan Ridenour), Beth Ehlers (Nancy Kester), Jesse Schwartz (Jacob Nesbit)

Reviewing the Case: Marilyn Nesbit is a super-creepy mom who turns paranoia into a parenting style that stifles her children— and mutates into murder. Novak decides that the trigger-puller is less guilty than the mother who poisoned his outlook on the world, and decides to put the parent on trial. But it will take a back-from-the-dead surprise witness to drive the final nail in the coffin of the prosecution's case.

Noteworthy Discoveries: Onetime *That Girl* (ABC, 1966–1971) Marlo Thomas returns to television in the first of four appearances as "That Judge"—Novak's friend and former boss; one of the *Designing Women,* Dixie Carter, also guests as the strident homeschool association lawyer.

Episode 108: Mean

Original air date: February 24, 2004
Teleplay by Michele Fazekas and Tara Butters, directed by Constantine Makris

Additional Cast: Blair Brown (Lynne Riff), Robert Iler (Troy Linsky), David Thornton (Lionel Granger), Ned Eisenberg (Roger

Kressler), Lindsay Hollister (Agnes Linsky), Kelli Garner (Brittany O'Malley), Zachary Knighton (Lukas Ian Croft), Shayna Ferm (Terri Welsh), Arielle Kebbel (Andrea Kent), Kimberly McConnell (Paige Summerbee), Brad Holbrook (Greg Sullivan), John Ahlin (Pat Linsky), Jake Robards (Assistant Medical Examiner Cardillo), Kimberly Ross (Sarah O'Malley), Elizabeth Fye (Shauna Goletz)

Reviewing the Case: A young bully is found dead in the trunk of her car, and at first the obvious suspect is the target of the girl's tormenting. But after a psych evaluation and the M.E.'s report come in, detectives turn their attention to the girl's circle of so-called friends. Unfortunately, even a conviction isn't enough to prevent yet another tragic twist in the tale.

Noteworthy Discoveries: Jake Robards, who makes a brief appearance, is the son of legendary actor Jason Robards. Robert Iler was thrust into the spotlight as the troubled son of a Jersey mob boss on HBO's *The Sopranos*.

Episode 109: Careless

Original air date: March 2, 2004
Teleplay by Patrick Harbinson, directed by Steve Shill

Additional Cast: Julie Hagerty (Mariel Plummer), CCH Pounder (Carolyn Maddox), Malinda Williams (Lori-Ann Dufoy), Cress Williams (Sam Dufoy), Jazz Raycole (Megan Rose), Keith Randolph Smith (Father Lucas Hendry), Michole Briana White (Tamara Semple), Stephen Schnetzer (Dr. Engles), Pilar Witherspoon (Julia Hynton), Sue-Anne Morrow (Dr. Angela Chuny), Steven G. Smith II (Jamie Semple)

Reviewing the Case: A young boy dies in foster care and there's no end of suspects, from a clueless church leader to the foster father who was in charge of him when he died, to his overburdened social worker. One of them ends up going to trial, but a witness hidden in a mental institution provides the ultimate answer everyone seeks.

Noteworthy Discoveries: Julie Hagerty is perhaps best known from her roles in the 1980 and 1982 *Airplane!* movies.

Meanwhile, Ice-T delivers a "cool" performance underscored by his roiling disillusion with the human race; he's an overlooked, powerful actor.

Episode 110: Sick

Original air date: March 3, 2004
Teleplay by Dawn DeNoon, directed by David Platt

Additional Cast: Cindy Williams (Nora Hodges), Philip Bosco (Judge Joseph P. Terhune), Peter Riegert (Chauncey Zierko), Jill Marie Lawrence (Cleo Conrad), Will Keenan (Billy Tripley), Madeleine Martin (April Hodges), Shane Haboucha (J.J. Ostilow), James Colby (Jeremy Ostilow), Jennifer Van Dyck (Ann Ostilow), Nick Cubbler (Mitchell Edison), Ryan Simpkins (Lisette Ostilow), Tim Ewing (Jonas Haase)

Reviewing the Case: A vengeful boy whose molestation was silenced with a payoff to his parents, who scoot him out of the country to avoid giving up their hush money, is linked to a physically ill young girl and her mentally unstable grandmother. Everyone in this episode is, indeed, sick. All of them circle around a Michael Jackson-esque man-boy who is nicknamed "the Teflon pedophile" for good reason.

Noteworthy Discoveries: Former *Laverne & Shirley* fans should appreciate seeing Cindy Williams pop up as the bad granny.

Relevant Testimony: "There had been allegations about (Michael Jackson) that kind of went away, and someone who had done research into that, I knew that person, so I had some information that wasn't even ripped from the headlines—just things that didn't get into the trial because they couldn't. The guy was named Billy, which is based on (Jackson's hit song) 'Billie Jean.' A lot of times we go further from the (headlines) story, but in this one it seemed that justice needed to be done. Justice wasn't done in the real arena, so I kept closer to the true story in this one than in most of them."—Dawn DeNoon

Episode 111: Lowdown

Original air date: April 6, 2004
Teleplay by Robert Nathan, directed by Jud Taylor

Additional Cast: Peter Riegert (Chauncey Zierko), Michael Beach (Andy Abbott), Bethany Butler (Maryellen Abbott), Romi Dias (Tina Gardner), Moet Meira (Belinda), David Aron Damane (DuShawn McGovern), Robert Jason Jackson (Jerome Adams), Roger Pretto (Francisco Martinez), Benton Greene (Terrence Baker), Curt Karibalis (Charlie Horner), Carlos Pizarro (Hector Alvarez), Dean Strange (Jeff York)

Reviewing the Case: A group of black men gather each week for a sex party with each other, but tell their significant female others that it's a poker game. Oh, and none believe they're gay. Tutuola informs the SVU squad that it's known as being on the "down low," and is generally unique to black experience. It's not necessarily illegal, but once HIV and a dead white Bronx ADA who wasn't dealt a full hand get involved, there are no more secrets.

Noteworthy Discoveries: Benson dated the victim for a month five years ago, but broke it off due to no chemistry, though they did sleep together. That's enough to give her an HIV scare, though she's found to be negative.

Relevant Testimony: "It's funny when writers try to write slang. There's this one show where they talked about the 'down low' and (Tutuola) has to explain what that is—black men who're gay and can't go home with it—and everybody looks at me: 'A little too much information, Ice.' And (as Tutuola) I go, 'Don't look at me, I just know stuff.' I wrote that line. Because at the end of the day, I'm like, 'How do I know so much damn information about this?'"—Ice-T

Episode 112: Criminal

Original air date: April 20, 2004
Teleplay by Jose Molina, directed by Alex Zakrzewski

Additional Cast: James McDaniel (Javier Vega), Doug E. Doug (Rudy Lemcke), Michael Boatman (Dave Seaver), Zoe Saldana

(Gabrielle Vega), Charlayne Woodard (Sister Peg), Joe Towne (Kyle Luhrmann), John C. Vennema (Ian Busch), Joanna Rhinehart (Kianna Lemcke), Triney Sandoval (Echevarria), Joey Diaz (Elijah Coney), Jason Marr (Dave)

Reviewing the Case: When a professor is pinpointed as a suspect in an investigation of his student's murder, Cragen recognizes the teacher as an ex-con he once prosecuted—and based on the strangulation M.O. appears back in business. But after a homeless witness steps forward, the captain has to look for the less-obvious perpetrator, who may not survive being outed as the killer.

Noteworthy Discoveries: James McDaniel, formerly Lt. Fancy on *NYPD Blue,* turns in a powerful, emotional performance.

Episode 113: Painless

Original air date: April 27, 2004
Teleplay by Jonathan Greene, directed by Juan J. Campanella

Additional Cast: Marlee Matlin (Dr. Amy Solwey), John Cullum (Barry Moredock), Sheila Tousey (Judge Danielle Larson), Peter McRobbie (Judge Walter Bradley), Karen Young (Christina Nerrit), John Robert Lupone (Brooks Harmon), Annie Campbell (Allison Nerrit), Peter Appel (Marvin Friedman), Richmond Hoxie (Dr. Ben Fletcher), Adam Kulbersh (C.C. Det. Ben Suarato)

Reviewing the Case: Crying rape is an unusual way to cover a failed suicide attempt, but that's what Christina Nerrit does when she's discovered half-dead. She succeeds later at the hospital thanks to Internet friend Dr. Amy Solwey—a deaf woman with a terminal disease who's devoted to helping the suicidal go quietly. During the legal battle that ensues, Munch identifies with Solwey's struggle, and becomes a key factor in her will to survive.

Noteworthy Discoveries: Oscar-winner (the 1986 film *Children of a Lesser God*) Matlin receives an Emmy nomination for her performance in this episode, but the real crime is that Belzer—who delivers the most moving performance he's had in this series when Munch reveals he was a boy when his father shot himself—did not receive a nod of his own. He knows of what he speaks, too; in real life Belzer's father also committed suicide. (This may have been a canonical error, however; on *Homicide: Life on the Street*, Belzer's father, a cop, was shot.)

Relevant Testimony: "I remember watching Richard struggle with the scene (where Munch talks about his father's suicide). I recall the producers saying that they had never had the chance to watch Richard dig so deep emotionally as they did in that scene and I remember Richard having a hard time with it at first. I figured there must have been some personal connection there and I believe he told me afterwards."—Marlee Matlin

Episode 114: Bound

Original air date: May 4, 2004
Teleplay by Barbie Kligman, directed by Constantine Makris

Additional Cast: Anthony Rapp (Dr. Matt Spevak), Jane Krakowski (Emma Spevak), Callie Thorne (Nikki Staines), Philip Bosco (Judge Joseph P. Terhune), Richard Easton (Richard Sutton), Daniel Pearce (Gary DeVaal), Isabel Glasser (Josette Brooks), Edmund Lyndeck (Marvin Zelmann), James A. Stephens (Harvey Cohen), Eunice Anderson (Alexis Sutton), Paul Urcioli (Eddie Wooding), Michael W. Howell (John Ridley), Mark Fairchild (Dr. David Brelsford), Gibson Frazier (Pat Fisher), Lisa Leguillou (Lisa DiMarco), Tara Greenway (Lori Smith), Diane Bradley (Estelle Garson), Trevor Jones (Ben Pawler)

Reviewing the Case: After three older women are found strangled, detectives go to the common denominator: A caregiver service with an owner who has a gambling problem. But when yet another senior has a stroke just after apparently shooting the deadbeat owner, Benson and Stabler must do a little playacting to get to the perpetrator, who turns out to have been even more of a monster than they realized.

Noteworthy Discoveries: Novak needs a speedy motion signed by a friendly judge—and ends up in the midst of Judge Terhune's poker match, which includes many other familiar justices from the *SVU* world.

Episode 115: Poison

Original air date: May 11, 2004
Teleplay by Michele Fazekas and Tara Butters, directed by David Platt

Additional Cast: Tom Skerritt (Judge Oliver Taft), Barry Bostwick (Oliver Gates), Peter McRobbie (Judge Walter Bradley), Craig Wroe (James Woodrow), Cynthia Gibb (Karen Campbell), Rebecca Luker (Wendy Campbell), Sloane Momsen (Katie Campbell), Alicia Goranson (Rosalin Silvo), Sean Cullen (Pete Campbell), Matthew Sussman (Lawrence Alcott), Michael Goodwin (William Keldon), William Whitehead (Judge Phillip Wyler)

Reviewing the Case: A seemingly easy abuse case in which a mother's punishment that led to the brain-death of her adopted daughter ends up pitting Novak against autocratic Judge Oliver Taft. Novak's subsequent investigation into his case history reveals he has sent an innocent woman to jail—and when the adoptee is smothered, Novak redeems her credibility while putting Taft on trial.

Noteworthy Discoveries: There's some excellent legal maneuvering in this episode, which explores the concept of judicial immunity and rights. There's also a battle of magnificent gray heads between returnee Bostwick and Skerritt, who won a 1993 Emmy for *Picket Fences*.

Episode 116: Head

Original air date: May 18, 2004
Teleplay by Dawn DeNoon and Lisa Marie Petersen, directed by Juan J. Campanella

Additional Cast: Amy Sedaris (Charlie Donato), Robert John Burke (Ed Tucker), Jill Marie Lawrence (Cleo Conrad), Diana Scarwid (Jackie Madden), Stacy Edwards (Meredith Rice), Tyler Hudson (Jason Rice), D.L. Shroder (Phil Gordon), Jenny Fellner (Cindy Bellamy), Chuck Montgomery (Vic Spinella), Brian Maillard (Gil Tanner), Elisabeth S. Rodgers (Vanessa Henderson), Oliver Solomon (Rudy Norwick), Mischa Kischkum (Fred Moynihan), Coco

NBCU PHOTOBANK

Christopher Meloni, Diana Scarwid (Jackie Madden), Mariska Hargitay in "Head"

(Porn Queen), Jake Weary (Shane Madden), James Urbaniak (Wade Donato)

Reviewing the Case: A hidden camera in a toilet captures a young boy being raped and leads detectives to a woman with no history of such incidents—but who has started having sudden sexual urges. A medical condition appears to prevent her from being responsible for her actions, including the molestation, but Novak is unconvinced. A deal is struck, but in a soap-opera twist, there's even one more indignity for everyone in the case.

Noteworthy Discoveries: The "porn queen" is played by Coco (a.k.a. Nicole Austin), who married Ice-T in 2004. Comedienne Amy Sedaris (sister of memoirist/comedian David Sedaris) makes a brief appearance.

SEASON SIX

September 2004–May 2005

Regular Cast: Christopher Meloni (Det. Elliot Stabler), Mariska Hargitay (Det. Olivia Benson), Richard Belzer (Det. John Munch), Ice-T (Det. Odafin "Fin" Tutuola), Dann Florek (Capt. Donald Cragen), Stephanie March (ADA Alexandra Cabot), Tamara Tunie (M.E. Melinda Warner), and B.D. Wong (Dr. George Huang)

Recurring Cast: Judith Light (SVU Bureau Chief Elizabeth Donnelly), Isabel Gillies (Kathy Stabler), Jeffrey Scaperrotta (Dickie Stabler), Patricia Cook (Elizabeth Stabler), Erin Broderick (Maureen Stabler), Allison Siko (Kathleen Stabler), Daniel Sunjata (CSU Tech Burt Trevor), Lou Carbonneau (CSU Tech), Welly Yang (CSU Tech Georgie), Jordan Gelber (CSU Tech Layton), Sheila Tousey (Judge Danielle Larson), Harvey Atkin (Judge Alan Ridenour), Tom O'Rourke (Judge Mark Seligman), Joanna Merlin (Judge Lena Petrovsky), Philip Bosco (Judge Joseph P. Terhune), Joel de la Fuente (TARU Tech Ruben Morales), Caren Browning (CSU Capt. Judith Siper), Peter Hermann (Trevor Langan), Ned Eisenberg (Roger Kressler), Mike Doyle (Forensics Tech Ryan O'Halloran)

SEASON SIX OVERVIEW: The *SVU* gang is still chasing after serial abuse, contemporary sexual practices among high schoolers, child abductions, false accusations of rape, and mothers from hell. And Dr. Huang is still coming up with a wide range of psychological explanations for why the warped perps do what they do. Through it all, as usual, the detectives take turns becoming rattled by their difficult work.

There's a crossover episode with the short-lived and underappreciated *Law & Order: Trial by Jury*, with the formidable star power of Angela Lansbury, a role for which she receives an Emmy nomination. In various episodes, Martin Short, Alfred Molina, Matthew Modine, and John Savage all seem to enjoy portraying truly despicable human beings. This is the kind of program that welcomes such descents.

Ratings Recap for Season: 8.3 rating / 14 share / 12,070,000 viewers

EPISODE DESCRIPTIONS

Episode 117: Birthright

Original Air Date: September 21, 2004
Teleplay by Jonathan Greene, directed by Arthur W. Forney

Addiitional Cast: Abigail Breslin (Patty Branson), Lea Thompson (Michele Osborne), Peter McRobbie (Judge Walter Bradley), Viola Davis (Donna Emmett), Beau Gravitte (Matt Branson), Camilla Scott (Sarah Branson), Tobias Segal (Kenny Pratt), Ned Bellamy (Peter Carson), Gibson Frazier (CSU Tech Fisher), David Forsythe (Dr. Stanley Norton), Leslie J. Frye (Mrs. Molina)

Reviewing the Case: What initially seems to be a typical case of child abduction by predators turns into a far thornier situation. Although her biological mother's name is Michele, six-year-old Patty was born to parents Sarah and Matt by virtue of an in-vitro fertilization clinic's unethical practices. While the detectives and prosecutors struggle with this fuzzy area of the law, Michele keeps trying to kidnap the daughter who calls someone else "Mommy."

Noteworthy Discoveries: Abigail Breslin would go on to gain wide attention and acclaim as a beauty-pageant wannabe in *Little Miss Sunshine* (2006). Before Michele's DNA links her to Patty, Dr. Huang theorizes that she is tormented by "a single fixed illusion."

Relevant Testimony: "(Abigail Breslin's) mother told me, 'She can cry with her left eye or her right, whichever you want.' When Mariska asked how she learned to cry on cue like that, Abigail said, 'Family fights.' The girl was unbelievable. I'd never seen that in a child actor before."—Arthur Forney

Episode 118: Debt

Original Air Date: September 28, 2004
Teleplay by Amanda Green, directed by David Platt

Additional Cast: Ming-Na (Li Mei Wu), Loren Dean (Roger Baker), Jack Yang (Ricky Yao), Aaron Yoo (Tommy), James Hong

(Laundry Supervisor), Donnetta Lavinia Grays (Off. Ramirez), Elizabeth Flax (Nurse), Jenny Wong (Ping Wu), Kim Chan (Mr. Zhang), Gene Canfield (Det. D'Allesandro), Craig Walker (Howard Kendall), Sabrina Jiang (Hannah Wu), Jake Robards (Assistant Medical Examiner Cardillo), Margaret Reed (Felicia Chatham), Karen Tsen Lee (Penny Chen), Cindy Lee Moon (Jade) Helen Palladino (Mrs. Armita), Andrew T. Lee (Charlie Ping)

Reviewing the Case: In a departure from the typical black or Hispanic diversity seen on *SVU*, this episode presents a fascinating glimpse of New York's Chinese community. When the mother of two little girls disappears, the detectives confront a nasty underworld filled with people who prey on undocumented refugees. The sister of the missing woman is torn between helping the police and fearing for her family's safety if she cooperates. Dr. Huang is a key player, both as translator and undercover operative.

Noteworthy Discoveries: Benson poses as a well-heeled shopper hunting for bargains, specifically a Hermes bag, in a marketplace known for illegal knockoffs. Stabler runs afoul of the IAB yet again.

Relevant Testimony: "(This episode) required not the traditional actors you normally see on TV. Early on I had developed an extensive database so I had in mind some actors of Asian ethnicity—but not enough of them. We also held auditions in L.A., a rare thing. There, I found Jack Yang, who portrays the suave, charismatic villain. I probably had the most trouble so far in the series finding characters for that episode."—Jonathan Strauss, casting director

Episode 119: Obscene

Original Air Date: October 12, 2004
Teleplay by Jose Molina, directed by Constantine Makris

Additional Cast: Dana Delany (Carolyn Spencer), Lewis Black (B.J. Cameron), Maggie Grace (Jessie Dawning), Nestor Serrano (Franco Marquez), Lauren Velez (Stephanie Jameau), Ricky Ullman (Danny Spencer), Michael Boatman (Dave Seaver), Jason Antoon (B.J.'s Producer), Joseph E. Murray (EMT Olson), Jesse Marchant

(Trip Willis), Josh Tower (Vijay), Jane Kim (Susie Yen), David Gerald (Jim Willoughby), Tessa Auberjonois (Dr. Payne)

Reviewing the Case: Jessie, the sixteen-year-old star of a controversial TV show, has been raped in her trailer. The program's middle-aged producer is ruled out as a suspect when detectives learn he's married to the preternaturally mature actress. Meanwhile, an activist who sees Jessie's sexually provocative performance as a bad role model for girls clashes with a radio shock-jock. There are very few nice characters in this dynamic episode, which weighs free speech against the valid concerns of parents.

Noteworthy Discoveries: Dana Delany was the star of *China Beach* (1988–91), an ABC show on which *SVU* showrunner Neal Baer once worked. Lewis Black goes on to gain fame as a *Daily Show* comic on Comedy Central. Maggie Grace later does not fare well as a marooned plane crash survivor on ABC's *Lost*.

Episode 120: Scavenger

Original Air Date: October 19, 2004
Teleplay by Dawn DeNoon and Lisa Marie Petersen, directed by Daniel Sackheim

Additional Cast: Anne Meara (Ida Becker), Doug Hutchison (Humphrey Becker), Elizabeth Franz (Jeannette Henley), Kent Cassella (Uniform Officer), Remy Auberjonois (Eric Liebert), Paul Harman (Bernie), Roxane Barlow (Red Watts), Alex Wipf (Clive Bremsler), Oliver Wadsworth (Rupert Daniel Kilmore), Rony Clanton (Heroin Addict), Madison Arnold (Morty Graf)

Reviewing the Case: Serial killers invariably are portrayed as clever masterminds who devise intricate clues to baffle the police. The perp in "Scavenger" leaves little poems at each crime scene, so he appears to have a lot of time on his hands—the detectives even first suspect an innocent clockmaker. This guy might be a copycat patterning his murders on the work of a maniac from more than two decades earlier, but the significant difference is that the contemporary victims are mothers. Is he Oedipal?

Episode 121: Outcry

Original Air Date: October 26, 2004
Teleplay by Patrick Harbinson, directed by Constantine Makris

Additional Cast: Michael O'Keefe (Ronald McCain), Blair Brown (Lynne Riff), Amanda Seyfried (Tandi McCain), Joseph Lyle Taylor (Jamie Barrigan), John Bedford Lloyd (Mike Tucker), Jim Coleman (Rico), Stewart J. Zully (Jeff), Sewell Whitney (Dr. Lyne), Gordon Joseph Weiss (Fred), Neal Lerner (Lawrence Ullman), Jake Mosser (Luke Delvecchio), Emma Bell (Allison Luhan), Christopher Moccia (Larry O'Connor), Keith Jamal Downing (Joseph Eglee), Jarrett Willis (Tony Storr), Cady McClain (Alice McCain), John Schuck (Chief of Detectives)

Reviewing the Case: Detectives have trouble investigating the kidnapping and rape of a teenager who has been missing for days after attending a college party. She accuses three military cadets before changing her story several times—lies that lead to unforeseen tragedy. The episode contends that the girl's behavior has been prompted by a noble if misguided attempt to protect her family. Even so, this knowledge doesn't engender much sympathy for her choices.

Relevant Testimony: "This was inspired by the Tawana Brawley case (upstate New York, 1987). We wanted to look at how the media handles these things. As a storyteller, how am I going to show this girl lying, lying, lying?"—Patrick Harbinson

Episode 122: Conscience

Original Air Date: November 9, 2004
Teleplay by Roger Wolfson and Robert Nathan, directed by David Platt

Additional Cast: Kyle MacLachlan (Dr. Brett Morton), Peter Riegert (Zierko), Jordan Garrett (Jake O'Hara), Johanna Day (Leslie O'Hara), Novella Nelson (Judge Anne Sciola), Jill Marie Lawrence (Cleo Conrad), Audrie J. Neenan (Judge Lois Preston), Ian Bedford (Off. Bamford), P.J. Brown (Billy Turner), Bruce Kirkpatrick (Malcolm

Wolinsky), Kathleen McNenny (Mrs. Morton), Jeff Gurner (Dr. Burt Gleason), Wiley Moore (SOMU Det. Monahan), Mark Aldrich (Jeffrey Jackson), Brendan McVeigh (Theo Morton), Michael Iles (Henry Morton)

Reviewing the Case: Although not necessarily recognized in law, sometimes denial can be as much of a crime as homicide. When his son is murdered, a psychiatrist blames the system for failing the tormented thirteen-year-old killer, who he had once recommended attend a tough-love camp. The kid's mother lives in her own world of rationalizations. The boy with blood on his hands is smarter than both of these adults.

Episode 123: Charisma

Original Air Date: November 16, 2004
Teleplay by Michele Fazekas and Tara Butters, directed by Arthur W. Forney

Additional Cast: Holliston Coleman (Melanie Cramer), Jeff Kober (Eugene Hoff), Shannon Cochran (Cindy Cramer), Peter Maloney (Geoffrey Downs), Bruce Norris (Reg), William H. Burns (Off. Robbins), Margaret Reed (Sarah's Attorney), Ali Reza (Dr. Mehta), Christopher Durham (Carl Buchman), Laura Sametz (Simone Buchman), Michael Cullen (Det. Stu MacKenzie), Munson Hicks (Rev. Tucker), Emilio Del Pozo (Duty Capt. Claros)

Reviewing the Case: Freckle-faced Melanie, pregnant at age twelve, tells detectives that the father is her "husband" Abraham. Turns out he's a self-styled preacher—a.k.a. a con man named Eugene—with an obedient cult following, most of them women or young girls. When police raid one of his households, they find children shot to death in their beds and cribs. Melanie's brainwashed mom must be convinced that Abraham/Eugene has a hidden and far more earthly agenda.

Notable Discoveries: The shot of so many dead children precedes a long silence, a chillingly effective way to end the scene. "Charisma" as a whole is altogether chilling. The detectives are shaken and ordered to talk with Dr. Huang in a long stretch of soul-searching.

Munch: "The human race is ever-evolving and we'll always come up with elaborate, repulsive, and depraved ways to kill each other."

Relevant Testimony: "We lay the kids down, put fake blood all around and told them to go to sleep. But the image, even when you know it's not real, is striking. I looked at pictures of the 700 dead people at the Jim Jones compound in Guyana. I kept that photo on my script book, in fact, and showed it to Mariska. That was a great motivator."—Arthur Forney

Episode 124: Doubt

Original Air Date: November 23, 2004
Teleplay by Marjorie David, directed by Ted Kotcheff

Additional Cast: Bill Campbell (Ron Polikoff), Shannyn Sossamon (Myra Dempsey), Viola Davis (Donna Emmett), Mariette Hartley (Lorna Scarry), Patricia Kalember (Judge K. Taten), Wynter Kullman (Jenny West), Jeffrey Carlson (Justin Wexler), Carolyn Miller (Sophie Polikoff)

Reviewing the Case: A grad student claims to have been raped by a womanizing art professor. The evidence—bruises on her throat, deep scratches his back—seems conclusive and yet. . . . A sequence in which the duo take off their clothing for separate forensics exams is conveyed with split-screen parallel views, a very effective way to underscore the he said/she said nature of this case with an ambiguous conclusion.

Noteworthy Discoveries: Stabler reveals that his wife has left him, a shock to Benson and the start of a long story arc.

Relevant Testimony: "The actor, Bill Campbell, asked: 'Did I rape her?' I said, 'Of course you didn't, Billy.' The actress, Shannyn Sossamon, asked: 'Did he rape me?' I told her, 'Of course he raped you, darling.' I wanted to give the sense of how difficult it is to make a decision sometimes about guilt."—Ted Kotcheff

Episode 125: Weak

Original Air Date: November 30, 2004
Teleplay by Michele Fazekas and Tara Butters, directed by David Platt

Additional Cast: Mary Stuart Masterson (Dr. Rebecca Hendrix), Amanda Plummer (Miranda Cole), Dallas Roberts (Thomas Mathers), Joselin Reyes (Martinez), Angela Pietropinto (Mrs. Mathers), Greg Vaccarello (Off. Galloway), Ward Horton (Alan Richter), Justine Boyriven (Samantha Trager), Adara Almonte (Gina Kownacki), Casey Spindler (Raymond Ettinger), Geneva Carr (Margo Sanders), Becki Newton (Colleen Heaton)

Reviewing the Case: Predators come in all sizes, shapes, and sexual predilections. The guilty party in "Weak" is a true surprise. He favors the most helpless people, including a paranoid schizophrenic woman prone to wild hallucinations when she stops taking her meds. A psychiatrist at Bellevue, who happens to be a former cop, works on the case with Benson and Stabler. The ending is not happily-ever-after.

Noteworthy Discoveries: Amanda Plummer's Emmy-winning turn as a madwoman seems like a familiar one for the quirky actress. Benson seems wary of Stabler's willingness to work with Dr. Hendrix, perhaps suspecting it has something to do with his marital woes.

Relevant Testimony: "Amanda is actually the sweetest, meekest, most introspective kind of person. . . . Mary Stuart Masterson's character got under the audience's skin a little bit. People thought she was coming between Stabler and Benson."—Jonathan Strauss, casting director

Episode 126: Haunted

Original Air Date: December 7, 2004
Teleplay by Amanda Green, directed by Juan J. Campanella

Additional Cast: Nicholas Gonzalez (Det. Miguel Sandoval), Kent Cassella (ND Detective), Katie McGee (Reporter), Jeffrey V.

Thompson (Fat Tony), Jeanetta Arnette (Sandra Knowles), Kevin Pinassi (Vance Dennis), Ernest Waddell (Ken Randall), Emma Myles (Lizzie Jones), John Schuck (Chief of Detectives), Gene Silvers (T.D. Beeman), Albert Insinnia (Lt. Pizzelli), Kevin Nagle (Joey Bosco), Tijuana Ricks (Dr. Marnie Aiken), Francis Jue (Dr. Fong), Jaime Rodriguez (Crazy Jim), Georgienne Millen (Paula Beeman)

Reviewing the Case: Tutuola is wounded in the process of killing two robbers in a convenience store holdup. This is merely a prelude to another case, from the days when he was an undercover narc. A distraught woman sees his picture in the newspaper and demands to know why he dropped the ball on finding her daughter, who disappeared into the underworld of drugs. After reluctantly teaming up with a rookie, a young whippersnapper who proves to be quite savvy, Fin retraces his steps.

Noteworthy Discoveries: Tutuola, whose *nom de guerre* in Narcotics was Terry Brown, sees his estranged son Ken after a separation of many years. Their meeting isn't exactly warm and fuzzy. An especially poetic scene at Potter's Field gives Warner a chance to talk about some New York history.

Episode 127: Contagious

Original Air Date: January 11, 2005
Teleplay by Jonathan Greene, directed by Aaron Lipstadt

Additional Cast: Mary Stuart Masterson (Dr. Rebecca Hendrix), Jennette McCurdy (Holly Purcell), David Lansbury (Larry Purcell), David Lipman (Judge Arthur Cohen), Caitlin Muelder (Donna Pellegrino), Maggie Kiley (Terry Van Houten), Daniel Hugh Kelly (Mark Dobbins), Rebecca Lowman (Julie Dobbins), Pamela Holden Stewart (Sonya Purcell), Zach Gilford (Kevin Wilcox), Mariah Fresse (Nicole Van Houten), Courtney Taylor Burness (Danielle Pellegrino), Laura Kai Chen (Dr. Sanada), Angela Robinson (Mrs. Wheeler)

Reviewing the Case: Doctors determine that a prepubescent girl named Holly, brought into the ER after a car accident, has been molested. She eventually pinpoints a friend of the family who coaches girls' soccer at her school. When other students come forward with similar accusations, the hysteria begins to resemble that of Salem in the late 1600s. But the truth eventually emerges, leaving several casualties in its wake.

Episode 128: Identity

Original Air Date: January 18, 2005
Teleplay by Lisa Marie Petersen and Dawn DeNoon, directed by Rick Wallace

Additional Cast: Charlayne Woodard (Sister Peg), Peter Firth (Dr. Preston Blair), Mary Stuart Masterson (Dr. Rebecca Hendrix), Donnetta Lavinia Grays (Off. Ramirez), Reiley McClendon (Logan Stanton/Lindsay Stanton), Regan Thompson (Katie), Hillary Bailey Smith (Amelia Stanton), John Bolger (Clark Stanton), Denise Ramirez (Claudia Hernandez), Michael Ray Escamilla (Hector Ramirez), Ron Scott (Jerry DelVecchio), Ana Maria Andricain (Housekeeper), William Paulson (Agent McClosky)

Reviewing the Case: This episode travels a very long distance, from an apparent gang-related homicide to the bizarre psychology of identical twins. These prep-school adolescents are wannabe graffiti artists, so their involvement in the crime is derived from a desire to "tag" like the street kids. Lurking beneath the surface, however, is a social engineering experiment that makes Manhattan seem a bit like *Village of the Damned* (1960 and remake in 1995).

Relevant Testimony: "The casting process was murder. We needed to see hundreds of kids—twins, bother-sister combos. Reiley McClendon came to audition for the boy's role and still had that sort of androgynous quality of young guys. He said, 'You know, I could do the girl's part as well.' When he came back for another audition, he'd glammed himself up a bit. As the boy, we put him in lifts to distinguish between the twins. That was (executive producer) Ted Kotcheff's idea."—Jonathan Strauss, casting director

Episode 129: Quarry

Original Air Date: January 25, 2005
Teleplay by Jose Molina, directed by Constantine Makris

Additional Cast: John Savage (Lucas Biggs), Michael Shannon (Avery Shaw), Terry Serpico (Deacon Brinn), Angelica Torn (Julia Brinn), Jill Marie Lawrence (Public Defender Conrad), Bill Buell (Terry Ronsen), Suzanne Grodner (Lynne Ronsen), Julie Lund (Kimber Faulk), Kathryn Rossetter (Vivian Tate), Corey Carthew (ESU Leader), Jack Pavlinec (Zeke Brinin)

Reviewing the Case: Every now and then, *SVU* comes up with a predator so repulsive that even a devoted fan of the show might want to switch channels. That's the reaction prompted by baseball player Lucas Biggs, who gleefully enumerates his extensive abuse of adolescent boys while awaiting execution. The repeated rape of one particular child has set off a chain of events that, twenty-five years later, sparks tragic repercussions for an entire community.

Episode 130: Game

Original Air Date: February 8, 2005
Teleplay by Patrick Harbinson, directed by David Platt

Additional Cast: Barry Bostwick (Oliver Gates), Seth Gabel (Garrett Perle), Robert Montano (U.S. Attorney Raul Menendez), Matthew Faber (Stuart Davis), Geoffrey Arend (Game Creator)

Reviewing the Case: A brutal attack on a prostitute seems to emulate a particularly nasty video game, so the detectives begin tracking down the denizens of virtual reality. After questioning a few pathetic nerds, they arrest a seventeen-year-old boy who's a sociopath and proud of it, along with his I'll-do-anything-for-him girlfriend. Dr. Huang surmises the young man's "an adrenaline junkie and narcissist." The defense? Blame it on the dopamine.

Noteworthy Discoveries: There's nothing like a case with demented teenagers to get Stabler worrying about his own children. Sweet little Dickie gives his dad reason to ponder.

Relevant Testimony: "That look at the end between Dickie Stabler and (his father) is implied in the script but I might have taken it another step."—David Platt, episode director

Episode 131: Hooked

Original Air Date: February 15, 2005
Teleplay by Joshua Kotcheff, directed by Jean de Segonzac

Additional Cast: Hayden Panettiere (Angela Agnelli), Janae Kram (Lisa Downey), Shuler Hensley (Tim Downey), Matt Malloy (Max Long), Alex Cranmer (Dr. Derek Tanner), Ivan Martin (Jerome), Jessica Dunphy (Allison Downey), Sharon Washington (Jenny Anderson), Aaron Staton (Andy Wall), Annie McGreevey (Mrs. Downey), Patrick Frederic (Troop Leader), Michael Drayer (Nicky Sims)

Reviewing the Case: Lisa Downey, a fifteen-year-old last seen in her high school uniform, has been found dead wearing an $800 cocktail dress. She and her classmates sported "sex bracelets" to boast about their levels of promiscuity. But Lisa and her BFF Angela had gone way beyond teen hanky-panky. Adult predators, HIV, pornography, and prostitution all come into play as this complicated girls-gone-wild episode unfolds, with a few sly references to Monica Lewinsky along the way.

Episode 132: Ghost

Original Air Date: February 22, 2005
Teleplay by Amanda Green, directed by David Platt

Additional Cast: Mitch Pileggi (DEA Agent Hammond), Brian F. O'Byrne (Liam Connors), Stephanie March (Alexandra Cabot), Nicholas Gonzalez (Det. Miguel Sandoval), Joselin Reyes (Paramedic Martinez), Audrie J. Neenan (Judge Lois Preston), Natascia A. Diaz (Mrs. Delgado), Robert Turano (DEA Agent Trayne), Millie Tirelli (Elvira Castilla), Maury Ginsberg (Assistant M.E. Fielding), Mickey

Kelly (Doyle Shanahan), Lori Prince (Patty Kerner), Raymond Witt-mann (Antonio Montoya), Ali Reza (Dr. Mehta)

Reviewing the Case: The husband-and-wife owners of a private hedge fund are murdered. Ditto for an Hispanic couple, whose son Antonio is left for dead. These crimes are linked to an earlier case ("Loss," season five), in which ADA Cabot was shot while investigating a notorious Colombian narco-baron. His elusive hit man—a former IRA operative—figures in the current situation. Full of surprises, this episode is a bit like the movie *Traffic* in addressing the futility of America's war on drugs.

Noteworthy Discoveries: Mitch Pileggi, who appeared as an FBI official on *The X-Files*, shows up here as a top DEA agent.

Relevant Testimony: "I was desperately homesick for New York when I wrote that, so when Cabot talks mournfully about the Mister Softee song, that was me missing Mister Softee in Santa Monica. We have one in my neighborhood in Pasadena that just doesn't play the song."—Amanda Green

Episode 133: Rage

Original Air Date: March 1, 2005
Teleplay by Michele Fazekas and Tara Butters, directed by Juan J. Campanella

Additional Cast: Matthew Modine (Gordon Rickett), Anne Pitoniak (Mrs. Larsen), Michele Santopietro (Linda Cusick), Anthony Inneo (Antoine), Barbara Rosenblatt (Nurse), Ashley Lopez (Emily Barrington)

Reviewing the Case: The usual *SVU* format—discovery of a crime in the teaser, police investigation, courtroom showdown—is abandoned in favor of an intimate drama. At times, the dialogue almost seems as if it had been written by Samuel Beckett. Instead of *Waiting for Godot*, the squad is waiting for a confession when Stabler interrogates Gordon Rickett, a suspected serial rapist who slipped through the system's cracks fourteen years earlier.

Relevant Testimony: "Plays are very much dialogue, whereas TV and film are action-driven. So on this type of episode, the only thing you have to keep the drama going is the words. You can't blow up a car. . . . We read a lot of actual interview transcripts to understand the rhythms and how detectives try to trap people with their own words."—Michele Fazekas

Episode 134: Pure

Original Air Date: March 8, 2005
Teleplay by Dawn DeNoon, directed by Aaron Lipstadt

Additional Cast: Martin Short (Sebastian Ballentine), Charlayne Woodard (Sister Peg), Marianne Hagan (Mrs. Sellers), Mary Mara (Carlene Ballentine), Taylor Spreitler (Chloe Sellers), David Deblinger (Harlan Beaumont), Adam Kulbersh (Det. Ben Suarato), Luke Robertson (Jake Ostrander), Dina Pearlman (Mindy Mayhern), Nicole Guidetti (Bernadette), Ben Mostyn (Off. Kivlahan), Monica K. Ross (Suzie), Lou Savarese (Off. Baxter), Molly Bea Spears (Kaley Sellers)

Reviewing the Case: Martin Short's comedic skills are set aside in his role as Sebastian, a purported psychic trying to help the SVU solve the disappearance of Kaley Sellers. The teenager's mother bypasses the detectives in hiring him to find her daughter. Stabler thinks he's a charlatan; Benson's not quite so sure. But Kaley had some dark secrets, including an attempt to sell her virginity to the highest bidder on a website. And Sebastian's wife reveals that wedded bliss was never evident in their marriage.

Relevant Testimony: "We had Martin Short in mind (when we wrote this script). We had to find something that would be fun. . . . Neal (Baer) and I met with him, had lunch at Spago, and it was so great. We had a few ideas, so it was looking into what would stretch him the most. I'd never seen him do an evil character before, because he's so likable."—Dawn DeNoon

Episode 135: Intoxicated

Original Air Date: March 29, 2005
Teleplay by Jonathan Greene, directed by Marita Grabiak

Additional Cast: Cathy Moriarty (Denise Eldridge), Danielle Panabaker (Carrie Eldridge), Glenne Headly (Attorney Simone Bryce), Stephen Gregory (Dr. Beresford), William H. Burns (Off. Robbins), Saundra McClain (Principal), Stephanie Cozart (Marissa Tatro), Bruce Turk (Neighbor), Nat deWolf (Trooper Linden), Lee Camp (Bart), Jennifer Abrams (Nomi), Jon Foster (Justin Sharp)

Reviewing the Case: In 1980's *Raging Bull*, actress Cathy Moriarty portrayed the trophy wife of an abusive boxer. On *SVU* twenty-five years later, she's a raging alcoholic mother who insists that her adolescent daughter's older boyfriend should be charged with statutory rape. Before the dust settles, the kids are on the run, leaving mom's bludgeoned body behind. "Premenstrual dysphoric disorder" may be a factor, according to a defense attorney. Blame it on the blood flow.

Episode 136: Night

Original Air Date: May 3, 2005
Teleplay by Amanda Green, story by Amanda Green and Chris Levinson, directed by Arthur W. Forney and Juan J. Campanella

Additional Cast: Angela Lansbury (Eleanor Duvall), Alfred Molina (Gabriel Duvall), Rita Moreno (Mildred Quintana), David Thornton (Lionel Granger), Bebe Neuwirth (ADA Tracey Kibre), Kirk Acevedo (DA Investigator Hector Salazar), Fred Dalton Thompson (DA Arthur Branch), Bradley Cooper (Jason Whitaker), Anya Migdal (Nina Zergin), Stelio Savante (Milan Zergin), Lou Ferguson (Beauclaire), Marlyne N. Afflack (Sarah Miller)

Reviewing the Case: When the rape of a young Haitian woman with a bad heart causes her death, the crime is linked to a series of similar attacks. The plight of poor, undocumented immigrants in America is treated with great compassion. In counterpoint, the wealthy come under fire, specifically the unhinged son of a well-connected matriarch who'll do anything to get him off the hook. His bizarre personality puzzles the detectives. Things don't go especially well for the justice system until the story continues in a crossover episode on the short-lived *Law & Order: Trial by Jury*.

Noteworthy Discoveries: Angela Lansbury, nominated for an Emmy, appears as a character not unlike her coldly calculating mother in 1962's *The Manchurian Candidate*. Rita Moreno, here an activist for refugees, later portrays Detective Goren's schizophrenic mom on *Law & Order: Criminal Intent*.

Relevant Testimony: "We wanted one of those fantastic grand dames . . . Angela Lansbury's such a huge star, but Charlie Engel (NBC Universal executive vice-president for programming) had worked closely with her on *Murder, She Wrote*. So he broke the ice for us."—Jonathan Strauss, casting director

Episode 137: Blood

Original Air Date: May 10, 2005
Teleplay by Patrick Harbinson, directed by Felix Enriquez Alcala

Additional Cast: Melinda Dillion (Jenny Rogers), Matt Schulze (Kevin Rogers), Christine Elise McCarthy (Carol Rogers), Brian Gant (Jake Lumet), J. Paul Nicholas (Attorney Linden Delroy), Réal Andrews (Sgt. Ray Crawford), Lauren Hodges (Samantha Beavans), Rafael Sardina (Naldo)

Reviewing the Case: A security camera has documented a woman beaten outside a club and the subsequent injuries to an infant tossed out of her hijacked car. That leads to a perp named Jake, though his accomplice's face is obscured. But why was the baby left alone in the vehicle? And why are doses of oxycodone prescribed for slightly senile Jenny Rogers being sold on the street? Moreover, why does she insist on protecting her dysfunctional son and daughter-in-law?

Noteworthy Discoveries: Everyone refers to Melinda Dillon's Jenny as a "little old lady," despite the fact that she's still quite a babe. When Stabler's daughter Kathleen is arrested for DUI, he makes the charge go away. Cragen asks him: "How many times do you think you can break the rules and get away with it?" After six seasons of similar shenanigans, the answer apparently is "indefinitely."

Episode 138: Parts

Original Air Date: May 17, 2005
Teleplay by David Foster, directed by Matt Earl Beesley

Additional Cast: Marlee Matlin (Amy Solwey), Glenn Kessler (Leon Shragewitz), Marc Grapey (Russ Bianco), Kevin Carroll (James McGovern), Alex Burns (Mark Mogan), Tyler James Williams (Kyle McGovern), Isiah Whitlock Jr. (NTCC Representative), Amir Arison (Dr. Ghupta)

Reviewing the Case: This episode begins with semen in the throat of a severed head. From there the story spirals into a fish market's worth of red herrings: The victim returned from a tour of duty in Iraq with an injury that led her to heroin as a painkiller and prostitution to support the habit. But she was stalked by a lovelorn Orthodox Jewish butcher. Eventually, it all comes down to an illicit scheme to supply surgeons with transplant organs. This tragedy encompasses two very sick people awaiting kidneys: Amy Solwey, last seen in season five's "Painless," and a little boy whose father resorts to desperate measures.

Noteworthy Discoveries: Stabler poses as a morgue worker to deliver a corpse to a suspect. Munch crosses the line in his compassion—perhaps even passion?—for Amy Solwey. A debate about the country's organ donation system hits all the ethical, medical and legal viewpoints.

Relevant Testimony:

"Clearly, Munch falls for her, and that was implicit in the script. . . . She said she's gotten more reaction from that (episode) than anything she's done, and she'd like to come back, so we're working on that. Keep your fingers crossed."—Richard Belzer

"(I'd return to *SVU*) in a heartbeat."—Marlee Matlin

Episode 139: Goliath

Original Air Date: May 24, 2005
Teleplay by Michele Fazekas and Tara Butters, directed by Peter Leto

Additional Cast: Fred Dalton Thompson (DA Arthur Branch), Gina Tognoni (Off. Kristen Vaill), William Ullrich (Anthony Myers), Brian Hutchison (Off. Wes Myers), Stuart Burney (Colonel Gage), Julian Gamble (Koehler), Jon Bernthal (Sherm Hempell), R.E. Rodgers (Off. Tommy Callahan), John Dossett (Dr. P. Trainer)

Reviewing the Case: When *SVU* takes on the U.S. military in the midst of a war, sparks are sure to fly. In this episode, two former soldiers now working as police become homicidal and suicidal. Both served with the same unit in Afghanistan, where the Army administered an experimental drug to protect troops against malaria but without their informed consent. The vets who suffer continuing side effects such as paranoia are considered collateral damage.

Noteworthy Discoveries: The story draws on actual 2002 murder-suicides at Fort Bragg by soldiers given a similar drug in Afghanistan. Stabler was a Marine fighting in Operation Desert Storm. Novak's father, we learn, earned a Purple Heart in Vietnam.

Relevant Testimony:

"I was a little nervous. I had visions of a knock on the door and being taken away. We had real reporting, real facts, the real cover-up. It went to the highest levels of government."—Peter Leto

"We made Novak's father a Vietnam vet. My father was a gunner on a Huey in Vietnam. Tara's father was in the Big Red One unit there. We're children of veterans and that's why we felt completely fine about writing this episode. . . . We had a tabloid reporter refer to Munch and Novak as 'Scully and Mulder.' That was a little bit of a shout-out for us. And Belzer had been Munch once on *The X-Files*."—Michele Fazekas who along with writing partner Tara Butters formerly worked on *The X-Files*.

SEASON SEVEN

September 2005–May 2006

Regular Cast: Christopher Meloni (Det. Elliot Stabler), Mariska Hargitay (Det. Olivia Benson), Richard Belzer (Det. John Munch), Ice-T (Det. Odafin "Fin" Tutuola), Dann Florek (Capt. Donald

NBCU PHOTOBANK

Season seven cast, from l.-r.: Diane Neal, B.D. Wong, Dann Florek, Christopher Meloni, Mariska Hargitay, Ice-T, Tamara Tunie, Richard Belzer

Cragen), Tamara Tunie (M.E. Melinda Warner); B.D. Wong (Dr. George Huang), Diane Neal (ADA Casey Novak)

Recurring Cast: Fred Dalton Thompson (DA Arthur Branch); Judith Light (Judge Elizabeth Donnelly); Audrie Neenan (Judge Lois Preston); Joanna Merlin (Judge Lena Petrovsky), Stephen Gregory (Dr. Kyle Beresford), Joel de la Fuente (TARU Tech Ruben Morales), Paula Garcés (CSU Tech Millie Vizcarrondo), Mike Doyle (Forensics Tech Ryan O'Halloran), Caren Browning (CSU Capt. Judith Siper)

SEASON SEVEN OVERVIEW: Late in the season, M.E. Warner notes wryly about Det. Stabler: "Sometimes, all that brooding intensity is just annoying." And after seven seasons, the show has more than earned the right to contain a little meta focus on characters' personal lives, exchanging it for an increasingly mature, layered, and complex series of stories, for the most part intriguingly well-told. (Tunie's Warner also gets a bump up this season to appear in the opening credits as well as the squad room group shot, which now includes Novak, Huang, Cragen, Stabler, Benson, Tutuola, Warner; and Munch.) Meanwhile, the series continues to project its own style, rarely adhering to the strict book 'em and cook 'em approach of the franchise, spending whole episodes on the chase or in the legal system, as nearly every major player gets his or her own spotlight. Outside the show, Christopher Meloni earns his first Emmy nomination, but that goes largely unnoticed when Mariska Hargitay finds a third time is the charm—and wins not only a Golden Globe but an Emmy, largely based on her efforts in the gripping "911." Off-camera, Hargitay (and husband Peter Hermann, who plays recurring defense lawyer Trevor Langam) produce their first child. All brooding intensity aside, seven is a magic season for the program.

Ratings Recap for Season: 8.2 rating / 13 share / 12,111,000 viewers

EPISODE DESCRIPTIONS

Episode 140: Demons

Original air date: September 20, 2005
Teleplay by Amanda Green, directed by David Platt

Additional Cast: Robert Patrick (Ray Schenkel), Robert Walden (William Dorsey), Joe Lisi (Greg Lennon), Brittany Underwood (Kelly Browning), Carrie MacLemore (Lucy Kozlowski)
Reviewing the Case: A retired NYPD officer familiar with the particulars of a recently released rapist named Ray Schenkel alerts Stabler to the danger after a rape near the Port Authority Bus Terminal, so the SVU detective goes undercover to keep an eye on the perp. An initial sting operation fails to net him, but soon Ray takes matters into his own hands, and Stabler has reason to fear for his life in this thriller of a season-opening episode.

Noteworthy Discoveries: Meloni's excellent, conflicted performance may have led to his eventual first nomination this season, but all those years of not being nominated didn't faze him—even if it did seem to faze his co-workers.

Relevant Testimony: "I still remember the first time Mariska (Hargitay) got nominated and I didn't. And it was so weird on the set—I didn't try to convince anyone, but people would be like, 'Man, you should have been nominated, too!' And I'm like, 'I'm OK.' And not that I was trying to convince them, but I'd be like 'I'm OK' and they'd be like, '*Sure*. You soldier on, cowboy.' You can't win."—Christopher Meloni

Episode 141: Design

Original air date: September 27, 2005
Teleplay by Lisa Marie Petersen, directed by David Platt

Additional Cast: Lynda Carter (Lorraine Dillon), Estella Warren (April Troost), Ronny Cox (Dr. McManus), Julian Sands (Barclay Pallister), Peter Riegert (Pallister's Attorney), Mark McGrath (J.J. Price), Bobby Flay (Leo Ashford), Tom O'Rourke (Judge Mark Seligman), Jeffrey Doornbos (Roger Mason), Caroline McMahon (Monica Mason), Jesse Palmer (Don Lacey)

Reviewing the Case: A mother/daughter con artist team first trick a wealthy man into believing he has raped and impregnated the younger woman, then run a baby-selling scam on several would-be parents. But when the daughter appears to have died in a car crash, the scam unravels and it's up to the detectives—and Novak—to try and find some justice, even if it's just for the baby.

Noteworthy Discoveries: The men tricked into sharing their ejaculate are all playing versions of their real-life selves: Mark McGrath is Sugar Ray's ex-singer, Bobby Flay is a famous chef (who married former *SVU* star Stephanie March in February 2005), and Jesse Palmer is a former NFL player.

Episode 142: 911

Original air date: October 4, 2005
Teleplay by Patrick Harbinson, directed by Ted Kotcheff

Additional Cast: John Herrera (Consul Duarte Farias), Zabryna Guevara (Julia Ortiz), Rachel Diaz-Stand (Maria Recinos), Christopher Evan Welch (Richard Dwyer), Chandra Wilson (Rachel Sorannis), Jessica Pimentel (Selma Garcia), Chris Mendoza (Ricardo Garcia), Jeanine Monterroza (Voice of Maria Recinos)
Reviewing the Case: A 911 call from a terrified young girl locked in a mysterious location is transferred to Benson, who tries to extract details without much success. Though detectives initially think it's a hoax, slowly details emerge revealing the caller, a Honduran girl named Maria, has been sold to a child pornographer. But when her "owner" comes home and cuts off the connection, the SVU has to beat the clock to find Maria alive in this nail-biter of an episode that effectively explores Benson's humanity.
Noteworthy Discoveries: Mariska Hargitay takes home the L&O franchise's first lead-actor Emmy.
Relevant Testimony: "When we finished the episode, I knew this was going to be nominated. In 1967 I did a TV movie, *The Human Voice*, with Ingrid Bergman. She gets on the phone with a lover and off the phone. As her mood changed, the walls subtly changed colors to objectify her feelings. That movie in no way informed '911' but the script did come to me because of (that film): 'Let's put Mariska (Hargitay) on the phone for an hour.'"—Ted Kotcheff

Episode 143: Ripped

Original air date: October 11, 2005
Teleplay by Jonathan Greene, directed by Rick Wallace

Additional Cast: Mary Stuart Masterson (Dr. Rebecca Hendrix), Noah Emmerich (Pete Breslin), Peter McRobbie (Judge Walter Bradley), Julia Weldon (Pamela), Paul Wesley (Luke Thomas Breslin), Rich Washburn (Buster Flynn), Bob Walton (Carl Sawyer), Elizabeth Duff (Emily Sawyer)

Reviewing the Case: Stabler is suspended for trying to shield his old partner Pete Breslin's son, Paul, a star school pitcher who has beaten up a friend. But after Stabler knocks Pete unconscious, it emerges that both Breslins were hopped up on steroids. As Stabler fights his own demons in a revealing discussion with Dr. Hendrix, Paul throws his father a curve no one expected—and it takes the detective to help keep 'roid rage from turning into 'roid tragedy.

Noteworthy Discoveries: Stabler, whose badge is No. 6313, had a very controlling father who would beat him with a belt if he cried.

Episode 144: Strain

Original air date: October 18, 2005
Teleplay by Robert Nathan, directed by Constantine Makris

Additional Cast: CCH Pounder (Attorney Carolyn Maddox), Brian Bloom (Gabriel Thomason), Bill Smitrovich (Liam Weller), Ernest Waddell (Ken Randall), Adam Kulbersh (Ben Suarato), Jason Manuel Olazabal (Sascha Hart), Brendan Griffin (Jason Haig), James O'Toole (Henry Fanello)

Reviewing the Case: In this timely and thought-provoking episode, two men infected with a virulent strain of AIDS are found murdered with the word "killer" written nearby, leading detectives to a gay activist leader who claims he did it in self-defense: The perps were infecting others in the same way they'd infected his now-deceased younger brother, therefore, he's done the world a favor by taking them out. Novak disagrees—but will the jury?

Noteworthy Discoveries: During the investigation, Tutuola discovers that his son (Ken Randall) is gay. The detective isn't thrilled, but doesn't judge—and Ken even helps on the case.

Relevant Testimony: "When they first said, 'OK, Ice, you're going to have a son who's gay,' I think they thought I was going to have a problem with that, but I'm like, 'Yo, I'm acting.' I'm an adult man, I know how to deal with issues like that. My real son saw the show and said, 'Ohhh, your son on TV is gay!' and I'm like, 'What about you? How you doin' with the girls?' It is what it is. I rolled with that."—Ice-T

Episode 145: Raw

Original air date: November 1, 2005
Teleplay by Dawn DeNoon, directed by Jonathan Kaplan

Additional Cast: Marcia Gay Harden (Star Morrison), John Cullum (Barry Moredock), John Rubinstein (Judge T. Schuyler), Lucian Maisel (Danny Kohler), J.C. MacKenzie (Brian Ackerman), Joe Grifasi ("Heshy" Horowitz), Sima Bissette (Tawndra), Sophia Barricelli (Annabelle Paoletti), Brian Letscher (Patrick McCorkle), Suzanne Di Donna (Lana Mayhew), Marin Hinkle (Mrs. Whitlock), Cassidy Hinkle (Maddy McCorkle), Ana Reeder (Mrs. McCorkle), Myk Watford (Mark Whitlock), Cody Kasch (Kyle Ackerman), Joel Marsh Garland (Brannon Lee Redding), Keith Siglinger (Christopher Rawlings), Harry Madsen (Mr. Buggesi), Jess le Protto (Johnny Mayhew)

Reviewing the Case: A schoolyard shooting leaves the black foster child of a white correctional officer dead. The gun leads detectives to a white supremacist group and a mouthy racist named Star, a teen who wants to join the group, and a father who's leading the charge. But when the shooter takes the stand, bullets fly inside the courtroom and Star turns out to have a secret identity that takes detectives back to investigate the real motivations of the dead boy's foster parents.

Noteworthy Discoveries: Munch is shot in the posterior during the courtroom battle. Stabler, recovering from a similar wound to his arm, tells Benson that his wife has started divorce proceedings. Oscar-winner Marcia Gay Harden (2001's *Pollock*) is both hateful and delightful at the same time in her racist role.

Relevant Testimony: "Dawn (DeNoon) did all this research (for 'Raw') and one detail was that in the home of some neo-Nazi somewhere, he'd made a giant swastika on his ceiling out of beer bottle caps. Six feet in diameter. That's a great detail; you couldn't make that up. Does she put that into her script? Yeah. All that you see on the screen is that the camera starts on the ceiling and pans down into the home of this neo-Nazi, but that's stuff you can't make up."—Amanda Green, co-executive producer

Episode 146: Name

Original air date: November 8, 2005
Teleplay by Michele Fazekas, directed by David Platt

Additional Cast: Ruben Santiago-Hudson (Carlos Guzman), J. Paul Nicholas (Attorney Linden Delroy), Angel Desai (M.E. Tech Tatum), Brigitte Viellieu-Davis (Principal Arroyo), Richard Bright (Robert Sawyer), Madhur Jaffrey (Dr. Indira Singh), Lisa Emery (Anna Gable)

Reviewing the Case: Get your scorecard out for this one: Four Hispanic boys went missing in 1978, and when one child's skeleton turns up, a crusading CSU tech named Millie Vizcarrondo partners with Stabler to find his killer. Along the way, they cross-reference the decades-old murder with a more recent one, quiz a drugged-out space cadet and convince an alibi witness to rethink his story from thirty years ago to nab the perp—who still may not end up giving the detectives what they want.

Noteworthy Discoveries: Paula Garcés (who plays Millie) has a long history with the L&O franchise—she first appeared on the original show in 1991 as a teen.

Episode 147: Starved

Original air date: November 15, 2005
Teleplay by Lisa Marie Petersen, directed by David Platt

Additional Cast: Dean Cain (Dr. Mike Jergens), Teri Garr (Minerva Grahame-Bishop), Tina Holmes (Cora Kennison Jergens), Fred Dalton Thompson (DA Arthur Branch), Veronica Cartwright (Virginia Kennison), Kelly Miller (Janice Clay), Julie White (Dr. Anne Morella)

Reviewing the Case: Benson bonds with Cora, a serial rapist's damaged girlfriend who refuses to believe he's guilty and self-medicates with alcohol. After a sudden wedding, the girlfriend and the rapist vow a suicide pact—and Cora ends up brain dead. Suddenly, this already overly complex story upends as (in the words of one character) "the wrong person tries to do the right thing" by pulling the life-support plug. But her erstwhile mother—and Novak—want to fight back.

Noteworthy Discoveries: Judith Light returns as Elizabeth Donnelly, now a judge. Teri Garr (best known as the frustrated wife in 1977's *Close Encounters of the Third Kind*) pops in as a lawyer. And former superhero Dean Cain from *Lois & Clark: The New Adventures of Superman* turns up as a very un-super person.

Episode 148: Rockabye

Original air date: November 22, 2005
Teleplay by Patrick Harbinson, directed by Peter Leto

Additional Cast: Annie Potts (Sophie Devere), Skipp Sudduth (Philip Westley), Fred Dalton Thompson (DA Arthur Branch), Robert Foxworth (Dr. Lett), J. Paul Nicholas (Attorney Linden Delroy), Keri Lynn Pratt (Lauren Westley), John Patrick Amedori (Wayne Mortens), Adriane Lenox (Judy Galton)

Reviewing the Case: A pregnant teen is beaten with a lamp badly enough to cause her child to be stillborn a few days later, but after detectives arrest her boyfriend, forensics indicate she had a hand (literally) in the baby's death. Once both teens take the stand, the rest of the story emerges: That they were thwarted at all turns in trying to have a legal abortion, as well as stymied by anti-choicers in the guise of pharmacists and a supposed abortion doctor—which draws the attention of prosecutors.

Noteworthy Discoveries: Judge Donnelly holds feminist, pro-choice views; DA Branch is of the opposite bent. In New York, a fetus is not legally a person after birth unless it takes a breath. Spunky Annie Potts should be recognizable to viewers from *Designing Women* and *Any Day Now*.

Episode 149: Storm

Original air date: November 29, 2005
Teleplay by Neal Baer and Amanda Green, directed by David Platt

Additional Cast: Russell Hornsby (Alvin Dutch), Nickayla Tucker (Nicki Wright), Drucie McDaniel (Felicity Gill), Lou Sumrall (Clayton Miles), Matthew Settle (Jackson Zane), Barbara Lee GoVan (Mrs. Fontenont), Leo Marks (Michael Delphit), Birdie M. Hale (Goldie Prioleaux), Keke Palmer (Tasha Wright)

Reviewing the Case: A convicted sex offender saves, then "adopts," three sisters orphaned on the Gulf Coast after Hurricane Katrina and brings them to New York, but two escape. Detectives arrest the criminal, who promptly drops dead from anthrax, which journeyed from the Big Easy to the Big Apple in a van. The Feds hush up the details and try to wrest the case away, so Benson leans on a pesky *Ledger* reporter to get the real story out.

Noteworthy Discoveries: Some episodes seem overly complicated, with elements that don't mesh, but there's enough story in "Storm" to pack a feature film, and all of it riveting. Bonus points for finally giving Tamara Tunie more to do than poke around in corpses; pairing her up with Benson proves they're a formidable team.

Episode 150: Alien

Original air date: December 6, 2005
Teleplay by Jose Molina, directed by Constantine Makris

Additional Cast: Raquel Castro (Emma Boyd), Patricia Kalember (Judge K. Taten), Stephen McKinley Henderson (Judge Bernard), Ned Eisenberg (Roger Kressler), Sarah Knapp (Kate Boyd), Daniel Manche (Sean Hamill), Heather Fairfield (Lenore Hamill), Jack Koenig (Edgar Hamill), Amy Pietz (Zoe Dunlop), Sasha Neulinger (Charlie Monaghan), Todd Gearhart (Garrett Gillespie), Mary Beth Peil (Debra Boyd), Daniel Jenkins (Father Justin Miller), Stephen Bogardus (James Decker), Adam LeFevre (Ray Monaghan), Edmond Genest (Oliver Decker)

Reviewing the Case: When a little girl named Emma is bullied at her Catholic school for having two women as parents, she lashes out at her tormentor, paralyzing him. But that's only half the battle: Her hospitalized biological mom Kate worsens and her other mother Zoe has no legal custody of Emma, so the child is temporarily placed with Kate's homophobic parents. While there, Emma claims that Zoe molested her—a charge buoyed by some questionable photographs. It will take a court case to sort out the truth from propaganda.

Noteworthy Discoveries: Raquel Castro held her own with J. Lo and Ben Affleck the year before this episode, as the titular *Jersey Girl* (2004 movie).

Episode 151: Infected

Original air date: January 3, 2006
Teleplay by Tara Butters and Michele Fazekas, directed by Michelle MacLaren

Additional Cast: Annie Potts (Sophie Devere), Gordon Clapp (Ted Carthage), Malcolm David Kelley (Nathan Phelps), Ron McLarty (Judge Joseph Malloy), Nancy Opel (Mrs. Carthage), David Aaron Baker (Attorney Mike Getty), Glynn Turman (Dr. Young), Spencer Grammer (Katie), April Nixon (Monica Phelps), Amanda Plant (Candace Tanner), David Thornton (Lionel Granger)

Reviewing the Case: After young Nathan Phelps' meth-addicted mother is shot while he hides in a closet, Benson takes him under her wing but fails to see the warning signs that lead him to gun down his mother's killer. The case seems clear-cut, but a novel defense strategy—that witnessing a shooting makes a person more likely to shoot someone—gets the go-ahead from Judge Donnelly. A plea bargain is interrupted and stayed temporarily by the gun industry, which wants such a defense quashed for good.

Noteworthy Discoveries: Gordon Clapp will be most recognizable to fans of ABC's *NYPD Blue*, on which he played Det. Greg Medavoy from 1993–2005. And trivia alert: The briefly seen Spencer

Grammer is the daughter of Kelsey Grammer, of *Cheers* and *Frasier* fame.

Episode 152: Blast

Original air date: January 10, 2006
Teleplay by Amanda Green, directed by Peter Leto

Additional Cast: Tom Verica (Jake Hunter), Joe Lisi (Craig Lennon), Shawn Reaves (Daniel Hunter), Kaitlin Hopkins (Pamela Hunter), Gabrielle Brennan (Carly Hunter), Traci Lynne Kindell (Yvette Fennessy)

Reviewing the Case: A kidnapper snatches leukemia-ridden young Carly Hunter from outside her school and demands no cops—but M.E. Warner is drawn in by circumstance and tries to help. The missing girl is recovered, but Stabler thinks her father may know more about the kidnapper than he's letting on, and the detective is right: It's the Hunters' older, heroin-addicted son Daniel, who takes everyone hostage at a bank to get the money he needs. After an accidental shooting, Daniel becomes suicidal—and it requires an M.E. with nerves of steel to help this episode come to a conclusion.

Noteworthy Discoveries: Tamara Tunie's M.E. Warner gets out of the lab again, thankfully, and her expanded role not only makes sense but is well-played. Viewers also learn that the character had two tours of Air Force duty at the Ramstein base in Germany during Operation Desert Storm, and once worked in a methadone clinic.

Relevant Testimony: "The writers decided they were going to give Warner a show she was the catalyst for, and before Amanda Green put it on paper she talked to me. So I knew from the inception what it was going to be about, some of the new history we're going to find out about Warner, all of that. There isn't a lot of information out there about Warner. There's still a lot of room to fill in the blanks about her. I did like the idea that she got a lot of her medical training through military service (discovered in 'Blast'), so when it came time for her to have to handle a gun, to think under a duress-like situation she was cool, calm, collected, and able to do it. But still ultimately affected by it."—Tamara Tunie

Episode 153: Taboo

Original air date: January 17, 2006
Teleplay by Dawn DeNoon, directed by Arthur W. Forney

Additional Cast: Zeljko Ivanek (Everett Drake), Michael Lerner (Morty Berger), Patricia Kalember (Judge Taten), Schuyler Fisk (Ella Christiansen), Brandon Bales (Vincent Wensel), Piter Marek (Dr. Palshikar), Jack Mulcahy (Det. Brian Beal), Tijuana Ricks (Dr. Marnie Aiken), Greta Lee (Heather Kim), Curt Hostetter (Joe Shepherd), Gloria Biegler (Candace Shepherd), Anthony Bishop (Danny Hayes), Curtis Mark Williams (Jerry Spencer)

Reviewing the Case: Brilliant college student Ella claims not to have known she was pregnant, and that she blacked out after giving birth, so doesn't recall tossing the baby in the trash. Huang suspects post-partum psychosis. Benson thinks they're being scammed, and then it gets creepy: The surviving baby's DNA reveals an unholy union between Ella and her only recently discovered biological father. Still, the question remaining in a story V.C. Andrews would have approved of remains: Is Ella a sociopath, or truly off-the-beam?

Noteworthy Discoveries: Guest Schuyler Fisk is Sissy Spacek's daughter, and has the same haunting beauty as her mother. Stabler is feeling traumatized by his pending divorce and is let off of the case early (after an uncontrolled outburst) in order to spend more time with his kids. Zeljko Ivanek probably is familiar to fans of *Homicide: Life on the Street*, *Oz*, and *Law & Order*, among other shows. He won a 2008 Emmy for best supporting actor in *Damages* (FX).

Episode 154: Manipulated

Original air date: February 7, 2006
Teleplay by Jose Molina, directed by Matt Earl Beesley

Additional Cast: Rebecca DeMornay (Tessa McKellen), Betty Buckley (Attorney Collette Walsh), Ned Eisenberg (Roger Kressler), Faina Vitebsky (Josie Post), Matthew Maher (Tim), Mark Love (Wally Rimaldi), Kevin Carrigan (Jeffrey Sobchak), Brian Slaten (Alan Winchell), Chris Potter (Linus McKellen), Holt McCallany (Walter Inman)

Reviewing the Case: A murdered lawyer has been living a double life—stripping on the side, and sleeping with her paralyzed boss' husband. At first, he seems a natural suspect, but when a second stripper is found dead in a locked room, that seems less likely. Detectives turn back to boss Tessa and expose more double lives, including a case of Munchausen's syndrome and a guilt-ridden spouse who's been framed and duped.

Noteworthy Discoveries: Rebecca DeMornay has the face of an angel, but routinely plays women one sandwich short of a picnic; she's electrifying here in a story that feels more like a feature film. Her character's lawyer is played by Betty Buckley, known as the "voice of Broadway" who sang the definitive version of "Memory" from *Cats* (1982–2000). The episode is excellent, but that said, no *L&O* final reveal should echo a 1976 episode of *Little House on the Prairie*. *SVU* has offered Betty Buckley "various psychopathic roles" over the years.

Relevant Testimony: "I wasn't that gung-ho about them. I love to play crazy people, but I kept opting for something more normal because I wanted the ability to come back! When I first met Mariska and told her, she thought I was nuts, because apparently all of the (*SVU*) parts I'd turned down, the actresses had gotten Emmy nominations."—Betty Buckley

Episode 155: Gone

Original air date: February 28, 2006
Teleplay by Jonathan Greene, directed by George Pattison

Additional Cast: Susan Saint James (Attorney Bradshaw), Fred Dalton Thompson (DA Arthur Branch), Anna Holbrook (Roberta King), Barry Bostwick (Oliver Gates), Harvey Atkin (Judge Ridenour),

Haythem Noor (Sharif Damavandi), Ray Luetters (Sanford Warren), Rebecca Baxter (Amanda Durning), Edmund Davys (William King), Maggie Siff (Emily McCooper), Paul David Story (Nick Pratt), Teddy Eck (Doug Waverly), Barbara King (Jennifer Durning), Harry Zittel (Jason King), Sandor Tecsy (Keith Willis), Katie Bowden (Dana Simpson)

Reviewing the Case: Students Doug Waverly, Jason King, and Nick Pratt are clearly guilty of something in the gang rape and disappearance of a visiting Canadian, but detectives have a hard time making anything stick until videotapes and pressure cause one of the young men to crack. But after his grand jury testimony, King goes missing and everyone fears the worst, except for Waverly and Pratt, who may get away with murder—twice. A sequence of scenes with Judge Donnelly, DA Branch, and Novak is worth the price of admission.

Noteworthy Discoveries: Guest star Susan Saint James is a TV veteran who first came to wide notice as Rock Hudson's spouse in *McMillan & Wife.*

Episode 156: Class

Original air date: March 21, 2006
Teleplay by Paul Grellong, directed by Aaron Lipstadt

Additional Cast: Mathew St. Patrick (Roddy Franklin), Trieste Dunn (Gloria Culhane), Joey Slotnick (Walter Camp), Tess Soltau (Caroline Pereira), Michael Jay Bressman (Mark Duffy), Will Estes (Adam Halder), Jenelle Lynn Randall (Angela Franklin), Michael de Nola (Diamond Dov), Anjali Bhimani (Dr. Farouq), Scott Bailey (Brian Townsend), Nick Sandow (Doug Kirsten)

Reviewing the Case: Police suspect a college student is prostituting herself through school when she's found dead with a lot of cash, but it turns out she's a poker player running with big boys. But when they turn up her ace in the hole—a silent partner who helped her scam an online poker site, where she lost a large sum of money—detectives discover that what motivates her killer all has to do with class. A well-woven episode that still requires a scorecard to keep track of the details.

Noteworthy Discoveries: Mathew St. Patrick is most recognizable from his multi-year run on *Six Feet Under* (HBO, 2001–2005). Stabler identifies with the perpetrator's upwardly-mobile notions, and reveals that when he was the young man's age he got into a scuffle while working in his uncle's bar. He was arrested, but his father the cop made the charge disappear. It would have been possible for Stabler to both go to night school and work at a bar, apparently.

Episode 157: Venom

Original air date: March 28, 2006
Teleplay by Judith McCreary, directed by Peter Leto

Additional Cast: Lisagay Hamilton (Teresa Randall), Chris "Ludacris" Bridges (Darius Parker), Stephanie Berry (Kathleen Summers), Darnell Williams (Steven Stansfield), Tiffany Thompson (Angela Bowden), Ernest Waddell (Ken Randall), Joe Grifasi ("Heshy" Horowitz)

Reviewing the Case: Tutuola's son Ken reports a crime he overheard in a bar—and is an initial suspect, until he points to his "cousin" Darius. Until now, Tutuola never realized that this grown man is the long-rejected son of his ex-wife Teresa, Ken's mother. Darius seems willing to confess to his role in the old crime, but he quickly turns jailhouse lawyer and almost wriggles away—leaving Tutuola with this parting message: Take this case to court, and I'll expose all of your ugly family secrets.

Noteworthy Discoveries: Rapper/actor Ludacris is equally sympathetic and frightening; he almost has more charisma than Ice-T. Tutuola's ex-wife, known as "Tessie," gave birth to Darius at sixteen and never told Fin. She let her mother raise the boy because he reminded her too much of his father (who wasn't Fin).

Relevant Testimony: "Ludacris is one of my spawn!"—Ice-T

Episode 158: Fault

Original air date: April 4, 2006
Teleplay by Tara Butters and Michele Fazekas, directed by Paul McCrane

Additional Cast: Lou Diamond Phillips (Victor Paul Gitano), Rebecca Wisocky (Dr. Paula Greenfield), Steven Hinkle (Ryan Clifford), Tristen Douglass (Rebecca Clifford), Matt Landers (Glen Porter), Craig McEldowney (Calvin Porter), David Colburn (Eddie Loomis)

Reviewing the Case: The show breaks further from tradition, digging perhaps more deeply into the personal realm with an affecting episode that evolves almost entirely on the run. A violent pedophile is quickly determined to be the killer of three family members—and the kidnapper of the two youngest. Pursuit leads to Benson being injured and Stabler questioning their long-term partnership. But when the perp takes Stabler hostage, leaving Benson concerned about shooting him while trying to get to their killer, the two detectives have to reassess their long connection.

Noteworthy Discoveries: After the case is resolved, Stabler tells Benson that in two life-and-death situations they "chose each other over the job," and that can't happen, so Benson asks Cragen for a new partner. Director Paul McCrane will be familiar to long-time *ER* fans as the testy but doomed Dr. Romano, while guest star Lou Diamond Phillips has a long history in feature films, including 1987's *La Bamba* and 1988's *Young Guns*. During this episode, Hargitay is seven months pregnant—but still had to do stunts. Crew members set up padding on the floor where she can fall so her belly would be protected, but then she has to leap to her feet while brandishing a gun and talking. It's far from easy.

Relevant Testimony: "Everybody's crying; they had to cry between takes because it was so hilarious. (Executive producer) Ted (Kotcheff) was like, 'Well, darling, we'll take care of you (while you're pregnant)' and of course I had to do all these scenes running full speed through Port Authority, running with my belly at full speed! It's amazing (my son August) came out all right, but he was fine."—Mariska Hargitay

Episode 159: Fat

Original air date: May 2, 2006
Teleplay by Patrick Harbinson, directed by Juan J. Campanella

Additional Cast: Anthony Anderson (Det. Lucius Blaine), Natalie Cole (Attorney Waldron), Ted Sod (Hamzid Latif), Shahidah McIntosh (Mia Bixton), Wallace J. Little (Kenny Bixton), J. Paul Nicholas (Attorney Linden Delroy), Billy Wheelan (Tommy Strahan), Peter McRobbie (Judge Walter Bradley), David Bishins (Rufus Brownell), Tricia Mara (Jessica DeLay), David Thornton (Lionel Granger), Paul Calderon (Eric Molina), Omar Benson Miller (Rudi Bixton)

Reviewing the Case: With Benson reassigned to "computer crimes," Cragen punishes Stabler by pairing him up with a detective even more of a blowhard than he is: Det. Lucius Blaine, of the Queens SVU. Though they don't get along, the duo investigates the rape and assault of a high school girl by two overweight siblings. This proves to be a revenge attack in defense of their similarly overweight brother Rudi. Police finally sort out all of the beatings and come up with a suspect—but then Rudi takes the law into his own substantial hands.

Noteworthy Discoveries: Benson and Stabler have been partners for seven years, which means the show runs in real time. In 2008, Anderson was hired by *Law & Order* to portray Det. Kevin Bernard.

Relevant Testimony: "What convinced me (to get Anthony) on (the Mother Ship) was actually the *SVU* episode. There was a scene where (Stabler) had been making Anthony's character totally nuts during the whole episode. And he was over by the coffee stand and (Stabler) came up to bug him about something else and (Anthony's character) turned on him and went, 'What!' It was such a pure human moment and a non-acting moment that it was just one of those wonderful things that convinced you that this guy can really act in a way that you can't teach. He's a guy you want on your show."—*SVU* creator Dick Wolf (as told to Troy Rogers on thedeadbolt.com)

Episode 160: Web

Original air date: May 9, 2006
Teleplay by Paul Grellong, directed by Peter Leto

Additional Cast: Kate Mulgrew (Donna), Jack Vignone (Jake Winnock), Drew Battles (Ralph Zessner), Peter Hermann (Trevor Langan), Dana Eskelson (Ms. Winnock), Marla Sucharetza (Hensal's Sister), Tim Hopper (Gregory Hensal), Connor Paolo (Teddy Winnock), Charley Scalies (Bert Ferrara), Christen Simon (Elaine Norman), Maximillian Sherer (Colin), Pasha Pellosie (Gordy Richards), Gregg Edelman (Dr. Lucas)

Reviewing the Case: A boy abused by his father has grown into a damaged teen who now sells himself through his own online business to subscribing pedophiles—and sometimes incorporates his younger brother in the porn videos he makes. But when police close in, one of those "customers" decides to protect his interests by kidnapping the elder boy, which leads to a network of Web-connected predators that can only be unraveled by the department's newest computer crimes expert: Benson.

Noteworthy Discoveries: Recurring character Ruben Morales has a nephew who was lured by a pedophile on the Web. At the episode's end, Benson returns to her desk. Canny viewers will know that Hargitay was very close to giving birth at this stage, which explains the unusually high and tight camera shots.

Episode 161: Influence

Original air date: May 16, 2006
Teleplay by Ian Biederman, directed by Norberto Barba

Additional Cast: Brittany Snow (Jamie Hoskins), Peter Riegert (Chauncey Zeirko), Stella Maeve (Leslie Sweeney), Zachary Booth (Trevor Olsen), Ron Scott (Malcolm Shaw), Chris Lindsay-Abaire (Barbara Collins), Norman Reedus (Derek Lord), Teddy Cañez (Mr. Ramirez), John Sutherland (Danny Morrison), Brandon Gill (Cameron Shaw), Tom O'Rourke (Judge Mark Seligman), Jeff McCarthy (Mr. Hoskins), Marsha Dietlein Bennett (Mrs. Hoskins)

Reviewing the Case: Bipolar teen Jamie goes off her meds after hearing her rock idol Derek Lord preach that they're "poison." Subsequently, she's deflowered in the school bathroom and mows down pedestrians with her parents' car, killing one. Novak's sympathies fade after the death and Jamie is charged with vehicular manslaughter, while all along Derek champions the girl's right to refuse medication.

Noteworthy Discoveries: Brittany Snow got her start as a child in soaps (*The Guiding Light*), but quickly became an American sweetheart as the lead adolescent on *American Dreams*.

SEASON EIGHT

September 2006–May 2007

Regular Cast: Christopher Meloni (Det. Elliot Stabler), Mariska Hargitay (Det. Olivia Benson), Richard Belzer (Det. John Munch), Ice-T (Det. Odafin "Fin" Tutuola), Dann Florek (Capt. Donald Cragen), Stephanie March (ADA Alexandra Cabot), Tamara Tunie (M.E. Melinda Warner), and B.D. Wong (Dr. George Huang)

Recurring Cast: Connie Nielsen (Det. Dani Beck), Adam Beach (Det. Chester Lake), Judith Light (SVU Bureau Chief Elizabeth Donnelly), Isabel Gillies (Kathy Stabler), Jeffrey Scaperrotta (Dickie Stabler), Patricia Cook (Elizabeth Stabler), Erin Broderick (Maureen Stabler), Allison Siko (Kathleen Stabler), Daniel Sunjata (CSU Tech Burt Trevor), Lou Carbonneau (CSU Tech), Welly Yang (CSU Tech Georgie), Jordan Gelber (CSU Tech Layton), Sheila Tousey (Judge Danielle Larson), Harvey Atkin (Judge Alan Ridenour), Tom O'Rourke (Judge Mark Seligman), Joanna Merlin (Judge Lena Petrovsky), Philip Bosco (Judge Joseph P. Terhune), Joel de la Fuente (TARU Tech Ruben Morales), Caren Browning (CSU Capt. Judith Siper), Peter Hermann (Trevor Langan), Ned Eisenberg (Roger Kressler), Mike Doyle (Forensics Tech Ryan O'Halloran)

SEASON EIGHT OVERVIEW: Oy, vey. Characters on the show probably ought to be taking anti-anxiety meds by now. When Benson goes undercover in Oregon (while Mariska Hargitay is pregnant and then on maternity leave), Dani Beck steps in as Stabler's SVU partner and—maybe—as his lover. In a moment of revelation, Benson's own subconscious carnal desire for him becomes evident. The Stabler marriage has gone from bad to worse, but eventually settles back on perhaps. Tutuola is plagued by questions about his history in Narcotics and Cragen is constantly threatening his employees for various transgressions. Viewers meet Munch's uncle, Benson's half-brother, and Detective Chester Lake—who is introduced briefly before later joining the series as a regular. Now there will be nine actors assembled around a squad room desk at the beginning of each episode.

Ratings Recap for Season: 7.2 rating / 12 share / 10,621,000 viewers

EPISODE DESCRIPTIONS

Episode 162: Informed

Original Air Date: September 19, 2006
Teleplay by Dawn DeNoon, directed by Peter Leto

Additional Cast: Marcia Gay Harden (Star Morrison/Dana Lewis), Kristen Bush (Haley Kerns), Alan C. Campbell (Mitchell Hissam), Ebon Moss-Bachrach (Justin), Joanna P. Adler (Persephone James), John O'Creagh (Sheriff Bailey), Lisa Strum (Tonya Majeski), Jefferson Breland (Adam Porter), Christopher Sapienza (Roy Delphy), David Dollase (Agent Lockwood), Gerrianne Raphael (Mrs. Weiman)

Reviewing the Case: A rape investigation quickly leads to an eco-terrorism conspiracy in a story arc that will disrupt the SVU squad for some time to come. A young woman, bleeding and her head crudely shaved after a sexual assault, refuses to cooperate with police. She's involved with an underground environmental organization, which brings the FBI's Star Morrison back on the scene and propels Benson out of it on a secret assignment.

Noteworthy Discoveries: Warner to Benson: "Did I ever tell you about the year I spent in Paris?" A plot device allows Benson to disappear for several episodes, giving Hargitay real-life maternity leave.

Relevant Testimony: "What a pleasure it was working with Marcia Gay! She's so talented and never even needed to rehearse. Each take had a little something extra."—Peter Leto

Episode 163: Clock

Original Air Date: September 26, 2006
Teleplay by Allison Intrieri, directed by Jim Hayman

Additional Cast: Gregory Harrison (Nathan Speer), Betsy Hogg (Jamey Speer), Deborah Raffin (Maia Graves), Betty Buckley (Attorney Walsh), Robert Vaughn (Tate Speer), Jason Butler Harner (Greg Hartley), Larry Pine (Attorney Van Allen), Stephen Gregory (Dr. Kyle Beresford), Stephen McKinley Henderson (Judge Bernard)

Reviewing the Case: With Benson mysteriously gone, the detectives search for a missing seventeen-year-old who looks much younger. Jamey Speer suffers from Turner syndrome, a rare genetic disorder that inhibits normal development yet can result in early aging. Consequently, she is ridiculed at school, tormented by her parents' nasty custody battle, and anxious to speed up her love life with a guy in his thirties. This is a situation that the detectives don't quite know how to tackle.

Noteworthy Discoveries: Det. Dani Beck shows up at the end of this episode to fill in for Benson. In court, we learn that Stabler has roughed up a boy named Kevin who was dating his daughter Kathleen. As SVU cops debate the complexity of sexual relationships, Dr. Huang talks about the romance between two men, one of whom looked like a woman—much like the plot of *M. Butterfly*, the 1988 Broadway show that starred B.D. Wong.

Episode 164: Recall

Original Air Date: October 3, 2006
Teleplay by Jonathan Greene, directed by Juan J. Campanella

Additional Cast: Leslie Caron (Lorraine Delmas), Charles Shaughnessy (Martin Trenway), Robin Weigert (Heather Stark),

Lily Rabe (Nikki), Meg Gibson (Dr. Polk), James Naughteon (Trenway's Lawyer), Philip Levy (Off. Fineman), Kris Eivers (Barry Cole), Rozie Bacchi (Ophelia Jones), Laura Kai Chen (Dr. Sanada), Chinasa Ogbuagu (Off. Scott)

Reviewing the Case: The action begins with a chase in progress, as Beck and Stabler try to catch up with a rapist. Eventually the most likely candidate, identified in an unusual lineup involving only men's hands, is a respected attorney. But evidence and reliable witnesses evaporate. An elusive woman from France may provide important clues, especially when she and Beck converse in French—with English subtitles. The detective is the only one likely to coax the older woman out of her long-term denial.

Noteworthy Discoveries: Cragen tells Stabler that Danish-born Beck had a reputation for being overzealous when she worked in Warrants. After meeting her American husband in Germany, the couple came to the US. He became a cop, and was killed four years ago.

Relevant Testimony: "(Dani Beck) was very balls-to-the-wall, my way or the highway, this is how we do business in the Warrants (division). . . . What she learns is that Special Victims is a people job and you have to spend your time trying to understand what's in people's minds."—Jonathan Greene

Episode 165: Uncle

Original Air Date: October 10, 2006
Teleplay by Dawn DeNoon, directed by David Platt

Additional Cast: Jerry Lewis (Andre Munch), Timothy Adams (Brent Allen Banks), William Hill (Landlord), Peter McRobbie (Judge Walter Bradley), Jill Marie Lawrence (Cleo Conrad), Ali Reza (D. Rohit Mehta), Ryan Brown (Trey Williams), Jana Robbins (Sean Darringer), Tara Bast (Maryellen Seaver), Sam Riley (Patrolman Eric Bruny), Roxane Carrasco (Mrs. Rojas), Caitlin Sanchez (Lupe Rojas)

Reviewing the Case: A mother and her young daughter have been raped, killed, and wrapped in acrylic tape. The chief suspect is an incoherent homeless man with blood on his hands and clippings about the SVU in the cardboard box where he sleeps. He's also "Uncle Andrew" to Munch. Even once the crime is solved, this episode focuses on the issue of taking responsibility for acts of violence, no matter the cause.

Noteworthy Discoveries: The kid who killed Beck's husband is doing life in Attica. Munch's father committed suicide when his son was thirteen; the detective now lives at 80 West 183rd Street, in a briefly glimpsed apartment.

Relevant Testimony: "Jerry Lewis is a good friend of Richard Belzer's . . . Richard idolizes Jerry Lewis. I idolize Jerry Lewis. When he was sick, he used to watch *SVU* marathons and fell in love with the show. He (normally) doesn't do television and that was a huge blessing to get him."—Dawn DeNoon

Episode 166: Confrontation

Original Air Date: October 17, 2006
Teleplay by Judith McCreary, directed by David Platt

Additional Cast: Michael Kelly (Luke Dixon), Kerr O'Malley (Megan Carlisle), Matthew Arkin (Barry Carlisle), Marin Ireland (Gina Maylor), Patricia Kalember (Judge Taten), John Michael Bolger (Det. Geiger), Eleanor Hutchins (Elizabeth Hassenback), Mariette Hartley (Attorney Lorna Scarry), Tug Coker (Ted Wilmington), J. Paul Nicholas (Attorney Linden Delroy), Jessi Campbell (Off. Randa Lewis)

Reviewing the Case: A serial attacker invariably comes back to assault his victims a second time, always taking their urine when he goes. Dr. Huang speculates he may be a "power reassurance rapist" with "urolangia," the need to demonstrate total control of his victims—even their bladders. Maybe so, but the rationale for these crimes is even stranger—think Adolf Hitler. Yet the episode ends on a grace note about the healing power of, if not forgiveness, then letting go of hatred.

Noteworthy Discoveries: Two fifteen-year-olds murdered Beck's husband, Mike. But the shooter has since died in a prison fight. Stabler tells her that she might not belong in the SVU. Novak lectures her about the use of excessive force.

Relevant Testimony: "Urolangia is often when perps drink the urine of their victims. I don't know how rare it is. Maybe less so than we think. There's a lot of aberrant behavior going on out there."—Judith McCreary

Episode 167: Infiltrated

Original Air Date: October 31, 2006
Teleplay by Dawn DeNoon, directed by David Platt

Additional Cast: Charles Martin Smith (Sheriff Bartley), Vincent Spano (FBI Agent Porter), Debra Jo Rupp (Debra Hartnell), Steven Rishard (Deputy Jimmy Ibold), Chris Bowers (T-Bone), Maria Thayer (Hope), Frederick Strother (Judge Siburt), Kelly McAndrew (Deputy Trudi Minehart), Molly Camp (Britney Dunlap), Candace Thompson (Chelsea Arndale), Keri Setaro (Kristy Shutt), David Dollase (SAC Lockwood), Joe Tapper (Attorney Delray Mellott), J.B. Adams (Dr. Richard White)

Reviewing the Case: When the possible outcome of a New York City rape trial turns on DNA from chewing gum, Benson is called to testify. Only one problem: The detective is clear across the country, posing as an environmental activist in Oregon. At a demonstration there, she's knocked out by a local cop, then arrested for assault. After the head of a Pacific Northwest company that pollutes is found floating in the river, Benson realizes he was also a pedophile and begins sleuthing.

Noteworthy Discoveries: While Benson's unconscious, she mutters the name "Elliot" several times.

Relevant Testimony: "I thought I'd give the fans a little 'something-something'. . . . Dreams don't mean anything really. It could have been a nightmare!"—Dawn DeNoon

Episode 168: Underbelly

Original Air Date: November 14, 2006
Teleplay by Amanda Green, directed by Jonathan Kaplan

Additional Cast: Michael K. Williams (Victor Bodine), Charlayne Woodard (Sister Peg), Charlie Ray (Belinda Holt), Victor Slezak (Blake Peters), Joanna Rhinehart (Venice Jones), Joe Grifasi (Hashi Horowitz), Lynda Gravatt (Mrs. Mason), Julito McCullum (Jason Young), Luther Creek (Miguel Alvarez), David Lipman (Judge Arthur Cohen), Constance Wu (Candy), Gary Cowling (Caseworker Hecht), Sanjiv Jhaveri (Mr. Singh)

Reviewing the Case: Three rape-homicide victims, discovered separately, have tattoos of a dog's paw on their backs. All from troubled backgrounds, they were prostitutes and proud of it. Their smug pimp is only slightly more revolting than the older married man who "adopts" such girls to live with him at a Fifth Avenue apartment. Sister Peg is back to help but gets clobbered for her effort.

Noteworthy Discoveries: A phone call interrupts Beck and Stabler in the midst of kissing while out for a drink after work. Benson inadvertently meets Beck but decides to remain anonymous and does not immediately return to her job.

Relevant Testimony: "What does (Stabler) get with his wife? 'Mow the lawn. Take out the trash. I need a check for the tuition. Spank Dickie, he was bad at school today.' The mundane side of life is what we have when we come home. At work you have the very highs and very lows but it's never going to be, 'Take out the trash.'"—Amanda Green

Episode 169: Cage

Original Air Date: November 21, 2006
Teleplay by Patrick Harbinson, directed by David Platt

Additional Cast: Elle Fanning (Eden), Margo Martindale (Rita Gabler), Ken Howard (Dr. Arlen Rieff), Viola Davis (Donna Emmett), Leo Burmeister (Bud Gabler), Philip Bosco (Judge Joseph Terhune), Marlyne N. Afflack (Alma Cordoza), Louis Mustillo (Frank Hovis), Bob Ari (Ignatius Petty), Marilyn Chris (Dora Hovis), Linda Powell (Lauren White)

Reviewing the Case: Two kids survive in a van that crashes into a river, despite being handcuffed to their seats. The young boy, diagnosed by Dr. Huang as suffering from "reactive detachment disorder," stabs Stabler with a pen. The sweet little girl initially seems less deranged. Both had been captives at a group home run by a middle-aged couple that practices controversial rebirthing therapy and keeps disobedient youngsters confined. As the perps go to trial, Beck bonds with the adorable child but there's only heartbreak ahead.

Noteworthy Discoveries: At the hospital Stabler and Beck are about to share another intimate moment, when his wife Kathy suddenly appears. Elle Fanning is the younger sister of Dakota Fanning.

Relevant Testimony:

"I did a lot of research and spoke to a lot of shrinks. . . . There's detective work in storytelling. These are impossible children (with detachment disorder)."—Patrick Harbinson

"When I asked (Elle Fanning) what her process is, she told me: 'I sit and think about the character and it comes.'"—David Platt

Episode 170: Choreographed

Original Air Date: November 28, 2006
Teleplay by Paul Grellong, directed by Peter Leto

Additonal Cast: Bob Saget (Glenn Cheales), Catherine Bell (Naomi Cheales), Chris Sarandon (Wesley Masoner), Bernadette Peters (Attorney Stella Danquiss), Alan Davidson (Mr. Keener), Sean Haberle (Steve), Kristine Szabo (Danielle Masoner), Al Brown (Corrections Commissioner Tom Sablone), David Wilson Bernes (Agent Hellerman), Anne James (Dr. June Larom), Richmond Hoxie (Dr. Reed Vineland)

Reviewing the Case: The director of a modern dance company—known for his womanizing—falls under suspicion when his wife succumbs to an apparent coronary after indicating she was raped. But the true cause of death is more labyrinthine, involving layers of deceit among supposed friends and lovers.

Noteworthy Discoveries: Beck has left the building, unable to cope with the SVU job stress. Benson and Stabler both have

A-positive blood. Munch, discussing how some people seek revenge in an angry divorce: "My four exes never made good on their threats." Fin: "Except for your Warren Commission memorabilia."

Relevant Testimony:

"Like the real people doing this kind of work, our characters occasionally lighten the mood with a wisecrack. In that instance, the set design for Munch's desk includes books on the Warren Commission and the JFK assassination. Nice little touches."—Paul Grellong

"(We're) a kind of a comedy team in a way. Fin is on to Munch's conspiracies and sarcasm, and they have a great back and forth repartee, but there have been episodes that have revealed a deep connection between them that comes out when it's important. We're very good in the interrogation room, when we dance around the suspect, and we really know how to work them over psychologically."—Richard Belzer

"There was nothing comic in Bob Saget's performance but whenever we yelled 'Cut!' he went right back into the dirty jokes."—Peter Leto

Episode 171: Scheherazade

Original Air Date: January 2, 2007
Teleplay by Amanda Green. directed by David Platt

Additional Cast: Brian Dennehy (Judson Tierney), Paget Brewster (Sheila Tierney), John Doman (Mike Mollinax), Karen Ziemba (Tierney's Doctor), Victoria Wyndham (Rita Colina), Karl Kenzler (Father Denis), Malachy Cleary (Asst. Warden McFarland), Erickka Sy Savane (FBI Agent Peters)

Reviewing the Case: A family priest asks Stabler to visit Judson Tierney, a dying Queens man with a dark past. But his story, like those in "1001 Arabian Nights," cannot be told all at once and he first wants the detective to find his estranged daughter Sheila. What unfolds is a series of crimes—bank robbery and murder, in particular—that stretch back more than four decades.

Noteworthy Discoveries: The Stabler twins, Dickie and Elizabeth, are confirmed in a church ceremony with the names Michael and Claire. Dad finds out his daughter Kathleen is a vegetarian. Fans of *Another World* should be delighted to see Victoria Wyndham resurfacing; she played Rachel Cory on the NBC soap from 1975–99 but has rarely been seen on TV since.

Episode 172: Burned

Original Air Date: January 9, 2007
Teleplay by Judith McCreary, directed by Eriq La Salle

Additional Cast: Blair Underwood (Miles Sennet), Michael Michele (Valerie Sennet), Tiffany Evans (Tessa Sennet), Peter Gerety (Judge Harrison), Maureen Mueller (Social Worker Jenner), Danny Johnson (Phillip Anderson), Connie Teng (Denise Fielding)

Reviewing the Case: A divorced couple fights over their daughter. The husband, who has anger-management problems, can only see the girl in brief supervised visits and must obey a restraining order. When his wife claims he raped her, SVU detectives try to separate truth from mendacity. Benson and Stabler take sides, threatening their own professional equilibrium. "I'm the longest relationship you've ever had with a man," he says. She later snaps back that his point of view is questionable, coming from someone "with a dying marriage and a history of violence." And that's not the most painful sequence in a truly wrenching episode.

Noteworthy Discoveries: Tutuola to Munch: "One divorce was enough for me. I can't figure out how you did it four times." After acknowledging she never liked Dani Beck, Kathy Stabler suggests to Benson that "Elliot is what we have in common," even though she was always worried "he preferred to spend time with you." Director La Salle had a long-running role on NBC's *ER* as Dr. Peter Benton (1994–2002).

Relevant Testimony: "I like it when things get ugly (between the detectives). I had a lot of fun writing Meloni's dialogue."—Judith McCreary

Episode 173: Loophole

Original Air Date: February 6, 2007
Teleplay by Jonathan Greene, directed by David Platt

Additional Cast: Ray Wise (CEO Roger Hanley), James Naughton (Charlie Moss), Peter Riegert (Chauncey Zeirko), Casey Siemazko (EPA Official), Wayne Duvall (Seth Milsted), Karen Olivo (Jennifer Benitez), Marquis Rodriguez (Diego Benitez), Justin McCarthy (Raymond Nesbitt), Bill Goldberg (Cupid), Anne James (Dr. Jane Larom), Peter McRobbie (Judge Walter Bradley)

Reviewing the Case: When SVU detectives busts the superintendent of a Washington Heights tenement, what initially seems like child pornography is soon revealed as clues in a governmental/corporate conspiracy. Before long the EPA, Homeland Security, and the Terrorism Task Force are either investigating or stonewalling. M.E. Warner admits, "This time, Munch isn't crazy." But it all boils down to Benson's dogged detective work in this rage-against-the-machine episode.

Noteworthy Discoveries: Benson and SVU techie Morales hide in the stall of a men's room to hack into a sinister company's computers.

Relevant Testimony: "We got a lot of response to this show; in fact, the EPA put up a rebuttal on their website. This is not to rabble-rouse. This is about how does the government of the United States allow human testing of these horrible chemicals on children? . . . . (*SVU*) is a place where you can do a lot more than just write fiction, because most of the time it is true."—Jonathan Greene

Episode 174: Dependent

Original Air Date: February 13, 2007
Teleplay by Ken Storer, directed by Peter Leto

Additional Cast: Carey Elwes (Sidney Truex), Emily VanCamp (Charlotte Truex), Robert John Burke (IAB Sgt. Ed Tucker), Seamus Davey-Fitzpatrick (Tommy Truex), Albert Jones (ADA Fritz), Justin Klosky (Ryan Bedford), Allison Hirschlag (Jane Williams)

Reviewing the Case: A small boy says he saw "a monster" knock his father unconscious; his mother is found sodomized and bludgeoned to death in her bed. Their rebellious adolescent daughter Charlotte supposedly was at the home of her nineteen-year-old boyfriend. Various alibis begin to crumble in light of a "pharm party"— when teenagers raid their parents' medicine cabinets to get high. The story takes a sharp left turn after it appears that Stabler may have killed a suspect.

Noteworthy Discoveries: "Here comes the rat squad," Stabler mutters when he spots the IAB's Ed Tucker, who later enumerates the SVU detective's many potentially unethical activities: He shot an unarmed suspect during a chase, held a man underwater, beat an ex-partner, impersonated a pedophile. To which Benson replies, "That was all to save lives." The case convinces Stabler to seek a rapprochement with his wife.

Episode 175: Outsider

Original Air Date: January 16, 2007
Teleplay by Paul Grellong, directed by Arthur W. Forney

Additional Cast: Kal Penn (Henry Chanoor), Navid Negahban (Dr. Rankesh Chanoor), Tiffany Pao (Ming Hao), Ernest Waddell (Ken Randall), Sakina Jaffrey (Geeta Chanoor), Pooja Kumar (Debi Chanoor), Kelli Giddish (Yin Chang-Chun Hao), Mark La Mura (Tom Bawson), Carmen Goodine (Edie Rimpo), Sharon Wilkins (Nurse Manager)

Reviewing the Case: Det. Chester Lake ambles in from the Brooklyn SVU to help solve a series of cross-borough murders and rapes, and temporarily pairs with Tutuola. He's an American Indian but the trail leads to an Indian-American doctor notorious for sexual harassment in the workplace. His family is soon embroiled in the investigation, with lifelong father-son tensions taking center stage.

Noteworthy Discoveries: Kal Penn has gained notoriety in two popular stoner movies, *Harold & Kumar Go to White Castle* (2004) and *Harold & Kumar Escape From Guantanamo Bay* (2008), as well as a recurring role on the Fox series *House*. In 2009 he left show business altogether to become an advisor to President Barack Obama. Tutuola's college-kid son Ken initially figures in the case. Lake flirts with Novak and she doesn't seem to mind. The men in his family, going back three generations, were ironworkers who built New York City. Tutuola is initially testy with him.

Relevant Testimony:

"(The Tutuola-Lake clash) is territorial, borough-based antagonism, Manhattan versus Brooklyn. You protect your turf. They come from different sides of the bridge. So that's enough (reason for) fireworks right there."—Paul Grellong

"Cops don't like to share their information with other cops. They're proprietary. So we had two-tier tension: cop to cop and a culture clash in the family."—Arthur Forney

Episode 176: Haystack

Original Air Date: February 20, 2007
Teleplay by Amanda Green, directed Peter Leto

Additional Cast: Marian Seldes (Peggy Kendall), Judith Light (Judge Elizabeth Donnelly), Ashley Williams (Laura Kozlowski), Pablo Schreiber (Dan Kozlowski), Dana Ashbrook (Paddy Kendall), Kali Rocha (Cindy Marino), David Thornton (Lionel Granger), Kathleen Chalfant (Judge Cutress), Jack O'Connell (George Kendall), Ali Reza (Dr. Rohit Mehta), Linda Powell (Lauren White), Stephen Guarino (Garrett), Santo Fazio (Bernardo)

Reviewing the Case: When a baby is abducted, his father and mother take turns as suspects. Both have a history of using illegal substances, though hers seems no worse than marijuana. His drug of choice is cocaine and gambling debts have forced him to deal. But even after an unethical tabloid-television reporter—a "poor man's Geraldo," as Stabler calls her—devastates the estranged couple, an entirely different scenario threatens the kidnapped child's well-being.

Noteworthy Discoveries: A suspect sues Stabler and Novak for violation of civil rights. Former SVU Bureau Chief Elizabeth Donnelly steps out of her judge's robes to defend them, citing his eighteen years on the force with a 97 percent case-closure rate and her six years as a prosecutor with a 71 percent conviction rate. Benson, employing a DNA kinship analysis test that M.E. Warner (who refers to her own child) has talked about, learns that she has a brother.

Relevant Testimony: "There's always been that question for Benson: Why do people do what they do? If it's genetic, do you carry it?"—Amanda Green

Episode 177: Philadelphia

Original Air Date: February 27, 2007
Teleplay by Patrick Harbinson, directed by Peter Leto

Additional Cast: Kim Delaney (Capt. Julia Millfield), Mary Stuart Masterson (Dr. Rebecca Hendrix), Michael Weston (Simon Marsden), Roberto Purvis (Bobby Trapido), Greg Alan Williams (Det. Folkner), Rick Otto (Det. Joyce), Jonathan Kells Phillips (Ronnie Cavelle), Arian Moayed (Amal Qinawi), Annie Meisels (Lucy), Michael Carbanaro (Jeff Trapido), Brian Rogalski (Brent)

Reviewing the Case: An unseen woman questions Stabler about Benson and vice-versa. But the details of these interviews will only be revealed at the end of the episode, which begins a narrative thread that continues through the rest of the season. Meanwhile, the two detectives are detained by a New Jersey cop, Julia Millfield, for interrupting a stakeout at the home of Simon Marsden—Benson's half-brother, now a suspect in several rapes. She's torn between believing he's innocent and her natural SVU instincts.

Noteworthy Discoveries: Kim Delaney appeared on *NYPD Blue*. "I've been alone my whole life," Benson laments after finding out through DNA that she had a brother. Distracted, she allows another suspect to get away during a chase. Cragen chews out Benson and Stabler for their Jersey detour: "Why should I keep you two together? Why should I keep you at all?" It's a cliffhanger.

Relevant Testimony: "(We) wanted to explore what it's like to discover family for a woman who all her life thought she had none."—Patrick Harbinson

Episode 178: Sin

Original Air Date: March 27, 2007
Teleplay by Patrick Harbinson, directed by George Pattison

Additional Cast: Tim Daley (Rev. Jeb Curtis), Kathy Baker (Hannah Curtis), John Cullum (Attorney Barry Moredock), Corey Sorenson (Paul Curtis), Manny Perez (DEA agent), Chad Hoeppner (Trent Labette), Amie Tedesco (Lucy Curtis), Karl Kenzler (Father Denis), Sandra Shipley (Rhona Antrim), David Lipman (Judge Arthur Cohen)

Reviewing the Case: The mutilation death of a male prostitute at first appears to be related to narcotics from Southeast Asia. Instead, the detectives come upon a homegrown source for the crime: a sect of homophobic fundamentalist Christians. A preacher, his wife, and their nine children figure in the whodunit of this episode, in which the cup of schmaltz nearly runneth over.

Noteworthy Discoveries: A confession that Stabler inspires by reciting his own prayer of repentance in a church is later tossed out of court as coercion.

Episode 179: Responsible

Original Air Date: April 3, 2007
Teleplay by Allison Intieri, directed by Yelena Lanskaya and David Platt

Additional Cast: Laura Leighton (Lillian Rice), Judith Light (Judge Elizabeth Donnelly), Hunter Parrish (Jordan Owens), Sarah Drew (Becca Rice), Leven Rambin (Regan Michaels), Van Hughes (Luke Young), Rob Mayes (Matt Schroeffel), Neal Matarazzo (Mr. Tomkin), Kelly Rebecca Walsh (Sheila Banks), Joseph Ricci (Kevin Banks), Linda Powell (Lauren White), Denise Lute (Eve Wilson), Lynn Hawley (Rose Tamkin)

Reviewing the Case: A teenage girl, partying with high-school pals in the apartment of strangers on vacation, drinks herself to death. The kids flee rather than call for help or face the consequences. A seductive single mom and her seemingly straitlaced daughter are involved in this episode about the importance being accountable for our decisions.

Noteworthy Discoveries: Expect a poignant epiphany after the years of angst about family matters that Stabler has endured. His daughter Kathleen teaches him the intricacies of Internet postings favored by her age group. He later acts privately on his remorse for having used police connections to erase her DUI charge in 2005 ("Blood," season six).

Relevant Testimony: "I had to take over because the other (director) had some problems. So for me it was cramming. I didn't know the locations and didn't really know the script. That was a different way of working. Usually, I make meticulous notes. But the whole thing was actually fun, as it turned out."—David Platt

Episode 180: Florida

Original Air Date: May 1, 2007
Teleplay by Jonathan Greene, directed by David Platt

Additional Cast: Kim Delaney (Capt. Julia Millfield), Vincent Spano (FBI Agent Dean Porter), Michael Weston (Simon Marsden), Frankie Faison (FBI Agent Tom Nickerson), Josh Casaubon (Michael Thatcher), Kathryn Hays (Jane Willet), Alex Wipf (Dr. Pressman), Catrina Ganey (Nurse Parmenter), Chance Kelly (State Trooper Lawley), John Rue (Desk Sgt. Ludlow)

Reviewing the Case: FBI Agent Porter, who has switched from domestic terrorism to "sexual offender fugitive apprehension," asks Benson to disclose her brother Simon's whereabouts. It's been two months since he disappeared at the end of "Philadelphia" earlier this season, and New Jersey detective Julia Millfield's still obsessed with tracking him down. Benson's obsessed with understanding if the father she never knew was indeed a rapist as she has always believed. This packed-to-the-gills story is a tangle of incest, sexual assault, drug use, alcoholism, depression, and suicide.

Noteworthy Discoveries: Cragen to Benson, who has just repeatedly kicked a suspect: "I have had it with your crap." Ordered to go home, she snaps at Stabler: "Oh, the poster boy for rage is going to tell me how to control my anger?" In a lighter moment, Benson (born in 1967) later admits that in high school she "had feathered hair and wore acid-washed jeans."

Relevant Testimony: "(For Benson,) it's not a question of wanting to create somebody who has misery, it's wanting to create somebody who wants to know why they are who they are. Though this was (her) personal story, there was also a crime involved, and I think as long you keep your eyes on the road you're not going to crash. And as far as I'm concerned we haven't just kept out eyes on the road, we've been paving it as we go along."—Jonathan Greene

Episode 181: Annihilated

Original Air Date: May 8, 2007
Teleplay by Amanda Green, directed by Peter Leto

Additional Cast: Dylan Walsh (Malcolm Royce), Kelly Dead-mon (Lindsay Royce), John Douglas Thompson (Mel Cantor), Paolo Montalban (Wahid), Reade Kelly (Bud Yellin), Annie McGreevey (Janet Yellin), Paul Urcioli (CIA Off. Chase), Rachel Stern (Millie Lefkowtiz), Lucas Delvasto (Tyler Royce)

Reviewing the Case: Malcolm Royce, who leads a double life, is the most likely perp in the murder of a bride-to-be. He's already got a wife named Lindsay and three kids in Staten Island, but kept his mistress at bay by pretending to be a covert CIA agent. There's also a *Desperate Housewives*–like scenario when Lindsay and a divorced friend vent about the frustrations of suburban existence, where things soon go from frustrating to deadly.

Noteworthy Discoveries: Munch, after pinpointing the suspect's home via a satellite image: "Aren't we lucky Big Brother's watching us from outer space?" Stabler's daughter Kathleen warns him: "We're your family, not some booty call." Nonetheless, he and his wife re-consummate their marriage—male partial buttock alert!

Relevant Testimony: "I wanted (Stabler) naked in that scene and figured what better place to see than his rear end? NBC has a two-inch crack rule."—Peter Leto

Episode 182: Pretend

Original Air Date: May 15, 2007
Teleplay by Dawn DeNoon, directed by David Platt

Additional Cast: Barry Bostwick (Oliver Gates), Misti Traya (Cassandra Sullivan), Michael Welch (Scott Heston), Ylfa Edelstein (Sonia Briglund), Patricia Kelember (Judge Taten), Peter McRobbie (Judge Walter Bradley), Clark Middleton (Landlord), Scott Sowers (Tim), Tibor Feldman (Dr. Cohen)

Reviewing the Case: The title of this episode, about a girl grasping for eternal youth, could just as easily be "Deluded." A boy's death while "extreme fighting" is quickly attributed to his classmate Scott Heston, only sixteen and claiming to be clinically depressed. But petite, innocent-looking Cassandra Sullivan is at the center of a romantic triangle that somehow sparked the tragedy. There's a bombshell regarding her identity, as she turns into one creepy chick.

Episode 183: Screwed

Original Air Date: May 22, 2007
Teleplay by Judith McCreary, directed by Arthur W. Forney

Additional Cast: Adam Beach (Det. Chester Lake), Steven Weber (Matthew Braden), Chris "Ludacris" Bridges (Darius Parker), Vincent Spano (FBI Agent Dean Porter), Lindsay Hamilton (Teresa Randall), Peter Gerety (Judge Harrison), Judith Light (Judge Elizabeth Donnelly), Michael Weston (Simon Marsden), Ernest Waddell (Ken Randall), John Schuck (Chief of Detectives), Nancy Grace (Herself), Star Jones (Herself)

Reviewing the Case: Darius Parker, the son of Tutuola's ex-wife Teresa, is accused of murder and the courtroom becomes a confessional for the entire SVU. A disgruntled former colleague targets Cragen. Benson is under fire for giving money to her brother Simon when he was a fugitive. Fin's record as a narc is questioned. Judge Donnelly recuses herself from the trial because she knows how Stabler helped his daughter Kathleen beat a 2005 DUI rap. On TV, Nancy Grace and Star Jones debate Novak's prosecutorial skills.

Noteworthy Discoveries: Tutuola, a cop for twenty-two years, was twice suspected of sampling the merchandise while an undercover narc. But he explains that in each instance he merely got a contact high. Kathleen Stabler's in for a big, nasty surprise regarding a previous DUI charge that had been erased. Det. Chester Lake returns to help out while the squad is immersed in chaos.

Relevant Testimony: "I wanted to explore chickens coming home to roost. A lot of shit these cops have been doing they haven't paid for. Benson committed a felony; she should've been kicked off the force and gone to prison. I also wanted someone to unmask all the secrets—that's what the defense attorney does. It's possible to show a jury that sometimes a cop's behavior suits his or her whim when it applies to their own families."—Judith McCreary

SEASON NINE

September 2007–May 2008

Regular Cast: Christopher Meloni (Det. Elliot Stabler), Mariska Hargitay (Det. Olivia Benson), Richard Belzer (Det. John Munch), Ice-T (Det. Odafin "Fin" Tutuola), Adam Beach (Det. Chester Lake); Dann Florek (Capt. Donald Cragen), Tamara Tunie (M.E. Melinda Warner); B.D. Wong (Dr. George Huang), Diane Neal (ADA Casey Novak)

Recurring Cast: Isabel Gillies (Kathy Stabler), Allison Siko (Kathleen Stabler), Joel de la Fuente (TARU Tech Ruben Morales), Mike Doyle (Forensics Tech Ryan O'Halloran), Caren Browning (CSU Capt. Judith Siper), Joanna Merlin (Judge Lena Petrovsky), Peter McRobbie (Judge Walter Bradley), David Lipman (Judge Arthur Cohen)

SEASON NINE OVERVIEW: After several seasons of relative stability within ranks, season nine made Det. Chester Lake (Adam Beach) a regular, partnering the hunky squad member with Fin—thus dialing back Det. Munch's appearances considerably—only to yank the new guy out permanently at the end of the season, which

MITCHELL HAASETH/NBC UNIVERSAL

Season nine cast, from l.-r.: Richard Belzer, Christopher Meloni, Tamara Tunie, B.D. Wong, Diane Neal, Mariska Hargitay, Ice-T, Adam Beach, Dann Florek

also saw the departure of the longest-running ADA in Law & Order franchise history: Diane Neal's Casey Novak. Those surprises aside, it was a season of extremes, with several overly fanciful storylines, including a very underground sex party, retrograde amnesia, Stabler's near-blinding, and Benson's abduction and near-rape. Nevertheless, the season proved remarkably strong as it hit its 200th episode (with a turn by Robin Williams at its center) and effectively moving, particularly when Benson has to help an injured Kathy Stabler deliver the family's latest addition—under the greatest of duress possible. All of this led to three Emmy nominations for *SVU* performers, with a possible second statuette in the offing for Mariska Hargitay; Cynthia Nixon picked up a guest Emmy for her role on the season's lead-off episode, "Alternate."

Ratings Recap for Season: 9.3 rating /17 share / 13,499,000 viewers

EPISODE DESCRIPTIONS

Episode 184: Alternate

Original Air Date: September 25, 2007
Teleplay by Neal Baer and Dawn DeNoon, directed by David Platt

Additional Cast: Cynthia Nixon (Janis Donovan), Bronson Pinchot (Dr. Henry Carlisle), Laura Allen (Cass Magnall), Stephen Spinella (Morgan), Joe Grifasi (Heshy Horowitz), Quincy Tyler Bernstine (Sheri Simkins), Amy Tribbey (Penny Taylor), Tamela Aldridge (Carla Sexton), Katy Grenfell (Mrs. Lynde), Donnetta Lavinia Grays (Off. Ramirez)

Reviewing the Case: "Dissociative identity disorder" dominates this episode, which centers on a Museum of Natural Science arachnologist who ensnares the SVU in her web of multiple personalities. A missing baby heightens the tension, but eventually incest and murder become the issues. Cynthia Nixon gives a bravura, Emmy-winning performance as a gal with many dimensions.

Noteworthy Discoveries: Benson returns from suspension, just as Cragen is temporarily reassigned for supporting his many wayward detectives in season eight. Munch, who took the sergeant's exam the previous year on a lark, finds himself appointed commanding officer. We're reminded that he was shot in the derriere by a white supremacist in "Raw" (season seven).

Relevant Testimony:
"There are case studies in law journals about when you can put an alternate (personality) on trial just because they're in the same body as the person who committed the crime. That just fascinated me."—Neal Baer, executive producer

"I was so thrilled to appear on *Law & Order: SVU*. I read all about multiple personalities—it was such a juicy part!"—Cynthia Nixon (as told to reporter Cameron Rose)

Episode 185: Avatar

Original Air Date: October 2, 2007
Teleplay by Paul Grellong, directed by Peter Leto

Additional Cast: Kevin Tighe (Julian Cooper), Florencia Lozano (Lauren Molby), Christina Brucato (Rachel McGarrett), Richard Short (Eric Winton), Teddy Bergman (Nestor Buchanan), Ryan Lynn (Dan Friedich), Lisa Joyce (Kristi McGarrett), John Hickok (Mr. McGarrett), Lou Martini Jr. (Robert Solomon), Paul Klementowicz (Tobin Willis), Doan Ly (Anne Bentley), Anne James (Dr. Jane Larom)

Reviewing the Case: The abduction of Rachel McGarrett isn't linked to her boyfriend's involuntary nocturnal lust: "sexsomnia" to Dr. Huang and "sleepsexing" to Stabler. Instead, she has become the victim of a grotesque predator attracted by her racy virtual-reality persona in an online game. He's also behind the disappearance of a fifteen-year-old a quarter-century earlier. "Avatar" is a somewhat far-fetched exercise in a high-tech world.

Relevant Testimony: "The diagnosis turned up in our medical research as a way into the story, but I didn't want to use (sexsomnia) for the whole episode. . . . I had to familiarize myself with virtual reality, but I do read a lot about technology. I thought it would be great to have our detectives solving one crime in two worlds at once."—Paul Grellong

Episode 186: Impulsive

Original Air Date: October 9, 2007
Teleplay by Jonathan Greene, directed by David Platt

Additional Cast: Melissa Joan Hart (Sarah Trent), Kyle Gallner (Shane Mills), Annie Potts (Sophie Devere), Quincy Dunn-Baker (Mr. Trent), Austin Lysy (Russell Hunter), Elizabeth Keifer (Mrs. Mills), Richard Joseph Paul (Mr. Mills), Danny Rutigliano (David Feldron), David P. Conley (Earl Romaine), Robert Vincent Smith (Dr. Drucker), Liam McMullan (Ryan Bluth)

Reviewing the Case: A recent American trend—female teachers sexually involved with high school boys—gets a distinctive *SVU* spin, going in various unexpected directions. Kyle, just fifteen and suffering from gonorrhea, accuses educator Sarah Trent of seducing him two months earlier. She claims to be the victim of an unreported rape. Her subsequent abortion sets off a chain reaction, beginning with a husband angry about the procedure on moral grounds. A my-abnormal-brain-made-me-do-it defense is juxtaposed with the kind of illustrations regularly seen on rival CBS show *CSI: Crime Scene Investigation.*

Noteworthy Discoveries: Novak assaults the director of a privatized juvenile detention center and Benson warns she might have to arrest her.

Relevant Testimony: "The truth is worse than our fiction. It's stunning the depravity that exists out there; we can't fully portray it on network TV. We have to shake that stuff off because we've got a job to do. But in order to educate people, we do it with gallows humor. It helps to have a funny cast and crew."—David Platt

Episode 187: Savant

Original Air Date: October 16, 2007
Teleplay by Judith McCreary, directed by Kate Woods

Additional Cast: Aidan Quinn (Ben Nicholson), Judy Kuhn (Corrine Nicholson), Paulina Gerzon (Katie Nicholson), Vincent Spano (FBI Agent Dean Porter), Jayne Atkinson (Assistant U.S. Attorney Marion Springer), Peter Riegert (Chauncey Zierko), Geraldine Hughes (Tina Parven), Josh Caras (Alex Parven), Robert Clohessy (Joel Parven), David Andrew MacDonald (Dr. Gerald Morgan), John Henry Cox (Judge Trenton), Kathleen Tipton (Jordana Weitz), Robert Kim (Paul Wei), Lia Yang (Ursula Wei), Julie White (Dr. Anne Morella)

Reviewing the Case: The bedroom of Corinne Nicholson was a remarkably busy place on the night of the beating that leaves her with retrograde amnesia. All three people in question can be quoted verbatim by her daughter Katie, a savant with super-sensitive hearing. The prime suspect is her father Ben, a biochemical engineer doing clandestine work for the government that shields him from SVU detectives. After many double-crosses, the conclusion is fierce.

Noteworthy Discoveries: Cragen tells Novak, "The Patriot Act trumps rape and attempted murder every time." She later observes: "That convoluted piece of legislation isn't worth the paper it's written on." Jayne Atkinson, formerly a White House terrorism expert on the Fox series *24*, portrays a terrorism-wary Fed.

Relevant Testimony: "Paulina Gerzon is very much not a savant, just a great actor. She had done 'Serendipity' (season five). . . . Writer Judy McCreary sent me videos from a fundraiser held to heighten awareness about it and a *60 Minutes* piece on Asperger's Syndrome, a form of autism. Paulina has an angular, elf-ish quality and the right sort of energy. She agreed to do the show before even reading the script."—Jonathan Strauss, casting director

Episode 188: Harm

Original Air Date: October 23, 2007
Teleplay by Josh Singer, directed by Peter Leto

Additional Cast: Steven Weber (Attorney Matthew Braden), Elizabeth McGovern (Dr. Faith Sutton), Liz Morton (Kate Simes), Elaine Bromka (Arlene Simes), Patrick Page (Jack Rexton), Jennifer Van Dyck (Dr. Kelly Alvin), Marjan Neshat (Mrs. Abbas), Jarreth Merz (Haroun Abbas), Audrie Neenan (Judge Lois Preston), Libya Pugh (Women's Refugee Coalition Center Director), Lou Martini Jr. (Robert Solomon), Leon Addison Brown (Clifton Mitchell), Karen Shallo (Paula Deeks), Jules Hartley (Jackie Solomon), Eddie Furs (Manny Jaworski), Kevin Cutts (Off. Louie Velchik)

Reviewing the Case: A profound ethical debate runs though much of "Harm," an engrossing episode that provides no easy answers. The murder of Kate Simes, an Arabic speaker who volunteered at a refugee center, winds back to Iraq. A cab driver from Baghdad is also dead from a sudden shock, a result of the post-9/11 interrogation by U.S. mercenaries that ruined his health. Complicity goes on trial, as M.E. Warner challenges a respected psychiatrist who sees torture as a necessary evil.

Noteworthy Discoveries: Stabler concedes that nine out of ten instances of police coercion are counterproductive. When a defense attorney quips that Novak might even want to indict the Secretary of Defense (then Donald Rumsfeld), she mutters, "Don't tempt me." An Abu Ghraib photo is introduced into evidence. A scene of torture victims from various countries testifying has a stark documentary quality.

Relevant Testimony: "I pushed myself visually in that scene. I thought of *Reds* (Warren Beatty's 1981 feature, which includes interviews with genuine elderly radicals). On *SVU*, they were speaking in their native tongues and the stories were all true. One woman from the Philippines was a survivor of the Marcos regime. She was a Muslim and they'd starve her and then offer only pork. We wanted to make the audience pay attention; we wanted it to really sink in about how America has been treating people from other nations. The country was still thinking you're unpatriotic to speak out, but you've got to stand up for the things you believe in."—Peter Leto

Episode 189: Svengali

Original Air Date: November 11, 2007
Teleplay by Kam Miller, directed by David Platt

Additional Cast: Beverly D'Angelo (Attorney Rebecca Balthus), Jared Harris (Robert Morton), Shannon Marie Woodward (Cecilia Strayer), Alex Organ (Damien), Mitchell Jarvis (Jasper Grace), Margaret Devine (Susan Goodman), Kerisse Hutchinson (Lashena Reynolds), Samantha Jacobs (Tina Snow), Gareth Saxe (Harrison Thomas), Justin Blanchard (Edgar Rabinowicz), Adam Heller (Ed Brown), Alexandra Rhodie (Jann Brown)

Reviewing the Case: Are there really noir fantasy clubs for people in retro finery staged in filthy abandoned subway stations? That's the passing conceit of this episode, which is actually about a sexually demented serial killer doing eight life terms in prison yet still manipulating his many fans. Revered for his "outsider art" (work by people not part of mainstream society), he's almost as sinister a villain as Hannibal Lecter thanks to a riveting portrayal by Jared Harris. Otherwise, "Svengali" is bursting at the seams with improbabilities.

Noteworthy Discoveries: When Lake knows about a defunct platform under the Waldorf-Astoria, Tutuola muses that the

Mohawks probably built New York's subway system as well as its above-ground structures.

Episode 190: Blinded

Original Air Date: November 13, 2007
Teleplay by Jonathan Greene, directed by David Platt

Additional Cast: John Cullum (Attorney Barry Moredock), Arye Gross (Saul Picard), Sam Waterston (DA Jack McCoy), Heather Braverman (Sabrina Farmer), Sylvia Kauders (Anna), Anne James (Dr. Jane Larom), Howard W. Overshown (Lt. Shea), Daniel Cantor (Special Agent Nelson), Diane Cossa (Dr. Merrins), Sam Riley (Uni Bruny), Joseph Vincent Gay (Uni Walker), Cassady Leonard (Eve Holland)

Reviewing the Case: This episode adds physical turmoil to the heap of emotional stress Stabler endured in season eight. His sight is reduced to blurred images after an escaping suspect bonks him in the head. Although the perp from Louisiana has kidnapped and raped eleven-year-old girls, he's a schizophrenic acting out a childhood trauma rather than a genuine pedophile. Novak bends the law, defies the FBI, and joins forces with a defense attorney. Cragen's not happy, but when is he ever? "Blinded" ultimately depicts a paradox, the perfect *SVU* conclusion.

Noteworthy Discoveries: Novak's onetime fiancé Charlie attacked her when he stopped taking his anti-psychotic meds. She had the charges dropped but he later died after walking into traffic. The defense attorney refers to her "new boss" Jack McCoy, the Mother Ship regular who's displeased with the way she's handling the case.

Relevant Testimony: "The idea was that (the death penalty for child rape) has just been approved by the Louisiana Supreme Court and they're going to need a test case. . . . Right now in Louisiana, as far as I know, you can charge someone who rapes a child with a capital crime and that's a really important question."—Jonathan Greene

(AUTHORS' NOTE: In June 2008, the U.S. Supreme Court ruled it unconstitutional for a child rapist to be sentenced to death if there's no murder involved.)

Episode 191: Fight

Original air date: November 20, 2007
Teleplay by Mick Betancourt, directed by Juan J. Campanella

Additional Cast: Steve Earle (Prison Teacher), Coco Nicole Austin (Traci Bell), Gaius Charles (Jadon Odami), Adina Porter (Janelle Odami), Forrest Griffin (Mike Kona), Lenny Venito (Terry Donovan), Arlen Escarpeta (Ezra Odami), Anwan Glover (James McDonnell), Josh Clayton (Dan Duebler), Stephanie Lee Andujar (Latrice Munez)

Reviewing the Case: A murdered teenage girl leads first to the world of mixed martial arts (with which Lake has more than a passing connection), then to a racist fraternity and its two brothers of color, one of whom confesses to the crime. But Lake's further inquiries cause him and Stabler to question the motives behind the confession. When gangs get involved, it turns out the victim was in deeper, darker territory than she could ever have known. Plus, there's a particularly gruesome death by trash compactor not to be missed.

Noteworthy Discoveries: Lake was known as "Naptime" when he participated in amateur mixed martial arts, but was sidelined by an injury. He also came up in the foster care system, and has an almost-didn't-make-it-as-a-cop story similar to a Stabler tale of woe. Additionally, there's a new power couple on the set—and it isn't Mariska Hargitay/Peter Hermann: Ice-T's wife Coco returns as the gold-digging fiancée of an ultimate fighter, and has some amusing scenes with her hubby. And finally, singer Steve Earle puts in a brief performance as the prison teacher.

Relevant Testimony:

"Ice and me, we rehearsed at home. He's a good coach and helps me out . . . I did theater when I was in school, and I learned from my mother because she's an actress herself. I have a little background."—Coco

"I don't think she got one bad review. Everybody said she did a good job, so it made my household happy, and I had a good time with her."—Ice-T

Episode 192: Paternity

Original air date: November 27, 2007
Teleplay by Amanda Green, directed by Kate Woods

Additional Cast: Mark Valley (Jake Keegan), Anastasia Griffith (Leah Keegan), Lawrence Saint-Victor (Paramedic Jackson), Steven Bauer (Raphael Gardner), Isabel Gillies (Kathy Stabler), Matthew Nicklaw (Matt Kramer), Thomas Langston (Tommy Keegan), Korey Jackson (Gilbert Matthews)

Reviewing the Case: A little boy lost is only the start of an investigation into a murdered nanny looking for love on the Internet, but also to the revelation that he and his father don't share the same DNA. Dad kills Mom and plans to commit suicide until Stabler intercedes—leaving Benson to transport a very pregnant Kathy Stabler to a doctor's appointment. But the two women are in a terrible car accident, and the baby decides it's time to come out, ready or not. It'll be up to everyone but Stabler to make sure the child arrives safely in this gripping, ultimately moving episode.

Noteworthy Discoveries: The Stablers live at 72-12 Castleside Street, Glenoaks, Queens. The new baby is named Elliot, Jr.

Relevant Testimony: "We figured let's have the other woman in his life deliver Kathy's baby. When we screened that episode in the editing room, everyone was startled by the auto accident. They didn't see it coming."—Neal Baer, executive producer

Episode 193: Snitch

Original air date: December 4, 2007
Teleplay by Mark Goffman, directed by Jonathan Kaplan

Additional Cast: Method Man (Dennis King), Steven Weber (Matthew Braden), Gloria Reuben (ADA Bureau Chief Christine Danielson), Hakeem Kae-Kazim (Chuckwei Bothame), Tracy Middendorf (Sarah Flint), Muna Otaru (Almani Bothame), Julie White (Dr. Anne Morella), Justin McCarthy (Adam Clayton Powell), Aixa Kendrick (Mira Otame), Frank Pando (Jesse Bleyer), Yasha Jackson (Courtney Williams)

Reviewing the Case: What seems like a case of witness intimidation by a local thug against the only person who'll come forward to testify against him unearths Nigerian cultural customs, including female circumcision and polygamy. And while much energy is expended by the cops—and new ADA Bureau Chief Danielsen—to make sure their witness and his family remain safe, the real threat apparently comes from within in this fast-moving, timely story that nevertheless dodges the real problem of modern witness intimidation.

Noteworthy Discoveries: Stabler's stable of beauties continue to pile up: While separated from Kathy he briefly saw Agent Courtney Williams in Immigration. Wu-tang Clan member Method Man is suitably intimidating as the thug in question, while Gloria Reuben (*ER*) is a welcome addition to the district attorney's office.

Episode 194: Streetwise

Original air date: January 1, 2008
Teleplay by Paul Grellong, directed by Helen Shaver

Additional Cast: Mae Whitman (Cassidy Cornell), Thom Bishops (Cole Roderick), Patricia Charboneau (Paige), Bill Winkler (Mr. Braidwell), Jeremy Jordan (Doug Walshen), Emily Meade (Anna), Fiona Hutchison (Lydia Crawford), Latham Gaines (Mr. Crawford), Johnny Hopkins (Tony Ramirez), Kathleen Garrett (Mrs. Braidwell), Natalie Hall (Shelby Crawford), Madeline Taylor (Josie)

Reviewing the Case: A street "family" of runaways is revealed when Benson and Stabler investigate the robbery and beating death of a debutante. The sociopathic "father" of the clan, Cole, temporarily eludes capture. But after one of the "children" turns up dead, "Mom" Cassidy's testimony and a child's stories of her life in the family put him away for multiple murders. But then "Mom" turns out to have a very different past than the one she's been peddling on the street, and detectives wonder how much blame sits on her shoulders for the teen's death.

Noteworthy Discoveries: The concept of a street "family" with its own sense of justice is intriguing and worth exploring further; hopefully the show will find other areas about this to mine down the road. Director Helen Shaver is a veteran actress best known in her home country of Canada.

Relevant Testimony: "(Street families) exist all over the country, often with that kind of hierarchical structure. I based the episode on a murder case in the Pacific Northwest."—Paul Grellong

Episode 195: Signature

Original air date: January 8, 2008
Teleplay by Judith McCreary, directed by Arthur W. Forney

Additional Cast: Erika Christensen (FBI Special Agent Lauren Cooper), Jane Cronin (Helen Moore), Rosemary De Angelis (Mrs. Tillman), Cindy Katz (Valerie Barrow), Patricia Kalember (Judge Taten), Jill Marie Lawrence (Cleo Conrad), Priscilla Lopez (EADA Lydia Ramos), Frankie Faison (FBI Agent Tom Nickerson), Roscoe Orman (Bryant Davis), Macon Blair (Conner Robb), Bill Phillips (Charles Barrow), Vaneik Echeverria (Aaron Winters), Amanda Leigh Cobb (Amy Doe)

Reviewing the Case: FBI Agent Cooper is called in by M.E. Warner, who recognizes a particular serial killer's ("the Woodsman") signature in at least one body found in Central Park. Cooper has worked to find the Woodsman for years, and lost her mentor in the process when he shot himself over the stress. But as the detectives dig through the profile and its discrepancies, they soon learn that Cooper is more deeply entrenched than anyone would have believed. At episode's end, there's still one final victim of the Woodsman left.

Noteworthy Discoveries: Forney has framed the episode's opening and closing scenes with an elegant series of slow dissolves as the caretakers of crime scenes arrive; but by the time Benson and Cooper have walked through the killer's *Saw*-like holding cell and taken pictures of the not-yet-dead Amy Doe's horrific mutilations, it all begins to feel like torture porn.

Relevant Testimony: "You have to get graphic but not too graphic. When the bodies are found in the woods, there are leaves to cover them up. We wanted the torture chamber to look authentic, not like some Gothic horror house. . . . The sex crimes on *SVU* are hard to digest, especially for single women out there. The trick is to make the characters warm enough. That's important if you're not going to throw up on the floor."—Arthur Forney

Episode 196: Unorthodox

Original air date: January 15, 2008
Teleplay by Josh Singer, directed by David Platt

Additional Cast: Rhea Perlman (Roxana Fox), Bob Dishy (Rabbi Iscowitz), Mike McGlone (George Trembley), Cara Buono (Rachel Zelinsky), Alexander Gould (Jack Trembley), Braeden Lemasters (David Zelinsky), Adam Stein (Avi Zelinsky), Linda Emond (Dr. Emily Sopher), Noel Joseph Allain (Jacob Ribowsky), Jake Goldberg (Adam Trembley)

Reviewing the Case: When an Orthodox Jewish community closes ranks around a young boy who has been repeatedly raped, at first detectives think they're going to have to deal with Talmudic law. But quickly—and more shockingly—the perpetrator turns out to be one of the boy's fellow schoolmates, who has been over-influenced by what he's been watching on television. Worse: The kid isn't violent; he just didn't think he was doing anything wrong. The story's well told, but it's a hard episode to watch.

Noteworthy Discoveries: *Cheers* star Rhea Perlman has an all-too-brief role as a legal aid lawyer. Director David Platt on how *SVU* directors coax performances from youngsters in episodes with very grim material:

Relevant Testimony: "Whether the kids fully comprehend the script is another matter, but these children were so self-possessed. My philosophy is: I've got two things to do, tell the story and get a great performance. Sometimes it's not about camera moves, it's about telling the story. If I make a comfortable environment for actors, within that comfort zone they'll go further."— David Platt

Episode 197: Inconceivable

Original air date: January 22, 2008
Teleplay by Dawn DeNoon, directed by Chris Zalla

Additional Cast: Janine Turner (Victoria Grall), Gabrielle Anwar (Eva Sintzel), Mark Moses (James Grall), Austin Lysy (Russell Hunter), Meredith Eaton (Jocelyn Miller), John Schuck (Chief of Detectives), James Waterston (Mr. Harvey), Danielle Skraastad (Paige Harvey), Kevin Kane (Scott Ryland), Richard Masur (Dr. Berletch), Meredith Zinner (Maya Jorgensen), Darrin Baker (Stan Jorgensen), Emilio Delgado (Enrique Diaz), Rightor Doyle (Chad Ogilvy)

Reviewing the Case: Activists steal a vat full of frozen embryos to prove a point, which leads detectives to the doorsteps of a number of aspiring parents in desperate situations, including a cancer patient with whom Benson bonds. When the return of the embryos goes wrong the activists are arrested, but before trial can begin one grieving parent takes justice into his own hands, and further tragedy ensues.

Noteworthy Discoveries: Elliot, Jr. is called "Eli." Benson reveals that she wants children, but was turned down by an adoption agency. Munch says he was dumped as Tutuola's partner once Det. Lake came along—and only seems to be half-joking. James Waterston (Sam's son) has a small role in the episode; Janine Turner should be recognizable to fans of *Northern Exposure*.

Episode 198: Undercover

Original Air Date: April 15, 2008
Teleplay by Mark Goffman, directed by David Platt

Additional Cast: Johnny Messner (Lowell Harris), Shareeka Epps (Ashley Tyler), Todd Stashwick (Matthew Parker), LaChanze (Amber), Hassan Johnson (Rick Tyler), Austin Lysy (Russell Hunter), Dinah Lenney (Prison Warden), Melanie Nicholls-King (Jill Botas), Eric L. Abrams (Henry Botas), Tawney Cypress (Shauna)

Reviewing the Case: Last time Benson changed her identity to venture deep into the criminal world it was for an investigation of ultimately harmless environmental activists ("Infiltrated," season eight). Now she really enters the belly of the beast as a make-believe drug addict incarcerated at a prison where female convicts are being raped by guards. It all begins with the New York City assault of a teenager whose mother is behind bars at the hellhole of a prison.

Noteworthy Discoveries: Stabler gets into the act posing as a defense attorney and Fin shows up incognito with a surprise hairstyle, as well.

Relevant Testimony: "I was getting tired of just wearing (my hair) pinned back all the time, and it was hot. So I went to Ted (Kotcheff): 'I want to cut my hair off,' and he's like, 'Ice, I don't wanna have to do a reshoot (and) stick a ponytail on your head.' Then, when the writers' strike hit, they said, 'If you still want to cut your hair, you can cut your hair.' . . . So I went and whacked it off. I was like, 'I'll be the same, don't worry about it.'"—Ice-T

Episode 199: Closet

Original Air Date: April 22, 2008
Teleplay by Ken Storer, directed by Peter Leto

Additional Cast: Bill Pullman (Kurt Moss), Bailey Chase (Lincoln Haven), Beverly D'Angelo (Rebecca Balthus), Richard Lewis (voice of Sportsman Larry), Rick Hoffman (Gary Lesley), Robert John Burke (IAB Sgt. Ed Tucker), Peter Gerety (Judge Harrison), Ian Alda (Sam Edelstein), Chloe Cmarada (Natasha), David Del Rio (Freddie Ramirez), Cortez Nance, Jr. (Elias San Oro), Darren Kelly (William Breckenridge), Deep Katdare (Dr. Parnell)

Reviewing the Case: A popular athlete is implicated in the murder of a businessman, seemingly during a gay S&M encounter. The chief suspect, a football player hesitant about going public with his sexual preference, becomes more of a victim than a perp. His agent apparently is shocked. His narcissistic girlfriend-of-convenience seemingly blabs to the press—specifically, a tabloid where the editor has been dating Benson.

Noteworthy Discoveries: Benson is once again questioned—and suspended without pay—by IAB Sgt. Ed Tucker, who's surely growing weary of these SVU troublemakers. Her affable gentleman caller, Kurt Moss (Bill Pullman), asks: "Why is it you won't move in with me?"

Relevant Testimony: "That was challenging with Bill Pullman for just one scene because it had to cover months of backstory about his relationship with Benson."—Peter Leto

Episode 200: Authority

Original air date: April 29, 2008
Teleplay by Neal Baer and Amanda Green, directed by David Platt

Additional Cast: Robin Williams (Merritt Rook), Didi Conn (Nurse), Monica Raymund (Trini Martinez), Ka-Ling Cheung (Dr. Cheng), Audrie Neenan (Judge Lois Preston), Joe Scarborough (Himself), Scott Adsit (Dwight Lomax), Mo Rocca (Protest Leader), Matthew Stadelmann (Joel)

Reviewing the Case: A charismatic but damaged widower named Merritt Rook takes everyone from a fast food restaurant manager to Benson and Stabler for a ride while trying to convince them not to be "sheep" and follow authority blindly. Unfortunately, this means he gets the manager to strip search an employee—and then disproves the adage about going *pro se* at your trial. But he meets his match in the very un-sheep-like Stabler, who has to undergo his own psychological experiment to free Benson once Rook draws her into his lair.

Noteworthy Discoveries: The milestone 200th episode takes a journey through recent real-life pop culture events: In late 2007 a young woman received $6.1 million after suing McDonalds when her manager got a call from a so-called policeman, and strip-searched her; for several years, urban prankster groups like Improv Everywhere have been staging random acts of weirdness like the pillow fight and "Frozen Grand Central" that are aped in the episode—the real-life version occurred in January 2008. Stabler has been a detective for sixteen years.

Relevant Testimony: "Robin's synapses work at a rate that is absolutely ungodly. At any given moment, he can spin off into astrology, astronomy, philosophy, history. At the same time, he's an incredible professional and very talented actor. He took notes."—David Platt

Episode 201: Trade

Original Air Date: May 6, 2008
Teleplay by Jonathan Greene, directed by Peter Leto

Additional Cast: Stephen Collins (Pierson Bartlett), Matthew Davis (P.J. Barlett), Clea Lewis (Heaven Moscowitz), P.J. Benjamin (Eddie Rincado), Michalle Barth (Avery Hemmings), Jennifer Simard (Debra Jackson), Darlesia Cearcy (Viola), Brandi Burkhardt (Jenna Ludlow)

Reviewing the Case: Some studies contend coffee is bad for people; others indicate it's good. On *SVU*, a cuppa joe is downright deadly when it comes to a family business thriving on the java commodities exchange. A prosperous father and son are alternately suspected in the killing of a beautiful temptress in this caffeinated melodrama with a stunning rooftop denouement.

Noteworthy Discoveries: Fin and Munch question Heaven Moscowitz, a wonderfully flaky "angel-healing" practitioner who ought to be a recurring character on the show.

Relevant Testimony: "That rooftop scene took a lot of careful planning. It was the fourth time I'd shot a sequence like that. I was the first person on location at 6:30 A.M. A helicopter was hovering overhead. I think it was Homeland Security. They took a good look at me and I made the traditional 'I'm-shooting-a-movie' signal."—Peter Leto

Episode 202: Cold

Original Air Date: May 13, 2008
Teleplay by Judith McCreary, directed by David Platt

Additional Cast: Deidre Lovejoy (Penelope Fielding), Victoria Cartagena (Celina Cruz), Jack Gwaltney (Bill Jensen), Anthony

Ruiz (Hector Hernandez), Robert Turano (Wesley Meadows), Viola Davis (Donna Emmett), Torsten Hillhouse (Det. Dave Foster), Lawrence Ballard (Bret Smith), Philip Levy (Off. Fineman), Eva Kaminsky (Mary Kralik)

Reviewing the Case: Under suspicion in the shooting death of a cop linked to the decade-old rape and murder of an adolescent Brooklyn girl, Chester Lake goes rogue. His Manhattan SVU squad is divided on how to react. Stabler treats him like a perp; Fin keeps trying to help his enigmatic new partner. Anxious to see justice done, Novak skirts the law. In this season finale, there are a lot of jobs on the line.

Noteworthy Discoveries: Angry about how Stabler has been treating Lake, Tutuloa says: "That makes for a good cop but a lousy human being. You will still be the same old rat-bastard tomorrow." Lake and a private investigator named Penelope Fielding have gone to Philadelphia to attend a meeting of the Vidocq Society, a real-life organization that revisits unsolved crimes.

Relevant Testimony: "Our (high) rate of closure on the show is a fantasy. The resources aren't available. In real life, police don't have enough cars. I know of cops in Manhattan and Brooklyn who have to travel to crime scenes by bus."—Judith McCreary

SEASON TEN

September 2008–June 2009

Regular Cast: Christopher Meloni (Det. Elliot Stabler), Mariska Hargitay (Det. Olivia Benson), Richard Belzer (Det. John Munch), Ice-T (Det. Odafin "Fin" Tutuola), Dann Florek (Capt. Donald Cragen), Tamara Tunie (M.E. Melinda Warner), B.D. Wong (Dr. George Huang), Michaela McManus (ADA Kim Greylek)

Recurring Cast: Stephanie March (ADA Alexandra Cabot), Mike Doyle (Forensic Tech Ryan O'Halloran), Noel Fisher (CSU Tech Dale Stuckey), Amir Arison (Dr. Manning), Joanna Merlin (Judge Lena Petrovsky), Edelen McWilliams (CSU Tech Martin), Allison Siko (Kathleen Stabler), Joel de la Fuente (TARU Tech Ruben Morales)

SEASON TEN OVERVIEW: After a decade of watching a favorite TV show, the characters should read like an open book. Surprise, surprise. The show's introductory cast shot isn't the only thing to change this year (though it features, from left to right: Michaela McManus, B.D. Wong, Tamara Tunie, Christopher Meloni, Mariska Hargitay, Dann Florek, Richard Belzer, and Ice-T, all standing in front of desks). Instead, *SVU*'s tenth season is full of new details, anomalies, and a sort of what-goes-around-comes-around karma.

Det. Elliot Stabler has an estranged mother! And she's got the family crazy gene! Not only that, the detective has links to NASA and even named his son after an old Marine pal who's since become a legendary astronaut.

Det. Olivia Benson, haunted by her near-rape from season nine, finally seeks psychiatric help. In real life, the actress is twice hospitalized for a partially collapsed lung in early 2009, later telling People.com that she was injured doing her own stunts. She misses one full episode ("Baggage") while recuperating.

Perhaps strangest of all, former ADA Alexandra Cabot (Stephanie March) returns for a six-episode arc, despite the fact that she was forced to accept a second round of witness protection in "Ghost" (season six). This contemporary switcheroo is precipitated by one of those revolving doors endemic to all Law & Order shows: Actress Michaela McManus, who began playing ADA Kim Greylek in September 2008, abruptly departs. In fiction, the excuse is that she has been recalled to the Justice Department in D.C. by the new administration (presumably President Barack Obama's). Real life seems to have been more complicated. Showrunner Neal Baer describes the McManus fare-thee-well as "a mutual decision. Sometimes, the part and the actor don't mesh."

Casey Novak—the ADA played by Diane Neal from 2001 to 2008, when the character crossed an ethical line—remains "disbarred for at least a year," according to Baer.

A network decision apparently prevails when only two fresh episodes air in May, an all-important "sweeps" month in which big ratings hopefully draw big bucks from advertisers. Baer says NBC wanted the season finale as a strong lead-in for Conan O'Brien's June debut as *The Tonight Show* replacement for Jay Leno, who then becomes the host of a new talkfest every week night at 10 in September. At that point *SVU* moves to 9 P.M. each Wednesday.

Is Baer OK with his series taking a less drama-friendly time slot? "Sure," he insists. "It's always on at 9 in Chicago and Denver. And we're much beloved there."

An even thornier dilemma was shaping up as a true cliffhanger, however. With both Hargitay and Meloni negotiating for salary increases, NBC Universal threatened to replace them rather than give into their demands. But all was well by the official start of summer and, with his two lead actors once again on board, Baer envisions a continuum for the future: "We'll still be exploring travesties of the human psyche."

Meanwhile, one such travesty ends season ten with the departure of a long-time recurring cast member, whose character meets a sad fate at the hands of the strangest duck ever to be hired by the City of New York. The same finale, "Zebras," offers another quirky situation when one of Munch's many ex-wives—last seen in *Homicide: Life on the Street* during the late 1990s—reappears. Plot-wise, this gambit means the popular detective, too often consigned by the writers to just a few lines of witty dialogue, has an opportunity to stretch.

In the previous SVU episode, "Liberties," there's a fleeting reference to Munch's "girl." This particular Man in Black may be a Man in Love.

In early June, there was an announcement that Stephanie March signed on for another ten episodes in season eleven while the show seeks a permanent ADA. "I have no clue what I will be doing," says March, "but likely it will include getting reprimanded by a judge and losing a fair number of cases."

Ratings Recap for Season: 6.8 rating / 11 share / 10,251,000 viewers

EPISODE DESCRIPTIONS

Episode 203: Trials

Original Air Date: September 23, 2008
Teleplay by Dawn DeNoon, directed by David Platt

Additional Cast: Julie Bowen (Gwen Sibert), Jae Head (Christopher Ryan), Mary Beth Evans (Dr. Eichenberry), Sara Gilbert (Caitlyn Ryan), Luke Perry (Noah Sibert), Julia Knight (Emily Johannsen), Lisa Strum (Tonya Majeski), Carolyn Morrison (Natalie Clay), Walter Masterson (Jayden Bierce), Peter Dylan Richards (Dietrich Strauss)

Reviewing the Case: Noah and Gwen Sibert are at their wits' end with foster child Christopher, who "escapes" from them by stealing a van. But when Benson realizes Christopher's biological mother Caitlyn was part of a rape case she oversaw, she visits the victim and convinces her to try getting her son back. That's when it all starts to unravel, as Noah becomes a linchpin in not just Caitlyn's rape—but several others, some quite close to home.

Noteworthy Discoveries: Eager-beaver ADA Kim Greylek shows up ready for work, telling Stabler she's made a "lateral move" from the Office of Violence Against Women in D.C., where she was known as "The Crusader." Benson is having flashbacks to her prison assault from last season ("Undercover") and goes to a therapist. Stabler's credit card is "borrowed"—by his daughter Kathleen's boyfriend. Tutuola learns his transfer won't go through because the officer in charge of allowing transfers has a beef with him.

Episode 204: Confession

Original Air Date: September 30, 2008
Teleplay by Judith McCreary, directed by Arthur W. Forney

Additional Cast: Teri Polo (Dana Kelley), Marshall Allman (Eric Byers), Stephen Schnetzer (Dr. Engles), Ned Eisenberg (Roger Kressler), Ann James (Dr. Jane Larom), Caren Browning (CSU Capt. Judith Siper), Tom Noonan (Jake Berlin), Josh Charles (Sean Kelley), Kristen Pozanski (Lisa Deering), Gabe Duran (Frank Deering), Aaron Mayer (Cory Kelley)

Reviewing the Case: A teen confesses pedophilic longings for his young stepbrother, which tears his family apart—his stepfather seems homicidal and mother is a basket case. Detectives are also led to the one "friend" the teen found on the Internet: The owner of a Web site (PediaPhax) devoted to helping pedophiles restrain their actions while indulging their desires with pictures online. But then the teen runs away from home and turns up brutally murdered and there's no shortage of suspects.

Noteworthy Discoveries: Stabler is suspended without pay after beating up Jake, the owner of the PediaPhax Web site, who posts a photo of the detective's daughter, Kathleen, on the pages.

Episode 205: Swing

Original Air Date: October 14, 2008
Teleplay by Amanda Green, directed by David Platt

Additional Cast: Ellen Burstyn (Bernie Stabler), Isabel Gillies (Kathy Stabler), Fiona Dourif (Nikki), Steven Flynn (Mr. Foster), Lizette Carrion (ADA Kristen Torres), Harvey Atkin (Judge Alan Ridenour), CCH Pounder (Carolyn Maddox), Sarah Bennett (Ronda Foster), Deep Katdare (Dr. Parrell)

Reviewing the Case: When Stabler's daughter Kathleen begins exhibiting wild behavior (including breaking into a house, showering, and stealing jewelry), her father is at first reluctant to admit she might be bipolar (as the doctors say she is). But after speaking to his mother, who has never before been seen on the show, he understands how the illness travels in families—and the real key is to get Kathleen to accept her diagnosis before she is sent to jail.

Noteworthy Discoveries: Stabler's mom Bernie is a piece of work: She lives in Long Beach and raised her children in a wild, unstable environment (she "chased snowflakes" once in a New York City blizzard, wrecked the car, and broke young Elliot's arm). However, she's a devoted mother and shows Benson a photo of the future detective (who she insists wanted to be an architect) dressed as a carrot for a Thanksgiving play.

Episode 206: Lunacy

Original Air Date: October 21, 2008
Teleplay by Daniel Truly, directed by Peter Leto

Additional Cast: James Brolin (Col. Richard Finley), Danny Mastrogiorgio (McTeer), Dane DeHaan (Vincent Beckwith), Annika Boras (Leslie Schuster), Kristina Klebe (Marga Janssen), Betty Buckley (Attorney Collette Walsh), Chris Elliott (Anton Thibodaux), Fiona Dourif (Nikki)

Reviewing the Case: When an astronaut is found dead in the Hudson, detectives seek help from Stabler's old mentor, another astronaut named Dick Finley—the namesake of Stabler's youngest child. But as rivalries (and stalkers) within the space organization are revealed, attention turns to an unexpected source, and the detective has to take it on the chin.

Noteworthy Discoveries: This episode is covered in great detail in Chapter 26, "Diary: A Week in the Life of an Episode."

Episode 207: Retro

Original Air Date: October 28, 2008
Teleplay by Jonathan Greene, story by Joshua Kotcheff and Jonathan Greene, directed by Peter Leto

Additional Cast: Martin Mull (Dr. Gideon Hutton), Paula Malcomson (Susan Ross), Aidan Mitchell (Tommy Ross), Babs Olusanmokun (Mr. Marong), Austin Lysy (Russell Hunter), Peter McRobbie (Judge Walter Bradley), Richard Joseph Paul (Jack Luftin), Viola Davis (Donna Emmett), Donna Murphy (Dr. Raye Massey), Samantha Ryan Maisano (Roberta Nolan), Jessica Pimentel (Joanne Suarez), Chris Rivaro (Daniel Ramirez)

Reviewing the Case: A renegade doctor disputes the existence of AIDS, claiming it is a drug company conspiracy, and so treats his patients with unusual cures, which leads to the death of a young girl. Meanwhile, her mother is also an AIDS-denier (despite having HIV) and is also blamed for the death of her child. But has she been lying to everyone, including her older son?

Noteworthy Discoveries: This is Viola Davis' seventh appearance on *SVU* as defense attorney Emmett; the veteran actress went on to score her first Best Performance by an Actress in a Supporting Role Academy Award nomination for *Doubt* shortly after her appearance here.

Episode 208: Babes

Original Air Date: November 11, 2008
Teleplay by Daniel Truly, directed by David Platt

Additional Cast: Jesse McCartney (Max Matarazzo), John Cullum (Judge Barry Moredock), Geoff Wigdor (Dizzer), Bridget Barkan (Sara), David Thornton (Lionel Granger), Frederick Strother (Judge Milton Siburt), Philip Ettinger (Alec Bernardi), Jessica Varley (Fidelia Vidal), Ray Abruzzo (Gordon Vidal), Kathrine Narducci (Adrianna Vidal), Michael Badalucco (Tom Galli), Britt Robertson (Tina Bernardi), Debi Mazar (Peggy Bernardi)

Reviewing the Case: This is something of a hodgepodge mess of a show, tacking together several real-life headline cases (the teenage pregnancy pact, a mother who harrasses a teen online, resulting in her eventual suicide, videotaped beatings of the homeless) that never quite jells. A schizophrenic young man impregnates one teen, then is burned alive by her brother. Mom learns the daughter got pregnant on purpose to be part of the crowd of girls at school who were doing the same thing, then the ringleader tuns up a suicide. But in the end, Stabler manages to put a big bow on top of the mess in what feels like an afterschool special ending.

Noteworthy Discoveries: John Cullum's recurring Barry Moredock has been promoted to a judgeship here; Jesse McCartney is a teen pop singer who once toured with Britney Spears; and Kathrine Narducci is back in the *L&O* fold after a long stint on *The Sopranos*—and in her second penis-severing episode of the franchise (*Law & Order*'s "Mayhem" episode, 1994).

Episode 209: Wildlife

Original Air Date: November 18, 2008
Teleplay by Mick Betancourt, directed by Peter Leto

Additional Cast: Andrew Divoff (Andre Bushido), Reg E. Cathey (Det. Victor Tibor), Isabel Gillies (Kathy Stabler), Vanessa Aspillaga (Agent Brianna Kalke), Carlos Leon (Oscar Assadorian), Caitlin Fitzgerald (Anna/Natalie), Antwan "Big Boi" Andre Patton (Gotz Money), John Bianco (Michael Solano),

Reviewing the Case: An episode light on story, heavy on stylish point-of-view perspectives, flashbacks, and wild animals: A model is mauled by a tiger and turns out to be a rare-animal smuggler with a less-than-successful rapper as one of her clients. Stabler goes undercover where the wild things are as a dirty customs agent, but quickly his life is put in danger. Can Benson find her partner as he tries to catch the smugglers (bloody) red handed?

Noteworthy Discoveries: Antwan Andre Patton is better known as real-life rapper "Big Boi" and this is his first appearance on a dramatic TV series. Fans of *The Wire* and *Oz* will recognize Cathey, who usually plays a stand-up guy—and may be playing to type in this episode, too.

Episode 210: Persona

Original Air Date: November 25, 2008
Teleplay by Amanda Green, directed by Helen Shaver

Additional Cast: Brenda Blethyn (Linnie Malcolm), Clea DuVall (Mia Latimer), Nathaniel Marston (Brent Latimer), Peter Hermann (Trevor Langan), Didi Conn (Nurse), Audrie Neenan (Judge Lois Preston), Kelly Bishop (Attorney Julia Zimmer), Judith Light (Elizabeth Donnelly), Mike Farrell (Jonah Malcolm)

Reviewing the Case: A domestic abuse case that ultimately leads to tragedy also leads detectives to unearth a long-sought-after fugitive who's been on the run for thirty years. But once Benson hears the captured fugitive's story, her heart softens. It seems the woman will simply get probation, until the former prosecutor on the case, Elizabeth Donnelly, takes off her judge robes and returns to the DA's office to exercise a little vengeance on the escapee who made her look like a fool.

Noteworthy Discoveries: Brenda Blethyn is a veteran British actress with two Oscar nominations; Mike Farrell is best-recognized from his work on *M*A*S*H*.

Episode 211: PTSD

Original Air Date: December 2, 2008
Teleplay by Judith McCreary, directed by Eriq La Salle

Additional Cast: Ryan Kwanten (Master Sgt. Pruett), Dominic Fumusa (Lt. Gary Rosten), Amy Spanger (Marlene Ross), Rosa Arredondo (Rochelle Rodriguez), Karen Mason (Ann Crewes), Jay Patterson (Lt. James Reed), Brooke Adams (Margo), Frank Whaley (Navy Commander Grant Marcus), Robert C. Kirk (General Bolinger), Samantha Zweben (Jessica Crewes)

Reviewing the Case: While undergoing therapy for her assault six months earlier, Benson's therapist asks her to locate a missing patient from another group—a Marine who was raped and impregnated. Benson finds the AWOL soldier dead in a trunk, the baby cut out of her, and clues all point back to the military. Greylek and a Judge Advocate General attorney battle over jurisdiction and Benson (paired with Fin) battles her demons as they locate two likely suspects. But when DNA points only to one, there's a last surprise over who else was responsible.

Noteworthy Discoveries: Longtime *ER* actor Eriq La Salle also directed Episode 172, "Burned," in 2007 for *SVU*. Fin was in Mogadishu as a U.S. Army Ranger in 1993.

Episode 212: Smut

Original Air Date: December 9, 2008
Teleplay by Kam Miller, directed by Chris Eyre

Additional Cast: Michael Trucco (Eric Lutz), John Cullum (Judge Barry Moredock), Christine Ebersole (Hilary Regnier), Christy Pusz (Laurel Andrews), Ryan Dunn (Riley Slade), Sharon Washington (Dr. Crosthwaite), Stephen Gregory (Dr. Kyle Beresford), Kelly Hu (Kelly Sun), Asa Somers (Colin Andrews), Christina Hogue (Shannon Browning)

Reviewing the Case: Porn made me do it! At least, that's what a serial rapist claims when the detectives catch him with multiple videos, in which he forces sex on women while demanding they pretend to love it. But the rapist has a secret up his sleeve—he drugs them with a rare substance that paralyzes victims' ability to fight back, and leaves them without memories later.

Noteworthy Discoveries: Clearly, Stabler lives deep in Queens; he notes at one point: "A thousand people go through Grand Central every day." Commuters only wish that were so—stats prove it's more like 500,000 visitors, with 125,000 of them trying to get to work.

Episode 213: Stranger

Original air date: January 8, 2009
Teleplay by Dawn DeNoon, directed by David Platt

Additional Cast: Tess Harper (Mrs. Hallander), Kate Baldwin (Erica Hallander), Ellen Waglom (Heather Hallander), Natalia Payne (Nikki Hallander), Patrick Collins (Mr. Hallander), Lindsay Crouse (Judge), Peter Lewis (Carl Vasko), Christopher Mann (Det. Stu Freeland), Margaret Reed (Defense Attorney)

Reviewing the Case: A teenager, missing for years, suddenly shows up at the door of the family she insists is her own. Nobody quite recognizes the girl, but there is a familiar four-leaf clover tattoo on her wrist. As with any twisty *SVU* plot, this story unveils many deep, dark secrets and an alarming sex-slave situation before arriving at a resolution that's both happy and tragic.

Episode 214: Hothouse

Original air date: January 13, 2009
Teleplay by Charley Davis, directed by Peter Leto

Additional Cast: George Tasudis (Joseph Lychkoff), Neal Matarazzo (Ezra Kriegel), Misha Kuznetsov (Alik), Aya Cash (Katrina Lychkoff), Juliet Brett (Elisa Lychkoff), Sarah Hyland (Jennifer Banks), Funda Duval (Mrs. Lychkoff), Gretchen Egolf (ADA Gil), Will Rogers (Danny Burke), Enid Graham (Suzanne Banks), Anna Stone (Grace Metcalf), Eric Gores (Brian Walem), Carol Jacobanis (Jane Siddons), Gabriela Modorcea (Veronica Pankovich), Ian McWethy (Andrew)

Reviewing the Case: The murder of an adolescent math prodigy is only a proverbial tip of the iceberg in a case that involves immigrant smuggling, forced prostitution, and drug addiction. Not to mention a Russian pimp. Plus, the dead girl's volatile father has an approach to educating his daughters that borders on torture. There's also a battle of wills a between New York and New Jersey prosecutors.

Noteworthy Discoveries: Benson poses as "Claudia," a fashionably dressed woman from Chicago trying to procure young girls for her pedophile clients.

Episode 215: Snatched

Original air date: February 3, 2009
Teleplay by Mick Betancourt, directed by David Platt

Additional Cast: Dabney Coleman (Frank Hagar), Ron Eldard (Geno Parnell), Burt Young (Eddy Mack), Wallace Shawn (Prof. Ray Batters), Michelle Ray Smith (Liz Rinaldi), Michael C. Williams (Pete Rinaldi), Daisy Tahan (Rosie Rinaldi), Anthony J. Gallo (Louie Buratta), Alyssa May Gold (Amy Sarkis), Joe Lisi (Parole Off. Craig Lennon), Chadwick Brown (Jake)

Reviewing the Case: When little Rosie is abducted, the child's mother blames her jailbird ex-husband. He's out of the slammer but, in proclaiming innocence, seems more determined to find his daughter than anyone else. Stabler believes him. The trail takes them to the girl's maternal grandfather, a jewel thief slowly succumbing to dementia. The police aren't sure who to trust, as the burden of guilt keeps shifting.

Noteworthy Discoveries: Ron Eldard, who once portrayed a medical professional on *ER*, delivers a moving performance as the conflicted ex-con.

Episode 216: Transitions

Original air date: February 17, 2009
Teleplay by Ken Storer, directed by Peter Leto

Additional Cast: Alex Kingston (Miranda Pond), Bridger Zadina (Henry/Haley Van Kuren), Frank Grillo (Mark Van Kuren), Wendy Makkena (Ellen), Daniela Shea (Blake), Heidi Marnhout (Molly "Misty" Lambert), Paul Lazar (Sid Gabbert), Lea DeLaria (Frankie), Dequina Moore (Sapphire), Aisha Hinds (Jackie Blaine), Audrie Neenan (Judge Lois Preston), J. Paul Nicholas (Attorney Linden Delroy), Barbara Rosenblatt (Selma Peters)

Reviewing the Case: Sexual identity sits on the front burner in this whodunit, in which the father of a teenage boy who feels more like a girl is savagely beaten. The son wants to take hormone blockers that would fend off female puberty to make later gender-reassignment surgery easier. Although Dad doesn't want his offspring to undergo the operation, a social worker at the kid's school is particularly simpatico about the choice to change.

Noteworthy Discoveries: Alex Kingston has a cameo as an honorable defense attorney. She played a doctor on *ER*, which also featured Mariska Hargitay in a recurring role during the 1997-98 season. *SVU* showrunner Neal Baer was an executive producer on that now-defunct medical show. Taucher-Leto Pharmaceticals, which figures in a red herring subplot, is a playful nod to *SVU* production designer Dean Taucher and episode director Peter Leto.

Episode 217: Lead

Original air date: March 10, 2009
Teleplay by Jonathan Greene, directed by David Platt

Additional Cast: John Gallagher Jr. (Jeff Lynwood), John Cullum (Judge Barry Moredock), Mariette Hartley (Lorna Scarry), Lawrence Arancio (Gilbert Keppler), Tim Ransom (Logan Coldwell), Robert John Burke (Lt. Ed Tucker), David Thornton (Lionel Granger), Fredric Lehne (Clive Lynwood), Laura Leigh Hughes (Virginia Lynwood), Ann Dowd (Lillian Siefeld), Ross Bickell (Michael Rowan)

Reviewing the Case: After a prolonged stay in witness protection, Cabot suddenly shows up at a crime scene. The SVU detectives are astonished to learn she stopped hiding three years earlier but never contacted them. There's also an explanation that defies all odds about why it's now safe to reassume her own identity. Don't ask, don't tell. Earlier, Greylek makes a brief appearance, never to be seen again. None of which has much to do with the story, about a doctor who's a sexual predator and a developmentally delayed young man who reacts to ridicule with unbridled anger. Justice is multifaceted in this case because corporate malfeasance once again figures in the mix.

Episode 218: Ballerina

Original air date: March 17, 2009
Teleplay by Daniel Truly, directed by Peter Leto

Additional Cast: Carol Burnett (Bridget "Birdie" Sulloway), Vincent Curatola (Marv Sulloway), Matthew Lillard (Chet), Lindsay Crouse (Judge), Robert Klein (Mr. Stannich), Yuval Boim (Efraim), Raquel Almazan (Maricela), Daniel Frith (Kevin), James Stahl (Stan), Dominic Colon (Leo Morales), Eliezer Meyer (Rabbi Elli), Enrique Sebastian Rivas (Alejandro Reyes)

Reviewing the Case: Like Norma Desmond in *Sunset Boulevard*, aging entertainer Birdie Sulloway relishes her bygone glory days. She shares a posh apartment with a thuggish but age-

PHOTO BY: WILL HART/NBCU PHOTO BANK

Carol Burnett (as Birdie Sulloway) and B.D. Wong in season ten's "Ballerina"

appropriate husband and a much younger "nephew," who is slavishly devoted to her. After various people bite the dust, however, the faded superstar's self-centered lifestyle begins to unravel.

Noteworthy Discoveries: This episode introduces a new CSU tech named Dale Stuckey, who's prone to making inappropriate statements at inopportune times. Actual footage of Carol Burnett's early performances on *The Garry Moore Show* is used when the character, looking much like the deranged diva from *Sunset Boulevard*, watches her younger self on TV.

Relevant Testimony: "'The specific Norma Desmond feel in that scene actually evolved from something Carol asked to do [to show Birdie's vulnerability] by shedding the wig she wore in previous scenes and just wearing a turban as she watched her old films. When I wrote the script, I didn't have any actual footage in mind. . . . Then [showrunner] Neal Baer mentioned seeing Carol on *The Garry Moore Show* when he was a kid. . . . It was an inspired idea (and typical of Neal). Carol hadn't actually seen the clips for years and years

(since they aired live decades ago) and loved seeing them again."—
Daniel Truly

Episode 219: Hell

Original air date: March 31, 2009
Teleplay by Amanda Green, directed by David Platt

Additional Cast: Robert Wisdom (Father Theo Burdett),
Gbenga Akinnagbe (Elijah Okello), Cicely Tyson (Ondine Burdett),
Mike Colter (Samuel/Joseph), Julyza Commodore (Miriam Bur-
dett), Sean Cullen (Brett Trask), Stephen Gregory (Dr. Kyle Beres-
ford), Joanna Bonaro (Doris DiNuzio), Pietro Gonzalez (Felipe), Kola
Ogundiran (Nathaniel), Andrew Guilarte (Rajiv)

Reviewing the Case: *SVU* has always been sensitive to the
plight of refugees, a topic frequently eclipsed in the heated national
debate about immigration. "Hell" examines the problem of child soldiers forced to fight in Africa's many civil wars, which may eventually find their way onto the streets of New York. The throat of a little
girl, possibly from Sudan, has been slashed. The initial suspect hails
from Uganda. A more likely perp has somehow eluded capture for
crimes against humanity.

Noteworthy Discoveries: Seeking help on the case, Cabot
meets with a fellow Harvard alum who is now an official at the
UN—marking the first time in its six-decade history that the international organization allowed a major network television production
to film on the premises.

Relevant Testimony: While shooting the episode in March
2009, Stephanie March told CNN.com, "I have a great job but really
all I want to do is actually work with the UN. . . . It's been a lifelong
dream to be part of it in some way."

Episode 220: Baggage

Original air date: April 7, 2009
Teleplay by Judith McCreary, directed by Chris Zalla

Additional Cast: Delroy Lindo (Det. Victor Moran), Jeri Ryan (Patrice Larue), Nelson Vasquez (Mike Ocurro), Judith Delgado (Elena Ocurro), John Ashton (Chief of Detectives), Victor Anthony (Stefan Henriquez), Lisa London (Debra Huggins), Joe Passano (Supervisor), Jasmin Tavarez (Angela Ocurro), Dawn Yanek (Evie), Keith Baker (Oswald), Rick Younger (David Paige), Isaiah Stokes (Tyrone Beckwith), Timothy Mitchum (Paul), Deirdre Lorenz (Det. Nina Gardner), Nicole Mangi (Vicky Henningen)

Reviewing the Case: A gruesome murder is attributed to a serial rapist whose crimes have begun to escalate. The city's chief of detectives demands that the SVU squad play second fiddle to a seasoned cop from another precinct who is already on the case. He clashes with Stabler at first, but the two men establish mutual respect in an effort to catch the elusive and prolific killer.

Noteworthy Discoveries: Benson is unexpectedly absent from this episode due to Mariska Hargitay's hospitalization for a collapsed lung. CSU Tech Mike Doyle's lament to the SVU detectives is, "Now you know what I have to put up with," when they witness annoying behavior by his colleague Dale Stuckey. Later the newcomer says something that causes Stabler to repeat three times in succession: "What's the matter with you?"

Episode 221: Selfish

Original air date: April 28, 2009
Teleplay by Mick Betancourt, directed by David Platt

Additional Cast: Hilary Duff (Ashlee Walker), Gail O'Grady (Ruth Walker), Annie Potts (Sophie Devere), Mike Pniewski (Ralph Walker), Anastasia Barzee (Monica Potter), Peter Hermann (Trevor Langan), Marilyn Torres (Maria), Miriam Colon (Yolanda), Tonye Patano (Judge Maskin), David Lipman (Judge Arthur Cohen), Deidre Goodwin (Nanny), Tracy Griswold (Uriah Faber), Ryan Raftery (Dennis Faber)

Reviewing the Case: Commentator Nancy Grace of cable's HLN (Headline News) may think she has cornered the market on murdered toddler Caylee Anthony, but *SVU* sure knows how to present a fictionalized mirror image of that genuine Florida case. A reckless young single mom reports the child's disappearance and, despite numerous discrepancies in the story she tells police, is backed by her parents. In this instance, though, the grandmother is a harpy and another crime scenario comes into play regarding a disease that can be deadly.

Noteworthy Discoveries: That old *Law & Order* ripped-from-the-headlines routine seems more cogent than ever with lines such as, "This car smells like a dead body!"—an exact quote lifted from the Sunshine State saga. Do the writers ever worry about scripts borrowing too much from their sources?

Relevant Testimony: "If there are ever any similarities to real world events, the story always winds up going in a different direction than the original, almost always ending by shining a light on a social or ethical issue, leaving the last opinion up to the audience. We always run our stories and research through our legal department which checks and double checks all facts and similarities."—Mick Betancourt

Episode 222: Crush

Original air date: May 5, 2009
Teleplay by Jonathan Greene, directed by Peter Leto

Additional Cast: Swoosie Kurtz (Judge Hilda Marsden), Alex Kingston (Miranda Pond), Carly Schroeder (Kim Garnet), Melinda McGraw (Samantha Copeland), Kellie Overbey (Mrs. Garnet), Scott Bryce (Bill Garnet), Ezra Miller (Ethan Morse), Alexander Nifong (Steve Walker), Geoffrey Cantor (Ed Mangini), Jennifer Regan (Janice Morse), Nicholas J. Giangiulio (Mort), Brian Rogalski (Little Pete), Bill Winkler (Mark Walker), Conrad Woolfe (Rick Edwards), Kelly Kunkel (Daniela)

Reviewing the Case: When the police question a high school girl who has foolishly sexted a boyfriend risqué photos of herself, they find evidence of battering. Although she remains mum on the subject, two male classmates come under scrutiny. All the kiddie porn concerns that emerge are merely a platform for launching an episode about a corrupt judicial process.

Noteworthy Discoveries: Stabler refers to the CSU's Dale Stuckey as "the talk-too-much tech." The officious Melinda McGraw is identified as a "corporation counsel," an attorney for the city rather than the DA's office. She handles civil legal matters, in this case the prosecution of a juvenile. The fifteen-year-old victim's salacious pictures go viral, prompting others to taunt her as she navigates the school hallways—very much like the ubiquitous real-life TV public service ad warning teens about the dangers of internet intimacy.

Relevant Testimony: "To this day, have not seen the (public service) ad. . . . Sometimes we'll come up with a scenario in which we'll put together a story for an episode, only to see our fictional story play out in real life just before the episode airs (what Neal calls 'the headlines being ripped from us'). Other times, we hear about a case, use it for an episode, and all of a sudden, as we're writing the episode, the momentum on the issue behind said case builds. That's basically what happened with the naked-photo storyline in 'Crush.'"—Jonathan Greene

Episode 223: Liberties

Original air date: May 19, 2009
Teleplay by Dawn DeNoon, directed by Juan J. Campanella

Additional Cast: Alan Dale (Judge Joshua Koehler), Sprague Grayden (Pamela Galliano), Jon Patrick Walker (Tyler Brunson), Attorney Heshy Horowitz (Joe Grifasi), Silas Weir Mitchell (Owen Walters), Victor Arnold (Roy Lee Dodson), Linda Park (TARU Tech)

Reviewing the Case: When a stalker/rape-provocateur is captured, he deserves some compassion for having been the victim of persistent childhood sexual abuse by his father. But this is not the only issue weighing on the young man's trial judge, an otherwise law-abiding jurist whose own son was abducted as a toddler thirty years earlier.

Noteworthy Discoveries: Stabler agrees to do whatever it takes to elicit information from a repellent, unrepentant serial pedophile dying of emphysema in prison; It's essentially a moment of torture-light. Munch tells Cragen: "I'm going out of town this weekend with my girl." Fans of the acerbic and much-divorced detective are no doubt be left to wonder if he might take yet another trip down the aisle. But who is this mystery woman?

Relevant Testimony: "(That dialogue about Munch's 'girl') was the lone remnant of a story line that ended up getting cut out of my original script. It was to set up a possible new romance in a future episode, and was not referring to any of his many exes."— Dawn DeNoon

"We're thinking it could be Marlee Matlin's character (assisted-suicide advocate Dr. Amy Solwey, seen in seasons five and six). She might come back."—showrunner Neal Baer

Episode 224: Zebras

Original air date: June 2, 2009
Teleplay by Amanda Green & Daniel Truly, directed by Peter Leto

Additional Cast: Carol Kane (Gwen Munch), Tim Bohn (Jacob Nauss), Judith Light (Judge Elizabeth Donnelly), Nick Stahl (Peter Harrison), Lizette Carrion (ADA Kristen Torres), Ronald Guttman (Edgar Radzinski), Kelly Bishop (Attorney Julia Zimmer), Tim Bohn (Jacob Nauss)

Reviewing the Case: When a tourist's body is found in Central Park with the word "guilty" written on her forehead, a suspect with paranoid delusions of governmental conspiracy quickly emerges. He eludes prosecution thanks to a mistake by CSU Tech Stuckey, and following his release murders and attempted murders begin piling up as detectives try to pin a crime on him. Munch turns to his ex-wife Gwen for assistance—but when a final piece of DNA falls into place, suddenly a new danger emerges from inside the department.

Noteworthy Discoveries: Carol Kane played Gwen Munch on the sixth season of *Homicide: Life on the Streets*. This *SVU* season concludes with Stabler looking at two bodies and noting, "What a way to end." Since both Christopher Meloni and Mariska Hargitay were still in negotiations at that point to re-sign their contracts, the line takes on a particular poignancy.

PRODUCTION TEAMS FOR ALL SEASONS

Creator/Executive Producer

Seasons one–ten: Dick Wolf

Executive Producer

Season one: Robert Palm, David Burke
Season two: David Burke, Ted Kotcheff, Neal Baer
Season three–ten: Neal Baer, Ted Kotcheff, Peter Jankowski

Co-Executive Producer

Season one: Peter Jankowski, Ted Kotcheff
Season two: Peter Jankowski, Arthur W. Forney, Judith McCreary, Martin Weiss
Season three: Arthur W. Forney, Judith McCreary
Season four: Arthur W. Forney, Judith McCreary, Patrick Harbinson
Season five: Arthur W. Forney, Patrick Harbinson, Robert Nathan, Dawn DeNoon and Lisa Marie Petersen, Roz Weinman
Season six: Arthur W. Forney, Patrick Harbinson, Robert Nathan, Dawn DeNoon and Lisa Marie Petersen, Roz Weinman, Jonathan Greene, Michele Fazekas and Tara Butters
Season seven: Arthur W. Forney, Patrick Harbinson, Robert Nathan, Dawn DeNoon and Lisa Marie Petersen, Jonathan Green, Michele Fazekas and Tara Butters, Ian Biederman
Season eight: Arthur W. Forney, Patrick Harbinson, Jonathan Greene, Amanda Green, Dawn DeNoon
Season nine: Arthur W. Forney, Jonathan Greene, Amanda Green, Dawn DeNoon
Season ten: Arthur Forney, Amanda Green, Jonathan Greene, Dawn DeNoon, David Platt, Peter Leto

Produced By

Seasons one–ten: David DeClerque

Supervising Producer

Season one: None
Season two: Judith McCreary
Season three: Jeff Eckerle
Season four: Patrick Harbinson, Dawn DeNoon and Lisa Marie Petersen, Roz Weinman
Season five: Jonathan Green, Michele Fazekas and Tara Butters, Randy Roberts
Season six: Randy Roberts
Season seven: Randy Roberts, Amanda Green
Season eight: Randy Roberts, Peter Leto
Season nine: Randy Roberts, Peter Leto, Mark Goffman
Season ten: Randy Roberts, Daniel Truly

Co-Producers

Season one: Joe Lazarov
Season two: Lynn Goldman, Wendy West
Season three: Randy Roberts, Lynn Goldman, Jonathan Greene and Robert F. Campbell
Season four: Peter Leto, Michele Fazekas and Tara Butters
Season five: Gail Barringer
Season six: Amanda Green, Jose Molina, Gail Barringer
Season seven: None
Season eight: Sheyna Kathleen Smith
Season nine: Sheyna Kathleen Smith, Paul Grellong
Season ten: Sheyna Kathleen Smith

Producers

Season one: Michael R. Perry
Season two: Jeff Eckerle, Joe Lazarov, Roz Weinman

Season three: Joe Lazarov, Lisa Marie Petersen and Dawn DeNoon, Roz Weinman
Season four: Randy Roberts, Jonathan Greene and Robert F. Campbell
Season five: Peter Leto
Season six: Peter Leto
Season seven: Peter Leto, Jose Molina, Gail Barringer, Sheyna Kathleen Smith
Season eight: Gail Barrringer
Season nine: Gail Barringer, Josh Singer, David Platt
Season ten: Gail Barrringer

Associate Producer

Season one: Lynn Goldman
Season two–three: None
Season four–six: Sheyna Smith
Season seven–ten: None

Consulting Producer

Season one: Billy Fox
Season two: None
Season three: Eric Overmyer, Samantha Howard Corbin
Season four–seven: None
Season eight–ten: Judith McCreary

Casting

Seasons one–four: Julie Tucker, Lynn Kressel Casting
Season five: Julie Tucker, Jonathan Strauss, Lynn Kressel Casting
Seasons six–ten: Jonathan Strauss, Lynn Kressel Casting

Executive Story Editor

Season one: John Chambers
Season two: Dawn DeNoon and Lisa Marie Petersen
Season three: Michele Fazekas and Tara Butters

Season four: None
Season five: Amanda Green, Jose Molina
Season six–seven: None
Season eight: Paul Grellong
Season nine–ten: None

Story Editors

Season one: Wendy West
Season two: Robert F. Campbell and Jonathan Greene
Season three–five: None
Season six: Roger Wolfson
Season seven–ten: None

Music

Seasons one–ten: Mike Post

Editor

Season one: Doug Ibold, Karen Stern, Scott Boyd
Season two: Doug Ibold, Karen Stern, Scott Boyd, Risa Blewitt, Maja Vrvilo
Season three: Karen Stern, Doug Ibold, Bonnie Koehler
Season four: Doug Ibold, Karen Stern, Bonnie Koehler
Season five: Karen Stern, Doug Ibold, Nancy Forner
Season six: Karen Stern, Doug Ibold, Nancy Forner, Steve Polivka,
Season seven: Doug Ibold, Karen Stern, Nancy Forner, Jim Stewart
Season eight: Karen Stern, Nancy Forner, Jim Stewart, Daniel J. Simmons, Jon Koslowsky
Season nine–ten: Karen Stern, Nancy Forner, Steve Polivka

Unit Production Manager

Season one: Lynn Goldman
Season two: Lynn Goldman, Robert E. Warren

Season three: Lynn Goldman, Peter Leto, Robert E. Warren
Season four: Peter Leto, Howard McMaster, Gail Barringer
Season five–seven: Gail Barringer
Season eight: Howard McMaster, Gail Barringer
Season nine–ten: Gail Barringer

First Assistant Director

Season one: Robert E. Warren, Rebecca Saionz, Peter Leto
Season two: Robert E. Warren, Peter Leto, Jono Oliver
Season three: Robert E. Warren, Peter Leto, Terry Ham, Jono Oliver, Howard McMaster, Mary Rae Thewlis
Season four: Robert E. Warren, Terry Ham, Jono Oliver, Howard McMaster, Kenneth Brown
Season five: Howard McMaster, Kenneth Brown, Denis Doyle
Season six: Howard McMaster, Kenneth Brown
Season seven: Howard McMaster, Kenneth Brown, Denis Doyle, Christo Morse, Jay Tobias
Season eight: Howard McMaster, Kenneth Brown, Denis Doyle, Jay Tobias, Stacey Beneville, Rebecca Saionz
Season nine: Howard McMaster, Kenneth Brown, Jamie Sheridan, Stuart Feldman
Season ten: Howard McMaster, Kenneth Brown

Second Assistant Director

Season one: Terry Ham, Peter Leto, Kim Kennedy
Season two: Terry Ham, Kim Kennedy, Don Julian, Roger Lee
Season three: Terry Ham, Kim Kennedy, Mike Pitt, Roger McDonald Lee
Season four: Terry Ham, Kim Kennedy, Denis Doyle, Samantha Lavin, Linda Perkins
Season five: Kim Kennedy, Denis Doyle, Mark Garland, Mikki Ziska
Season six: Kim Kennedy, Denis Doyle, Mikki Ziska, Alexa Steele-Brown, Mark Garland
Season seven: Kim Kennedy, Denis Doyle, Mikki Ziska, Mark Garland, Colin A.J. MacLell, Vanessa Hoffman,

Season eight: Kim Kennedy, Denis Doyle, Vanessa Hoffman, Michelle Regina, Greg White
Season nine: Kim Kennedy, Michelle Regina, Jim Nickas
Season ten: Kim Kennedy, Michelle Regina Jacobelli, Alexa Steele

Director of Photography

Season one: Anthony Jannelli
Season two–six: Geoffrey Erb, George Pattison
Season seven: Geoffrey Erb, George Pattison, Peter Reniers
Season eight: Geoffrey Erb, George Pattison, Phil Oetiker
Season nine: George Pattison, Phil Oetiker
Season ten: George Pattison

Production Designer

Season one: Dean Taucher, Teresa Carriker-Thayer
Season two: Dean Taucher, Darrell K. Keister
Season three: Dean Taucher, Richard Bianchi, Gregory Hill
Season four–five: Dean Taucher, Melanie Baker, Wing Lee
Season six: Dean Taucher, Melanie Baker, Fred Kolo
Season seven: Dean Taucher, Sarah Frank, Jeff Crye
Season eight: Dean Taucher, Sarah Frank
Season nine: Dean Taucher, Jeff Crye
Season ten: Dean Taucher

Location Manager

Season one: Trish Adlesic, Maria Bierniak
Season two: Trish Adlesic, David Graham
Season three: Trish Adlesic, Anne Kuronyi, Tim Robbins
Season four: Trish Adlesic, Timothy Robbins, Randy Manion
Season five: Trish Adlesic, Timothy Robbins, Frank Covino
Season six: Trish Adlesic, Frank Covino, Shannon Bowen
Season seven: Trish Adlesic, James Adlesic, Frank Covino, Thomas Scutro
Season eight: Trish Adelsic, James Adlesic

Season nine: Trish Adlesic, James Adlesic, Thomas Scutro
Season eight: Trish Adelsic

Costume Designer

Season one: Leslie Yarmo
Season two: Leslie Yarmo, Rhonda Roper
Season three: Leslie Yarmo, Rhonda Roper-Shear
Season four: Leslie Yarmo, Thomas L. Keller, Kim Wilcox
Season five–eight: Thomas L. Keller, Kim Wilcox
Season nine: Tina Nigro, Jessica Sinoway
Season ten: Tina Nigro

CHAPTER TWENTY-THREE

HOW THE NUMBERS ADD UP

*L*aw & Order: SVU has never been a numerical powerhouse. It's never hit No. 1 in the Nielsen household ratings, and only come within sniffing distance of the Top 10.

For many years, those numbers were the only ones that could possibly matter to a show—the higher it ranked, the more the network could sell space to advertisers for, so the more money the show made. But when "repurposing" came into vogue in the 1990s, a show didn't have to wait weeks, months, or years for a rerun; it could air within days on a different channel and pull in even more viewers. Few series could handle that much repetition but *SVU*, like the Mother Ship, was a workhorse.

All of which means that household ratings were never the end product of *SVU*'s success story, though they are parsed minutely first thing the morning after a show. On average over nine seasons (all numbers are according to Nielsen Media Research), *SVU* brought in 10.7 million viewers. It hit its high point in season four with 13.7 million viewers and a 9.4 household rating, higher than its debut season of 11.2 million viewers and an 8.1 household rating, but not even scraping the tip of the iceberg that was the year's No. 1 show— CBS' *CSI: Crime Scene Investigation*, which brought in a 13.7 household rating and 21.6 million viewers.

Season seven, the year Mariska Hargitay won the show's sole lead-acting Emmy, failed to see a significant bump (12.1 million viewers with an 8.2 household rating), nor did the Emmy encourage more viewers to turn in—viewership dropped in season eight to 10.6 million viewers and a 7.2 household rating. (Note: season seven inaugurated Nielsen's counting what it calls "Live+7"—namely, the live rating for the show as it airs, plus seven days of viewership subsequent from DVRs.)

Yet the bigger picture deserves a moment of mention. As the industry routinely laments, all TV shows have a shrinking viewership. Arguably, a show still can pull in impressive numbers—the No. 1 show for 2007–08 (*SVU*'s season nine) was Tuesday's *American Idol* on Fox and it had 30.6 million viewers for a 16.1 household rating.

But those numbers are paltry compared to just a decade or two ago, and they're largely linked to zeitgeist shows—the *Survivor* finales, or any one of the *American Idol* nights. Over a ten-year period *SVU* has managed to hold a firm average of between 10–13 million viewers, which proves its durability. And unlike the *Survivors* and *American Idols*, it retains its repeat viewability.

Additionally, it might be said that Dick Wolf's height (6'4") matches his stature in the industry. According to a 2006 list of the top 100 celebrities published by *Forbes*, the Law & Order magnate ranked number 50 in terms of power and number 12 in terms of money. According to the magazine, his earnings totaled $70 million, primarily from syndication deals.

Summary of Seasonal Household Ratings for *L&O*, *SVU* and *CI*, 1999–Present

1999–2000
SVU: 8.1/14 (11,169,000 viewers)
L&O: 10.8/18

2000–01
SVU: 8.5/16 (11,944,000 viewers)
L&O: 11.1/19

2001–02
SVU: 9.3/17 (13,499,000 viewers)
L&O: 11.4/19

2002–03
SVU: 9.4/17 (13,772,000 viewers)
L&O: 10.5/18
CI: 8.4/13

2003–04
SVU: 8.3/14 (12,059,000 viewers)
L&O: 10.0/17
CI: 8.0/12

2004–05
SVU: 8.3/14 (12,070,000 viewers)
L&O: 8.1/13
CI: 7.1/11

2005–06
SVU: 8.2/13 (12,111,000 viewers)
L&O: 7.0/11
CI: 6.5/10

2006–07
SVU: 7.2/12 (10,621,000 viewers)
L&O: 5.9/10
CI: 6.0/9

2007–08
SVU: 7.6/12 (11,374,000 viewers)
L&O: 7.2/12
CI: 5.1/8

2008–09
SVU: 6.8/11 (10,251,000 viewers)
L&O: 5.5/9
CI: 2.8/4

SOURCE: *Nielsen Media Research Galaxy Explorer*

SVU BIOGRAPHIES

Dick Wolf

CREATOR, EXECUTIVE PRODUCER

Television has many producers, writers, and directors, but relatively few architects. Dick Wolf, who currently oversees three of NBC Universal's most profitable and long-running projects—all part of the Law & Order brand—is just such a designer.

Wolf grew up in and around television; his father worked in press relations for NBC, which gave the son access as a child to the *Howdy Doody* peanut gallery. An education at prestigious prep schools (one of Wolf's schoolmates was future President George W. Bush) led him to a career in advertising, where he coined such slogans as National Airline's "Fly Me" and "You can't beat Crest for fighting cavities," a saying he admits actually means nothing at all.

Wolf shifted into film and television in the late 1970s and hit an early stride as a producer and writer on NBC's *Miami Vice*, where he first began developing the concept that would become *Law & Order*. The idea did not catch on immediately, and the Mother Ship's pilot was rejected at every network before NBC incorporated it as an episode in the series almost two years later. The show was initially set up so that it could be run as two "strips" of thirty minutes each, which would make it easier to sell in syndication—but none of the L&O shows have ever run that way. Instead, audiences showed they liked them in full, sixty-minute versions.

With branding learned from his Procter & Gamble days, Wolf knew that once *Law & Order* caught on it could work in several different iterations. *L&O* debuted on NBC in 1990 and is set to become television's longest-running drama (barring any short-sightedness in NBC's executive offices) once it reaches its twentieth season. Not long after the Mother Ship won the primetime Emmy for Outstanding Drama in 1997, the idea for a second series (*Law & Order: SVU*) was born; it premiered in 1999. *Law & Order: Criminal Intent* followed in 2001 and ultimately shifted from NBC to USA Network. But audiences have felt satiated—*Law & Order: Trial By Jury* was canceled after just thirteen episodes in 2005. In ensuing years, L&O shows have also taken off overseas; both France and England are producing their own, localized versions.

While the Law & Order shows are his most successful ventures, Wolf has hardly restrained himself to just those programs. His company, Wolf Films, produced *Twin Towers*, which won a 2003 Oscar in the Short Documentary category; in 2007 he won six Emmy Awards (out of seventeen nominations) for his HBO original movie *Bury My Heart at Wounded Knee*.

His upcoming projects include a documentary on The Doors, to be narrated by Johnny Depp. As a college student, Wolf booked rock bands for live shows; he tapped Jim Morrison's legendary group for a performance early in its career. At the moment the film is "in the pipeline," according to a representative. Wolf also has completed a pilot called *Lost and Found* for NBC.

Neal Baer

EXECUTIVE PRODUCER/SHOWRUNNER

Sometimes, it just helps to have a physician on call. *Law & Order: SVU* wasn't quite on life support when Dr. Neal Baer was ordered in, but it's likely that, without him, the show's plug would have been pulled long before it really got going.

But to backtrack a bit: Baer has more degrees and awards on his shelf than you can shake a stethoscope at, including master's in education and sociology and a doctorate of laws; he's taught elementary school and worked in Africa to help HIV/AIDS mothers tell their stories via photography. And that's just scraping the surface. Yet almost since he entered the medical profession, Neal Baer—who earned his M.D. from Harvard University and interned in pediatrics at a Los Angeles hospital—has found ways to merge his interest in television with his scientific expertise.

One of his earliest television jobs involved writing for boyhood pal John Wells on ABC's *China Beach* in the 1990s; that relationship led to a longer-term gig as writer and executive producer on NBC's *ER*, which Wells also executive produced. While there, Baer used his medical know-how to lend the show verisimilitude; by the time *SVU* was ready to bring him aboard in 2000, he has mastered the art of showrunning as well as translating complex stories for the small screen.

And his arrival on *SVU*, by all accounts, saved the show—which had floundered in its first season. Baer brought with him a compelling vision of what the series could be, weaving his interests in public policy, medicine, and sexual issues to help create a potent, fascinating array of stories that have both entertained and educated viewers. With seven Emmy nominations (all for *ER* thus far), it's surely only a matter of time before he's recognized in a similar fashion for his *SVU* contributions.

For now, Baer will just have to be satisfied with other prizes, including the Valentine Davies Award, given in 2004 by the Writers Guild of America, West for "public service efforts in both the entertainment industry and the community at large, bringing dignity to and raising the standard for writers everywhere"; the Special

Individual Achievement Award from the Media Project, given in 2003; the Leadership Award from NOFAS; the Loop Award from Lupus LA for educating the public about lupus and autoimmune diseases; and the Socially Responsible Medicine Award from Physicians for Social Responsibility for "accomplishment in crafting compelling health messages."

During his initial *ER* gig as a writer in 1994, Baer was spending every Saturday as a doctor at the Venice Family Clinic, doing ambulatory medicine. He then had a residency from 1997 through 2002 at Children's Hospital in Los Angeles, all the while still working for the NBC show. To this day, despite a hectic *SVU* schedule, "I go to Africa a lot during hiatus," he says. "Two summers ago, I treated 240 kids in Kenya."

Why? "Because there's life outside of television," Baer points out. "It's very curative for me. It grounds me."

(Baer's medical charities: www.thehouseissmall.org and www.joinipe.org)

Ted Kotcheff

EXECUTIVE PRODUCER/EPISODE DIRECTOR

Finding your niche in the entertainment industry can take years for even the most talented, but there are those—like Ted Kotcheff—who are lucky enough to find their calling from the start.

Kotcheff is a director, an organized man who can see the shots before the camera does and get his actors to do what he needs to tell the story. That he serves as an executive producer on *Law & Order: SVU* is a function of his veteran status in the industry—producing comes naturally after over fifty years behind the scenes—and he still directs the occasional episode.

In those five decades Kotcheff's gone from being the youngest drama director in Canada (at twenty-four) thanks to his work at the Canadian Broadcasting Corporation Television Service, to a director of plays and musicals in London's West End, to a feature film director with such credits as *The Apprenticeship of Duddy Kravitz* (1974, a film based on a book by his good friend Mordecai Richter; eleven years later Kotcheff would make *Joshua Then and Now*, also by Richter), *Fun with Dick and Jane* (1977), and *North Dallas Forty* (1979), which he also wrote.

His work covers a wide swath of subject matter and, periodically, more lowbrow fare: the wildly successful *First Blood* (the 1982 Rambo movie) and the wildly juvenile *Weekend at Bernie's* (1989), both of which he directed.

His long stint with *SVU* ranks was unplanned; he had been working on a film about Hitler in the late 1990s, but it fell through. His agent informed him that Dick Wolf was planning a new TV series. A friend of Kotcheff's had been a producer on the Wolf-penned 1992 feature film *School Ties*, so it seemed the two were destined to meet. The radical nature of what *SVU* wanted to do appealed to Kotcheff, who signed on at the series' inception.

And he's been one of the few constants at *SVU* from Day One, riding with the lows (that difficult first season, the loss of several writers) and the highs (the Emmy nominations, Mariska Hargitay's win, the critical acclaim). Over the years, "Uncle Ted" (as he's been dubbed) has become not just an *eminence grise* on the New Jersey set, but a calm center around which cast and crew seem to gather.

AWARDS WON

Emmy Awards

2006–07 Season Outstanding Guest Actress in a Drama Series: Leslie Caron, "Recall"

2005–06 Season Outstanding Lead Actress in a Drama Series: Mariska Hargitay

2004–05 Season Outstanding Guest Actress in a Drama Series: Amanda Plummer, "Weak"

2007–08 Season Outstanding Guest Actress in a Drama Series: Cynthia Nixon, "Alternate"

SVU *Emmy 2008 Button (from NBC)*

RANDEE DAWN

Golden Globe Awards

2004–05 Season Best Actress in a Drama: Mariska Hargitay

Edgar Allan Poe Awards

2002–03 Season Best Television Episode: "Waste"
2000–01 Season Best Television Episode: "Limitations"

BMI Film & TV Awards

2007–08 Season TV Music Award: Mike Post
2006–07 Season TV Music Award: Mike Post
2005–06 Season TV Music Award: Mike Post
2004–05 Season TV Music Award: Mike Post
2003–04 Season TV Music Award: Mike Post
2002–03 Season TV Music Award: Mike Post
2001–02 Season TV Music Award: Mike Post
2000–01 Season TV Music Award: Mike Post

Image Awards

2001–02 Season Outstanding Supporting Actor in a Drama Series: Ice-T

Shine Awards

2003–04 Season Drama: "Lowdown"
2002–03 Season Special Individual Achievement Award: Neal Baer—Honored for positive portrayals of sexuality and reproductive health issues
2002–03 Season Drama Episode: "Fallacy"

Golden PSI Award

2003–04 Season Honored for their positive portrayal of mental health professionals

Valentine Davies Award

2003–04 Season: Neal Baer Honored by the Writers Guild of America, West for bringing dignity and honor to the profession of writing

Gracie Allen Award

2006–07 Season Outstanding Drama Series
2005–06 Season Outstanding Drama Program: "Fault"
2003–04 Season Best Female Lead, Drama Series: Mariska Hargitay

ASCAP Film & Television Music Award

2005–06 Season Top TV Series: Atli Orvarsson
2004–05 Season Top TV Series: Atli Orvarsson

Prism Award

2007–08 Season Commendation, Mental Health Depiction Award: "Alternate"
2007–08 Season Commendation, Mental Health Depiction Award: "Blinded"
2006–07 Season Commendation, TV Drama Series Episode: "Dependent"
2006–07 Season Commendation, TV Drama Series Episode: "Loophole"
2006–07 Season Performance in a Drama Series Episode: Mariska Hargitay
2004–05 Season Commendation, TV Drama Series Episode: "Criminal"
2004–05 Season Commendation, TV Drama Series Episode: "Haunted"
2003–04 Season TV Drama Series Episode: "Choice"
1999–00 Season Commendation, TV Drama Series Episode: "Wanderlust"

ALMA Awards

2005–06 Season Outstanding Script for a Television Drama or Comedy: Jose Molina, "Alien"

Environmental Media Awards

2005–06 Season Turner Prize for Primetime Television: "Rockabye"

Satellite Awards

2005–06 Season Outstanding Guest Star: Jerry Lewis, "Uncle"

APPENDIX C

LINKS

The *Law & Order: SVU* Lineup on the Web

At the time this book was published, these websites and URLs were still valid, but due to the ever-changing nature of the Internet, links may change or go dark in time. For continuous updates, check in at UnofficialCompanion.com, which will be updated by the authors. Any future links of interest should be sent to UnofficialCompanion@gmail.com.

Show-Related Sites

OFFICIAL NBC SITE

http://www.nbc.com/Law_&_Order:_Special_Victims_Unit/
      Lots of great photos and interactive content, plus the show's production blog, short video recaps, desktop images and a quiz.

THE INTERNET MOVIE DATABASE SITE

http://www.imdb.com/title/tt0203259/
      Basic information on cast, filming locations and classic quotes.

WIKIPEDIA ENTRY

http://en.wikipedia.org/wiki/Law_&_Order:_Special_Victims_Unit

Generally reliable, succinct history of the show. Can be added to by volunteers, so veracity of information should be taken with a grain of salt.

TV GUIDE SITE

http://www.tvguide.com/tvshows/law-order-special/100257

Aggregator for *TV Guide* news on the show, plus photos.

USA NETWORK SITE

http://www.usanetwork.com/series/svu2/

Community message board, exclusive clips of actors providing character insights.

TV.COM SITE

http://www.tv.com/law-and-order-special-victims-unit/show/334/summary.html

Extensive listing of each episode with a short summary. Well-organized, but not a lot of bells and whistles.

FANLISTING SITE

http://www.specialvictimsunit.org/

Organized by an individual fan out of the U.K., this is part of the generic "fanlisting" sites around the Internet. Provides basic information about characters and the show, and has an unusual pink background. Requests registration.

FANPOP SITE

http://www.fanpop.com/spots/law-and-order-svu

Much like Fanlisting, FanPop provides a relatively generic home for fans to set up their worship; this one has a lot of quizzes, a message board, and photos, among other things.

BRANDON BIRD'S *SVU* VALENTINES

http://www.brandonbird.com/svutines.html

Brandon Bird is a talented artist based in California who has an intense interest in all things Law & Order—and he's created T-shirts, original art, and even valentines to prove it.

SVUFANS.NET

http://www.svufans.net/forums/

Extensive message board for discussions of all things *SVU*

Actor/Character-Specific Sites

MARISKA HARGITAY / DET. OLIVIA BENSON

OFFICIAL MARISKA HARGITAY SITE

http://mariska.com/

Comes with blog (and guest bloggers), merchandise (not the obvious stuff, either), and links Hargitay's Joyful Heart Foundation, among other things.

INTERNET MOVIE DATABASE SITE

http://www.imdb.com/name/nm0002127/

WIKIPEDIA ENTRIES

http://en.wikipedia.org/wiki/Mariska_Hargitay
http://en.wikipedia.org/wiki/Olivia_Benson

MARISKAHARTIGAY.ORG

http://mariskahargitay.org/

Spare site with photos (requires email contact), message board, chat room.

MARISKA RESOURCE

http://www.mariskaresource.com/
A fan page with an elegant design; even includes a Mariska-based hangman game.

MARISKA ONLINE

http://www.mariska-hargitay.org/
At press time was "undergoing a total revamp" and had no current content.
http://www.mariska-hargitay.org/law&order/
This part of the site contains information on Benson and links to articles.

DEDICATED: THE OLIVIA BENSON FANLISTING

http://fan.harmony-bunny.net/olivia/
Minimal content, a few graphics.

CHRISTOPHER MELONI / DET. ELLIOT STABLER

OFFICIAL CHRISTOPHER MELONI SITE

http://www.christopher-meloni.com
http://www.christophermeloni.com/
A well-organized, meat-and-potatoes site (you expected something less?) with questions answered by Meloni, events at which he has and will appear, and articles, among other goodies.

INTERNET MOVIE DATABASE SITE

http://www.imdb.com/name/nm0005221/

WIKIPEDIA ENTRIES

http://en.wikipedia.org/wiki/Christopher_Meloni
http://en.wikipedia.org/wiki/Elliot_Stabler

MR. NEW YORK (THE CHRIS MELONI FANLISTING)

http://fan.velvetysmooth.net/cmeloni/
    A fanlisting with virtually nothing except a place to register. (Maybe by registering you get access to other areas.)

TO SERVE AND PROTECT

http://fan.lucid-star.net/stabler/
    Another fanlisting with virtually nothing to offer except registration.

ICE-T / DET. ODAFIN "FIN" TUTUOLA

OFFICIAL ICE-T SITE

http://www.icet.com/

INTERNET MOVIE DATABASE SITE

http://www.imdb.com/name/nm0001384/

WIKIPEDIA ENTRIES

http://en.wikipedia.org/wiki/Ice-T
http://en.wikipedia.org/wiki/Fin_Tutuola

RICHARD BELZER / SGT. DET. JOHN MUNCH

INTERNET MOVIE DATABASE SITE

http://www.imdb.com/name/nm0001938/

WIKIPEDIA ENTRIES

http://en.wikipedia.org/wiki/Richard_Belzer
http://en.wikipedia.org/wiki/John_Munch

DANN FLOREK / CAPT. DON CRAGEN

INTERNET MOVIE DATABASE SITE

http://www.imdb.com/name/nm0282648/

WIKIPEDIA ENTRIES

http://en.wikipedia.org/wiki/Dann_Florek
http://en.wikipedia.org/wiki/Donald_Cragen

MICHAELA MCMANUS / ADA KIM GREYLEK

INTERNET MOVIE DATABASE SITE

http://www.imdb.com/name/nm2288842/

WIKIPEDIA ENTRIES

http://en.wikipedia.org/wiki/Michaela_McManus

MICHAELA MCMANUS ONLINE

http://michaelamcmanus.net/
    An early fansite set up when McManus was still on *One Tree Hill*, and regularly updated.

MICHAELA MCMANUS FAN

http://michaela-m.org/
    A fan site apparently connected to Celebuzz.

TAMARA TUNIE / M.E. MELINDA WARNER

INTERNET MOVIE DATABASE SITE

http://www.imdb.com/name/nm0876645/

WIKIPEDIA ENTRIES

http://en.wikipedia.org/wiki/Tamara_Tunie
http://en.wikipedia.org/wiki/Melinda_Warner

B.D. WONG / DR. GEORGE HUANG

THE UNOFFICIAL B.D. WONG SITE

http://www.unofficialbdwong.com/
Basic in design, but very informative.

INTERNET MOVIE DATABASE SITE

http://www.imdb.com/name/nm0000703/

WIKIPEDIA ENTRIES

http://en.wikipedia.org/wiki/B._D._Wong
http://en.wikipedia.org/wiki/George_Huang_(Law_%26_Order)

PANDORA'S BOX

http://www.fullcirclenausea.com/huang/
Beautifully designed, but sparse. Requests registration.

B.D. WONG APPRECIATION PAGE

http://www.geocities.com/Hollywood/Film/6371/
Not appreciative lately; last update was 1999.

Fan Fiction Sites

For those who don't know what fan fiction is, it's basically fans writing stories based on the characters—stories that have never appeared on camera and are never likely to. Some of it is amateurish, some of it is quite good, and some of it is explicit, so it's not for everyone. Be sure to look for ratings before reading.

SVU FICTION

http://www.svufiction.com/index.php
A couple thousand stories written about the characters, by fans. Ratings indicated.

PASSION AND PERFECTION: *LAW & ORDER: SVU* STORIES

http://www.ralst.com/storiesLO.html

Unusually grouped by authors' last names. Also includes story ratings.

LAW & ORDER: SVU FEMSLASH SITE

http://xenawp.org/svu/

Stories restricted to female/female relationships between characters on the show.

UNNAMED SITE

http://www.bdwong.com/index.html

Just a photo and a note saying "Coming Soon."

THE *SVU* CONNECTION

http://svu.doriennesmith.com/fiction.php

Fiction written by Dorienne Smith, who runs this site, among others.

BIBLIOGRAPHY

Andreeva, Nellie. "Beach Retires from *SVU*." *The Hollywood Reporter*, April 21, 2008

Ausiello, Michael. "Exclusive: Diane Neal Bails on *Law & Order: SVU*." *TV Guide*, April 28, 2008

Battaglio, Stephen. "Which TV Stars Earn What." *TV Guide*, July 26, 2007

Blakeley, Kiri and Goldman, Lea (editors). "The Celebrity 100." *Forbes* magazine, June 15, 2006

Collins, Monica. "Success on His Own Terms." *USA Weekend*, September 12–14, 2008

Courrier, Kevin and Green, Susan. *Law & Order: The Unofficial Companion*. Renaissance Books, 1999

Gonshor, Adam. "Adam Beach Conquers His Demons." Andpop.com, May 11, 2007

Goodman, Tim. "Lucrative Law & Order Brand Deserves Limelight, Wolf Whines." *The San Francisco Chronicle*, March 3, 2006

Green, Susan. "Collecting Evidence: A Look At Dick Wolf's TV Canon." *The Hollywood Reporter*, March 29, 2007

Kalat, David P. *Homicide: Life on the Street—The Unofficial Companion*. 1998, Renaissance Books

Miranda, Carolina A. "Q&A with Adam Beach." Time.com, February 2, 2007

"Producing Excellence (An Interview with Dick Wolf)." *Produced By (The Official Magazine of the Producers Guild of America)*, 2000

Rose, Lacey. "Prime-Time TV's 20 Top-Earning Women." Forbes .com, September 2008

Roth, Richard and Buxbaum, Evan. "U.N. hosts filming of 'Law & Order: SVU' episode." CNN.com, March 30, 2009

Slonim, Jeffrey and Silverman, Stephen M. "Mariska Hargitay's Health Mystery Revealed." People.com, May 19, 2009

Tucker, Ken. "Crime Doesn't Pay." *Entertainment Weekly*, February 26, 1993.

ABOUT THE AUTHORS

SUSAN GREEN

An award-winning journalist, Susan Green freelances for *Vermont Life*, a quarterly magazine; the *Burlington Free Press*, the Green Mountain State's major daily newspaper; and *Seven Days*, an alternative weekly there. She also has reviewed films for *BoxOffice* magazine and written entertainment stories for *The Hollywood Reporter*. Her articles have appeared in *Rolling Stone, Premiere,* and *USA Today*, among other national periodicals.

With Kevin Courrier, Green co-authored two editions of *Law & Order: The Unofficial Companion* (Renaissance/St. Martin's Press, 1998 and 1999). Her coffee-table book about Bread & Puppet Theater came out in 1986 (Green Valley Media). She contributed a chapter to *Backstory 3: Interviews with Screenwriters of the '60s* (University of California Press, 1997) and her short fiction has been published in several literary journals.

RANDEE DAWN

New York–based journalist and critic Randee Dawn is an entertainment writer for such publications as *The Hollywood Reporter, The L.A.*

Times, and FoxNews.com. She has previously worked for *Soap Opera Digest,* National Public Radio's *Living on Earth,* and WGBH-TV's *The Ten O'Clock News.* In the past twenty years she has covered the entertainment industry for *Billboard, The Boston Phoenix,* E! Online, *New Musical Express,* and other national and international publications. She also contributed to the first edition of *Les Séries Télé,* a French book about American television, and has a paralegal certificate from New York University.

Her short fiction has appeared online in *3AM Magazine* and on the *Well-Told Tales* podcast.

She is raising a Cairn Terrier named Ciara.

INDEX